Alcohol, Violence, and Disorder in Traditional Europe

Habent sua fata libelli

EARLY MODERN STUDIES SERIES

GENERAL EDITOR
MICHAEL WOLFE
St. John's University

Alcohol, Violence, and Disorder
in Traditional Europe

A. Lynn Martin

Early Modern Studies 2
Truman State University Press

Copyright © 2009 Truman State University Press, Kirksville, Missouri USA
All rights reserved
tsup.truman.edu

Cover: *Corpo di Guardia*, a fresco by Colin in the Castello di Issogne, Val d'Aosta, ca. 1500, shows soldiers relaxing. In what could be a scene from a tavern, on the far left two men play backgammon, the two men to their right play a board game, a woman joins two other men for drinks, while on the far right one man attacks the sitting man with his sword, while the third uses his drinking cup to ward off the attack. Photograph by Ars Una, 1976, from the Archivio fotografico dell'Assessorato istruzione e cultura-Soprintendenza per i beni e le attività culturali. Used courtesy of the Regione Autonoma Valle d'Aosta.

Cover design: Teresa Wheeler
Type: Minion Pro and Galahad © Adobe Systems Inc.,
Printed by: Sheridan Books, Ann Arbor, Michigan USA

Library of Congress Cataloging-in-Publication Data

Martin, A. Lynn.
Alcohol, violence, and disorder in traditional Europe / A. Lynn Martin.
    p. cm. — (Early modern studies series ; v. 2)
Includes bibliographical references and index.
ISBN 978-1-931112-96-3 (hbk. : alk. paper)
1. Drinking of alcoholic beverages—Europe—History. 2. Violence—Europe—History.
3. Disorderly conduct—Europe—History. I. Title.
HV5438.M373 2009
303.6094—dc22

                                                                        2009028696

The paper in this publication meets or exceeds the minimum requirements of the American National Standard for Information Sciences—Permanence of Paper for Printed Library Materials, ANSI Z39.48–1992.

Contents

Figures and Tables

Figures

Tables

Acknowledgments

To begin at the end, the task of bringing this book to publication became a pleasant one as a result of the efficiency and consideration of Michael Wolfe, general editor of Truman State University Press's Early Modern Studies series, Nancy Rediger, director and editor-in-chief of the Press, and Barbara Smith-Mandell, copy editor. I am especially grateful to Smith-Mandell for her attention to detail and her facilitation of the process of bringing a manuscript to press. I also wish to acknowledge the contribution of the two anonymous readers whose constructive criticism helped me tie loose ends together and clarify my arguments.

During the years that I have worked on the topic of drinking in traditional Europe, many librarians, academics, and friends—too many to mention—have helped me find sources, provided me with information, sharpened my understanding, and expressed their interest and encouragement. I thank them all, especially one whom I will mention, Barbara Santich, who worked as my research assistant. My lively group of postgraduate students, Andrea Cast, Angela Heuzenroeder, Craig Hill, Jennifer Jones, Nadia Postiglione, and Peter Stawhan, deserve acknowledgment for keeping my wits sharp. Special thanks go to Nadia for obtaining permission to use the cover illustration. As usual my warmest thanks go to my best friend and life's companion, Noreen.

To end at the beginning, I dedicate this book to the memory of my parents, AA and MM.

Chapter 1

The Problem of Alcohol and Violence

S tudies of modern societies demonstrate a link between the consumption of alcohol and crimes of violence. Late medieval and early modern Europe had plenty of both, so much so that the levels of violence and drinking were higher than they are today. This book attempts to determine if the link between violence and alcohol demonstrated by studies of modern societies can help explain the violence of the past, using an approach similar to that in my 2001 *Alcohol, Sex, and Gender in Late Medieval and Early Modern Europe.* That book used an anthropological perspective to address the assumption evident in Ogden Nash's witticism, "Candy is dandy, but liquor is quicker"; that is, the consumption of alcohol makes a person inclined to have sex. The evidence showed that the relationship between alcohol and sexual activity is culturally mediated rather than physiologically determined. Drinking behavior, in other words, is learned behavior, and consequently it varies from one culture to another. This book also adopts an anthropological perspective to examine the relationship between the consumption of alcoholic beverages and violent and antisocial behavior. In some cultures drinking leads to violent behavior; in other cultures it has the opposite effect with drinkers less prone to violence than when they are sober. Many factors—cultural, social, and psychological—affect drinking behavior. Take the man who drinks at the same bar on three successive nights. On the first night the drink makes him morose, withdrawn, and uncommunicative, on the second night he is full of good fellowship and is the life of the party, and on the third night he becomes belligerent, threatening, and disorderly: same man, same

1

drink, same bar, but with three different outcomes. The physiological effects of alcohol cannot be responsible for all three.

The focus is England, France, and Italy during the late medieval and early modern periods, roughly 1300 to 1700, what I prefer to call traditional Europe. The geographical limits permit a comparison of the wine-producing south with the beer-drinking north and of Catholic France and Italy with, from the mid-sixteenth century, Protestant England. The four-hundred-year period reflects the preference of the *annaliste* school of history for analysis over long periods of time, the *longue durée,* with 1700 heralding the commencement of significant changes in the consumption of alcohol, changes that eventually brought an end to the traditional drinking pattern. In late medieval and early modern Europe men, women, and children consumed enormous amounts of alcoholic beverages, primarily wine or ale and beer, as part of their daily diet. People drank water, of course, but in the period before safe drinking water and alternatives such as tea and coffee, alcohol was the beverage of choice. During the eighteenth century the consumption of spirits increased dramatically, especially in England, and tea and coffee gradually became popular drinks; both developments were responsible for a new drinking pattern. On the positive side, tea- and coffee-infused water was safe to drink because of the need to boil it. The widespread consumption of spirits, on the other hand, had negative consequences including increased social problems, exacerbated by the effects of nascent industrialization.

For many contemporary commentators and observers, wine and beer drinking in traditional Europe likewise created problems. Drunkenness was the gateway to all the other sins as well as to economic ruin, or so they argued, and they perceived too many drunkards, too many sins, and too much ruin. One of the better expressions of this attitude is the preamble to the English law against drunkenness enacted in 1606: "The loathsome and odious sin of drunkenness is of late grown into common use within this realm, being the root and foundation of many other enormous sins, as bloodshed, stabbing, murder, swearing, fornification [*sic*], adultery, and such like, to the great dishonor of God, and of our nation, the overthrow of many good arts and manual trades, the disabling of diverse workmen, and the general impoverishing of many good subjects, abusively wasting the good creatures of God."[1] Most people, however, daily drank such large amounts of alcohol that they would be considered problem drinkers today. One of the better indications of this

---

[1] Baird, "Alcohol Problem and the Law: II," 144. Here and elsewhere I have modernized the spelling.

practice is the young Benjamin Franklin's account of the drinking habits at the printer's shop in London in the early eighteenth century: "We had an alehouse boy who attended always in the house to supply the workmen. My companion at the press drank every day a pint before breakfast; a pint at breakfast with his bread and cheese; a pint between breakfast and dinner; a pint at dinner; a pint in the afternoon about six o'clock, and another when he had done his day's work." He drank six imperial pints, which equals 3.6 US quarts or 3.4 liters. That much beer did not make him drunk, lead him to other sins, result in economic ruin, or even leave him incapable of working; indeed the drinker felt he must, in the words of Franklin, "drink strong beer that he might be strong to labor."[2]

In addition to its dietary role, alcohol had other functions that made it an indispensable social lubricant and led to multiple occasions for binge drinking. Christian festivals, for example, were occasions for recreational drinking that promoted celebration, jollification, and socialization. Christmas was an occasion for massive drinking, as the bitter winter weather and the long, cold nights combined with the festive cheer to encourage the consumption of special alcoholic beverages. Festivals of the agricultural calendar, the rites of passage of birth, marriage, and death, and municipal, national, confraternal, and occupational festivals had similar functions. Many of these were so important to communal solidarity that local authorities sometimes suspended the collection of taxes on the drinks consumed. Closely linked to all of these festive occasions were the alehouses and the taverns that increasingly replaced the church as the venue for popular recreation and the associated recreational drinking. During the late medieval and early modern period, alehouses and taverns developed from institutions that primarily catered to travelers or sold drink to be consumed off premises to ones that were centers of popular culture.

The moralists of course viewed the rise of taverns and alehouses with alarm, for they believed that drinking establishments were centers of disorderly conduct. According to their view, alehouses and taverns promoted drunkenness, idleness, and profanity, they served customers during divine services, and they violated the curfew, entertained vagabonds, and permitted gambling. They likewise harbored thieves, gangs of criminals, prostitutes, and political and religious dissidents. Religious and political authorities feared that drinking in taverns and alehouses could foster enemies of church

---

[2] Franklin, *Autobiography*, ed. Lemay and Zall, 46.

and state through heresy and treason. Early in the seventeenth century, an English bishop complained of the possibility of men going into alehouses "and there upon their ale-benches talk of matters of the church or state, or else into conventicles."[3] Often setting a bad example for their customers were the alehouse and tavern keepers themselves, the keepers from hell, who flaunted the authorities and set poor examples for their customers. Aside from the establishments and their keepers, individuals were often guilty of disorderly conduct. Much of the disorderly conduct by individuals was the result of drunkenness, and "drunk and disorderly" was a frequent charge then as it is today. Much was also a mirror image of the disorder in alehouses, as drunkards wasted their time, swore, missed church services, stumbled home after curfew, gambled, and fornicated. The disorderly conduct associated with drinking and drinking establishments was usually victimless, but it could result in brawls, wounds, and murders among friends, enemies, and strangers. In other words, the celebration, jollification, and socialization that accompanied recreational drinking could lead to violence after a night of sharing drinks with friends at a tavern or an alehouse. The disorder and violence captured the attention of the authorities. The maintenance of order was one of the primary concerns if not the primary concern of political authorities in traditional Europe. Reflecting this concern was legislation governing drinking and drinking establishments, such as the English law against drunkenness in 1606, whose preamble is quoted above. Throughout Europe, one of the most common methods of controlling the disorderly potential of alehouses and taverns was the enactment of curfews so that drinkers would cease their drinking and go home at a reasonable hour.

The above comments introduce the topics addressed in this book. The rest of this chapter examines, first, the relationship between alcohol and violence in modern societies and, second, the problem of disorder and violence in late medieval and early modern Europe. Chapter 2 focuses on contemporary perceptions of drunken disorder and disorderly drinking establishments through the complaints of moralists, humanists, and pedagogues. The documentation of the important role of drink in daily diets is the function of chapter 3, while chapter 4 discusses the recreational functions of alcohol. Chapters 5 and 6 examine disorderly places and persons, chapter 7 exposes the myriad faces of violence, and the regulation of drinking is the topic of chapter 8. As in *Alcohol, Sex, and Gender*, I have used a wide variety of primary and secondary sources,

---

[3] Hill, *Society and Puritanism*, 195.

but no archival sources. As is the case with other topics, early modern Europe is better documented than late medieval, and English sources have been more accessible than French or Italian.

Alcohol and Violence

Empirical studies have demonstrated a strong correlation between acts of violence and the consumption of alcohol. The correlation increases if both the victim and the assailant have been drinking. For example, an examination of 679 homicides in Philadelphia in 1978 revealed the presence of alcohol in 53 percent of the victims, 52 percent of the assailants, and 60 percent of the total cases. Other studies demonstrate a range of 36 to 68 percent of the victims, 48 to 66 percent of the assailants, and 52 to 79 percent of the total cases.[4] As summarized by one group of scholars, "criminal statistics link alcohol to violence in a pattern that is large in magnitude; consistent over the years; widespread in types of aggressive and violent acts; massive in cost to individual, family, and society; and serious in suffering and harm. ... Alcohol is associated with at least half of all murders, rapes, sexual violence such as incestuous offenses, family violence, and felonies."[5] In many societies, young adult males consume the most alcohol and commit the most crimes of violence. Unsurprisingly, the demographic group that produces the strongest correlation between alcohol and violent crime is young adult males.[6]

If these statistics are clear, their meaning is not. On a very elementary level a drunken criminal might be an easily caught criminal, thereby inflating the correlation between alcohol and crime in police reports. Similarly, because young adult males *both* drink much *and* commit many crimes the correlation is spurious; perhaps 100 percent of murderers drink water, but no one claims that water is the cause of the murders. Correlation does not equal cause. A study of the relationship between alcohol and aggression in youth suggests three different models, one that alcohol causes aggression, another that aggression leads to the heavy consumption of alcohol, and a third that aggression and drinking share common causes. The evidence supports the third model; "alcohol does not necessarily cause aggression but happens to be present when aggression, or violence, occurs."[7] Most people in Western

---

[4] Martin, "Epidemiology," 232.

[5] Miczek, Weerts, and DeBold, "Alcohol, Aggression," 83.

[6] Collins and Messerschmidt, "Epidemiology of Alcohol-Related Violence," 95.

[7] White, Hansell, and Brick, "Alcohol Use."

societies drink, and many drink daily, yet most—the vast majority—of this drinking does not lead to violence. In other words, there is nothing inherent in alcohol that produces aggressive behavior.

As already noted, anthropological studies have demonstrated that drunken comportment varies from one society to another. True, alcohol impairs sensorimotor skills and cognitive processes, but it does not affect a person's reason or conscience so that the brain cannot perform the functions of direction and inhibition. People learn how alcohol is supposed to make them act and then act accordingly. As stated by Craig MacAndrew and Robert B. Edgerton in *Drunken Comportment,* "Over the course of socialization, people learn about drunkenness what their society 'knows' about drunkenness; and, accepting and acting upon the understandings thus imparted to them, they become the living confirmation of their society's teachings."[8] To confuse the issue, some scholars argue that this picture is incomplete. They claim that social learning does not account for all of alcohol's effect on violent behavior; the link between alcohol and violence is far more complicated and includes pharmacological, physiological, psychological, and other factors. One of these factors is the impairment of cognitive processes that could increase the possibility of miscommunication between drinkers.[9] Nonetheless, alcohol does not produce a pharmacological trigger for violent or aggressive behavior, and people are far more likely to be jovial, agreeable, and sociable while drinking than the reverse.[10]

Despite cross-cultural variations in drunken comportment, anthropological studies have identified similarities in drinking behavior across many societies. The consumption of alcohol is usually a social rather than a solitary activity, and drinking has an important role in celebration and in social facilitation and jollification. In many societies, alcohol also has an important role in fostering durable same-sex friendship, camaraderie, and solidarity, especially among men,[11] whose drinking together results in a bonding brotherhood and a sense of identification.[12] Anthropologists also note that community rules and rituals, community authority, and community solidarity control drinking

---

[8] MacAndrew and Edgerton, *Drunken Comportment,* esp. 13–14, 88.

[9] Pernanen, *Alcohol in Human Violence,* esp. 220–21; and Collins, "Drinking and Violations," 654–55.

[10] Pernanen, *Alcohol in Human Violence,* 200–201; and Heath, *Drinking Occasions,* 132.

[11] Mandelbaum, "Alcohol and Culture," 17; Heath, "Decade of Development," 46; and Marshall, "Conclusions," 451–57.

[12] Jellinek, "Symbolism of Drinking," 859–61.

behavior.[13] For example, when studying the drinking behavior of rural Taiwan, Stevan Harrell found that the community rules are never drink alone, always drink with food, and continue contributing to the family and to the community.[14] In short, according to the anthropological perspective, rather than a social problem, drinking is a social act. All of these attributes of drinking behavior would tend to mitigate antisocial, aggressive, or violent tendencies.

Other attributes of drinking behavior would have the opposite effect. The strong ties of identification and camaraderie that result from drinking are capable of generating aggressive behavior towards strangers and others such as rival neighborhoods and different occupational and social groups.[15] Aggressive behavior towards the "other" increases the cohesion of the drinkers.[16] Because the sharing of a drink demonstrates friendship, a refusal could be interpreted as enmity, as a thirteenth-century rabbi advised his congregation: "Now of course you cannot eat with the Gentiles, because of the dietary laws. But do not refuse a drink—that would be going too far."[17] Several studies have emphasized the masculine nature of drinking establishments, which provide a refuge from women. In the secure environment of the tavern or pub, men can engage in macho drinking while escaping from their insecurity in the female-controlled households.[18] Another aspect of drinking that could lead to violent and aggressive behavior is the feeling of power that comes from the consumption of alcohol. As stated by one scholar, "men drink alcoholic beverages to attain, or regain, a feeling of strength," that is, "thoughts about being big, strong, and important, about having more impact on others, [and] dominating."[19] In other words, drinking results in Dutch courage (with apologies to the Dutch!). Taken together all of these factors, the cohesion directed against the "other," the refusal to share a drink, the male-dominated drinking establishments, and Dutch courage, make a dangerous brew.

This analysis of modern studies on the relationship between alcohol and violence has the character of a seesaw, now tilting one way, now the other, but that is the careful conclusion of modern scholarship on the topic,

[13] Douglas, "Distinctive Anthropological Perspective," esp. 3–4, 6.

[14] Harrell, "Normal and Deviant Drinking," 50.

[15] Marshall, "Conclusions," 455.

[16] Bruun, "Drinking Practices," 226.

[17] Jellinek, "Symbolism of Drinking," 861.

[18] Gefou-Madianou, "Introduction," 10–11; Driessen, "Drinking on Masculinity," 77; and Popham, "Social History," 227.

[19] Boyatzis, "Drinking as a Manifestation," 265. See also Schaefer, "Drunkenness and Culture Stress," 291; and Driessen, "Drinking on Masculinity," 77.

as best expressed by Alan R. Lang: "drinking can *cause* increases in aggressive behavior, at least in certain doses, in certain persons, and under certain circumstances. In many ways, however, this is really all we know. It is not clear which of the many potentially important aspects of the agent, the host, and the environment are critical to the interaction that produces increased aggression."[20] Sharing a drink can result in friendship or lead to violence; that is the nature of alcoholic beverages. As stated by a French scholar, "paradoxically, wine has the quality of construction and destruction,"[21] but all alcoholic drinks have this quality. An illustration of the quality of construction and destruction comes from the behavior of men in those male-dominated drinking establishments. The drink makes men transcend their everyday worries, their talk becomes animated and sentimental, and enduring friendships are forged around glasses of wine and bottles of beer. At the same time the men engage in systematic destruction of capital as they buy drinks for one another and engage in conspicuous consumption.[22] The destructive tendencies make the consumption of alcohol an obvious target for those responsible for the maintenance of law and order.

Violence and Disorder in Traditional Europe

In late medieval and early modern Europe, governments at every level grappled with the problems created by violence and disorder. The most serious was the recurrent threat of riots, rebellions, and revolutions, which could provoke the participation of people from all social classes. Less spectacular but more frequent was factional and familial violence that perpetuated murderous vendettas, especially among the privileged classes. In addition to the violence of the vendetta, many brawls, wounds, and murders resulted from spontaneous encounters such as public insults and challenges to honor. At another level was the criminal activity that ranged from the petty thefts of vagabonds to the armed robberies of organized bandits. Next in descending order of seriousness came a wide range of criminal activity, much of which was victimless, such as prostitution, gambling, sodomy, and excessive expenditure on attire and entertainment. Merging into this criminal activity was the disorderly or unruly behavior that accompanied popular recreation. The

---

[20] Lang, "Alcohol-Related Violence," 143.

[21] Romillat, "Femmes, la parole," 243.

[22] Gefou-Madianou, "Introduction," 13.

communal governments of Italy attempted to control the mounting tide of violence, crime, and disorder. The efforts began in the thirteenth and four-teenth centuries with an increasing number of statutes governing a wide va-riety of antisocial behavior including factional violence, adultery, conspicu-ous consumption at weddings and funerals, bathing in public, blasphemy, carrying arms, displaying partisan banners, gambling, sodomy, prostitution, and violating curfews. Accompanying the legislation was the establishment of policing agencies. For example, the Florentine government established the Otto di Guardia in 1378 and then the Ufficiali di Notte early in the following century. These and similar agencies in other cities had the power to enforce public morality in private space while attempting to eliminate activities such as sodomy and gambling.[23]

Perhaps Italy was precocious, but many historians have pointed to early modern rather than to medieval Europe as the important period for the development of government legislation and agencies, especially those con-cerned with the disorderly or unruly aspects of popular culture and recre-ation. Some of these historians have applied the theory of social discipline to the legislation and the agencies, arguing that the developments reflected the early modern state's concern to foster forms of socialization that would promote cooperation and harmony and result in a well-disciplined and well-ordered society. The goal of the early modern state was a pervasive discipline that ordered both work and play and governed all relationships and activity.[24] In his 1978 *Popular Culture in Early Modern Europe,* Peter Burke introduced the similar concept of the reform of popular culture and used Peter Brue-gel's famous painting of *The Combat between Carnival and Lent* to illustrate it. Carnival, symbolized by a fat man astride a beer barrel and armed with a spear laden with meat—a giant shish kebab—represents the disorder of popular culture. Surrounding him are scenes of carnival. Men and women dance, they crowd into a tavern, get drunk, play games, watch street theatre, ignore beggars, sneak inside for sex, play cruel tricks on others, gamble, eat, join masked processions, and make music; in short, they are unruly, profane, sexually promiscuous, spontaneous, and concerned with immediate gratifi-cation. Symbolizing Lent is a thin hag, armed with a long spatula holding fish. Surrounding her are scenes more appropriate to Lent. Men and women work, attend church, give alms to beggars and the poor; in short they are orderly,

[23] Crouzet-Pavan, "Sopra le acque salse," 799–802, 836–37.

[24] Oestreich, *Neostoicism and the Early Modern State.*

sober, devout, and disciplined. Lent represents the culture of the reformers, both Catholic and Protestant, and the values of "decency, diligence, gravity, modesty, orderliness, prudence, reason, self-control, sobriety, and thrift."[25] The reformers worked though religious and political authorities to replace the values of carnival with the values of Lent and to rid popular culture of its multiple manifestations of disorder.

Violence and disorder so exercised the attention of successive English governments that its examination has created a historical industry. Alison Wall has recently pointed out one product of this industry, namely, the large number of books and articles dealing with riots, rebellions, and revolts that present a collective picture of a country plagued by regional uprisings during the three centuries between the Peasants' Revolt in 1381 and Monmouth's Rebellion in 1685. The combined weight of the historiographical output makes Wall pose the questions, "Were the people really so rebellious?" and "Were the English really 'in contempt of all authority'?"[26] Accompanying the historiographical output are the inevitable disagreements among historians on the nature and the meaning of the violence and disorder. For example, Alan Macfarlane has argued that the nature of criminal activity supports his claim that England was not a peasant society because at least since the fourteenth century the typical peasant crimes of murder, arson, and rape were rare, but "capitalist" crimes such as theft and robbery were common.[27] Barbara Hanawalt, however, has demonstrated the high level of homicide in late medieval England. Although admitting that a comparison between modern and medieval statistics poses many problems, Hanawalt would argue that it was safer to walk the streets of Miami than those of medieval London. Far from fulfilling the model of a "capitalist" crime, Hanawalt's evidence indicates that passion rather than profit was the main cause of homicide with most murders resulting from arguments. This is her profile of the average homicide: The murderer "will be a man of middle means in the peasant society or a servant or tradesman in London. He is most likely to attack a man over forty who is a neighbor or an acquaintance rather than a family member, and he will kill with a knife or a staff."[28]

---

[25] Burke, *Popular Culture*, 213.

[26] Wall, *Power and Protest*, 1–6. See also Maddern, *Violence and Social Order*, 1.

[27] Macfarlane, *Justice and the Mare's Ale*, 186–87. Macfarlane is one of the historians who are "optimists" in arguing that high levels of violence were not a feature of English society, while others such as Lawrence Stone are "pessimists" in claiming the opposite. See the comments by Susan Dwyer Amussen, "Punishment, Discipline," 1–2.

[28] Hanawalt, "Violent Death," 302, 310–11.

Disagreements also exist among English historians over the attempts to reform popular culture or, if they do not accept Burke's concept of the reform of popular culture, the campaign against disorder. Significantly, historians are in agreement that the problem of order permeated the consciousness of authorities at every level of government, from royal ministers to local justices of the peace and the parish clergy. In the words of one historian, the concern for order "reached almost paranoid levels."[29] The disagreements are over the causes and the chronology of the consciousness. One group of historians has argued that the motivating force behind attempts to control unruly behavior was puritanism, the English strain of Calvinism that became influential especially among the local elites towards the end of the reign of Queen Elizabeth.[30] Other historians have noted that the campaign against disorder occurred in places that had no strong puritan presence and have stressed social and economic rather than religious explanations for the campaign against disorder.[31] One such explanation focuses on the widespread concern bordering on obsession among magistrates over the threat to order that came from vagrants and vagabonds. These were masterless men who were able-bodied yet unemployed and whose numbers seemed to increase at an alarming rate.[32] Another explanation points to the potential for disorder among apprentices, which could also be a source of anxiety for authorities, especially in London where, in the mid-sixteenth century, apprentices constituted about 12 percent of the population.[33] In the final analysis the distinction between religious and socioeconomic factors is decidedly blurred. Reforming and regulating magistrates would have found it difficult to separate moral from social reformation and regulation. For example, they would have considered idleness a moral sin as well as an economic offense. The social and economic welfare of the state was dependent in their view on morally revitalized Englishmen and women.[34]

Historians of England also disagree on the chronology of the campaign against disorderly conduct. The focus for much historical attention has been the early modern period, in particular the late sixteenth and early seventeenth

[29] Hindle, *State and Social Change,* 178.

[30] For example, Wrightson and Levine, *Poverty and Piety.*

[31] For example, Spufford, "Puritanism and Social Control," 41–57.

[32] Beier, *Masterless Men.*

[33] Archer, "Material Londoners?" 184–85.

[34] For a discussion of this debate, see Hindle, *State and Social Change,* 176–79; and Durston and Eales, "Introduction," 24–25. See also Wrightson, "Alehouses, Order."

centuries when the rise of puritanism coincided with social and economic dislocation. More recently, the work of Marjorie Keniston McIntosh has turned attention back to the late Middle Ages, and by doing so she has also addressed the role of puritanism in the campaign. McIntosh's study of the royal manor of Haverling between 1200 and 1500 had led her in 1986 to claim that at least some aspects of the campaign against disorder had medieval antecedents. In particular, she argued that the attempt by local authorities to reform the behavior of the poor was not a new development in the late sixteenth and early seventeenth centuries.[35] She returned to the argument in 1991 in her second book on Haverling that examined the period 1500–1620. This time she expressed her doubts about the role of puritanism in the campaign. The experience of medieval Haverling demonstrates, in her words, that "a high degree of social control could be present a century before the arrival of Calvinism in England."[36] The topic of social control formed only a relatively small part of the two books on Haverling, but her next book, *Controlling Misbehavior in England, 1370–1600*, published in 1998, focused on the topic. After reviewing the historical literature that points to the importance of the early modern period, particularly the decades around 1600, she states, "Evidence from medieval England, however, demonstrates that attempts to curtail wrongdoing had occurred in other periods and circumstances as well."[37]

The historical debates illustrate disagreements on causes but demonstrate unanimity on the concern of authorities with the problems of crime, violence, and disorder, even though no consensus exists on the chronology of this concern. The concern was well placed, because the evidence indicates that medieval and early modern societies were more violent and disorderly than modern societies. Not only is modern Miami safer than medieval London, but medieval and early modern society was on the whole more violent than modern societies, despite the impression gained from the enormous coverage of crime and violence in all the media. In 1990 the homicide rate in England was 1.5 murders per 100,000; in 1998 the rate in the United States was 6.3. The rates for European towns in the sixteenth century ranged from a low of 10 to a high of 60.[38] Just as traditional Europe had higher rates of

---

[35] McIntosh, *Autonomy and Community*, 260.

[36] McIntosh, *Community Transformed*, 250.

[37] McIntosh, *Controlling Misbehavior*, 4, 9–10. *Controlling Misbehavior* was the topic of a special issue of the *Journal of British Studies* 37 (July 1998). Paul Seaver's "Introduction" is a good summary of both the book and the debate.

[38] Ruff, *Violence in Early Modern Europe*, 120–21.

homicide, so also did it have higher rates of alcohol consumption than do modern societies. Contemporary moralists connected the drinking not only to the murders but also to all the other forms of violence and disorder. Oddly enough, few of the historians who examine violence and disorder in late medieval and early modern Europe direct much attention to the role of drinking and drinking establishments as agents. A good example is Julius R. Ruff's fine study of *Violence in Early Modern Europe*. Despite including examples of alcohol-related violence, Ruff spends less than a page analyzing the role of alcohol, taverns, and alehouses.[39] A bit better is the excellent book by Beat Kümin entitled *Drinking Matters: Public Houses and Social Exchange in Early Modern Central Europe* that has ten pages on the role of drinking establishments in disorder and violence, but he devotes the same number of pages to the food served in them.[40]

This book attempts to correct this lack of attention. It does so firstly by analyzing the condemnations of the moralists who blamed alcohol for the violence and disorder. Because of the important role of alcoholic beverages in most people's diets and in social interaction, the moralists did not advocate abstinence but only moderation and directed their criticism not at the drink but at the drunkenness and the drinking establishments. At first glance, the moralists appear correct in their assessment, for most people did consume vast amounts of alcohol, both as part of their daily sustenance and during recreation as a social lubricant. The latter often resulted in binge drinking, quite often in alehouses and taverns, that could provoke disorder and violence, but recreational drinking also promoted celebration, socialization, and jollification. These positive attributes of recreational drinking would mitigate rather than provoke disorder and violence. As it turned out, traditional Europe and especially England did have its disorderly places and disorderly persons, but a careful examination of the evidence reveals that drink's role in the disorder was ambivalent. Similarly, the alcohol-fueled violence that plagues many modern societies was not such a serious problem in traditional Europe. In short, the expectation that the high level of alcohol consumption in traditional Europe was responsible for the high level of violence is wrong. Government regulations demonstrate that it is wrong; despite the concern over violence and disorder, regulations focused more on the provision of good and cheap drink to citizens than on any disorder or violence

---

[39] Ruff, *Violence in Early Modern Europe*, 126, 187–88.

[40] Kümin, *Drinking Matters,* 102–11, 130–40.

that would result from this provision. That is not to say that the moralists got it completely wrong. The drunken disorder they perceived in drinking establishments did exist, but much of it existed because the moralists were the ones defining the drunken disorder, whether it be dancing in alehouses or drinking in taverns during divine service. Drinking behavior is not only culturally mediated; it is also socially mediated.

Chapter 2

The Condemnations
of the Moralists

Do not get drunk with wine, for that is debauchery.
—Ephesians 5:18

While medieval and early modern governments grappled with the problems of crime, violence, and disorder, many moralists were proclaiming that a major cause of the problems was the excessive consumption of alcohol. Drunkenness itself was a form of disorder, and it was the gateway to all other sins. Just as order existed in a moral society, immorality led to disorder. Drunkenness could result in thefts, in prostitution, fornication, and adultery, in brawls and violence leading to murder, and in treason and heresy. Alehouses and taverns were the devil's schools, where young people, students, servants, and apprentices strayed from the path of righteousness, where married men wasted their time and spent their wages while their wives and children starved at home. Drunken sacrilege and the drinking at alehouses or taverns on Sunday instead of attending church services could bring God's punishment on the entire community. Such was the message of the moralists. According to some historians, in the early modern period a shift occurred in the condemnations of drunkenness. It became less a religious sin and more an economic sin according to the ideology of nascent capitalism, a sin that violated the values of time, efficiency, and order.[1]

Moralists supported their condemnations with biblical citations and

[1] Austin, *Alcohol in Western Society*, 129–30.

quotations. However, the image of alcoholic beverages that emerged from the Bible was ambivalent. On the one hand were the shameful drunken nakedness of Noah, the first winemaker, and the incest of Lot with his daughters, who got him drunk. On the other hand was the wine of the Last Supper that became the blood of Christ in the Eucharist. Wine symbolized sex, negatively in the cases of Noah and Lot, but positively in the erotic poetry of the Song of Solomon. Neither bread nor wine existed in the primitive purity of the Garden of Eden, so both represented the passage to culture and were symbols of intelligence and knowledge. Paradoxically, through drunkenness wine could threaten culture by causing aggression, brawls, and rebellions. Likewise paradoxically, intoxication could threaten intelligence and knowledge by creating confusion.

Reinforcing the ambivalent meaning of wine were the differences between the Old and New Testaments. Jewish priests were forbidden to drink wine before their meetings, but Christ's disciples drank wine freely. Christ likened the Jewish people to a vineyard, he used the vine to represent himself, and his first miracle occurred during the marriage at Cana, when he turned water into wine. St. Paul could warn the Ephesians not to get drunk with wine, but the transubstantiation of wine into the blood shed by Christ to redeem the sins of mankind elevated wine to a position of enormous importance.[2] Beer-drinking areas of Europe were more likely to embrace Protestantism than were wine-producing regions, which remained Catholic and thereby retained the Eucharist. Perhaps the Protestants' rejection of transubstantiation also explains their tendency to demonize alcohol. Another explanation for Protestant antipathy towards alcohol derives from Harry G. Levine's examination of the temperance movements of the nineteenth and twentieth centuries. What Levine defines as temperance cultures were predominantly Protestant movements imbued with the Protestant ethos of individual responsibility and moral self-control. Wine drinkers in Catholic countries, even though they might consume far more alcohol than beer- and spirit-drinking Protestants, have not provoked the development of temperance movements.[3]

Woe to Drunkards

In the sixteenth and seventeenth centuries, English preachers and moralists published sermons and pamphlets attacking drunkenness. Although their

---

[2] Comet, "Iconographie du vin," 119–21; Courtois, "Ferments interdits," 63–75; and Unwin, *Wine and the Vine*, 139–41.

[3] Levine, "Temperance Cultures."

Italian and French counterparts condemned the excessive consumption of alcohol, these printed tracts were unique to England, indicating either that drunkenness was perceived to be a greater problem in England than it was on the Continent, or that it was in fact a greater problem. Another possible explanation is the demonization of alcohol by the Protestant authors. Most of the tracts date from the seventeenth century, and their titles leave little doubt about their contents: *The Deadly Danger of Drunkenness, The Scourge of Drunkenness, Warning to Drunkards, The Dreadful Character of a Drunkard, God's Sword Drawn against Drunkards,* and Samuel Ward's *Woe to Drunkards.*[4] Ward was a preacher who was briefly imprisoned and then dismissed from his position as a result of his extreme puritan beliefs. He delivered his sermon against drunkards in 1622 and published it five years later in 1627. His sermon was to a certain extent based on his own personal experience, because as a student at Cambridge he kept a diary that indicated he participated in the university's drinking culture.

Ward's *Woe to Drunkards* was neither a sophisticated analysis of the drinking problem nor a reasoned exhortation to drunkards to abandon their drunkenness. It was a polemic diatribe that condemned "these swinish herds of habitual drunkards, accustomed to wallow in their mire, yea deeply and irrecoverably plunged by legions of devils into the sea of their filthiness [who] turn again to their vomit." Ward devoted several pages to examples of the disastrous consequences that befell drunkards, comparable to the *exempla* of medieval preachers. An alewife at Kesgrave near Ipswich persuaded three young men to stay at her alehouse to continue their drinking, but as she brought them more ale she "was suddenly taken speechless and sick, her tongue swollen in her mouth, never recovered speech, the third day after died." At Barnwell near Cambridge four people drank a barrel of strong beer; three died within twenty-four hours and the fourth barely escaped. At Haslingfield a butcher in an alehouse ridiculed the minister for condemning drunkards; as he drank "something in the cup quackled him, stuck so in his throat that he could not get it up nor down, but strangled him presently." Woe to drunkards, indeed!

Ward informed his listeners/readers that the reason why drunkenness was not listed among the Ten Commandments was the fact that "it is no one sin but all sins, because it is the inlet and sluice to all other sins." As a result, drunkards violated all the commandments, even if Ward's list covered social

---

[4] French, *Nineteen Centuries of Drink*, xi–xx.

as well as moral misbehavior: the drunkard "swears, blasphemes, rages, strikes, talks filthy, blabs all secrets, commits folly, knows no difference of persons or sexes, becomes wholly at Satan's command." In particular Ward mocked the good fellowship and friendship that supposedly flowed from drinking sessions, claiming they were more likely to end in "frays and combats" with "wounds, broken heads, blue eyes, maimed limbs." Even if drinking sessions did not end in violence, they resulted in workers' consuming "the thrift and fruit of their labors... to the prejudice of their poor wives and children at home." In short, unless something was done about it, drunkenness would result in "the utter undoing... of health and wealth, piety and virtue, town and country, church and commonwealth."[5]

Ward's attack had precursors. In 1576 George Gascoigne published *A Delicate Diet for Dainty-Mouthed Drunkards, Wherein the Foul Abuse of Common Carousing and Quaffing with Hearty Draughts Is Honestly Admonished.* Gascoigne wrote with more wit and learning than Ward could muster; he cited the Bible of course but also St. Augustine as well as ancient Greek and Roman authors. What he called his general proposition was "that all drunkards are beasts." Some drunkards were like apes in their pursuit of pleasure, while others were comparable to bears and boars in their brawling and quarreling. Another sort attempted to deceive others as did foxes and wolves, others were as lecherous as goats, as proud as peacocks, or as sluggish as asses, while some belched and vomited like hogs. In short, excessive drinking transformed men into brute beasts, even worse because beasts were satisfied with drinking once or twice a day while men sat in alehouses and taverns night and day and thus misspent their time. What was even worse than being worse than beasts was being worse than Germans! The Germans had long held the reputation for their drunkenness, but nowadays, according to Gascoigne, "we surpass them very far."[6]

Phillip Stubbes was an Elizabethan puritan whose excessive prudishness continues to give puritanism a bad name. In 1583 he published *The Anatomie of Abuses,* attacking those customs that have become associated with the legend of Merry England and seeking to turn the nation into a puritanical commonwealth. Many parish churches supplemented their income through the custom of church ales, brewing ale, selling it to parishioners, and using the income for recurrent and special expenditures such as the repair of

[5] Ward, *Woe to Drunkards*, ed. Chandos, quotes at 233–36, 239–40.

[6] Gascoigne, *Delicate Diet*, ed. Cunliffe, quotes at 456, 467. And see Martin, "National Reputations."

the church tower. Stubbes was not impressed: "Do they think that the Lord will have his house built with drunkenness, gluttony, and such like abominations?" He condemned drunkards in his section on gluttony; his was not a pretty picture. "Every country, city, town, village and other has abundance of alehouses, taverns and inns, which are so fraught with malt-worms night and day, that you would wonder to see them. You shall have them there sitting at wine and good ale all the day long, yea all the night too, peradventure a whole week together, so long as any money is left, swilling, gulling, and carousing. ... How they strut and stammer, stagger and reel to and fro, like madmen, some vomiting, spewing, and disgorging their filthy stomachs, other some ... pissing under the board as they sit, which is most horrible." Although Stubbes admitted that God had ordained the use of drinks to sustain mankind, excessive use of them provoked blasphemy, swearing, deceit, dishonesty, lust, and murder.[7] Ward, Gascoigne, and Stubbes were all English Protestants who produced their condemnations of drunkenness in the space of fifty years, from 1576 to 1622. Protestants and especially puritans had reputations for greater moral severity than did Catholics, but both forms of Christianity demonstrated increased concerns with morality during the sixteenth and seventeenth centuries. The difference was one of degree, however, for the arguments against excessive drinking were essentially the same among medieval moralists and Protestant and Catholic reformers. In other words, the condemnations made by the English Protestants had medieval antecedents and Continental counterparts.

The Sin of Gluttony

Some medieval theologians and moralists considered drunkenness as a sin in its own right. However, most followed the classification of John Cassian and Gregory the Great in considering drunkenness to be a branch of gluttony, one of the seven deadly sins.[8] Books of penance often discussed the penalties for drunkenness under the heading of gluttony. For example, the section on gluttony in the seventh-century *Penitential of Cummean* began, "Those who are drunk with wine or beer ... shall expiate the fault for forty days with bread and water." The same penance applied to those who through

---

[7] Stubbes, *Anatomie of Abuses*, I1, I1v, I4, I4v, quotes at M5, I3v–I4.

[8] Magennis, *Anglo-Saxon Appetites*, 93; Bloomfield, *Seven Deadly Sins*, 147; and Owst, *Literature and Pulpit*, 442.

good fellowship made another drunk.[9] English homilies of the twelfth and thirteenth centuries warned that the sin of gluttony, taking too much to eat and to drink, destroyed both body and soul.[10] The section on gluttony in Robert Mannyng's *Handlyng Synne* (1303) began by proclaiming that immoderate consumption of meat and drink was shameful villainy and stinking abomination. Just as it was a sin to drink at a tavern until the loss of wit and clear speech, so also was it a sin to lead another to an alehouse and get him drunk.[11] Popular opinion could echo the views of the theologians; in the wake of the Black Death, survivors often faced condemnation for celebrating their good fortune by feasting and drinking rather than by praying and offering thanks.[12] Although a sin in itself, gluttony led to other sins such as lechery, and in the fourteenth-century *Vision of Piers Plowman,* William Langland explained the fate of Sodom and Gomorrah:

> Because they were immoderate in their eating and drinking,
> And did that deadly sin that the devil rejoiced at,
> For their vile vices, vengeance fell on them;
> And both of their cities sank into hell.[13]

Other authors were more inclusive in their warnings and claimed that the sin of gluttony was the gateway to all the other sins.[14]

Although the medieval church demonized Bacchus, the god of wine, medieval theologians and moralists did not demonize wine or alcoholic beverages and tended to follow the sentiments expressed by St. John Chrysostom: "wine is the work of God, drunkenness the work of the devil."[15] In the twelfth century the austere St. Bernard of Clairvaux put the case for wine: "Paul, after all, advised Timothy to take a little wine, and the Lord himself drank it and was even called a drunkard; he gave it, too, to his apostles to drink, and established in wine the sacrament of his blood."[16] Dante minutely catalogued God's punishment for every sin and reserved the first five circles

---

[9] *Medieval Handbooks*, trans. McNeill and Gamer, 101.

[10] Morris, *Old English Homilies and Homiletic Treatises*, 102.

[11] Mannyng of Brunne, *Handlyng Synne*, ed. Sullens, 162–63, 167.

[12] The chronicle of Matteo Villani, for example, cited in Fumi, "Economia e vita privata," 235–36.

[13] Latini, *Tesoretto*, trans. and ed. Holloway, 141; and Langland, *Vision of Piers Plowman*, trans. and ed. Tiller, 164.

[14] Scully, *Art of Cookery*, 182, citing *Grant kalendrier et compost des Bergiers*; *Jacob's Well*, ed. Brandeis, 145.

[15] Paronetto, *Chianti*, 82. See also Garrier, *Histoire sociale*, 78.

[16] Bernard of Clairvaux, "An Apologia for Abbot William," in Matarasso, *Cistercian World*, 46.

of his *Inferno* for sins of incontinence, but he had no place for habitual drunk-ards.[17] The typical view of medieval theologians was that food and drink in moderation were necessary for sustenance, but the excessive consumption of them led to the sin of gluttony; to drink more than necessary was a minor sin, but to drink to drunkenness was a deadly sin.[18]

As noted above, when writing *The Anatomie of Abuses,* Phillip Stubbes attacked drunkenness in his section on gluttony. In other words, the medieval theologians' practice of considering drunkenness as a branch of gluttony continued into the early modern period, and it also cast its shadow over Renaissance humanists. Two early humanists, Giovanni Conversini da Ravenna and Petrarch, denounced gluttony and its attendant drunkenness not as sins but for extinguishing reason and dulling the mind.[19] English Protestant clergymen were required to read the homily against gluttony and drunkenness once a year.[20] The homily began with a sentiment that would have been familiar to medieval preachers, "Now ye shall hear how foul a thing gluttony and drunkenness is before God."[21] The medieval moralists would have likewise listened with approving recognition to seventeenth-century English Protestant sermons. One stated that Adam, the father of the first world, sinned by eating, and Noah, the father of the second world, sinned by drinking, and another turned St. Paul's advice to the Corinthians, "Let us eat and drink, for tomorrow we die," into a warning to gluttons, "Let us eat and drink, for by this means tomorrow we shall die."[22] In short, medieval and early modern attitudes towards drunkenness were quite similar, at least as far as the sin of gluttony was concerned. Continuity is also evident in other aspects of the condemnations of moralists.[23]

Drunkenness

Modern definitions of drunkenness simply state that it is the condition of being overcome by alcohol. A definition from a medieval penitential was more

[17] Patrone, "Consumo del vino," 284.

[18] *Jacob's Well,* 142, 146.

[19] Conversini da Ravenna, *Dialogue,* ed. and trans. Eaker, 113; and *Petrarch's Remedies,* trans. and ed. Rawski, 1:57.

[20] Addy, *Sin and Society,* 29.

[21] *Sermons or Homilies,* 320.

[22] John Hales, "Of Gluttony," and Jeremy Taylor, "The Glutton's Way," in Chandos, *In God's Name,* 338, 499.

[23] A conclusion also suggested by Tlusty, *Bacchus and Civic Order,* 79.

descriptive: "This is drunkenness, when it changes the state of the mind, and the tongue babbles and the eyes are wild and there is dizziness and distension of the stomach and pain follows."[24] According to a seventeenth-century definition, it was the condition "where the same legs which carry a man into the house, cannot bring him out again."[25] Yet another seventeenth-century definition was "the privation of orderly motion and understanding," but the author claimed that definitions were unnecessary, since the streets were so full of drunkards that anyone could recognize "this detestable and odious vice."[26] Regardless of the definitions, many authors attempted to portray the condition in ways that combined humor, ridicule, and condemnation. William Langland described what happened to Gluttony after he drank a gallon of ale:

> He pissed four pints in the space of a Paternoster,
> And blew the round bugle at his backbone's end
> So that all who heard that horn held their noses,
> And wished that he had bunged it with a bunch of whins.[27]

Just as unflattering was the description in Geoffrey Chaucer's "Pardoner's Tale." After attacking the belly for sending forth its filthy music at either end, the pardoner proclaimed,

> O drunkard, how disfigured is thy face,
> How foul thy breath, how filthy thy embrace![28]

Later descriptions of drunkenness muted the scatology of the fourteenth-century versions by Langland and Chaucer, but they did not mute their condemnation. The anonymous author of *The Man in the Moon*, printed at London in 1609, called drunkenness "the mother of all mischiefs, the fuel of all filthiness, the root of all roguery, the distemperance of the head, the subversion of the senses, the shipwreck of honesty, the loss of time, and voluntary madness."[29] Further examples could be multiplied, as authors exercised their rhetorical abilities to create as ugly a portrait as possible.[30]

---

[24] *Medieval Handbooks*, trans. McNeill and Gamer, 230.

[25] Brinkworth and Gilkes, "*Bawdy Court*," 35, citing Dalton, *The Countrey Justice* (1655).

[26] French, *Nineteen Centuries of Drink*, 188; French does not identify the author but gives the date of 1627.

[27] Langland, *Vision of Piers Plowman*, trans. and ed. Tiller, 62.

[28] Chaucer, *Canterbury Tales*, trans. Coghill, 262–63.

[29] *Man in the Moone*, ed. Halliwell, 9.

[30] For example, Thomas Young, *Englands Bane: Or, the Description of Drunkennesse*, in Earnshaw, *Pub*

If the moralists are to be believed, drunkenness reached plague proportions in the sixteenth and seventeenth centuries, especially in England, less so in France, hardly at all in Italy. One of the few Italians to complain was the fifteenth-century Florentine poet Filippo Scarlatti, who attacked drunkards for their stupid behavior:

> I do not say this for one or two of them,
> But in the evening I find a good fifty of them.[31]

In the seventeenth century, Scipione Mercuri denounced the excessive consumption of spirits that he detected among lower-class Italians who began their drinking in the morning.[32] For France the key figure is Laffemas, economic adviser to Henry IV, who condemned his fellow countrymen for their drunkenness in treatises published in 1596 and 1600. According to the eminent historian of wine, Roger Dion, these treatises marked the first time anyone had expressed a concern about drunkenness in France.[33] However, other sources do not support Dion but reveal that moralists periodically expressed their concerns during the Middle Ages and continued doing so into the sixteenth and seventeenth centuries. Many condemned the drunkenness associated with festive drinking. Throughout the Middle Ages, French theologians were continually exasperated by the drunken revelry that occurred on feast days, so much so that they argued that the church should reduce the number of them to give people fewer occasions for misbehavior.[34] Both medieval and early modern clergymen complained of the drunkenness that accompanied carnival celebrations, while at the close of the seventeenth century the complaints focused on weddings.[35]

Festive drinking was not the focus of other French moralists, such as Nicolas de la Chesnaye, author of the morality play entitled *La condamnation de Banquet,* composed between 1503 and 1505. Towards the end of the play, Banquet admitted that by making people drink far too much he was responsible for the loss of reason and frequent illnesses; "I have committed many

---

in Literature, 10–11.

[31] Lanza, *Lirici toscani*, 2:565.

[32] *De gli errori popolari d'Italia* (1645), quoted in Camporesi, *Incorruptible Flesh*, 138.

[33] Barthélémy de Laffemas according to Dion, *Histoire de la vigne*, 488; Bernard de Laffemas according to Brennan, *Public Drinking*, 194.

[34] Rodgers, *Discussion of Holidays*, 69, 101, 108.

[35] Delumeau, *Mort des pays*, 28; Pellegrin, *Bachelleries*, 262n75; and Durand, *Vin, vigne*, 36.

crimes worthy of the gallows."[36] During the fourteenth and fifteenth centuries, preachers in the province of Artois attacked townsfolk for their drunkenness, and a priest in Limousin blamed a poor vintage and subsequent rise in the price of wine on the drunken behavior of rogues.[37] Complaints made during the sixteenth and seventeenth centuries condemned drunkenness on Sunday, drunkenness in taverns, and just plain drunkenness.[38]

In England the condemnations rose during the latter half of Elizabeth's reign, peaked during the reigns of James I and Charles I, and continued throughout the rest of the seventeenth century. The rise and peak coincided with the rise and peak of those spoilsport puritans, who were adept at making moral mountains out of moral molehills. Yet some of the condemnations came from those who were not puritans. The puritan credentials of Phillip Stubbes and Samuel Ward were well established, but George Gascoigne was hardly one; in fact, he faced accusations of atheism.[39] Whatever the frequency of drunkenness, many considered it to be increasing and becoming a cause for concern. John Stow, who began writing his famous *Survey of London* in 1590, claimed that "Immoderate quaffing among fools continues as before, or rather is mightily increased."[40] The capital was not the only place where observers perceived drunkards. The vicar at Cranbrook in Kent blamed an outbreak of the plague in 1597 on the town's sins, especially "that vice of drunkenness which did abound here."[41] Significantly, this period marked a decisive turning point in the presentation of drunkenness in Shakespeare's plays. Before 1601 he had only perceived the comic elements in drink; all was jovial and joyous frolic. Thereafter the function of drink was evil, provoking mayhem, murder, and madness. From the humorous Sir John Falstaff and Sir Toby Belch the bard moved to the tragic Cassio in *Othello* (2.3), who was filled with shame after his drunken brawl with Montano; "O God! that men should put an enemy in their mouths to steal away their brains!"[42]

The increasing chorus of complaints led to the enactment of the law against drunkenness in 1606, whose preamble was quoted in chapter 1. Of course, the law had little effect according to the perceptions of the moralists.

[36] La Chesnaye, *Condamnation de banquet*, ed. Koopmans and Verhuyck, 268.

[37] Muchembled, "Jeunes, les jeux," 572; and Bercé, *History of Peasant Revolts*, 35.

[38] Pellegrin, *Bachelleries*, 262n75; Norberg, *Rich and Poor*, 36; and Briggs, *Communities of Belief*, 313.

[39] Thomas, *Religion and the Decline of Magic*, 198.

[40] Rappaport, *Worlds Within Worlds*, 17.

[41] Collinson, "Cranbrook and the Fletchers," 186.

[42] Legouis, "Bacchic Element."

Thomas Dekker wrote in 1608 that in Westminster "drunkenness reels every day up and down my streets."[43] When the law of 1606 was renewed in 1609, the preamble complained that, "notwithstanding all former laws and provisions already made, the inordinate and extreme vice of excessive drinking and drunkenness doth more and more abound."[44] Despite the renewal of the act, the condemnations continued. A medical doctor observed in 1636 that many Englishmen and "too too many" in London "rise to drink, drink to fall, fall asleep of necessity, and ere they are half sober, fall a drinking drunk again."[45] As in the sixteenth century, the condemnations were not confined to London but continued in the provinces. In 1625 a preacher in Northamptonshire prayed, "We lift up our voices loud against drunkenness."[46] English moralists were like their French counterparts in connecting drunken behavior to festive occasions. In 1638 one preacher compared the drunkenness at fairs to a battleground: "Go but to the town's end where a fair is kept, and there they lie, as if some field had been fought; here lies one man, there another."[47]

The Civil War beginning in 1642 did not stifle the voices of the moralists. In 1645 Nicholas Proffet complained, "Hardly can men walk the streets, but to their grief they shall see of both sexes reel and vomit in a brutish manner."[48] A petition from the inhabitants of Warrington claimed that "the multitudes of alehouses, ales and merry-nights are occasions of drunkenness, robberies, and other sins."[49] The Restoration of the Stuart monarchy in 1660 supposedly marked the beginning of a period of massive drinking, as if the nation was celebrating freedom from its puritan yoke.[50] The condemnations continued, but they did not match the level of those earlier in the century, which might be an indication that religious ideology rather than the actual level of consumption was the driving force behind the condemnations. Both Edward Bury's *England's Bane, or the Deadly Danger of Drunkenness,* published in 1677, and Matthew Scrivener's *Treatise against Drunkenness,* published in 1680, likened drunkenness to an epidemic disease.[51] In their condemnations

[43] Dekker, *Dead Tearme*, ed. Grosart, 4:12.

[44] French, *Nineteen Centuries of Drink*, 185.

[45] Bradwell, *Physick for the Sicknesse*, 21.

[46] Clark, *English Alehouse*, 108.

[47] Thomas, *Religion and the Decline of Magic*, 21.

[48] Wrightson, "Alehouses, Order," 6, citing *Englands Impenitencie under Smiting.*

[49] Walter and Wrightson, "Dearth and the Social Order," 125.

[50] Austin, *Alcohol in Western Society*, 241–42.

[51] Warner, "Before There Was 'Alcoholism,'" 415.

of drunkenness, the English Protestants and particularly the puritans sang the loudest, but both medieval and early modern Catholics were singing the same song, that is, drunkenness was a sin that led to other sins, and it was a sin that was too widespread, especially on festive occasions.

Alehouses and Taverns: The Devil's Church

Inseparable from the condemnations of drunkenness was the attack on alehouses and taverns. According to the moralists, these establishments were a major cause of drunkenness, and they were also venues that promoted other sins, various forms of disorder, and violence. The attack on alehouses and taverns reveals the moralists' talent for colorful invective. Italian taverns were migraines of the brains, dropsies of the throat, dysenteries of the purse, cellars of the devil, fountains of sin, and haunts of all corrupt and depraved youths.[52] In France, taverns were cesspools of the devil, the devil's churches, and schools for mobs of delinquents.[53] English moralists easily surpassed their Italian and French counterparts, for they called alehouses the devil's chapels and schoolhouses; nests of Satan; breeders and nurseries of all vice and sin; secret dens of sheep stealers, rogues, robbers, quarrelers, and the like; common enemies to the peace and prosperity of the kingdom; greatest pests of the kingdom; public stages of drunkenness, violence, and disorder; rousy rakehells; puddles and sinks of all filthy livers and beastliness; seminaries of the greatest mischief; the very stakes and stays of all false thieves and vagabonds; resorts and harbors of idle and dissolute people; receptacles of baseness, naughtiness, and lewdness; wombs that bring forth all manner of wickedness; fountains and well-heads from whence spring all miseries; sties for swine; and cages for unclean birds.[54]

As indicated by much of the invective, the devil reigned rather than lurked in alehouses and taverns. Moralists viewed the tavern and the alehouse

---

[52] Basile, *Pentameron*, trans. Burton and intro. Vincent, 213; Buccellato, "Produzione, commercio," 166; and Francesco Guicciardini's *Storie Fiorentine* in Ross and McLaughlin, *Portable Renaissance Reader*, 649.

[53] Faral, *Vie quotidienne*, 76; *Goodman of Paris*, trans. and ed. Power, 84; and Mehl, *Jeux au royaume*, 248.

[54] This is a composite list based on the following sources: *Jacob's Well*, 147; Richardson, *Puritanism in North-West England*, 52; Ashton, "Popular Entertainment," 12; Clark, *English Alehouse*, 145; Lambarde, *Local Government*, ed. Read, 70; Dekker, *O Per Se O*, ed. Judges, 267; Fletcher, *Reform in the Provinces*, 239–40; French, *Nineteen Centuries of Drink*, 197; Harman, *Caveat or Warning*, ed. Judges, 65; Hindle, *State and Social Change*, 183; Leinwand, "Spongy Plebs," 161; Iles, "Early Stages," 260; Tawney and Power, *Tudor Economic Documents*, 1:330, 3:112; Thompson, *Wives, Widows*, 68; Wrightson, "Alehouses, Order," 12; and Wrightson, *English Society*, 170.

as an antichurch, their keepers as antipriests. The birth of Christ in a stable because there was no room at the inn represented the opposition between the church and inns and taverns.[55] An explicit expression of this view came from the fourteenth-century Parisian who wrote a manual of instructions for his young wife: "The tavern is the devil's church, where his disciples go to serve him and where he does his miracles." The tavern, he continued, turned good people into bad who swore, lied, and beat each other.[56] Fourteenth- and fifteenth-century English moralists made the same point and used almost the same language. The tavern was the devil's chapel and his school where his disciples studied and where he performed such miracles as taking away men's wits and strength.[57] In 1425 San Bernardino of Siena developed this theme in a sermon by comparing the tavern's swindlers with vicars, its drunkards with parishioners, its gamblers with priests, its prostitutes with nuns, and its pimps with cathedral officials. As an antichurch, the tavern celebrated an antimass; the sighs of losing gamblers corresponded to prayer, glasses of wine to the chalice, and coins to the host.[58]

Italian moralists were more concerned with the damaging effects of taverns than they were with the incidence of drunkenness. Even so most did not consider them the cause of murder and mayhem. The best illustration of this is the fifteenth-century clergyman who complained that taverns were places where men told dirty stories and lies.[59] At the other end of the scale were the warnings contained in the *Libro di buoni costumi,* written by Paolo da Certaldo, a fourteenth-century Florentine. According to Certaldo, the tavern was a very evil place where gluttons engaged in brawls and plots and lost their money.[60] Other Florentine moralists expressed concerns about the potential for taverns to corrupt the city's youth and supported efforts to close them.[61] Another concern of Italian moralists was the haunting of taverns, a practice condemned by relatives of students attending the university at Bologna in the fourteenth century, by San Bernardino of Siena in the fifteenth century,

---

[55] Cowell, *At Play in the Tavern,* 17, 27.

[56] *Goodman of Paris,* 84.

[57] *Ayenbite of Inwyt,* an English translation of Friar Laurent's *Somme le roy,* in Bloomfield, *Seven Deadly Sins,* 183; and *Jacob's Well,* 147–48.

[58] Cherubini, "Taverna nel basso medioevo," 204.

[59] Balestracci, *Renaissance in the Fields,* 4.

[60] Certaldo, *Libro di buoni costumi,* ed. Schiaffini, 133–34.

[61] *Storie Fiorentine,* in Ross and McLaughlin, *Portable Renaissance Reader,* 649; and Agostino Lapini's *Diario fiorentino dal 252 al 1596,* cited in Weissman, *Ritual Brotherhood,* 203.

Figure 1: Four men drinking at a fourteenth-century Italian tavern; the moderate drinker on the left drinks from a glass, the next one drinks from a large flagon while waiting for the cellarer to pass him a glass from the cellar, the man to his right drinks from both a flagon and a glass, while the last one has fallen off his chair and is vomiting. From a Latin prose treatise on the vices by a member of the Cocharelli family of Genoa, composed for the instruction of his children and especially his son Giovanni, written before 1324.

British Library, MS Additional 27695, fol. 14. Used by permission.

and by members of Jesuit sodalities at Barletta in the sixteenth.[62] An illustration (fig. 1) from a fourteenth-century Genoese treatise on vices depicts the drunkenness that could result from haunting a tavern, with one of the drinkers vomiting on the floor.

French moralists painted an unsavory picture of taverns. They served customers on Sundays and holy days; instead of acting with the piety and devotion appropriate to such days sinners became drunk, blasphemed the holy name of God, participated in obscene activities, and ate meat during Lent. Men dissipated their earnings and their time there while their wives and children went hungry at home. Taverns were haunts of criminals, who took refuge there after

---

[62] Cherubini, "Taverna nel basso medioevo," 219–20; Pullan, *History of Early Renaissance Italy*, 335; and Chatellier, *Europe of the Devout*, 25.

committing their crimes. They congregated in gangs, recruited new members, exchanged information, plotted new crimes, and sold stolen property. Prostitutes circulated among the clientele seeking customers, counterfeiters passed fake money, traitors schemed, and professional gamblers engaged the gullible in games with loaded dice. Brawls and fights broke out with the tavern keepers come time to pay and with strangers or with friends as a result of insults and slanders or for no reason at all. After a night at a tavern, men went home with bloodied faces as a result of the fights, or without cloaks and caps as a result of fraud or dissipation. Such were the characteristics of the devil's church.[63]

The English moralists' indictment of alehouses and taverns contained most of the charges made by the French and Italian attacks on taverns. Beginning in the thirteenth century, authorities and citizens in the towns of London, Nottingham, Southwark, Coventry, Worcester, and Chester condemned alehouses and taverns for promoting drunkenness, attracting criminals and prostitutes, violating curfews, causing brawls and murders, and impoverishing workers and their families.[64] These charges led to the Licensing Act of 1552, necessary because of the "intolerable hurts and troubles to the common wealth of this realm [that] doth daily grow and increase through such abuses and disorders as are had and used in common alehouses."[65] Thereafter the attacks on alehouses became inseparable from the attacks on unlicensed alehouses, and most towns and cities had too many of both according to the moralists. For example, in 1608 Thomas Dekker claimed the suburbs of London had "more alehouses than there are taverns in all Spain and France," and asserted that whole streets were now nothing but one alehouse after another; instead of workers in their shops, one only saw drinkers in the alehouses.[66] The pattern continued in the provinces. Throughout the sixteenth and seventeenth centuries authorities, preachers, and citizens in towns such as Hull, Colchester, Durham, Preston, and Cheshire complained of "the great number of alehouses" and "the multitude of alehouses."[67] After the Restoration the

---

[63] Pisan, *Medieval Woman's Mirror*, trans. Willard and ed. Cosman, 282; Cowell, *At Play in the Tavern*, 121, 229; Faral, *Vie quotidienne*, 76–77; Gauvard, "De Grace Especial," 803n51; Geremek, *Margins of Society*, 279–80; and Norberg, *Rich and Poor*, 36.

[64] Hanawalt, "Of Good and Ill Repute," 111; Iles, "Early Stages," 252; Karras, *Common Women*, 15; Owst, *Literature and Pulpit*, 427; Carlin, *Medieval Southwark*, 206; Bennett, *Ale, Beer, and Brewsters*, 142; and Monckton, *History of English Ale*, 99–100.

[65] Tanner, *Tudor Constitutional Documents*, 501.

[66] Dekker, *English Villainies*, ed. Pendry, 233, 281.

[67] Higgs, *Godliness and Governance*, 272, 323; Clark, *English Alehouse*, 39; Richardson, *Puritanism in North-West England*, 52; and Thirsk and Cooper, *Seventeenth-Century Economic Documents*, 359–60.

complaints waned, but in 1682 Thomas Browne still believed that the "unreasonable number of alehouses" in Norwich was "a great occasion of debauchery and poverty."[68] The chronology of the attack on taverns and alehouses in France and England was similar to that of the condemnations of drunkenness. Both had significant medieval antecedents and in France both continued into the early modern period, while in England the peak coincided with the rise of puritanism in the second half of Elizabeth's reign and in the first half of the seventeenth century. As already noted, the moralists in Italy had little to say about drunkenness, but they joined the assault on taverns.

The Gateway to Other Sins

Moralists feared the threatening potential of drunkenness to lead to other sins and crimes, especially when combined with the dangerous environment of taverns and alehouses. Just as medieval theologians condemned gluttony for being the "gate of sins," so also did medieval and early modern moralists condemn drunkenness. Although the English and Italians expressed similar sentiments, the comments of the French are especially revealing in view of the argument by Roger Dion that concerns about drunkenness did not surface in France until late in the sixteenth century. In 1413 Nicolas de Clamanges complained that people spent both days and nights in taverns, drinking too much yet always drinking more, resulting in oaths, blasphemies, lies, disputes, and brawls, and spending too much money while wives and children went hungry.[69] The religious drama *Le mystère de la résurrection,* written in 1456, likewise catalogued the sins resulting from too much wine: "murders, thefts and crimes, beatings and other misdeeds, suspicion and envy, dishonorable and dissolute games, gluttony and lusts, secrets revealed, promises broken, trouble and slander." That was just a small portion of the catalogue, for the anonymous author continued for several pages describing workers losing time and money, debauched women committing acts of vandalism, men beating wives, women and men losing their honor through fornication, and servants rebelling against their masters.[70] When the French government enacted a law against drunkenness in 1536, it declared the law necessary as a result of the "idleness, blasphemy, homicides, and other damage and harm

---

[68] Bretherton, "Country Inns," 161–62.

[69] Adam, *Vie paroissiale,* 262, citing *De novis celebritatibus.*

[70] *Mystère de la résurrection,* ed. Servet, 715–21.

that come from drunkenness."[71] The law might have reflected concern with the situation in Paris, but the provinces produced similar complaints. To cite two examples, in 1556 and 1576 the authorities at Rouen and Ervy complained of the consequences of haunting taverns, including illegal games, blasphemy, conspiracy, murder and other violence, and the abandonment of suffering wives and children.[72] All in all, the complaints of French moralists once again reveal that drunkenness was a concern before Laffemas' observations at the end of the sixteenth century.

One of the sins and crimes that moralists connected with drunkenness and drinking establishments was violence in all its various forms. The seventeenth-century English poet Samuel Butler captured the essence of this connection in his poem "Upon Drunkenness"; the drunkard neglected all better things,

> For madness, noise, and bloody fights;
> When nothing can decide, but swords
> And pots, the right or wrong of words.[73]

In his *Libro di buoni costumi,* Paolo da Certaldo demonstrated the connection when he advised his readers to avoid villages on feast days because peasants would be there with their weapons, full of wine and empty of respect for their superiors.[74] In 1627 authorities in Devonshire described alehouses as "the occasions of many manslaughters, bloodsheds, and affrays," and a magistrate in Surrey claimed in 1692 that drunkenness was "the root and foundation of bloodshed, stabbing, [and] murder."[75] Rather than merely condemn the drunken violence that occurred at taverns, Nicolas de Clamanges attempted to explain how it occurred: "the heart swells, anger erupts, threats fly, insults explode."[76] Another sin that moralists connected to drunkenness and drinking establishments was illicit sex. Much of my *Alcohol, Sex, and Gender* explores this relationship, and many of the moralists cited above connected the consumption of alcohol and drinking establishments with lechery, debauchery, incest, sodomy, and prostitution. For example, a sermon by Roger Edgeworth

---

[71] Brennan, *Public Drinking,* 199.

[72] Benedict, *Rouen during the Wars,* 16n3; and Babeau, *Village sous l'ancien régime,* 228n. For other cases see Bercé, *History of Peasant Revolts,* 35; and Gascon, *Grand commerce,* 737.

[73] Kiernan, *Duel in European History,* 120.

[74] Certaldo, *Libro di buoni costumi,* ed. Schiaffini, 91–92.

[75] Iles, "Early Stages," 260; and Fletcher, *Reform in the Provinces,* 275.

[76] Gauvard, "De Grace Especial," 803n51.

first cited St. Paul's letter to the Ephesians 5:18, which he rendered as "be not drunk with wine, for in wine is lechery," and then the ancient Roman author Valerius Maximus, who stated that Roman women were forbidden to drink wine so they would not commit adultery.[77]

According to an English proverb dating from 1530, "he that drinketh well sleepeth well, and he that sleepeth well thinketh no harm."[78] Many moralists would disagree, because drunkenness and drinking establishments were responsible in their opinion for seditious thoughts against church and state, leading to religious heresy and political treason. Some moralists blamed the drink. For example, Symphorien Champier, a doctor in Lyon, claimed that the popular revolt in 1529, La Grande Rebeyne, resulted from the strong wine consumed by the revolting workers.[79] In both England and France, however, the tendency was to include the tavern and the alehouse in the accusations. In his *Histoire veritable de la ville de Lyon,* published in 1604, the lawyer Claude de Rubys wrote how people congregated at taverns and while under the influence of wine criticized the king and the government and drafted "scandalous defamatory leaflets."[80] Across the Channel, the puritan John Downame expressed the same sentiments in 1613: "When the drunkard is seated upon the ale-bench and has got himself between the cup and the wall he presently becomes a reprover of magistrates, a controller of the state, a murmurer and repiner against the best established government."[81] Provoking the puritan protests was their perception that alehouses were subversive in general of both church and state and in particular of puritan pastors.[82] The puritans' campaign against alehouses and drunkards continued during the Civil War; they believed that their sectarian opponents sought recruits in alehouses, and that all the drunkards supported the king.[83]

If alehouses and taverns were the devil's churches, one would expect the moralists to include stories of encounters with Satan himself, at least in disguise, as a moral for drunkards. Surprisingly few such stories appear in the sources. One from France, dated 1701, told the story of three young men at a tavern trying to outdo each other in impiety. They decided that whoever

[77] Edgeworth, *Sermons Very Fruitfull,* ed. Wilson, 301.

[78] Apperson, *English Proverbs,* 165.

[79] Gascon, "France du mouvement," 260.

[80] Cited in Davis, *Society and Culture,* 97.

[81] Clark, *English Alehouse,* 145. For another example see Clark, "Alehouse and the Alternative Society," 47.

[82] Richardson, *Puritanism in North-West England,* 52.

[83] Hill, *World Turned Upside Down,* 198; and Walzer, *Revolution of the Saints,* 228.

could make the devil appear would not have to pay for his wine, so one of them cooked a crucifix in a pan. "To his surprise, thunder and lightning came flashing down the chimney, at which all three fled and have not been found since."[84] According to Johann Weyer, the sixteenth-century demonologist, the devil sometimes spoke through drunkards,[85] which would be a convenient way of denying responsibility for any blasphemies uttered while under the influence. An English homily from the twelfth century condemned drinking for leading people into witchcraft.[86] This was long before theologians had accepted the view that witchcraft resulted from a compact with the devil. The sources contain no cases of people making this compact while under the influence of drink. Once they made the compact, witches could enjoy a drink at their sabbats. At a sabbat in Italy they drank large amounts of wine, at one in England the devil furnished both wine and beer, at one in France, malmsey wine, but Spanish witches unfortunately had to drink wine that was "like black and clotted blood."[87]

For the moralists the drunken revelry at witches' sabbats mirrored the behavior of sinners on the Sabbath. Spending Sundays in taverns and alehouses was probably at the lower end of the charges leveled at drunkenness and drinking establishments, but the desecration of the Sabbath and other holy days through drinking was capable, like the sins of blasphemy and sacrilege, of bringing God's wrath down on the entire community. San Bernardino of Siena thundered from the pulpit, "You must not do as the country-folk do, who stay in the tavern drinking and filling their bellies until they hear the sacring bell, which announces the elevation of the Lord's Body; then they drink and run swiftly and, when the Lord's Body is elevated, then they go with their greasy lips, and often drunken, and kiss the altar; and then they run away and return to their wine; and in course of time mice come and nibble at the greasy altar-cloth and altar-linen."[88] Both French and English moralists complained of men spending their week's wages at the tavern or alehouse on Sunday.[89] Both likewise complained of the disorderly conduct, such as gambling, dancing, and whore-mongering that accompanied such

[84] Brennan, *Public Drinking*, 270–71.

[85] Weyer, *Witches, Devils*, ed. Mora and Kohl, trans. John Shea, 31–32.

[86] Morris, *Old English Homilies … From the Unique Ms.*, 212.

[87] Summers, *History of Witchcraft*, 119, 144–45.

[88] Coulton, *Medieval Village*, 247.

[89] Babeau, *Village sous l'ancien régime*, 228; and Rich, *Honestie of This Age*, ed. Cunningham, 54.

drinking.[90] English moralists were especially angered by the failure of sinners to attend church services. A bishop complained in 1560, "For come into a church on the Sabbath day, and you shall see but few, though there be a sermon; but the alehouse is ever full."[91]

Economic Ruin

As noted at the beginning of this chapter, according to some historians the attitudes towards drunkenness in the early modern period began to demonstrate the values of nascent capitalism, that is, time, efficiency, and order. A good illustration of these values comes from Daniel Defoe's *The Complete English Tradesman,* first published in 1726. Defoe began by criticizing the haunting of alehouses and taverns because of the loss of time. A young tradesman might claim that an afternoon at a tavern cost nothing because someone else purchased his drinks, "but at the same time … he spent five pounds worth of his time, his business being neglected, his shop unattended, his books not posted, his letters not written, and the like." Closely related to the first criticism is Defoe's comment that even short trips to the tavern could result in the loss of customers. Next, the loss of time and the loss of customers, combined with the cost of drinking and perhaps additional costs such as gambling, could result in the complete ruin of the tradesman. In summary, Defoe argued that wine, spirits, ale, and beer were innocent products and not guilty of any crimes committed by tradesmen, but "'tis the excess, 'tis drinking them extravagantly, taking an unreasonable quantity, loitering away an unreasonable deal of time, spending their money and starving their families; these are the vices."[92]

Defoe's analysis was explicit in its examination of the economic consequences of drunkenness and the haunting of taverns and alehouses, shorn of any religious moralizing. However, the substance of all of these points was present in medieval condemnations. One of the more explicit medieval manifestations of the values of "capitalism" was *De novis celebritatibus,* written in 1413 by Nicolas de Clamanges. He hoped to convince people that wasting time and money in taverns was folly; they should apply themselves instead to the values of industry, frugality, and temperance. Significantly, when Clamanges

---

[90] Palliser, *Tudor York,* 259; Sauzet, *Contre-réforme,* 274; and Underdown, *Revel, Riot,* 47.

[91] Collinson, *Religion of Protestants,* 203. For another example see Bretherton, "Country Inns," 154.

[92] [Defoe], *Complete English Tradesman,* 1.101, 107, 123, 2.2.119.

attacked the "detestable excesses" committed on holy days in taverns, he argued that the church should reduce the number of holy days so that people would work; instead of haunting taverns they would prune their vines and plant their crops.[93] Almost as explicit in its promotion of "capitalist" values was *Le mystère de la résurrection,* dated 1456. In his lengthy description of all the harm that came from drunkenness the author included indolence, idleness, deprivation, and poverty.[94] Clamanges and the anonymous author of *Le mystère de la résurrection* were by no means isolated medieval voices in the condemnation of the economic disorder associated with drunkenness and drinking establishments. Medieval poems, sermons, plays, and proverbs associated taverns and drunkenness with poverty.[95] The fourteenth-century English Dominican John Bromyard warned drunkards of their eventual impoverishment, and in the same century the theologian John Wyclif argued that poor workers should not spend all their money on drinks on holy days.[96] In the fourteenth century Paolo da Certaldo warned people against leaving their money in taverns, and in the fifteenth Christine de Pisan wrote that young artisans dissipated their earnings "with superfluous, outrageous expenses" at taverns.[97]

The final medieval example returns to Defoe's English tradesman, this time a carpenter. A humorous fifteenth-century poem, entitled *The Debate of the Carpenter's Tools,* described the ruin of the tools' master at an alehouse. When the whetstone claimed that he would earn his master much money by sharpening his axes, the adze expressed his doubts:

> For he will drink more on a day,
> Than you can lightly earn in two.

The plane and the broad axe agreed that they would help their master earn more silver in a year than anyone could carry, but the hammer repudiated their boasts:

> For he will drink more in an hour,
> Than two men may get in four.

---

[93] Rodgers, *Discussion of Holidays,* 100–102; and Adam, *Vie paroissiale,* 262.

[94] *Mystère de la résurrection,* ed. Servet, 715–21.

[95] Cowell, *At Play in the Tavern,* 111, 121; "How the Goodwife Taught her Daughter," in Goldberg, *Women in England,* 99; Morawski, *Proverbes français,* 58, 90; and Cherubini, "Taverna nel basso medioevo," 205.

[96] Owst, *Literature and Pulpit,* 434; and Wyclif, *Select English Works,* ed. Arnold, 3:158–60.

[97] Certaldo, *Libro di buoni costumi,* 133; and Pisan, *Medieval Woman's Mirror,* 210.

The carpenter's wife joined the debate and complained that he was also spending the money she earned by spinning:

> He will spend more in an hour,
> Than you and I can get in four.

In short, despite the best efforts of the tools to help him earn a comfortable living, the carpenter dissipated his wealth at the alehouse.[98]

The denunciations of the economic effects of drunkenness and drinking establishments intensified in the sixteenth and seventeenth centuries. When Laffemas expressed his concerns about the excessive consumption of wine in France towards the end of the sixteenth century, he focused on the economic consequences; drunkenness very often resulted in the ruin of households and families. According to French proverbs, the excessive consumption of wine resulted in ruin,[99] and, according to French moralists, the hungry wives and children that resulted from men drinking at taverns was proverbial. A farce performed for King Henry IV in 1607 put an amusing twist on the concerns of the moralists. A wife berated her husband for drinking too much; the money he spent on wine was supposed to go to the royal tax collectors. The husband replied that he would rather spend the money on more wine than see it go to the king. The wife in turn cursed him for ruining the family. When three tax collectors arrived, they forced open a trunk, out of which emerged three devils who, recognizing their own, carried the tax collectors away in the trunk.[100]

The dire economic consequences of drink were a popular theme in English literature during the sixteenth and seventeenth centuries, as poems, plays, songs, proverbs, sermons, treatises, and essays warned drunkards that poverty was their fate.[101] To give one example, Joseph Rigbie's poem, written in 1656, described "The Drunkard's Prospective":

> Health out of the body, wit out of the head,

---

[98] *Debate of the Carpenter's Tools*, in Hazlitt, *Remains of the Early Popular Poetry*, 1:79–90.

[99] Rivière, "Thème alimentaire," 204, 214.

[100] Lancaster, *History of French Dramatic Literature*, 1.1.19.

[101] Apperson, *English Proverbs*, 168; Barclay, *Eclogues*, ed. White, 505; "Toss the Pot," in Collier, *Illustrations of Early English Popular Literature*, 1:32–33; Copland, *Highway to the Spital-House*, in Judges, *Elizabethan Underworld*, 21; "The Drunkard's Legacy," in Dixon, *Ancient Poems, Ballads, and Songs*, 151–59; Earle, *Microcosmography*, ed. Osborne, 22; *Man in the Moone*, ed. Halliwell, 7–11; Rowlands, *Four Knaves*, ed. Rimbault, 59; "The Prodigal Son Converted," and "The Young Man's Counsellor: or, A Guide for New Beginners," in *Roxburghe Ballads*, ed. Chappell, 4:50, 75; and Warner, "Good Help," 264.

Strength out of the joints, and every one to bed,

All money's out of purse; drink out of the barrels,

Wife, children, out of doors, all into quarrels.[102]

As in France, the economic effects of alcohol and drinking establishments became a concern of the ruling class. The preamble to the licensing law of 1604 claimed that drinking establishments had become harbors of "lewd and idle people" who spent and consumed "their money and time in lewd and drunken manner."[103]

The moralists' condemnations of the economic effects of drinking targeted three groups of people. The first group comprised the young, including apprentices, servants, and students. As already noted, the potential of taverns to corrupt young men was a concern of moralists in Florence. Many feared the potential for sexual and violent disorder among the young who frequented taverns and alehouses, but the potential for economic disorder also concerned them. Young people were supposed to be learning the disciplined work habits and the respect for authority that would make them productive adults. Drinking and drinking establishments promoted the contrary values of idleness, profligacy, and insubordination. A sixteenth-century medical treatise claimed that few students gained "profound knowledge" because most of them drank too much wine.[104] Likewise, efforts to reform the behavior of students at Cambridge developed from the opinion that "excess in drinking" was one of the "sins of the university."[105] According to an order prepared by magistrates in Devonshire in 1627, the unlicensed alehouses drew "men's servants and young tradesmen and beginners from their lawful trades and labors to an idle and disordered course of life."[106] At about the same time a petition from Hatfield in Sussex expressed the fears of its citizens regarding one alehouse keeper, who by attracting the young was laying "a foundation of looseness" for the next generation.[107]

Another targeted group included vagabonds, beggars, and the poor. In times of economic hardship, such as the latter part of Elizabeth's reign,

---

[102] Hackwood, *Inns, Ales*, 161.

[103] French, *Nineteen Centuries of Drink*, 184. See also Harrison and Royston, *How They Lived*, 290; and Bretherton, "Country Inns," 161–62.

[104] O'Hara-May, *Elizabethan Dyetary*, 130.

[105] Griffiths, *Youth and Authority*, 187.

[106] Iles, "Early Stages," 260. See also Goldberg, "Masters and Men," 69.

[107] Fletcher, *Reform in the Provinces*, 239.

the large numbers of vagabonds roaming the roads and beggars clogging the streets posed a threat to the rest of society, at least in the view of many authorities. Moralists considered drunkenness and the frequenting of drinking establishments to be both cause and symptom of the problem. Poverty and drunkenness reinforced each other, as indicated by the perceptive words of the Water Poet John Taylor, "The meanest beggar dares to spend all he has at the alehouse ... for the poor man drinks stiffly to drive care away, and has nothing to lose."[108] Nonetheless, authorities considered the drinking beggar and vagabond and the drinking houses that harbored them to be a menace to order. In 1582 the magistrate William Lambarde condemned alehouses for providing relief and refuge to "idle rogues and vagabonds."[109] For the seventeenth-century puritan authorities at Northampton the drinking of the poor led to the daily increase in "the horrible and loathsome sin of drunkenness" and in turn increased "the impoverishing of this town and commonwealth."[110]

The final group targeted were workers, primarily tradesmen and craftsmen, the backbone of society, on whom the authorities depended for their industrious contributions to the public well-being by means of work and taxes. The town council and royal officers of Nantes complained in 1581 that the "artisans and craftspeople of the town and faubourgs ... pass the greater part of working days in taverns, gambling and getting drunk, rather than everyone sticking to his work to gain his living and serve the public and individuals."[111] Similar complaints came from the authorities at Rouen, Saint-Emillon, Dax, and Cognac.[112] Moralists in England likewise complained of the idleness and profligacy of craftsmen and tradesmen.[113] One particular custom that angered many was the observance of Saint Monday, that is, the practice among workers to continue their Sunday drinking at alehouses on Monday rather than return to work.[114]

Two seventeenth-century English commentators anticipated the economic analysis of Daniel Defoe. One, known only as S.T., included an appendix

---

[108] *A Discovery by Sea from London to Salisbury* (1623), cited by Slack, "Poverty and Politics," 182.

[109] Lambarde, *Local Government*, ed. Read, 70.

[110] Clark, "Alehouse and the Alternative Society," 47.

[111] Collins, *Classes, Estates*, 280.

[112] Benedict, *Rouen during the Wars*, 16n3; and Bercé, *History of Peasant Revolts*, 35.

[113] For two examples see Dekker, *Seven Deadly Sinnes*, ed. Grosart, 2:42–43; and Rich, *Honestie of This Age*, 54.

[114] Thompson, "Time, Work-Discipline," 72–73.

on the causes of vagabonds to his book entitled *Common Good,* published in 1652. The other, oddly enough known only as R.T., wrote a pamphlet, *The Art of Good Husbandry,* in 1675. Both proceeded to analyze the economic effects of alehouses and taverns. R.T. carefully calculated how much was lost in time, money, and opportunities by a "mechanic tradesman" who visited an alehouse or coffeehouse several times a day; "he cannot reckon less than seven groats; which comes to fourteen shillings a week (Sunday excepted) which is thirty-six pounds ten shillings a year."[115] S.T. began by reckoning that England had 200,000 alehouses, but for the sake of argument he was willing to concede only 100,000. If each alehouse sold two barrels weekly, the amount of barley malt wasted each week is worth 50,000 pounds or 2,600,000 pounds a year. Having made his mathematical calculations, S.T. joined the moralists and condemned the workers who sat in alehouses, "drinking themselves penniless, witless, and their wives and children bloodless."[116]

————  ————

The condemnations of the moralists demonstrate a large degree of continuity over time. The frequency of the condemnations ebbed and waned, but attitudes prevalent in the Middle Ages, such as considering drunkenness as a branch of gluttony, were still present in the early modern period. Conversely, the early modern "discovery" that drunkards were capitalistic sinners had medieval antecedents. The class specificity of the condemnations did change somewhat. The moralists targeted the poor and the working class, not just for their economic sins but for their drunken behavior in general. The best illustration of the class bias of this concern comes from the debates in the English Parliament over the introduction of laws against drunkenness in the late sixteenth and early seventeenth centuries. Many speakers expressed their concern that "the son of a good man" or "men of best quality" might face detention and whipping as a result of the proposed legislation and therefore sought amendments in the legislation to avoid the possibility of this happening.[117] In his *Description of England* (1587), William Harrison faulted "the meaner sort of husbandmen and country inhabitants" for their occasional drunkenness

---

[115] R.T., *Art of Good Husbandry,* in Thirsk and Cooper, *Seventeenth-Century Economic Documents,* 98.
[116] S.T., "Appendix Shewing the Chiefe Cause," ed. Martin, 38–41.
[117] Kent, "Attitudes of Members," 49.

but commended "the honorable and wiser sort" for their moderation.[118] In the seventeenth century, however, more and more moralists were pointing a collective finger at the gentry for their drinking binges. In his *Brief Lives,* John Aubrey claimed that nowadays the gentry met in an alehouse "to drink up a barrel of drink and lie drunk there two or three days together."[119] Other moralists agreed with Aubrey's observation, and one noted that no longer could people say "drunk like a beggar" since the gentry had earned this pejorative.[120] Another constant in the class specificity of the condemnations was the clergy, for they had a well-deserved reputation for their drinking.[121]

The gender specificity of the moralists' condemnations was overwhelmingly male. On the rare occasions when moralists included women in the accusations they served to demonstrate how absolutely terrible the situation had become, as when Nicholas Proffet complained of "both sexes" drunk in the street. Female keepers of taverns and alehouses could also be a target of the moralists' wrath, but the really notorious antipriests were male. The major exceptions to the male-specific nature of the condemnations were those involving sexual activity, which implicated women as well as men. Aside from these cases, women appeared as victims of their husbands' drinking behavior, the long-suffering wives who hungered or starved at home with their children while their husbands consumed their income at alehouses or taverns. Although age seldom featured in the condemnations, when mentioned it focused on the young, always young males. Since young males are the major consumers of alcohol in all societies, this is not at all surprising. If anything, what is surprising is the failure of the moralists to target young males more than they did.

While variations in the condemnations of moralists over time were negligible, variations over place were significant. England produced an enormous amount of evidence, France not as much but still substantial, Italy very little. Italy's situation might require further research; at any rate the uniqueness of Italy will be the subject of further analysis in subsequent chapters. The perception of French moralists was that France had a drinking problem throughout the period. The French historian Jean-Louis Flandrin would disagree with the perception; he argues that the French were moderate drinkers,

---

[118] Harrison, *Description of England,* ed. Edelen, 132.

[119] Aubrey, "*Brief Lives,*" ed. Clark, 2:267.

[120] Simon, *History of the Wine Trade,* 3:392, citing J. Hart's *Diet of the Diseased* (1633).

[121] Martin, "Alcohol and the Clergy," 23–39.

partly as a result of their practice of diluting wine with water.[122] As for England, the picture of the moralists almost suggests an entire nation staggering from one alehouse to another. Yet evidence presented in the next chapter indicates that Italy had a higher per capita consumption of alcohol than did the other two countries. The national differences in the condemnations of the moralists might result from culturally different attitudes. Just as anthropologists argue that drunken behavior is culturally mediated, perceptions of drinking problems are also culturally mediated. What constitutes a drunkard in a small town in America's Bible Belt would differ from what constitutes a drunkard in vodka-soaked Moscow.

The moralists, those who did the condemning, had diverse backgrounds, ranging from simple priests, monks, and pastors to people at the highest levels of political and religious life, including even one king in the person of James I.[123] All nevertheless belonged to that part of society that formed the religious, political, and literary elite, separated from the mass of the population through status, income, and/or literacy. During the Middle Ages, clergy dominated, although not completely, while increasingly during the early modern period, more and more laymen added their voices to the chorus of complaints. Male voices were likewise dominant throughout, with only the occasional female such as Christine de Pisan joining the attack. The elite background of the moralists and the content of their condemnations is suggestive of "the reform of popular culture," a phrase launched by Peter Burke in his book *Popular Culture in Early Modern Europe*. As noted in chapter 1, for Burke *The Combat between Carnival and Lent* was a metaphor for the concerted attempts to reform popular culture that occurred in the sixteenth and seventeenth centuries. Burke dismisses medieval reform efforts as ineffectual, but on that criterion many of the efforts of the early modern moralists to reform drinking patterns would likewise require dismissal. A safe conclusion would be that the condemnations of the moralists and Burke's "reform of popular culture" were part of the same tendency in both medieval and early modern Europe.

---

[122] Flandrin, "Boissons et manières," 309–14. Flandrin included this material in a longer article entitled "Diversité des goûts," 66–83.

[123] Monckton, *History of English Ale*, 113.

Chapter 3

The Consumption of Alcohol

No longer drink only water, but use a little wine.
                                                        —1 Timothy 5:23

The condemnations of the moralists give the impression that the English would be drowning in a sea of alcoholic beverages, the French would be knee deep in wine, and the Italians would be following the advice of St. Paul to Timothy to use a little wine. This chapter examines the consumption of alcohol in Italy, France, and England as well as the consumption by peasants. Very few people rejected Paul's advice and drank only water. Some religious ascetics such as Catherine of Siena did not drink wine.[1] Another total abstainer was a fourteenth-century Lollard heretic, who "renounced all pleasures" and also became a vegetarian.[2] In fact, in the 1460s Sir John Fortescue claimed that the English did not drink water, "unless at certain times upon a religious score and by way of doing penance."[3] He forgot the poor, who often had no choice but to drink water. The quality of water in traditional Europe was not yet as bad as it would later become as a result of urbanization and industrialization, but those who could afford alcoholic beverages preferred to drink them rather than water. Indicative of the situation were the reasons why London officials attempted to improve the quality

---

[1] Bell, *Holy Anorexia*, 43; see 122, 138, 165 for other examples.
[2] Hassall, *They Saw It Happen*, 187, citing the continuation of Henry Knighton's *Chronicle*.
[3] Barr, *Drink*, 257.

of the town's water supply in 1345; this was necessary to provide good water for people to prepare their food and for the poor to drink.[4]

Although voluntary abstention was rare, some individuals took pride in their temperance. The apostle of temperance was the Venetian Luigi Cornaro (1475–1566). He advocated moderation in all things, especially diet, and argued that a long life would result from his daily regimen of consuming only twelve ounces of solid food and fourteen ounces of liquid, mainly wine—not quite a half bottle a day. His longevity was his program's greatest recommendation, for he died at the age of ninety-one.[5] The early seventeenth-century Duke of Newcastle was praised by his wife for his temperance, which consisted in daily drinking a small glass of wine at breakfast, two "good glasses" of weak beer and a small glass of wine at dinner, and a draught of weak beer at supper.[6] This was indeed temperate when compared to the regulations of the Order of Temperance established at Hesse in 1600; its members pledged to drink no more than seven glasses of wine at each meal.[7]

Despite these examples of "temperance," the evidence indicates that Italians, French, and English consumed amounts that would be considered gargantuan by today's standards. The annual per capita consumption of wine in modern Italy is not quite 60 liters; in the Italian cities of the Renaissance it could be 300. At least that is what the statistical evidence reveals. Mark Twain's (or Benjamin Disraeli's) famous dictum concerning "lies, damned lies, and statistics" warns of the difficulties in using quantitative evidence, and to overcome these difficulties the tables in this chapter present four different types of statistics on the consumption of alcoholic beverages. Each of these has problems. The first is the annual per capita consumption of towns, usually based on municipal records of excise taxes. An obvious problem with these statistics concerns the alcoholic beverages that escaped taxation, and according to one estimate the records understated the consumption of wine by at least 25 percent.[8] These statistics also hide class-, age-, and gender-specific drinking. To take a hypothetical example, if the records reveal an annual per capita consumption of 365 liters of wine, that means a liter a day for each inhabitant. A high proportion of the population in preindustrial towns were too poor to consume much and a similar proportion were too young to drink much, meaning that the rest of

---

[4] Bennett, *Ale, Beer, and Brewsters,* 8–9; and Galloway, "Driven by Drink?" 95.

[5] Freeman, "Medical Perspectives," 14–15; and Porter, "Consumption," 60.

[6] Simon, *History of the Wine Trade,* 3:19.

[7] Austin, *Alcohol in Western Society,* 203.

[8] James B. Collins cited in Brennan, "Towards the Cultural History," 87n22.

the population could be drinking almost two liters a day. Although women did drink, they usually did not drink as much as men, leaving almost three liters for each adult male of means.

A second type of statistical evidence is the computation of annual per capita consumption from household accounts. The aggregate consumption of a household is of little value unless the accounts contain precise information on the number of people, whether ten or twenty, sharing the drink. The evidence from household accounts usually comes from the nobility or the middle class, who could afford to consume large amounts of expensive wine, but these households also contained servants who would figure in the computations even if they were drinking cheap wine or weak beer. Another factor is the sociable nature of the households of the privileged classes, as guests and visitors could consume alcoholic beverages. A third type of statistic derives from wills, maintenance contracts, and corrodies, which is a type of pension. A man's will might stipulate a precise amount of drink for his widow, or a couple might relinquish control of their land in return for a guaranteed amount of food and drink. Notarial records documented these arrangements, but they also documented cases of failure to adhere to them. A final type of statistic is the ration, particularly for sailors and soldiers. If anything, rations approximate the ideal rather than the real; many soldiers, especially those in the field, probably consumed a fraction of their ration of beer or wine. Nonetheless, rations are valuable in demonstrating expectations. Another problem with the use of rations to indicate per capita consumption is that a worker's wages could include a ration of wine that would then be consumed by members of his household. In addition to the specific problems for each type of statistic, other factors such as spoilage could alter the results, and the conversion of premodern measurements presents difficulties; for example, was the medieval gallon equal to the modern? Despite these problems and difficulties, as well as others considered below, the overwhelming impression is that people drank much.

Italy

Wine, according to the historian Antonio Ivan Pini, has had a very important, central role in Italian civilization, not only in the obvious areas "of food, of gastronomy, of agriculture, of commerce, and of economy, but also in the areas ... of poetry, of painting, of sculpture, of music, of myth, of religion, of spirituality, and of culture."[9] For Italians wine was one of life's necessities, an essential part of their diet. Perhaps the best expression of this comes from a statute protecting grapevines enacted in 1571 by a commune near Siena: "Vines are of as great importance as one can possibly say."[10] To quote Pini again, wine was of "prima ma non primissima necessità"—"prime but not primest necessity."[11] Bread was of "primest" necessity, but wine came before others, according to one historian, "with absolute precedence even over meat."[12] In his *Libri della famiglia*, written in the 1430s, Leon Battista Alberti stated that bread and wine were "the most necessary commodities" to feed a family.[13] To consume someone's bread and wine meant to live in his household or to be otherwise dependent on him.[14] Other alcoholic beverages such as beer and mead were almost unknown throughout the peninsula, although Italians did produce a small amount of fruit-based drinks such as cider and perry, and the consumption of spirits began to increase towards 1700. As a result of wine's importance, new rulers could obtain immediate pubic support by reducing the taxes on wine, as occurred at Florence in 1465.[15]

Studies of wine drinking in modern Italy indicate that "the average Italian rarely eats without drinking or drinks without eating."[16] The practice of drinking wine with food has a long history in Italy. A sixteenth-century novelist claimed that "all the foods in the world are insipid without wine, and, in truth, the better the wine, the greater the relish it gives meats."[17] When traveling in 1665, the priest Sebastiano Locatelli began his day with a large breakfast of rice pudding, eggs, bread, and sour wine.[18] Wine was not only a pleasing drink, it was also good for the health. At the beginning of the fourteenth century, a Florentine proclaimed that "Wine nourishes; it is a substantial food that becomes blood in the body."[19]

People of all classes drank wine regularly, except for the very poor, and one of the defining characteristics of the poor was their inability to purchase

[9] Pini, *Vite e vino,* 18.

[10] Imberciadori, "Vite e vigna," 319.

[11] Cited in Montanari, *Alimentazione contadina,* 377.

[12] Mazzi, "Note per una storia," 95.

[13] Alberti, *Family in Renaissance Florence,* 189.

[14] Cohen and Cohen, *Words and Deeds,* 73, 118, 221.

[15] Landucci, *Florentine Diary,* 4.

[16] Sadoun, Lolli, and Silverman, *Drinking in French Culture,* 54.

[17] Bandello, *Twelve Stories,* 10.

[18] Blunt, *Sebastiano,* 247.

[19] La Roncière, "Vignoble florentin," 125.

wine.[20] According to a thirteenth-century Franciscan, "those accustomed to drinking water are those who do not have wine."[21] A similar sentiment comes from the lament of the Italian peasant whose grapevines had withered during a drought: "For want of water, I am forced to drink water; if I had water, I would drink wine."[22] Had workers been forced to drink water, many of the monuments of the Italian Renaissance might have remained unfinished, for a condition of work was often a supply of wine. When overseeing the construction of the dome on Florence's cathedral in the fifteenth century, Filippo Brunelleschi arranged for a supply of wine to be carried to the workers so they would not waste time descending and ascending. The sculptor Nanni Grosso even refused to leave his shop to work unless he received free access to his employer's supply of wine.[23] The best example of drinking on the job occurred at the Arsenal in Venice. When it finished building a ship, the construction crew received two liters of wine to celebrate. This was pure, unadulterated wine; for daily drinking on the job workers drank watered wine, *bevanda,* diluted at a ratio of one part wine to two parts water. In the middle of the sixteenth century, the workers at the Arsenal drank on average 2.5 liters of *bevanda* a day; by 1615 to 1619, this had increased to 3.2, and was nearly 5 liters a day during the period of 1635 to 1639, when it flowed from a fountain. According to one observer, instead of making the workers unfit for work, *bevanda* restored their vitality and raised their spirits.[24]

When they finished work, men could continue drinking at home or in taverns. Florentines of all classes purchased barrels of wine for domestic consumption, sometimes buying a year's supply all at once, sometimes making several purchases throughout the year in the hope that the price might decline.[25] The figures in tables 3.1 through 3.4 are in liters; a liter is equal to 1.056 US quarts or .880 imperial quart. As already indicated, most of the figures in table 3.1 come from municipal tax records and a few are subject to debate among historians.[26] Some of the figures do in fact defy belief. For example, Florentine regulations forbidding the sale of wine in hotels permitted the owner of a hotel

---

[20] Balestracci, "Produzione e la vendità," 48.

[21] Jacapone da Todi, quoted in Soriga, "Vite e il vino," 153.

[22] Howell, *Epistolae Ho-Elianae,* ed. Jacobs, 2:450.

[23] Vasari, *Lives of the Artists,* trans. Bull, 157, 237–38.

[24] Davis, "Venetian Shipbuilders," 60–74.

[25] La Roncière, "Vignoble florentin," 127.

[26] For example see the comments on Villani's figures in Melis, *Vini italiani,* 90; Balestracci, "Consumo del vino," 1:27; and Balestracci, "Produzione e la vendità," 48.

to keep only enough wine to supply every member of his household with wine for a year, one *cogno* a person, that is, 406.8 liters.[27] Even more extraordinary is the figure of an annual per capita consumption of 740 liters at Turin in 1567, calculated from tax records. By way of conclusion, one historian reckons that in the fourteenth century, an adult worker in Florence drank much more than a liter a day, while another claims that in Bologna and Florence during the late Middle Ages each adult consumed almost two liters.[28] Perhaps a third historian, Anna Maria Nada Patrone, should have the last word: "It is not possible to calculate the average per capita consumption."[29]

Table 3.1: Italy: Annual per capita consumption of wine.

PLACE	DATE	AMOUNT (L)
Modena Adult male	1327	407–509
Florence Calculations of Giovanni Villani	1338	248–293
Siena	1350–1400	415
Volterra Each person above the age of three years	1367	335
Bologna	Early 1400s	200
Genoa	Early 1400s	286
Corleone	1437	124–148
Florence Estimate by Lodovico Ghetti	ca. 1445	288
Turin	1567	740
Bologna	17th century	300–350
Rome	1636	210
Rome	1660	270

SOURCES: Pini, *Vite e vino*, 133–34, 135nn315–16, 168–69n92; Fiumi, "Economia e vita privata," 231, 233n112; Stouff, *Ravitaillement et alimentation*, 92; Buccellato, "Produzione, commercio," 163; Goldthwaite, *Building of Renaissance Florence*, 346; Picco, "Viaggiatore in incognito," 249; and Revel, "Capital City's Privileges," 46.

The figures in tables 3.2 to 3.4 support the conclusions of the first two historians for the medieval period and suggest that they are also valid for the sixteenth and seventeenth centuries. Taking the example of Ser Ludovico from table 3.2, this Pisan notary's household comprised his wife, his mother,

[27] Fiumi, "Economia e vita privata," 233.

[28] La Roncière, "Alimentation et ravitaillement," 183; and Pini, *Vite e vino*, 27.

[29] Patrone, *Cibo del ricco*, 435.

a young male servant, and himself. Each day the household would consume more than the equivalent of six and a half modern bottles of wine. The proportion of household and institutional budgets spent on wine could be high. At the Genoese hospital for incurables in the early seventeenth century 26.5 percent of the budget for food was spent on wine; at the same time a college at Pavia spent 22 percent, and a Genoese noble family spent 17 percent.[30] The figure for the widows in table 3.3 derives from an examination of the annual maintenance stipulated in their husbands' wills. The figure that leaps from table 3.4 is the 1000 liters for the gravediggers during an epidemic of the plague in Turin. These were the notorious *monatti*, who removed the dead and buried them, a job perhaps requiring a state of inebriation.

Table 3.2: Italy: Annual per capita consumption of wine in households.

PLACE	DATE	AMOUNT (L)
Venice Household of Bernardo Morosini	1343–1344	720
Pisa Household of the notary Ser Ludovico	1428	455
Pisa Household of Giovanni Maggiolini	1428	683
Pavia Borromeo College	1609–1610	496
Montaldo Working family	1680–1688	300

SOURCES: Pini, *Vite e vino*, 135n316; and Wyczanski, "Structure sociale," 676.

Table 3.3: Italy: Annual per capita consumption of wine in contracts.

PLACE	DATE	AMOUNT (L)
Piedmont Half pure wine and half *mezzo vino*	1345	203
Chiesa, Piedmont Typical amount bequeathed to widow	1675–1706	246

SOURCES: Patrone, *Cibo del ricco*, 436; and Levi, *Inheriting Power*, 68–72.

[30] Spooner, "Régimes alimentaires," 37.

Table 3.4: Italy: Annual per capita rations of wine.

PLACE	DATE	AMOUNT (L)
Venice Sailor on galleys	1310	196
Piedmont Castellan	1329–1336	730–912
Sicily Adult laborer	1373	313
Florence Adult at the Hospital of San Gallo	1395–1405	255
Tuscany Sailor on galleys	1572, 1574	292
Turin Gravedigger during an epidemic of plague	1598–1600	1000
Piedmont Soldier	1617	500

SOURCES: Lane, *Venice and History,* 264; Stouff, "Approvisionnement des ménages," 666; Mazzi, "Note per una storia," 95; Goldthwaite, *Building of Renaissance Florence,* 344; Hémardinquer, "Sur les galères," 85; Picco, "Viaggiatore in incognito," 265; and Picco, "Gabelle, commerci," 201.

All of these statistics do not reveal how the primitive agriculture of the period was able to produce the wine that was consumed in such quantities. Some of it was imported and a brisk interregional trade in wine was the beneficiary of a revolution in transportation.[31] Nonetheless, the costs of transport dictated that the vast majority of wine, especially the cheap wine for the mass market, was local. Around Florence an enormous extension of vineyards occurred during the fourteenth century, including both the establishment of grape "plantations" on the plains and surrounding hills and the continuation of the more familiar type of mixed agriculture.[32]

The quality of the wines varied enormously from sweet varieties such as the malvasia imported from the eastern Mediterranean to the cheap watered *bevanda.* The quality of the wines rather than the quantity consumed was class specific, and each wine had its own clientele depending on price, with some imported wines costing ten times more than local wines. Most of the wine consumed was new wine from the last vintage. This was carefully rationed for a year until the next vintage produced a batch of new wine.[33] Even cheaper and weaker than *bevanda* was *mezzo vino,* the wine produced

[31] Melis, *Vini italiani,* 119.

[32] La Roncière, "Vignoble florentin," 143.

[33] Balestracci, "Consumo del vino," 18; and Melis, *Vini italiani,* 89–90.

by adding water during the process of fermentation. After crushing the grapes and drawing off the must, the winemaker poured water over the marc and let this set for several days before pouring it into barrels. The resulting drink was low in alcohol, but tart and refreshing, and consequently was even consumed by the wealthy.[34] It was mainly a drink for the lower classes, however, and in some parts of Italy, workers in both town and country received *mezzo vino* as part of their wages.[35]

The strength of normal wine is impossible to determine with any degree of accuracy. If the wine was low in alcoholic content, then the large amounts daily consumed by Italians of all classes would not appear so formidable, and some historians have assumed that the wine was relatively weak. Robert C. Davis, on the other hand, claims that the *bevanda* served at the Venetian Arsenal could be 4.5 to 5.5 percent alcohol, even after dilution with water, giving the original wine a strength of 13.5 to 16.5 percent[36]; 16.5 percent is high for unfortified wine even by modern standards. Other historians have come up with figures of 10 percent and 11 to 12 percent, making it similar to modern wine.[37] While on his travels, Sebastiano Locatelli, priest and bon vivant, encountered some strong wines. Four or five glasses of one especially potent wine were enough to put a person out for twenty-four hours. Another, which he drank with his lunch, "half fuddled" him. A third was so good that he and his companions consumed too much and subsequently could hardly remove their clothes before falling into such a deep sleep that a thunderstorm did not wake them.[38]

Despite the statistics and despite the strength of the wine, Italians enjoyed a reputation for moderation. The indefatigable English traveler Fynes Moryson believed that the Italians were one of the most sober people in Europe and wrote that "The Italians hold it a great shame to be drunken."[39] When Michel de Montaigne visited Florence in 1583, he contrasted Italian sobriety with German insobriety and believed that the size of the glasses was the cause; the Germans used big glasses, while the Italian glasses were "extraordinarily small."[40] However, given the statistics on per capita consumption, the Italians would

---

[34] Martin, "Baptism of Wine," 21–30.

[35] Patrone, "Consumo del vino," 286.

[36] Davis, "Venetian Shipbuilders," 62.

[37] Balestracci, "Produzione e la vendità," 43; and Mazzi, "Note per una storia," 96n138.

[38] Blunt, *Sebastiano*, 58–59, 67.

[39] Moryson, *Itinerary*, 117.

[40] Montaigne, *Travel Journal*, trans. Frame, 66.

have to refill those tiny glasses often. The drinking comportment of the Italians produces an enigma: the statistics reveal that Italians drank much, historians believe that the wine was not weak, and yet the Italians had a reputation for moderation. Likewise, the Italian moralists encountered in the previous chapter had few complaints about drunken behavior. One hundred years after Montaigne made his observations about the small glasses, a French Jesuit commented on the Italians in the region of Bologna: "Everyone drinks wine in this country, the women and children just as the men, even though they remain sober, and one can hardly reproach them on this."[41] This might be the best solution, albeit an incomplete one, for the Italian enigma: everyone drank, not to get drunk, but as part of their everyday life.

France

Wine has had a crucially important role in French civilization, as important as it has had in Italy. Wine is inseparable from what it means to be French; according to Roland Barthes, "Wine is felt by the French nation to be a possession which is its very own."[42] In attempting to explain how wine permeated the fabric of French society, one historian wrote, "Wine is a drink, it is also a luxury, a pleasure, and the church has made it a necessity. One gives it and receives it as a gift, one distributes it on feast days."[43] So important is wine that French poets often relegated love to second place behind it, and when they wrote of love they compared it to wine. To cite just one poet, Pierre de Ronsard (1524–1585) compared love to a cup of wine that made him drunk. Elsewhere he claimed that wine eased pain, banished troubles, repelled worries, drowned sorrows, and removed cares; a foolish man who washed his stomach with anything besides wine would have a bad end.[44] To a sixteenth-century poet, wine was "my most faithful brother and friend," a theme continued in the twentieth century by historian Roger Dion: "Man, in effect, loves wine as a friend he has chosen, by preference, not by obligation."[45] In short, wine has seeped into the soul of the French, helping them to overcome

---

[41] Flandrin, "Diversité des goûts," 70.

[42] Barthes, *Mythologies*, 58–59.

[43] Lachiver, *Vins, vignes et vignerons: Histoire*, 176.

[44] Ronsard, *Oeuvres complètes*, ed. Laumonier, Silver, and Lebègue, 17: 312–13; elsewhere 1:211; 2:9, 180; 5:45; 6:173; 17:329.

[45] Jean Fischart, quoted in Lachiver, *Vins, vignes et vignerons: Histoire*, 151; and Dion, *Histoire de la vigne*, 1.

adversity, and was treated with the respect deserving of a friend and lover.

Nonetheless, wine did not have the overwhelmingly predominant position in France that it had in Italy; the historical records document other alcoholic drinks, even if some were consumed due to the absence of wine, intended or not. An intended absence was the result of Lenten abstinence by King Louis IX—Saint Louis—who gave up wine and drank ale. Others joined the king in abandoning wine and drinking either ale or water during Lent, a practice that if anything demonstrated the low esteem of ale and water when compared to wine.[46] According to a contemporary journal, in 1428 the high price of wine in Paris led to the brewing of beer, and in 1447 wine was so expensive that "poor people drank ale or mead or beer or cider or perry and suchlike drinks."[47] For some the consumption of other alcoholic beverages was not just the result of penance or price. Although originally wine drinkers, Bretons switched to cider in the first half of the seventeenth century, a development that began in Normandy in the middle of the fifteenth century.[48] The cultivation of grapes extended farther north than it does today, but the lower classes of the northern areas of France such as Flanders shunned wine and preferred beer and ale.[49] Finally, as in Italy, towards 1700 spirits started to become a popular drink rather than just a medicine.

As in Italy, France had a long tradition of enjoying wine with food and enjoying food with wine. According to a fourteenth-century proverb, "to drink without eating is the meal of frogs."[50] Jean de la Fontaine (1621–1695) called the god of wine, Bacchus, "the soul of good meals."[51] Wine was included in breakfast, so much so that a moralist complained that the first words of people on waking were praises of wine rather than praises of God. At the end of the fifteenth century, municipal clerks in Troyes began their day with bread, roast meat, fruit, and wine.[52] Similarly, students attending the university at Montpellier in the sixteenth century met at a tavern for breakfasts of muscat and pork with mustard.[53] Medieval cooks also used wine in their recipes along with its cousins, vinegar, verjuice, and must, all

---

[46] Moulin, "Bière, houblon," 115, 118.

[47] *Parisian Journal*, trans. Shirley, 225, 365.

[48] Collins, *Classes, Estates*, 44; and Bois, *Crisis of Feudalism*, 197–98.

[49] Dion, *Histoire de la vigne*, 8–15.

[50] Morawski, *Proverbes français*, 10.

[51] Brereton, *Sixteenth to Eighteenth Centuries*, 239.

[52] Contamine, *Vie quotidienne*, 229, author not given.

[53] Platter, *Beloved Son Felix*, trans. Jennett, 55.

of which produced a "distinct tang" that was greatly appreciated by medieval palates.[54] The fourteenth-century cookbook by Taillevent used wine in 43 percent of its recipes, while in the fifteenth-century collection known as *Vivendier* the figure was 44 percent.[55] Medical and popular wisdom held that wine was healthy. According to one proverb, it was good in summer because of the great heat and good in winter because of the great cold, and according to others it aided digestion; one should always drink wine after eating salads, eggs, beef, and especially pears.[56]

In the mid-sixteenth-century *Débat des hérauts d'armes de France et d'Angleterre,* the herald of France proclaimed that his kingdom produced wine in such abundance that even workers consumed it.[57] This was not French propaganda. The best documented instances of this consumption come from research on the role of wine in the diets and payments of building workers at the end of the Middle Ages. Workers repairing a mill at Déville in 1391 received, in addition to their daily wage, "expenditures of mouth" that included cheese, eggs, and wine. In some cases, the wine was not a payment but a means of improving the conditions of work through the promotion of conviviality and sociability. For example, between 1461 and 1466, workers on the residence of an archbishop received periodic payments to permit them to drink at the surrounding taverns. Workers on the archbishop's residence were also rewarded with wine when they completed difficult work, such as raising the exterior staircase. When a cardinal visited the building site of his château in 1506, he demonstrated his satisfaction with the work by providing wine for the masons.[58] These practices were especially entrenched in the building industry, but other workers received the same benefits. At Nevers between 1398 and 1400 the town provided wine for ordinary laborers working on a road, and early in the sixteenth century the town of Dijon gave a supply of wine to its guards.[59]

Medieval workers were much better served with wine than their early modern counterparts. The change occurred during the sixteenth century as population pressure, which had been weak since the great mortality of the Black Death in the middle of the fourteenth century, eroded the favorable position

[54] Scully, *Art of Cookery,* 111.

[55] Taillevent, *Viandier of Taillevent,* ed. Scully; and *Vivendier,* ed. and trans. Scully.

[56] Rivière, "Thème alimentaire," 203.

[57] *Débat des hérauts,* ed. Pannier and Meyer, 44.

[58] Lardin, "Rôle du vin," 209–15.

[59] Dion, *Histoire de la vigne,* 476.

of workers. According to one estimate, during the late Middle Ages workers consumed large amounts of both bread and wine, 0.8 to 1.5 kilograms of bread and two liters of wine daily.[60] Similarly, the diets of workers at Déville in 1502 to 1503 contained large amounts of bread but also fish, meat, dairy products, and wine, with the wine constituting about 15 percent of a typical food budget. By the middle of the century, the price of wine had more than tripled, forcing workers to consume other beverages such as beer and cider.[61] As a result of the price inflation, during the sixteenth century the practice of providing workers with wine was gradually replaced with payments of money.[62] As for the poor, even in the relatively abundant Middle Ages they usually soaked their hard pieces of bread in water rather than wine.[63]

In the households of the wealthy large numbers of servants had access to their masters' wine,[64] but not only the wealthy had their own supply of wine. At Carpentras in the early fifteenth century, the vast majority of households had supplies, between 76 percent and 90 percent depending on the year and the vintage. Only about 15 percent of the households were so poor that they could never afford to purchase casks of wine for home consumption.[65] The figures in tables 3.5 to 3.8 are in liters. With the exception of Carpentras in 1405 and Toulouse late in the seventeenth century, all the figures in table 3.5 demonstrate an annual per capita consumption of 200 liters or less, significantly lower than what it was for Italy, but still two to three times the modern figure of not quite 60 liters. Variations in vintages account for the range of figures, such as at Carpentras and Metz in the fifteenth century and Nantes in the seventeenth. An indication of the variations in production comes from the early fifteenth-century records of the vineyards at Quinsac; in 1401 the vineyards produced 22,400 liters of wine but in 1404 only 6,800.[66] Regional variations, even within the same province, could result in some towns with ample supplies of wine and others where it was practically unknown.[67] These regional variations question the usefulness of the global computations made by one historian, who asserted that in the sixteenth century the 18 million inhabitants of France consumed 13

[60] Contamine, *Vie quotidienne*, 237.

[61] Bois, *Crisis of Feudalism*, 104–7.

[62] Lardin, "Rôle du vin," 214.

[63] Chevalier, *Bonnes villes de France*, 265.

[64] Bercé, *History of Peasant Revolts*, 35.

[65] Stouff, *Ravitaillement et alimentation*, 94–96.

[66] Marquette, "Vinification dans les domaines," 138.

[67] Charbonnier, *Autre France*, 157. Charbonnier uses the examples of Murol and Herment.

million hectoliters of wine a year, or 72 liters per inhabitant.[68] Many historians argue that the per capita consumption was lower in the sixteenth and seventeenth centuries than it had been in the late Middle Ages, but this development was apparently more notable in the countryside than in towns, which maintained or even increased their privileged position. An Italian visiting Lyon in 1664 claimed that the inhabitants consumed more wine than that consumed in a dozen towns of Italy.[69] This was hyperbole, but even workers in towns were able to consume more than their compatriots in the countryside, spending 25 to 30 percent of their wages on wine.[70]

Table 3.5: France: Annual per capita consumption of wine.

PLACE	DATE	AMOUNT (L)
Paris	1350–1450	100
Metz	15th century	50–150
Brittany	15th century	33
Lyon	15th century	200
Tours Each adult	15th century	148–178
Carpentras	1405	390
Carpentras	1406	210
Nantes	1500	100–120
Nantes	17th century	110–200
Paris	1637	155
Lyon	1680	200
Toulouse	Late 17th century	274

SOURCES: Garrier, *Histoire sociale*, 58; Lachiver, *Vins, vignes et vignerons: Histoire*, 140, 156; Leguay, *Rue au Moyen Age*, 155; Stouff, *Ravitaillement et alimentation*, 92; Collins, *Classes, Estates*, 247n40; Brennan, *Public Drinking*, 189; Durand, *Vin, vigne*, 48; and Bennassar and Goy, "Contribution à l'histoire," 416.

In contrast to the figures in table 3.5, those in tables 3.6 to 3.8 are similar to their Italian counterparts. The figure that stands out, comparable to that for the gravedigger at Turin, is the ration of 910 to 1095 liters for a fisherman working the Grand Banks off the shores of Newfoundland. Fishermen received their rations with their meals—2.5 to 3 liters a day. According to the authors of the study on the diet of the fishermen, the wine was well integrated

[68] Garrier, *Histoire sociale*, 76.

[69] Dion, *Histoire de la vigne*, 473.

[70] Brennan, *Public Drinking*, 191.

into life on board, and they "found only two examples of drunkenness in the records."[71] Some of the figures demonstrate that class, like towns, had its privileges. In addition to consuming better wines than the lower classes, middle-class and noble drinkers drank more. Hence, the apothecary and his assistants at the royal court in 1555 each had a ration of 680 liters, while for the laundress and her assistants the ration was 272. Similarly, the distribution of wine on feast days at the convent of the Hôtel-Dieu in Paris demonstrated the privilege of rank rather than the charity of Christianity; the master, prioress, and friars received almost two liters, the nuns received less than a liter, and the novices, the infants of the choir, and the servants received hardly half a liter.[72]

Table 3.6: France: Annual per capita consumption of wine in households.

PLACE	DATE	AMOUNT (L)
Vic Noble household	1320	664
Murol Noble household	1403–1420	730
Toul Female entourage of prioress	1410–1412	274
Arles Archbishop's household	1424–1468	784

SOURCES: Charbonnier, *Autre France,* 131–32; and Bennassar and Goy, "Contribution à l'histoire," 408.

Table 3.7: France: Annual per capita consumption of wine in contracts.

PLACE	DATE	AMOUNT (L)
St.-Bonnet Wife of lord	1369	750
Aix Pension for a man, plus 115 liters of *piquette*	1416	346
Bouc Pension for a man	1426	60
Barjols Pension for a widow	1441	360

SOURCES: Charbonnier, *Une autre France,* 490; and Stouff, *Ravitaillement et alimentation,* 230.

[71] Turgeon and Dickner, "Contraints et choix alimentaires," 236.

[72] Jéhanno, "Boire à Paris," 10.

Table 3.8: France: Annual per capita rations of wine.

PLACE	DATE	AMOUNT (L)
Burgundy Fisherman, wine or *piquette*	14th century	365–730
Aix Friar at the hospital	1338	460
Trets Student at papal school	1364	220
Auvergne Valet of count	1384	365
Saint-Pierre-de-Bèze Monk, plus a liter on feast days	Late 14th century	183
Châteaux de Custines Soldier, plus a daily supplement of 0.4 liters in summer	1406–1408	781
Gardanne Caretaker of royal property	1457	420
Vernines Chambermaid	1471	365
Narbonne Magistrate, plus 250 liters of *piquette*	1480	625
Grand Banks/Newfoundland Fisherman	16th century	910–1095
Paris Apothecary and assistants at the court	1555	680
Paris Laundress and assistants at the court	1555	272
Toul Worker on cathedral	1580	456
Murol Worker on construction of the château	1591	365
St. Germain des Prés Monk	17th century	438

SOURCES: Bennassar and Goy, "Contribution à l'histoire," 416; Stouff, *Ravitaillement et alimentation*, 230; Charbonnier, *Autre France*, 151, 785–86, 868–69; Moulin, *Vie quotidienne*, 118; Maguin, *Vigne et le vin*, 211; Turgeon and Dickner, "Contraints et choix alimentaires," 233; Boucher, "Alimentation en milieu," 167; Cabourdin, *Terre et Hommes*, 687; and Ultee, *Abbey of St. Germain des Prés*, 118.

The obvious question, as it was for Italy, is how did the primitive agriculture produce so much wine? Complicating the situation for France were several developments that would have opposing effects on the supply of wine. The first was the spread of vineyards during the Middle Ages to such an extent that they covered a larger area than they do in modern France.

The subsequent contraction of viticulture was mainly due to the spread of phylloxera in the nineteenth century, as winemakers fell back on the best vineyards. The ubiquity of the grape in traditional France meant that drinkers would have a large supply of wine, even if much of it was mediocre. Another development that would likewise increase the supply of wine was the tendency, especially around Paris beginning in the seventeenth century, for winemakers to focus on quantity at the expense of quality in catering for the mass market of the capital.[73] While these two developments helped increase the supply of wine for domestic consumption, France exported vast quantities of its wine. Bordeaux and the southwest exported so much wine at the beginning of the fourteenth century that the amount would not be surpassed until after World War II.[74] The low levels of productivity meant that a large amount of land was necessary to slake both the nation's thirst and the demand from abroad. The best productivity figure from the Middle Ages was a yield of 4,100 liters per hectare; the average for the sixteenth century was 1,500. By 1700 the yield around Paris ranged from 2,000 to 3,000, depending on whether the winemaker was using advanced methods of cultivation.[75]

The French drank new wine. If the previous vintage had produced such small yields that people did not have enough wine to last the year, they waited expectantly for the new wine of the next vintage, sometimes drinking it only six days after crushing, sometimes less.[76] The illustration of vintage from the *Compost et calendrier des bergers,* published at Paris in 1491 (fig. 2), shows a worker testing the new wine in barrels while the vintage proceeds around him. Although old wine was consumed, especially if it was sweet, widespread consumption of "vintage" wine would have to wait until the end of the seventeenth century and the use of glass bottles and corks.[77] Accompanying the bottles and corks were developments in viticulture and vinification, developments that combined with others to produce what Henri Enjalbert calls "la révolution des boissons."[78] In the meantime the French probably had to endure much wine that was mediocre to say the least. The strength of the

[73] Lorcin, "Usages du vin," 99; and Dion, *Histoire de la vigne,* 532.

[74] Lachiver, *Vins, vignes et vignerons: Histoire,* 118–19.

[75] Lachiver, *Vins, vignes et vignerons en région,* 140; Lorcin, *Campagnes de la région lyonnaise,* 66; and Garrier, *Histoire sociale,* 76.

[76] Marquette, "Vinification dans les domaines," 137–38.

[77] Renouard, "Vin vieux au Moyen Age," 447–55.

[78] Enjalbert, "Naissance des grands vins," 59, 71.

Figure 2: Illustration for the month of September depicting the vintage, from the *Compost et calendrier des bergers,* published at Paris in 1491. The busy vintage scene shows men moving through the vineyard picking grapes, others carrying grapes to the press, while the man crushing the grapes samples them as he works. A large barrel with a funnel is ready to receive the must. In the foreground a man takes a sample of the new wine.

Reproduced from Rudolf Weinhold, *Vivat Bacchus: A History of the Vine and its Wine,* 143. Watford, Hertfordshire, UK: Argus Books, 1978.

wine is impossible to determine, but one historian assumes that it was 10 percent alcohol, while another reckons that the peasants of Languedoc were drinking massive amounts of wine that was only 5 percent.[79] After sampling the strong wines of Italy, Sebastiano Locatelli encountered an even stronger one in Paris; he had to be carried to his inn and put unconscious on his bed, where he remained for "twenty-four hours without giving any sign of life," waking up bathed in sweat and piss.[80]

The French equivalent of *mezzo vino* was *piquette*; many historians assume that workers in town and country consumed it in large quantities, and one even asserts that in Lorraine the majority drank *piquette* rather than wine.[81] One problem with these assumptions and this assertion is that *piquette* was a by-product of winemaking, so the supply was not elastic. At one of the vineyards of the archbishop of Bordeaux in the fifteenth century, the vintage yielded 4,500 liters of red and white wine; the reworked marc produced only 500 liters of *piquette*.[82] If the majority in Lorraine were drinking *piquette*, then it was probably produced by another method than pouring water on the marc; the winemakers were adding water to the must before fermentation.

As noted in the previous chapter, Jean-Louis Flandrin argues that the French had a well-deserved reputation for temperance in drink, primarily as a result of their practice of adding water to their wine, that is, when they drank it rather than during the process of fermentation. However, France's reputation was not unanimous. Fynes Moryson provided support for Flandrin's contention by noting that "drunkenness is reproachful among the French, and the greater part drink water mingled with wine."[83] On the other hand, a thirteenth-century Franciscan condemned the French for drinking their wine undiluted.[84] Some foreigners wrote accounts commending the French and especially Frenchwomen for their sobriety and then added incidents that demonstrated the opposite. The best example of this is the Italian priest Sebastiano Locatelli, who might not be the best judge of temperance. He stated that Frenchwomen did not drink wine, but immediately qualified the statement: "if they did, they took care not to let anyone see." Then on several occasions during his travels in France, Locatelli encountered drunken

[79] Brennan, "Towards the Cultural History," 87n18; and Le Roy Ladurie, "Masses profondes," 783.

[80] Blunt, *Sebastiano*, 174.

[81] Maguin, *Vigne et le vin*, 191.

[82] Marquette, "Vinification dans les domaines," 138.

[83] Moryson, *Itinerary*, 135.

[84] Salimbene, *From St. Francis to Dante*, trans. G. G. Coulton, 139.

women, one of whom vomited all over him.[85] Just as Michel de Montaigne noted that the Italians used small glasses, the fourteenth-century Catalan Francesc Eiximenis stated in his encyclopedia that the French drank small amounts often rather than much at one time. Rather than consider this a sign of moderation, Eiximenis thought it led to excessive drinking because "those who drink small quantities never quench their thirst and thus have to drink continuously."[86] In the final analysis, the quantitative and qualitative evidence indicates that, if indeed the French were mixing water with their wine, they were drinking a lot of water.

England

Ceres is "our English Bacchus," proclaimed Thomas Fuller in 1662, referring to the Roman goddess of agriculture and the harvest. Instead of wine, the product of the vine, the typical drink of the English was the product of malted grain. Fuller continued by noting that ale "was our ancestors' common drink, many imputing the strength of their infantry (in drawing so stiff a bow) to their constant (but moderate) drinking thereof."[87] Traditional English ale was made with malted grain, water, and yeast, with at times the addition of herbs and spices to flavor it. By 1662 many English had abandoned their ancestors' ale for a new drink that was brewed with the addition of hops. This new drink was called beer. The preferred drink of the nobility, however, was wine, which was imported in vast quantities and even produced from England's own vineyards. In addition to ale, beer, and wine, other alcoholic drinks were popular over time and place. Mead was a favorite drink in medieval England but not as much during the sixteenth and seventeenth centuries, and cider and even perry were important in the west, especially in the counties of Hertfordshire, Worcestershire, and Gloucestershire. As in Italy and France, the consumption of spirits increased towards the end of the seventeenth century.

English drinkers were hence spoiled for choice, and each beverage had its champions as well as its detractors. Even water had a champion in Thomas Elyot, the author of *The Castel of Helth* (1541), who asserted, "Undoubtedly water has preeminence above all other liquors."[88] Most preferred to drink anything but

---

[85] Blunt, *Sebastiano*, 146; see 178, 185–86, 211.

[86] Gracia, "Rules and Regulations," 381.

[87] Fuller, *History of the Worthies*, ed. Nuttall, 1:367.

[88] Elyot, *Castel of Helth*, 31.

water. As already noted, in the fifteenth century Sir John Fortescue claimed that the English drank no water except for religious reasons. Early in the eighteenth century, a French visitor expressed his surprise at the same phenomenon: "Would you believe it, though water is to be had in abundance in London, and of fairly good quality, absolutely none is drunk?"[89] Perhaps many people concurred with the opinion of Andrew Boorde, who claimed in his *Dyetary of Helth*, published in 1542, that "water is not wholesome ... for an Englishman."[90]

The "natural drink" for an Englishman, according to Boorde, was ale. Beer, on the other hand, was a natural drink for a Dutchman; it was detrimental to the English and even capable, argued Boorde, of killing people with certain ailments. Barley was the most popular grain for the production of ale, but some brewers used oats, wheat, and a combination of oats and barley called dredge. Boorde claimed that the Cornish ale made from oats tasted as if pigs had wrestled in it, and the oat ale in Devon made those unaccustomed to drinking it vomit.[91] Boorde preferred plain ale brewed from malted barley with no additives; anything else would "sofystical" the ale, that is, corrupt it.[92] Nonetheless, brewers often added herbs and spices such as long-seeded pepper, wormwood, sage, rosemary, and scurvy grass, to name but a few, for flavoring as well as for medicinal purposes.[93] John Taylor, even more than Boorde, sang the praises of ale in his *Drinke and Welcome*, published in 1637: "it slides down merrily, ... it is most pleasing to the taste, ... it provokes men to singing and mirth, ... it will make a weeping widow laugh and forget sorrow. ... It will set a bashful suitor a wooing; it heats the chilled blood of the aged, ... it inspires the poor poet, ... it puts eloquence into the orator, ... it is a great friend to truth, ... it will put courage into a coward, ... and in conclusion it is such a nourisher of mankind that [I could never] speak or write the true worth and worthiness of ale."[94]

England first imported beer from the Netherlands and then began brewing it late in the fourteenth century. The addition of hops created a beverage that was cheaper and clearer than ale; it also did not spoil as quickly and was consequently easier to transport. Before the arrival of beer, brewing was a

---

[89] Barr, *Drink*, 257.

[90] Boorde, *Compendyous Regyment*, ed. Furnivall, 252.

[91] Hallam, Miller, and Thirsk, *Agrarian History*, 2:368, 3:304.

[92] Boorde, *Compendyous Regyment*, ed. Furnivall, 256.

[93] Sambrook, *Country House Brewing*, 144–52.

[94] Emerson, *Beverages, Past and Present*, 2:225–26.

domestic activity dominated by alewives who sold their surplus ale. The complexities of brewing with hops and the economies of scale resulted in large commercial breweries that had no place for alewives.[95] Beer slowly gained the ascendancy over ale, not without bitter opposition from some quarters. For example, in 1512 the magistrates of Shrewsbury forbade brewers to use "that wicked and pernicious weed," hops.[96] When William Harrison wrote *The Description of England* in 1587, beer had won the battle according to him, for he considered ale to be a drink only for the old or the sick.[97] That might have been the case around London, but elsewhere ale would continue to be the beverage of choice. Almost one hundred years later, the diary of Roger Lowe indicates that ale was still consumed in the alehouses of Lancashire, and the proverb, "Good ale is meat, drink, and cloth," dates from the seventeenth century.[98]

A warming trend in the climate during the Middle Ages permitted the spread of vineyards in England, especially on estates owned by the church, which required wine for the celebration of the Eucharist. According to William Harrison, the best English wine was called "theologicum" because it came from vineyards owned by the clergy,[99] but even that wine could be of questionable quality. When King John tasted the prized wine of Beaulieu Abbey in 1204, he immediately directed his steward, "Send ships forthwith to fetch some good French wine for the abbot!" At the time of the accession of Henry VIII in 1509 only 139 vineyards remained, and many of these disappeared with the dissolution of the monasteries.[100] Most of the wine and most of the better wine was imported, and different varieties found their champions. Shakespeare's Falstaff (*Henry IV, Part 2*, 4.3) claimed if he had a thousand sons, the first human principle he would teach them was to avoid all drinks but sack. For James Howell, canary was the "height of perfection," the consumption of which carried a man to heaven.[101]

While wine was the preferred drink at court, among the nobility, and for those who could afford it, cider and perry were predominantly drinks for servants and poor cottagers even in the areas of western England where

[95] Bennett, *Ale, Beer, and Brewsters*, 9.
[96] Hammond, *Food and Feast*, 87.
[97] Harrison, *Description of England*, ed. Edelen, 139.
[98] Lowe, *Diary of Roger Lowe*, ed. Sachse; and Apperson, *English Proverbs*, 255.
[99] Harrison, *Description of England*, ed. Edelen, 130.
[100] Barty-King, *Tradition of English Wine*, 40, 57.
[101] Howell, *Epistolae Ho-Elianae*, ed. Jacobs, 2:457.

they were popular drinks. Cider had its champions as well as its detractors. Among the latter was one who described the taste of cider as "steel filings mixed with vinegar and mud." Its champions considered it the "wine of Britain," and Daniel Defoe praised the cider he drank at alehouses in Hertfordshire as being "so very good, so fine and so cheap, that we never found fault with" it.[102] One of the main causes for the decline in popularity of mead was its cost; it was not cheap, and by the sixteenth century only the wealthy could afford it. Mead likewise had its champions, including Geoffrey Chaucer, who considered a gift of mead a means of wooing even the most recalcitrant woman.[103] While mead was in decline, spirits were on the rise. Before the end of the seventeenth century, people took spirits primarily for medicinal purposes, and few regarded them as a drink. The consumption of spirits increased from 527,000 gallons in 1684 to 8,203,000 in 1743,[104] a phenomenal increase that was responsible for Gin Lane and all of its unsavory implications. In 1700, wine, spirits, and cider each had about 5 percent of the market, while strong beer or ale accounted for more than 50 percent and weak beer and ale for more than 30 percent.[105] Despite the presence of other beverages, ale and beer remained the favored drinks; the English paid homage to Ceres rather than to Bacchus.

One of the advantages of paying homage to Ceres was the nutritional benefit of drinking ale and beer, a type of barley soup. Men doing heavy work who consumed a gallon a day obtained 2,000 calories plus B vitamins. As in Italy and France, breakfast included alcoholic beverages. A royal official claimed in 1575 that a large bowl of ale for breakfast was "very wholesome and good for the eyesight" and kept him fresh all morning.[106] At the court of Henry VIII, three ladies in waiting shared a piece of beef, two loaves of bread, and a gallon of ale for breakfast.[107] While ale was typical, some began their day with wine. For example, on a London morning in July 1557, Henry Machyn joined his fellow merchants for a breakfast of half a bushel of oysters with onions accompanied by red wine, claret, muscatel, and malmsey.[108] After breakfast, people continued to drink in between meals and at other

---

[102] Davies, " 'Vinetum Britannicum,'" 83, 91.

[103] Chaucer, *Canterbury Tales*, trans. Coghill, 108; and Gayre, *Wassail!* 101.

[104] Burnett, *Liquid Pleasures,* 163.

[105] Chartres, "No English Calvados?" 318–19.

[106] Morgan, *Readings in English Social History,* 300.

[107] French, *Nineteen Centuries of Drink*, 135.

[108] Machyn, *Diary of Henry Machyn*, ed. Nichols, 143–44.

meals. In two noble fifteenth-century households, the ration of ale was one-fourth a gallon at each of the two main meals, in addition to that consumed at breakfast and distributed at other times of the day.[109]

On special occasions, the amount of alcohol consumed could make "gargantuan" an understatement. At the ceremony installing William Warham as archbishop of Canterbury in 1504, guests were provided with "six pipes of red wine, four of claret, one of choice wine, one of white for the kitchen, one butt of Malmsey, one pipe of wine of Osey, two tierces of Rhenish wine ... four tuns of London ale, six of Kentish ale, and twenty of English beer."[110] Precision is difficult but that was probably close to 10,000 gallons of drink. The pipe of white wine for the kitchen indicates that English cooks, like their French counterparts, cooked with wine as well as with other alcoholic beverages. Almost one-fourth of the recipes in the seventeenth-century cookbook compiled by Rebecca Price used wine, while a few recipes called for ale.[111] As on the Continent, public opinion considered the consumption of alcohol to be good for the health. In 1633 a medical practitioner noted that most people "are persuaded that wine and strong drink will recover all diseases whatsoever."[112] Some doctors even recommended that people become drunk once a month as a result of the belief that the vomiting was good for the health.[113]

As indicated by the comment of the French Jesuit about people drinking in the area of Bologna, children throughout Europe were regular consumers of alcoholic beverages. Table 3.12 indicates that children, boys aged between ten and fourteen, at Christ's Hospital in the seventeenth century had a ration of three pints of beer a day. Just like adults, children began their day with a breakfast that included beer, ale, or wine. While Lord and Lady Percy of Northumberland shared bread, fish, a quart of beer, and a quart of wine for breakfast, their two children in the nursery shared bread and butter, fish, and a quart of beer.[114] In addition to their role in daily diets, alcoholic beverages were also used for medicinal purposes. When a two-and-a-half-year-old girl had "an extreme fit of the ague" in 1617, the doctor prescribed some salt powder to put in her beer.[115] Scurvy grass was another ingredient often

---

[109] Woolgar, "Fast and Feast."

[110] King, *Beer Has a History,* 57.

[111] Price, *Compleat Cook,* ed. Masson.

[112] Dr. J. Hart, *Diet of the Diseased,* quoted in Simon, *History of the Wine Trade,* 3:401.

[113] O'Hara-May, *Elizabethan Dyetary,* 129. For similar beliefs in Italy, see Patrone, "Consumo del vino," 294.

[114] Williams, *English Historical Documents,* 908.

[115] Clifford, *Diary of the Lady Anne Clifford,* ed. Sackville-West, 55.

added to children's beer as a result of the belief that it could prevent scurvy.[116] Children also consumed alcohol on festive occasions. In many places, children who took part in the Rogation Day perambulations around the parish boundaries received beer to go with their special treats of cakes and nuts.[117] In the fifteenth century, John Lydgate addressed the table manners of boys and included the advice that the young should be moderate in their consumption of ale and wine.[118] Such advice was evidently necessary, for Ralph Josselin, while discussing strange judgments and worse sins, recorded in his diary in March 1672 the case of an eight-year-old drunkard.[119]

While the wealthy could afford to drink much and well, the evidence indicates that all but the very poor consumed alcoholic beverages on a regular basis even if the quantity and quality were inferior. In the Middle Ages wine was so abundant that even workers could afford it.[120] The quality of ale or beer was usually a function of strength, so workers and servants often drank weak ale or beer. Monks, who had reputations for the quality of their brewing, reserved the best ale for themselves and let their servants consume the worst, often brewed with oats rather than barley. As in France, workers in the building industry in the fourteenth and fifteenth centuries received drinks as part of their wage, and they even enjoyed time off from work for their drinkings. They also received drinks for working on feast days, for working overtime, for completing the roof of a building, for working on hot days in summer, and to encourage their industry.[121] As in France, these practices also extended to other workers, especially servants, who could expect to receive a gallon of ale a day in some households.[122] Unlike France, these practices continued into the sixteenth and seventeenth centuries for servants and for workers.[123] Building workers received drinks when they signed on to work, when they completed crucial phases of the construction, when they had to endure unpleasant conditions, when they finished the project, and as part of their wages.[124]

---

[116] Sambrook, *Country House Brewing*, 149.

[117] Hutton, *Rise and Fall*, 176.

[118] *Stans Puer ad Mensam* in Coulton, *Social Life in Britain*, 92.

[119] Josselin, *Diary of Ralph Josselin*, ed. Macfarlane, 564.

[120] Barty-King, *Tradition of English Wine*, 35.

[121] Salzman, *Building in England*, 65, 77–79.

[122] Warner, "Good Help," 261.

[123] Wilson, "Keeping Hospitality," 49.

[124] Woodward, *Men at Work*, 147–59.

Tables 3.9 through 3.12 are in imperial gallons, slightly larger than the American gallon. For the sake of comparability with the tables for Italy and France, they perhaps should be converted to liters, but the different measurements stress the difference in the beverages, wine versus ale and beer. Unlike the similar tables for Italy and France, table 3.9 has only two figures for towns; the rest are estimates or calculations for the entire country. The figure for Coventry comes from calculations based on a census that determined the amount of barley used for brewing in the town. The amount would yield enough strong beer for every man, woman, and child to have one quart a day; if the brewers were extending the barley by making weak beer and more of it, then the per capita consumption would increase. The figure for England in 1684 comes from the records of the association of the Common Brewers and Brewing Victuallers combined with estimates for private brewing. In comparison, the modern figure is 22 gallons. In 1695 the English statistician Gregory King reckoned that beer and ale accounted for 28 percent of an average household's annual per capita expenditure on food.[125] Table 3.9 is also deficient in not having any figures for the Middle Ages. The consensus among historians is that following the depopulation of the Black Death in the middle of the fourteenth century, the consumption of ale increased among all classes to such an extent that a person's daily consumption of one gallon was the norm.[126] If this was indeed the case, consumption declined in the sixteenth and seventeenth centuries.

Table 3.9: England: Annual per capita consumption of ale/beer.

PLACE	DATE	AMOUNT (gal)
Coventry	1520	91
England	1684	105
England Estimate by John Houghton	1690s	91
London 64 gallons of strong beer, 38 of small beer	1700	102
England 16 gallons of strong beer, 10 of small beer	1700	26

SOURCES: Coulton, *Social Life*, 376; Burnett, *Liquid Pleasures*, 114; Clark, *English Alehouse*, 209; Chartres, "Food Consumption," 175, 193n17.

[125] Hallam, Miller, and Thirsk, *Agrarian History*, 5.2: 408.

[126] Bennett, *Ale, Beer, and Brewsters*, 43–44; Dyer, "Changes in Diet," 25–29; and Galloway, "Driven by Drink?" 94–95.

Table 3.10: England: Annual per capita consumption of ale/beer in households.

PLACE	DATE	AMOUNT (gal)
Sussex Servant in noble household	1382	365
Acton Hall, Suffolk Noble household	1412–1413	365
Earl of Northumberland Noble household	1512	137
English garrison at Boulogne Soldier	1545	234
Ingatestone Hall Estimated consumption on normal days in noble household	1550s	365
London Middle-class household	Mid-17th century	274
Arbury Servant in noble household, small beer	1670s	274

SOURCES: Sambrook, *Country House Brewing*, 228–29; Myatt-Price, "Tally of Ale," 65n; Hammond, *Food and Feast*, 78; Emmison, *Tudor Food*, 57; Clark, *English Alehouse*, 109; and King, *Beer Has a History*, 88–89.

Tables 3.10 to 3.12 support the contention that in the fourteenth and fifteenth centuries, people consumed a gallon of ale a day, and the figures, although mixed, tend to support the view that a decline in consumption occurred during the early modern period. The percentages of food budgets devoted to drink are similar to those from Italy. Chantry priests at Bridport in 1456 to 1457 spent 27 percent of their food budgets on ale, and during the years 1425 to 1426 a wealthy knight spent 23 percent, but another 23 percent went to wine.[127] Table 3.10 only records the consumption of ale or beer; the nobles' preference for wine is not indicated. Nobles could also consume ale and beer in vast quantities, as illustrated by the household account of the sixth Earl of Eglinton on 26 November 1646 that details the amount of beer served to him: "To your Lordship's morning drink, a pint; for my Lady's morning drink, 1 pint; to your Lordship's dinner, 2 pints; more, 3 pints; to the latter meal, 2 pints; after dinner, 1 pint; at four hours, 1 pint; one other pint; to your Lordship's supper, 3 pints."[128] Noble households hence consumed large amounts of drink, typically 20,000 to 40,000 gallons of ale or beer a year—a mere pittance, however, compared to the 600,000 gallons consumed by the household of Queen

[127] Dyer, *Standards of Living*, 55–56.

[128] Marchant, *In Praise of Ale*, 50.

Elizabeth.[129] Some of the corodies in table 3.11 seem excessive, especially since their purpose was to provide support for less active people in their retirement. Perhaps the solution would be that some of the corodies, such as the one for the prior at Bolton Priory, would include support for servants.

Table 3.11: England: Annual per capita consumption of ale/beer in contracts.

PLACE	DATE	AMOUNT (gal)
Abbot's Bromley Woman at a convent, either ale or cider	1295	730
Worcester Corody	1317	312
Carmelite Friary of Lynn Average corody for a couple	1368–1402	542
Bolton Priory Corody for retiring prior	15th century	730
Peterborough Corody for a couple	15th century	416
Blyth Priory Corody as a result of retirement	15th century?	1095

SOURCES: Hallam, Miller, and Thirsk, *Agrarian History,* 2:827; Titow, *English Rural Society,* 82; Little, "Corodies at the Carmelite Friary," 11–14; Kershaw, *Bolton Priory,* 133; Harper, "Note on Corodies," 96; and Rosenthal, *Old Age,* 108.

Table 3.12: England: Annual per capita rations of ale/beer.

PLACE	DATE	AMOUNT (gal)
English garrison in Scotland Soldier	1300	292
Royal army Soldier	Early 14th century	365
Beaulieu Abbey Monk, less for lay brothers and servants	14th century	365
Bolton Priory Canon	14th century	365
Nuneaton Nun	1328	183
Royal navy Sailor	1340	365

[129] Sambrook, *Country House Brewing,* 229; Hallam, Miller, and Thirsk, *Agrarian History,* 4:518.

Table 3.12: England: Annual per capita rations of ale/beer, *continued*

PLACE	DATE	AMOUNT (gal)
Westminster Monk	14th–15th century	365
Munden's Chantry Priest, plus cider, perry, and occasional wine	Mid–15th century	146
Durham Cathedral Priory Monk, plus 0.6 liters of wine per day	1464–1520	365
Earl of Northumberland Servant	1512	146
Royal navy Sailor	1565	365
St. Thomas Hospital, London	1570	91
Royal army in Ireland Soldier, plus a daily quart of wine	1585	183
Royal navy Sailor	1588	365
Christ's Hospital Child (3 pints a day)	17th century	137
London Servant of the bishop	1605	137
Yarmouth fishing fleets Fisherman	1615	365
Norwich Child at Children's Hospital, half pint a day	1632	46
Royal army Soldier	1639	183
Royal navy Sailor	1675, 1678	365
St. Bartholomew's Hospital 3 pints a day, plus an additional pint on Sunday	1687	143

SOURCES: Prestwich, "Victualling Estimates," 538; Bennett, *Ale, Beer, and Brewsters*, 17, 93; Kershaw, *Bolton Priory*, 133; Kerr, *Religious Life*, 167; Harvey, *Living and Dying*, 58, 64; Harvey, "Monastic Diet," 628; Hammond, *Food and Feast*, 63–65, 78; Threlfall-Holmes, "Durham Cathedral," 147; Clark, *English Alehouse*, 109; Davies, "Rations alimentaires," 93; Fissel, *English Warfare*, 197, 201; Black, "Survival Kit," 58; Burnett, *Liquid Pleasures*, 114; Gray, *Devon Household Accounts*, 1:xxv; Drummond and Wilbraham, *Englishman's Food*, 124, 126; Rees and Fenby, "Meals and Meal-Times," 212; and Mendelsohn, *Drinking with Pepys*, 83–84.

Paying homage to Ceres meant that the two main components of the English diet, ale/beer and bread, came from grain. Given the low levels of productivity during this period, the diet put pressure on arable land. This pressure relaxed after the Black Death but increased again in the sixteenth and seventeenth centuries. The area around London provides an indication of the demands that brewing could place on the supply of grain; at the end of the

demands that brewing could place on the supply of grain; at the end of the fourteenth century one-half of the grain marketed from manorial estates in this area went to brewing.[130] Poor harvests at the end of the sixteenth century led to accusations that brewing, especially the brewing of strong drinks, was taking bread from people's mouths, and several bills designed to curb this were introduced in Parliament early in the next century.[131] As for wine, at the end of the sixteenth century one estimate put the annual production of English wine at 630,000 gallons, which was insignificant in comparison to the amount imported. In the fourteenth century, England was importing 12,600,000 gallons from France every year, enough for an annual per capita consumption of 8 pints. That figure would not be reached again until 1972.[132]

The strength of ale and beer is more straightforward than that of wine. By controlling the amount of water added to the malted grain and the yeast, the brewers could control the strength of the product, all other things being equal. The additions of hops created a drink that was more durable and less likely to spoil; the resins in hops prevent infection by bacteria. To prevent such infection in ale, brewers had to increase the alcohol content by using more malted grain, which made beer brewing more efficient than ale brewing.[133] A by-product of both brewing processes was small ale or beer, made by pouring water over the used mash, which made a weak drink comparable to *mezzo vino* and *piquette*. Alternatively, brewers could simply add much more water at the beginning. As indicated in table 3.9, about a third of the drink consumed in 1700 was small beer, but alehouses competed to offer the strongest drink, a practice that drew the condemnation of constables and Parliament.[134] Medieval monks knew how to brew ale with several levels of strength, a practice that became widely disseminated, as indicated by the advice given to farmers in an early eighteenth-century treatise: "make three sorts of beer, the . . . strongest for your own use, the second is what is called best beer, whereof each man ought to have a pint in the morning before he goes to work, and as much at night as soon as he comes in. . . . Small beer they must also have in the field."[135] Although historians debate the issue, especially the strength of medieval ale,

[130] Galloway, "Driven by Drink?" 98.

[131] Lambarde, *Local Government*, ed. Read, 130; and Kent, "Attitudes of Members," 45.

[132] Barty-King, *Tradition of English Wine*, 57; Renouard, *Etudes d'histoire*, 243; Francis, *Wine Trade*, 10; and Burnett, *Liquid Pleasures*, 154.

[133] Unger, *Beer in the Middle Ages*, 55.

[134] Clark, *English Alehouse*, 96–99.

[135] Dyer, "Changes in Diet," 27.

the bulk of the evidence indicates that both ale and beer could be as strong as modern beers.[136]

Unlike the Italians and the French, the English had a reputation for drunkenness, not as bad as the Germans and the Dutch but bad enough for François Rabelais to use the phrase "as drunk as an Englishman."[137] The French in particular believed that the English were immoderate drinkers. The author of *Description d'Angleterre* reaffirmed Rabelais' comment in 1558: "The English are great drunkards."[138] The French condemnations continued in the seventeenth century, but a Dutch physician made quite different observations when he visited England in 1560; he found the English to be moderate drinkers who did not become drunk.[139] But then he was Dutch.

Did the Peasants Really Drink?

In traditional Europe, the vast majority of the population, 75 to 90 percent depending on the area, were agricultural workers. These were the peasants. Some peasants were relatively affluent, but the vast majority were not, which raises questions about their consumption of alcoholic beverages. When John Locke visited the wine-producing area surrounding Bordeaux in 1678, he talked to a poor peasant's wife about her life. Although she and her husband had a little vineyard, they drank no wine from it but subsisted on rye bread and water.[140] Many French historians concur with the wife's complaint; French peasants did not drink wine or did so rarely on festive occasions. Henri Enjalbert is the most adamant of these historians, claiming that until the end of the seventeenth century, wine was too expensive for the lower classes of society.[141] Roger Dion is a bit more circumspect. He begins by noting that the sources are inadequate to make a judgment until the seventeenth century. Then they indicate that peasant children did not drink wine at all, women drank wine very rarely and then usually just a bit in their water, while the men, even the vine-growers themselves, drank but little, and that was usually either diluted with water or just *piquette*. In short, according to Dion, the evidence demonstrates "a striking

[136] Galloway, "Driven by Drink?" 91; Bretherton, "Country Inns," 168–69; and Sambrook, *Country House Brewing*, 109–11.

[137] Rabelais, *Portable Rabelais*, trans. and ed. Putnam, 97.

[138] Rye, *England as Seen by Foreigners*, 190; and French, *Nineteen Centuries of Drink*, 209.

[139] Rye, *England as Seen by Foreigners*, 79.

[140] Locke, *Locke's Travels*, ed. Lough, 236–37.

[141] Enjalbert, "Comment naissent les grands crus," 315.

contrast between the peasants who drank very little wine and the workers in the towns who drank much."[142] Cicely Howell similarly doubts if English peasants consumed much ale. The brewing of ale was an inefficient way to utilize grain, and "the whole process of malting and then brewing ale requires space, fuel, equipment, time and much labor." Howell concludes that "porridge and pottage were thus probably the staple fare of the English peasant rather than bread and ale."[143] Other historians argue that it is wrong to claim that the peasants drank only water.[144]

Table 3.13: Italy: Peasants' annual per capita consumption of wine.

PLACE	DATE	AMOUNT (L)
Piedmont	14th–15th century	365
Sicily Ration for peasant	15th century	123–313
Appennino Modenese	15th century	407–509

SOURCES: Patrone, "Bere vino," 1:57; Bennassar and Goy, "Contribution à l'histoire," 416; and Pini, *Vite e vino*, 135n316.

Historians are in rare agreement on one point, however, and that concerns the consumption of wine by Italian peasants. Just as urban Italians of all classes except the very poor consumed wine, so also did the peasants. In his study of peasant diets in the late Middle Ages, Massimo Montanari asserts that peasants drank wine; the only difference between their consumption and that of their lords was the quality of the wine. Peasants were obliged to give one-third to one-half of the wine they produced to the lord, but much remained because of the tendency for viticultural practices to favor quantity over quality. Although Montanari believes that precision is impossible,[145] some historians have attempted to quantify the amount consumed, as indicated by table 3.13. Some of these quantities are considerable, such as that shown for the rural area of Appennino Modenese. All of this evidence comes from the medieval period, so perhaps judgment should be suspended for the consumption of wine by Italian peasants during the sixteenth and seventeenth centuries.

[142] Dion, *Histoire de la vigne*, 472–73. See also Lachiver, *Vins, vignes et vignerons: Histoire*, 310; and Brennan, "Towards the Cultural History," 77.

[143] Howell, *Land, Family*, 164–65.

[144] Jaritz, "Material Culture," 175–77; and Woolgar, Serjeantson, and Waldron, "Conclusion," 273.

[145] Montanari, *Alimentazione contadina*, 379–80, 382.

Contrary to Roger Dion's comment about the lack of evidence prior to the seventeenth century, historians have uncovered many medieval sources that indicate peasant consumption of wine. Peasants in the village of Montaillou drank little wine, but its distance from wine-producing areas meant that wine arrived on the backs of animals.[146] The peasants of Languedoc were, on the other hand, enormous consumers of wine, more than one and a half liters a day. Similar figures emerge from Auvergne. As indicated by table 3.14, part of the wages of a cowherd at Vernines in 1471 included a liter of wine a day, while at St. Amant in 1410 vine-growers received twice that amount. The assumption by Martine Maguin for Lorraine is that most people, including peasants, drank *piquette,* and much wine flowed to the towns from vineyards in the countryside, but she concedes that an immeasurable amount of wine remained in rural areas for consumption there.[147] The final province in this medieval tour of France's wine-consuming peasants is Normandy, where peasants consumed wine or cider. The key point here was the relatively favorable position of peasants in the late Middle Ages; in 1470 their real wages were three times that before the Black Death, and higher than they would be in the following centuries.[148] The testimony of the Norman Sire de Gouberville, writing about the condition of peasants in 1560, supports this analysis: "In the time of my father, they ate meat every day, food was abundant, they gulped down wine as if it were water. But today everything has changed."[149]

Nonetheless, some evidence indicates that peasants continued to consume wine in the sixteenth and seventeenth centuries. The peasants of Languedoc continued to drink large amounts of wine, although the alcohol content might have been only 5 percent. In contrast to the situation in Languedoc is the annual per capita consumption of 50 liters calculated for the rural areas of Brittany in the seventeenth century. If the poor and children did not drink, and if women did not drink much, this would still leave a half liter a day for the male peasants of means. In the province of Lorraine in 1575, the magistrates at Toul set a daily wage for the seasonal workers in the vineyards that included two and a half liters for males and half that for females. Likewise, in 1580 the lords of Tumejus gave their peasants a bit more than a half liter of wine a day when called upon to cart wood.[150] Other historians claim that the

[146] La Roy Ladurie, *Montaillou*, 9, 249, 264.

[147] Maguin, *Vigne et le vin*, 191, 202.

[148] Bois, *Crisis of Feudalism*, 104–7, 198, 354.

[149] Stouff, "Approvisionnement des ménages," 663.

[150] Cabourdin, *Terre et hommes*, 687.

normal drink for peasants was water, or at most *piquette*, even if they produced their own wine.[151] The peasant winemaker sold his wine to purchase food for his family, but he often kept some, *vin d'honneur*, for special occasions such as festivals and funerals.[152] Although much peasant drinking is hidden from historians, the most likely conclusion here is that the considerable consumption in the Middle Ages declined during the early modern period, but not as much as assumed by many historians.

Table 3.14: France: Peasants' annual per capita consumption of wine.

PLACE	DATE	AMOUNT (L)
Aix Cowherd	1338	230
St. Amant Wages of vine-growers	1410	730
Gardanne Cowherd, plus 240 liters of *piquette*	1457	360
Marseille Gardener, plus 430 liters of *piquette*	1461	315
Vernines Cowherd	1471	365
Languedoc Average consumption of farmworker	1480	624
Languedoc Consumption by male and female workers	16th–17th centuries	548–730
Brittany Estimate for countryside	17th century	50

SOURCES: Stouff, *Ravitaillement et alimentation*, 230; Charbonnier, *Autre France*, 785, 869; Le Roy Ladurie, *Peasants of Languedoc*, 63; Le Roy Ladurie, "Masses profondes," 783; Collins, *Classes, Estates*, 247.

The relaxation in demographic pressure following the Black Death also worked in favor of English peasants, so much so that they might have been consuming a gallon of ale a day. Judith M. Bennett refuses to quantify the amount but simply states that peasants were drinking "a *lot* of ale"—emphasis hers.[153] By the fifteenth century, peasants were becoming accustomed to drinking at alehouses that began appearing in even small villages. Many of these were informal establishments to say the least; an alewife with a surplus

[151] Blum, *End of the Old Order*, 184–85; Brennan, *Burgundy to Champagne*, 9; and Goubert, *French Peasantry*, 125.

[152] Garrier, *Histoire sociale*, 56.

[153] Bennett, *Ale, Beer, and Brewsters*, 43–44.

to sell would put a sign in front of her house.[154] Even in the period before the Black Death, peasants could expect to drink ale when they worked on their lord's lands, especially during haymaking and harvest times. At these "wet boons," the lord supplied abundant food, including meat, pottage, bread, and cheese, and ample "nut-brown" ale to wash it down.[155] Evidence from the fifteenth century indicates that some peasants received as much as two gallons of ale a day—a "wet boon" indeed.[156] Similarly, both before and after the Black Death, laborers hired to reap and bind received ale in addition to other food as part of their wages. On one manor in Norfolk, the amount increased from not quite three pints of ale a day in 1256 to over six pints in 1424.[157] Most of the figures in table 3.15 come from maintenance contracts that stipulated the amount of food and drink that the new holders, usually the heir, of peasant property would guarantee to deliver to the former holders. Some contracts merely stated a precise amount of malt, obviously intended for brewing rather than baking or making porridge.[158] The favorable demographic conditions of the late Middle Ages might not have been enough to create a golden age for the English peasantry, but they definitely created a nut-brown age.

As was the situation for Italy and France, less certainty exists about peasant consumption in the early modern period. Many of the same customs regarding the provision of drinks at harvest time continued into the sixteenth and seventeenth centuries. For example, on an estate in Sussex harvesters took breaks from their work for two "drinkings" in the morning and another two in the afternoon, and they likewise received drink with their midday meal and their dinner at the end of the day.[159] These occasions were enlivened by songs, such as the "Suffolk Harvest-Home Song" that toasted the master for supplying the drink and urged everyone to drink their fill:

> Drink, boys, drink, and see you do not spill,
> For if you do, you must drink two; it is your master's will.[160]

---

[154] Bailey, "Rural Society," 164; and Hanawalt, *Ties That Bound*, 28.

[155] Bennett, *Life on the English Manor*, 111.

[156] Hallam, Miller, and Thirsk, *Agrarian History*, 2:838.

[157] Dyer, "Changes in Diet," 26.

[158] Clark, "Quest for Security," 311.

[159] Warner, "Good Help," 261. See also Best, *Farming and Memorandum Books*, ed. Woodward, 20, 22–23, 101.

[160] Dixon, *Ancient Poems, Ballads, and Songs*, 190–91. See Hutton, *Stations of the Sun*, 333.

If ale or beer was not available, in some parts of England peasants consumed cider.[161] One of the figures in table 3.9 suggests that peasants did not drink much; the annual per capita consumption of beer in England in 1700 was only 26 gallons. This contrasts with the figure of 102 for London. These figures come from John Chartres' study of food consumption in London and are based on excise duties; he makes no allowance for private brewing.[162] As indicated by Pamela Sambrook's *Country House Brewing in England, 1500–1900*, enormous amounts of small ale and beer were privately brewed on country estates for consumption by servants and agricultural workers. In the last week of November 1634, the Cecil household at Quickswood in Hertfordshire consumed 702 gallons of small beer.[163] Similarly, some of the households mentioned in table 3.10 would include agricultural workers among the servants. After the nut-brown age of ale-drinking peasants, perhaps it would be incorrect to consider the early modern period the amber age of beer, but neither was it the age of water.

Table 3.15: England: Peasants' annual per capita consumption of ale/beer.

PLACE	DATE	AMOUNT (gal)
Girton, Cambridgeshire Maintenance contract for a woman	1291	120
Blackwell, Warwickshire Maintenance contract for a man	1347	137
Newbo, Lincolnshire Wage for a plowman	1394	365
Cranfield, Bedfordshire Maintenance contract for a woman	1437–1438	114
Bishop's Waltham, Hampshire Maintenance contract for a couple—cider	1457	120

SOURCES: Dyer, "English Diet," 202, 206, 213–14; and Dyer, *Standards of Living,* 153, 157.

Peasants had their preferred drinks, but they also were willing consumers of other fermented beverages. In France they made *frênette* from ash leaves, and in addition to the somewhat common drinks made from pear and apple trees, peasants also used the fruit of medlar, service, sorb, cornel, cherry, and juniper trees. Some of these fruits were added to the marc

[161] Davies, " 'Vinetum Britannicum,' " 85–87.

[162] Chartres, "Food Consumption," 175, 193n17.

[163] Sambrook, *Country House Brewing,* 190.

before making *piquette* and *mezzo vino* as a method of increasing the quantity and the strength of the drink.[164] On the whole, however, whether they were drinking products of the vine, of grain, or of something else, peasants often endured mediocre beverages that usually had a low alcoholic content. Just as the drink varied, so did the context of peasant drinking. This section has focused on the role of alcoholic beverages in the diet of peasants; the next chapter will examine their festive drinking. Jerome Blum has identified a different context, hopeless and desperate drinking by the oppressed masses who produced the wealth and the drinks consumed by their social superiors.[165]

The consumption of alcoholic beverages did not mirror the complaints of the moralists. Geographically, Italy and especially its towns consumed more wine than France and its towns, and yet French moralists were more vociferous than the Italian in their condemnations of the disorder and violence that accompanied drunkenness. Anthropologists make a distinction between "dry" and "wet" drinking cultures. The wet cultures are characterized by heavy daily drinking and high per capita consumption of alcohol; the dry, by low per capita consumption and binge drinking. Another difference is the tendency for dry cultures to associate drinking with social and economic problems and give it symbolic meanings that are strongly negative. Wet cultures have a more positive attitude towards drinking and do not demonize alcohol.[166] In the late medieval and early modern period, Italy demonstrated signs of a wet drinking culture, much more so than both France and England, which nonetheless could still be characterized as wet. Chronologically, the apparent decline in drinking, especially in the rural areas of England and France, during the sixteenth and seventeenth centuries did not match the rising chorus of complaints during this period, especially in England. The rise in beer's popularity at the expense of ale, at least in the area around London, coincided with the rise of the condemnations of the moralists. André Lascombes connects the two developments by arguing that ale was weaker than beer and was produced primarily for domestic consumption while the stronger beer was the drink at alehouses. In other words, the strength of beer combined with the

---

[164] Dupèbe, "Diététique et l'alimenation," 51–52; and Bechmann, *Trees and Man*, 19–21.

[165] Blum, *End of the Old Order*, 48.

[166] Heath, *Drinking Occasions*, 92, 121–22; and Levine, "Temperance cultures," 21.

volatile venue of the alehouse resulted in more disorder and violence than previously.[167] However, beer was cheaper than ale and could last longer, but it was not necessarily stronger; in fact, one way to keep ale from spoiling was to increase the alcohol content.[168] If there were something inherent in alcoholic beverages that caused disorderly and violent behavior, then the Italian towns of the Renaissance would have had continuous outbreaks of drunken violence. These towns were in fact notorious for their disorder and their violence, but the social and political struggles and family vendettas that characterized them have never been linked to the possibility that adult males of means were consuming three liters of wine a day. 🍇

---

[167] Lascombes, "Fortunes de l'ale," 132–33.
[168] Unger, *Beer in the Middle Ages*, 55.

Chapter 4

Recreational Drinking

Drink your wine with a merry heart.
—Ecclesiastes 9:7

In traditional Europe many occasions provided opportunities for recreational drinking. The occasions associated with the Christian and agricultural calendars were spread throughout the year, beginning with New Year's celebrations, continuing with carnival, Easter, Ascension Day with its rogation processions, May Day, Pentecost or Whitsunday, Midsummer's Night or St. John's Eve, harvest and vintage, and All Saints and All Souls, collectively known as the Feast of the Dead, and ending with the Christmas festivities that overlapped New Year. Interspersed with these major festivals were saints' days, many of which had significance for occupational groups, such as the feast of St. Vincent for the wine producers, and many of which had local significance as the patron saint of a town or village. An indication of the importance of these celebrations was the local regulation at Apt; citizens purchasing wine for any festival did not have to pay the customary taxes on it.[1] Other occasions for drinking resulted from the life cycle and rites of passage, most notably birth, marriage, and death, but also the beginning and end of apprenticeship and of education, and even the welcome of new neighbors and the farewell of old. Parish, municipal, national, confraternal, and occupational festivals provided other occasions. Closely linked to all of these occasions were the alehouses and the taverns that often provided venues for much of the recreational drinking. But not all of it; English peasants, for example, could enjoy their ale on the village green, in the churchyard, in the streets and lanes, and at the homes of

---

[1] Stouff, *Ravitaillement et alimentation*, 91.

friends and neighbors, as well as in the alehouses.[2]

The primary functions of recreational drinking were jollification, celebration, and socialization. Anthropologists have identified these and other reasons for drinking in societies around the world, but they also acknowledge the motives for drinking are often not discernible. The drinking at one festive occasion could have diverse functions depending on the participants, and some of these functions might be hidden from the eyes of observers. For example, a wedding's primary function was to celebrate the marriage of a couple, but the heavy drinking that accompanied weddings also provided enjoyment and merriment—the jollification, and it likewise brought friends, relatives, and neighbors, sometimes the entire village or neighborhood, together in a process of socialization. If invited, the village poor might use the occasion to become aggressively drunk as a result of their alienation and resentment, what anthropologists term "despair drinking."[3] An unlucky suitor might drown his sorrow, ease his pain, and forget his troubles, as suggested by the poets, while the youth of the village could express their collective disappointment at the loss of a marriageable lass by letting off steam through drunken violence.[4] Finally, for the parents of the bride and groom the occasion might have functioned primarily as a means of relaxation after the hectic preparations.

The jollification, celebration, and socialization that resulted from recreational drinking not only occurred during the occasions noted above; sometimes they occurred for no particular occasion at all, and at other times people seemed to be using an occasion as an excuse for drinking. For example, a custom in the village of Cahaignes during the fourteenth century was for a person to drink "the wine of the hiring" with the carpenter employed to build a house.[5] Other occasions demonstrate the jollification that could accompany such drinking. In 1392 Ser Lapo Mazzei wrote to his dear friend Francesco di Marco Datini, the merchant of Prato, after a drinking session, "In tasting those good wines we did nothing but laugh."[6] Similarly, Samuel Pepys recorded in his diary on 7 May 1660 that he was already in bed when two friends visited: "I gave them three bottles of Margate ale and sat laughing and very merry till

---

[2] Hanawalt, *Ties That Bound*, 26, 28.

[3] Heath, *Drinking Occasions*, 126, 165, 184.

[4] For alcohol as an escape valve, see Bacon, "Alcohol and Complex Society," 78.

[5] Vaultier, *Folklore pendant la Guerre*, 167, 180.

[6] Origo, *Merchant of Prato*, 296.

almost one o'clock in the morning."[7] Jollification was not restricted to men; in seventeenth-century Somerset a village girl brought some malt to a brewer and hired him to brew her some beer because "she together with some other maidens of her acquaintance had a desire to be merry together."[8]

As noted by the anthropologist Dwight B. Heath, "Some people make their lives more enjoyable by celebrating small things."[9] In the "pleasant and merry comedy entitled *Gammer Gurtons Nedle*," printed in 1575, Gammer Gurton celebrated the discovery of her lost needle by telling the deacon, "Let us go in and drink."[10] Such fictional celebrations no doubt had their counterparts in reality. Victories likewise deserved celebration; after capturing the castle of Fougeray in 1350, Bertrand du Guesclin and his men "drank the good wine and took good heart."[11] The Norman nobleman Gilles de Gouberville celebrated a different type of victory—a lengthy legal battle with the Sieur de Gatteville in 1556; the judges and his lawyers joined him in drinking nine gallons of wine.[12] When the city of Florence celebrated the visit of Pope Pius II in 1459, His Holiness expressed his disappointment with the tame entertainments arranged for his benefit, including tournaments "in which more wine was drunk than blood spilled."[13]

Just as important as the jollification and the celebration was the role of alcohol in socialization, which has received more attention than the others from anthropologists, who stress drinking as primarily a social activity. Socialization promotes the positive values of sociability, conviviality, hospitality, companionship, and integration. Drinking alone and refusing to drink with others can be forms of antisocial behavior.[14] Medieval poets likewise recognized these attributes of drink. In *Le mystère de la passion* (1452), Arnould Greban affirmed wine "nourishes love and peace," and according to Geoffrey Chaucer drink "can turn all rancour and dissension / To love and harmony and stop contention."[15] The bonds forged by drinking companions could be strong and they could manifest themselves in many ways. When

[7] Mendelsohn, *Drinking with Pepys*, 28.

[8] Quaife, "Consenting Spinster," 239.

[9] Heath, *Drinking Occasions*, 169.

[10] *Gammer Gurtons Nedle*, ed. Brett-Smith, 70.

[11] From a poem by the Picard minstrel Cuvelier translated in Coulton, *Life in the Middle Ages*, 3:107.

[12] Fedden, *Manor Life*, 153.

[13] Pius II, *Memoirs of a Renaissance Pope*, trans. Gragg and ed. Gabel, 110.

[14] Heath, *Drinking Occasions*, 172–73, 196; and Adler, "From Symbolic Exchange," 381.

[15] Greban, *Mystère de la passion*, ed. Paris and Raynaud, 399; and Chaucer, *Canterbury Tales*, trans. Coghill, 493.

Jaquet Le Roy finished work one day in 1380, he went to the workplace of his drinking companion, Jean Le Barbier, "his comrade and good friend," to ask him to go for a drink. Because Jean had not yet finished his work, Jaquet helped him so they could have more time for the wine.[16] The English custom of help-ale, also called bid-ale, demonstrates another way that drinking companionship could provide help to someone. When misfortune in the form of accident or crime struck, the victims or their friends and neighbors brewed ale and sold it, with the proceeds going to the victims. In 1605, for example, Henry Harris of Yatton Keynell lost his only possession, a cow; a friend told him to provide the ale, and the friend "would bring him company to help him towards his losses."[17]

In 1554 Thomas Platter and his fellow students befriended two soldiers in Montpellier. The soldiers admitted they had previously fought students but swore henceforth to take the students' side as a demonstration of their gratitude for the hospitality shown to them. To seal the friendship, the soldiers and students drank from the same cup, and the soldiers were baptized with a glass of wine poured over their heads.[18] Similar rituals were central to acts of reconciliation between foes, and the sharing of drinks even attained legal status in bringing peace to contending parties.[19] When Harry Martin and Thomas Hassel exchanged public insults, calling each other "knave," "Jack a napes," and "prating Jack," a court convened by the Pewterers' guild in 1552 ordered them to "be lovers and friends and ... to drink together before the master, wardens, and assistants."[20] In 1598 Thomas Bryant and John Spayne resolved their rivalry over the same woman by fighting at a sluice between Dimchurch and Romney; afterwards they drank together and "were good friends."[21] Similar rituals of reconciliation occurred in Italy and France. A nobleman persuaded the hot-tempered Benvenuto Cellini to make peace with an enemy by undertaking "the ceremony of drinking together and embracing."[22] When accused of attacking a man in 1609, Jacques Pié could assert his innocence by merely claiming they had "sealed their friendship in a drink."[23]

[16] Gauvard, *De Grace Especial,* 665–66.

[17] Ingram, *Church Courts,* 100. See also Hewitt, "Brewing," 2:401n3.

[18] Platter, *Beloved Son Felix,* trans. Jennett, 79.

[19] See Cohen, "Violence Control," 116.

[20] Rappaport, *Worlds Within Worlds,* 209. See also Hanawalt, *Of Good and Ill Repute,* 40.

[21] O'Hara, *Courtship and Constraint,* 143–44.

[22] Cellini, *Autobiography of Benvenuto Cellini,* trans. Bull, 69.

[23] Soman, "Deviance and Criminal Justice," 18.

Alehouses and Taverns

While alcohol was the ubiquitous social lubricant, alehouses and taverns were the ubiquitous venues of lubrication. Although originally intended to cater solely for travelers, taverns and alehouses gradually became the "third place," after the home (first place) and work (second place). As elaborated by anthropologists, the third place is public space that is relatively secure, a place where people can gather, talk, relax, and socialize.[24] The appeal of drinking establishments as a third place was particularly strong to the poor and to men. The poor congregated in taverns and alehouses because they offered alternative housing, companionship, and even family, while men considered them space that was free from the constraining female influences of the first place, home. For both groups, a man's house was not necessarily his dwelling place.[25] Around the Mediterranean, the piazza or the plaza competed with drinking establishments as the third place, but another competitor, the church, was losing ground in the sixteenth and seventeenth century. The parish church had long served as a venue for festive celebrations and had been intimately woven into the secular life of the community. Both Protestant and Catholic reformers resented this trespass and protested against the sacrilege of mixing the secular with the sacred. Reformers likewise protested against many of the festive celebrations, regardless of their venue. In 1628 Richard Rawlidge recalled that formerly people took part in the festive celebrations. Nowadays, he complained, as a result of the ranting of preachers against these public celebrations, people congregated instead in alehouses and taverns.[26] The decline of the parish church as a third place might have been one of the causes of the increase in the number of drinking establishments in the sixteenth and seventeenth centuries. The number had also been increasing earlier, as early as the decades following the Black Death.[27]

Italians of all classes, not just the poor, gathered to drink at taverns, day and night; lists of those prosecuted for violating the curfew at taverns included the social elite, municipal officials, clergy, pilgrims, and travelers in addition to prostitutes, rogues, procurers, gamblers, and criminals.[28] Other sources document the presence of many artisans, peasants, and soldiers.[29]

[24] Heath, *Drinking Occasions,* 50–51.

[25] Fumerton, "Not Home."

[26] *A Monster Lately Found, or, The Scourging of Tiplers,* in Wrightson, "Alehouses, Order," 10.

[27] Bennett, *Ale, Beer, and Brewsters,* 45; and Mehl, *Jeux au royaume,* 247.

[28] Patrone, "Consumo del vino," 286.

[29] Cherubini, "Taverna nel basso medioevo," 200.

Although the evidence is not as plentiful as it is for France and England, it nonetheless indicates that Italian towns had many taverns. In 1352 Florence had 62 taverns and another 55 wine shops, about one for every 500 inhabitants.[30] The smaller town of Orvieto had 237 taverns in 1400.[31] In 1450 Rome had a remarkable 1022 taverns, but many had been recently and temporarily established to cater for the pilgrims who flocked to the Holy City during the Jubilee.[32] The better taverns were furnished with tables, glasses, lanterns, a large cellar with room for as many as 100 barrels of wine, and possibly porticos or balconies for alfresco drinking.[33] Some sold large amounts of wine; one in Florence sold 21,000 liters in 1350, the equivalent of 460 modern glasses of wine a day.[34]

A sixteenth-century chronicler claimed the workers in Florence had a much more agreeable life than those above them; whenever they heard a tavern had good wine, without another thought except to live happily they went there to wallow in it.[35] In addition to good wine, Italian taverns offered their clientele a place to exchange gossip and news, a venue for weddings and gambling, an opportunity to make peace with enemies, occasions for laughing and dancing, and a focus of festive activities. According to a fifteenth century priest, "On holidays it is customary with peasants to spend the whole day and evening at the inn—drinking [and] gambling."[36] The *popolo minuto*, that is, the little people or lower-class workers, socialized with each other at taverns. Such socializing helped develop working-class solidarity, as indicated by a Florentine story explaining the origin of the word *ciompi*. During the fourteenth century French courtiers and soldiers in Florence asked the *popolo minuto* to join them as drinking comrades at taverns. The Florentines corrupted the French for "comrade" into *ciompo*, and in 1378 the Revolt of the Ciompi nearly succeeded in bringing down the Florentine government.[37]

The evidence from France reveals the large number of taverns that served villages, towns, and cities, as well as the increase in that number in the centuries following the Black Death. In 1320 Avignon had nine taverns, but

[30] Fiumi, "Economia e vita privata," 232.

[31] Riccetti, "Naso di Simone," 145.

[32] Ait, "Commercio delle derrate alimentari," 170.

[33] Cherubini, "Taverna nel basso medioevo," 201.

[34] La Roncière, "Vignoble florentin," 127.

[35] Cherubini, "Taverna nel basso medioevo," 212, citing Benedetto Varchia, *Storia fiorentina* (ca. 1529).

[36] Piovano Arlotto (1396–1484) in Speroni, *Wit and Wisdom*, 97.

[37] Cohn, *Laboring Classes*, 88–89, citing Stefani's *Cronaca fiorentina*.

between 1360 and 1370 that number had reached eighty, a figure that does not include several hundred little retailers of wine.[38] At Paris the number of taverns increased from 467 in 1313 to between 600 and 800 in 1400 and 1847 taverns in 1670.[39] In the fifteenth century Dol had one tavern for every sixty inhabitants, Antrain one for every sixty-five.[40] Even the smallest villages in France had at least one tavern, often located on the village square near the church and frequently serving as town hall.[41] The taverns in small villages probably did not sell much wine, but others did a roaring trade. An undated document from Avignon indicates that two taverns each had 24,000 liters of wine in their cellars.[42] Parisian taverns were notorious haunts for vagabonds, criminals, and prostitutes,[43] and of the 321 taverns at Rouen in 1597, 142 catered to the poor.[44] On the other hand, a study of the clientele in Parisian taverns at the end of the seventeenth century reveals that it mirrored French society, with a few noble and bourgeois customers and the majority being manual workers. As would be expected in a third place that appealed to married men fleeing domestic constraints, women seldom frequented taverns, but young, unmarried men did.[45]

French taverns were venues for recreation, jollification, and socialization, as indicated by the music, gambling, and reconciliation that occurred there. Men gathered at taverns for the purpose of learning songs, while some of the singing drew complaints from neighbors.[46] At a Paris tavern late in the seventeenth century, a painter gave his friends an impromptu performance with his flute, while they responded with an impromptu dance.[47] A popular game at taverns in the fourteenth century was "throwing the stone," and the stake was often a pot of wine to the winner. A much more brutal game of "throwing the stone" was a festive tradition at Langres in the fourteenth century, when the inhabitants of the town combated those from the surrounding area by throwing rocks at each other. Whenever someone was knocked down, his opponent

[38] Garrier, *Histoire sociale,* 60; and Chiffoleau, *Justices du pape,* 142.

[39] Contamine, *Vie quotidienne,* 226; Garrier, *Histoire sociale,* 60; and Trout, *City on the Seine,* 218.

[40] Leguay, *Rue au Moyen Age,* 156; and Collins, *Classes, Estates,* 62.

[41] Goubert, *French Peasantry,* 136–67.

[42] Chiffoleau, *Justices du pape,* 143.

[43] Geremek, *Margins of Society,* 278.

[44] Benedict, *Rouen during the Wars,* 16.

[45] Brennan, *Public Drinking,* 145–53.

[46] Vaultier, *Folklore pendant la Guerre,* 218.

[47] Brennan, *Public Drinking,* 261–62.

seized his hood and took it to the tavern, where he and the vanquished would drink a pint of wine together and "make peace as before."[48] Just as sociable was the custom of buying a drink for a newcomer to the tavern; when someone provided a welcome drink at a Parisian tavern, the recipient responded to his courtesy and drank to his health.[49]

Drinking with friends, neighbors, and workmates at taverns fostered a sense of solidarity and strengthened ties of companionship, as men became companions when they ate and drank together. A good illustration of this occurred at a tavern in Berry in 1392; when an acquaintance unexpectedly arrived, he joined a group of drinking companions and "became their companion and drank with them."[50] Pierre Ignace Chavatte, a seventeenth-century resident of Lille, was brief in describing why he visited the tavern of La Fleur de Lille: "I had fun with my comrades."[51] Young, unmarried men formed associations, often called the Abbeys of Misrule, whose functions centered on the local tavern, where the youths exhibited collective hostility and aggression towards the married men. The tavern became the third place for these associations, even more than it was for the married men, as the youth of a town or village ate at the tavern and elected their chief there. They set off from the tavern when they performed their charivaris, which often demanded drinking money from newlyweds, and returned to the tavern to spend their extorted money.[52] University students formed another group of young men who haunted taverns, and they were adept at seizing any and all occasions as an excuse to spend a large part of their budgets on wine: a new master, procurator, or receiver, the election of a new examiner, the conclusion of a peace between students of different nationalities, the renewal of the powers of a procurator, and the auditing of the accounts. Records from the fourteenth and fifteenth centuries show that the English students at the University of Paris spread their drinking around to sixty different taverns.[53]

Students at Oxford and Cambridge were likewise spoiled for choice of drinking places. Early in the seventeenth century, Oxford had 300 ale-

---

[48] Vaultier, *Folklore pendant la Guerre,* 177, 196–97.

[49] Brennan, *Public Drinking,* 222–23.

[50] Gauvard, *"De Grace Especial,"* 680–81.

[51] Lottin, *Chavatte, ouvrier lillois,* 346.

[52] Muchembled, "Jeunes, les jeux," 564; Bercé, *Fête et révolte,* 16; Hoffman, *Church and Community,* 141; and Collins, *Classes, Estates,* 72.

[53] Karras, "Sharing Wine," 193; and Chatelain, "Notes sur quelques tavernes," 87–109.

houses.[54] In the late 1620s, Cambridge had "only" 170, seventy of which were unlicensed, resulting in one for every fifty-two inhabitants. As in France the numbers of English drinking establishments kept increasing. An official census of thirty counties taken in 1577 indicated over 15,000 alehouses, leading Peter Clark to surmise the total number for England was 24,000. Later figures are not as precise, but Clark suggests that excise returns from the 1690s make a figure of 60,000 likely.[55] As revealing as all of these statistics are, probably the best illustration of the importance of the English alehouse is Chapel Ascote in Warwickshire; when its only alehouse closed in 1451, the few peasants living there abandoned the village.[56]

As mentioned in the previous chapter, the English could chose from a variety of alcoholic beverages; they also had a choice of drinking establishments—inns, taverns, and alehouses. The inn was increasingly a substantial and well-furnished enterprise, primarily serving travelers with food and lodging but also providing drinks to a better-class clientele. A tavern sold wine and consequently had a similar clientele; over time it likewise became better furnished and could offer its customers private drinking rooms. An alehouse sold ale and/or beer, while sometimes providing food and lodging, and attracted manual workers, peasants, tradesmen, and vagabonds. Some alehouses were bankers to the poor by providing credit on purchases of food and drink until the next payday.[57] Many alehouses were modest to say the least, often operating from the wretched accommodation of a poor widow, but by the end of the seventeenth century some had attained a respectable status.[58] Alehouses outnumbered inns and taverns; the 1577 census that counted over 15,000 alehouses listed 2,161 inns and 339 taverns.

Ned Ward described the cheerful ambience of a tavern in *The London Spy*, which he began writing in 1698: "After a friendly salutation, … down we sat, and when a glass or two had given fresh motion to our drowsy spirits, and we had abandoned all those careful thoughts which make man's life uneasy, wit begot wit, and wine a thirsty appetite to each succeeding glass: then open were our hearts and unconfined our fancies." What followed was song after song, including one whose lyrics proclaimed a bottle brought tunes to per-

---

[54] Crossley, "City and University," 131.

[55] Clark, *English Alehouse,* 43–44, 50.

[56] Dyer, *Making a Living,* 351.

[57] Earle, *Making of the English Middle Class,* 55.

[58] Clark, *English Alehouse,* 5. For Clark's analysis of the social class of the clientele, see ibid., 123–24, 222–23.

fection.[59] Nothing probably illustrates the jollification occurring in taverns and alehouses more than the singing. Customers often sang popular ballads about customers drinking at alehouses.[60] Unsurprisingly, ballad sellers visited alehouses on their rounds, and keepers bought copies to stick on the walls.[61] While drinking songs and ribald ballads were popular, professional music groups often performed at taverns and alehouses.[62]

Another perspective on the attractions of drinking establishments comes from a drunkard quoted by Owen Stockton in his tract entitled *A Warning to Drunkards* (1682): "methinks it is pleasant recreation to sit in an alehouse, and to hear and tell news, and talk of old stories over a pot of drink."[63] The drunkard highlighted two other activities that drew customers to drinking establishments: the exchange of news and the telling of stories. According to a sixteenth-century author, whenever someone bought a pint at a tavern, he kept his ears open to hear the news, and the common greeting was "What news?"[64] Samuel Pepys noted in his diary on 14 November 1660 that he joined some friends at the Dolphin, "and there we did drink a great quantity of sack and did tell many merry stories."[65] In addition to the news and the stories, drinkers could engage in political and religious discussions and debates, as Roger Lowe recorded in his diary. One of the debates on episcopacy versus presbytery with his good friend John Potter could have become, in Lowe's words, "hot, but the Lord prevented," while another debate with a Catholic ended in "love and peace."[66] In 1671 the Oxford antiquarian Anthony à Wood noted in his diary that he visited the King's Head, not to engage in discussion or debate, but for the more sensational purpose of seeing a giant who was seven and a half feet tall.[67] In addition to the music, news, stories, debates, and discussions, drinking establishments provided many other entertainments for the recreation, jollification, and socialization of their customers. Dancing accompanied the music, men on hobbyhorses performed tricks, wandering troupes staged plays, and customers gambled

[59] Ward, *London Spy,* ed. Hayward, 15–16.

[60] Capp, "Popular Literature," 203–4.

[61] Watt, *Cheap Print,* 194.

[62] Gouk, *Music, Science,* 48–49.

[63] Warner, "Good Help," 266.

[64] Spufford, *Small Books,* 65.

[65] Mendelsohn, *Drinking with Pepys,* 40.

[66] Lowe, *Diary of Roger Lowe,* ed. Sachse, 52, 54, 64, 89. See also Martin, "Drinking and Alehouses," 93–105.

[67] Wood, *The Life and Times,* ed. Powys, 193.

with dice and cards for pots of beer. Activities outside included bull and bearbaiting, football, and bowls.[68]

Not only did individuals resort to drinking establishments as their third place, but associations did also. Rather than use the church, parish councils often had their meetings in a neighboring alehouse or tavern, where they would spend parish funds on drinks, as occurred at Helmdon in Northamptonshire.[69] Parishes without licensed alehouses on occasion petitioned for permission to establish one so that parish business could be conducted there.[70] Guilds also used taverns and alehouses for meetings and celebrations. Although the Weavers of London had their own hall, in 1552 and 1553, they dined at the Gote, the Red Bull, the Horse Head, the White Horse, the Bishop's Head, and the Rose, some of them on five or six occasions.[71] Clubs were another type of association that utilized taverns and alehouses as meeting places, such as the group of mathematicians and physicians who met in the 1640s in London taverns for the purpose of discussing a wide range of scientific topics.[72] Political clubs such as those formed by Whigs and Tories in the 1680s also met at taverns; in 1682 Tory demonstrations in support of the Duke of York focused on the Dog-Wonder, the Dog, and the Globe, with bonfires, loyalist songs, and shouts of "No Whig, no Whig."[73] Finally, clubs and societies devoted to poetry likewise utilized taverns as a meeting place, sometimes consciously reviving the drinking customs of ancient Greek symposia.[74]

Alehouse and tavern space was male space, but women were more likely to visit drinking establishments in England than in France and Italy. One of the better illustrations of this is the diary kept by Roger Lowe at Ashton-in-Makerfield, Lancashire, between 1663 and 1674. The diary makes it obvious that women were free to visit alehouses, single women with other single women or with men, and wives with their husbands or by themselves. Lowe mentioned twenty-four women with whom he shared a drink, usually at alehouses. For example, when he accompanied Ellen Scott to a church service in a neighboring town, they spent eight pence at an alehouse before the service

---

[68] Wrightson, "Alehouses, Order," 9; Clark, *English Alehouse,* 152–57; and Clark, "Alehouse and the Alternative Society," 62.

[69] Harwood, "Public Houses," 55–56.

[70] Fletcher, *Reform in the Provinces,* 235.

[71] Schofield, *Medieval London Houses,* 54.

[72] Clark, *British Clubs,* 49.

[73] Harris, *London Crowds,* 170–71.

[74] Achilleos, "*Anacreontea,*" 21–35; and O'Callaghan, "Tavern Societies," 37–51.

began and returned to the alehouse after church with Ellen's sister. Similarly, Lowe courted his future wife, Emm Potter, at an alehouse, where "we professed each other's loves to each other." Despite the happy beginnings, eighteen months later they had "fallen out," so Lowe attempted a reconciliation at an alehouse, of course, but was unsuccessful.[75] Other sources indicate the experience of these women was not unusual, as other women drank together, received attention from suitors, played games with men, and took part in reconciliatory pledges at alehouses and taverns.[76] Drinking establishments could be a third place for women as well as men.

Festivals of the Christian and Agricultural Calendar

As taverns and alehouses increased in number and importance during the sixteenth and seventeenth centuries, many of the festivals of the Christian calendar declined. This was occurring throughout Europe in both Protestant and Catholic areas but was especially noticeable in England, as revealed by historians such as Ronald Hutton in *The Rise and Fall of Merry England: The Ritual Year, 1400–1700*. The title summarizes his argument: "Up till 1530 the English calendar of celebrations, like the religion to which so many of them were attached, was still flourishing and expanding rapidly along traditional lines. There was no sign of the changes which were soon to transform both almost out of recognition."[77] Nonetheless, many celebrations and their associated drinking customs survived and were still features of communal recreation, jollification, and socialization in the seventeenth century, even if historians know of them mainly through the writings of moralists who opposed them. In between these celebrations were those such as harvest and vintage associated with the agricultural calendar. According to a French sociologist, in traditional societies people live "in remembrance of one festival and in expectation of the next."[78] In traditional Europe people did not need long memories.

The New Year began in France with young people gathering at taverns for drinks or more likely participating in the festival of *aguilaneuf,* going

---

[75] Lowe, *Diary of Roger Lowe,* ed. Sachse, 23, 68–69, 97.

[76] For some examples, see Capp, "Separate Domains?" 128; Capp, *When Gossips Meet,* 331; Sharpe, "Such Disagreement," 175–76; Archer, *Pursuit of Stability,* 80; McIntosh, *Community Transformed,* 138–39; Crawford and Gowing, *Women's Worlds,* 138–40; and Shepard, *Meanings of Manhood,* 102. See also Cast, "Drinking Women."

[77] Hutton, *Rise and Fall,* 68.

[78] Cited in Burke, *Popular Culture,* 179.

from house to house begging for chickens, money, and wine, sometimes venturing far from home accompanied by fiddlers and pipers.[79] In 1552 London celebrated the Lord of Misrule on 4 January; the Lord and his magnificent retinue traveled by barge from Greenwich to the Tower, where morris dancers performed, and the Lord and his council broke open a large barrel of wine so that everyone could drink.[80] The festive drinking continued on Epiphany, the last of the twelve days of Christmas. In France people honored the day by eating and drinking with friends at a tavern, and in England, in addition to the traditional wassailing customs, farmers gathered in orchards to wassail their apple and pear trees by drinking to them to ensure their fertility in the coming year.[81] Plow Monday, the first Monday after Epiphany, was an occasion for English peasants to collect drinking money by dragging a decorated plow from house to house and staging a fight between a fool, supported by his clowns Pickle Herring and Pepper Breeches, and a dragon, ending with a merry dance as an occasion to make the collection.[82]

Carnival is revered by social historians as the most important popular festival in traditional Europe, and they have accordingly devoted much attention to dissecting it as an example of "the world turned upside down" and explaining its meanings and functions. Quite simply, carnival permitted people to feast and enjoy themselves before the rigors of Lent-imposed fasting and abstinence. Authorities did not proscribe alcohol during Lent, however, and this might explain why drinking was not as much a feature of carnival celebrations as food and entertainment, but it was still present. As a precursor to carnival, Venice celebrated the Festival of the Twelve Marys on 2 February, the Feast of the Purification, known as Candlemas. In addition to a reenactment of the annunciation, the festival featured heavy eating and drinking at banquets, "a barely Christianized fertility rite," according to one historian.[83] The San Zeno district of Verona inaugurated the carnival season by staging a *festa dei gnocchi* that featured feasting on gnocchi, of course, ribald costumes, and a great drinking binge.[84] Some communities in northern Italy supported the merrymaking by ordering taverns to sell wine

---

[79] Vaultier, *Folklore pendant la Guerre*, 93–94.

[80] Machyn, *Diary of Henry Machyn*, ed. Nichols, 13–14.

[81] Vaultier, *Folklore pendant la Guerre*, 99; and Harris, "Origin and Meaning," 34–35.

[82] Laroque, *Shakespeare's Festive World*, 94–95.

[83] Muir, *Ritual in Early Modern Europe*, 62–63.

[84] Heers, *Fêtes, jeux, et joutes*, 85.

at cost during the last three days of carnival.[85] On Shrove Monday, the crafts-men of Lille had the right according to an old tradition to ask the bourgeois and other inhabitants of the town for money to spend drinking at taverns.[86] Other towns provided free drinks to go with the festive fare and entertain-ment, some employers provided special carnival food and drinks for their workers, while the masons working on London Bridge received twenty gal-lons of ale on every Ash Wednesday, when carnival was over.[87]

Celebrations continued on the first Sunday of Lent, which was known in France as the Dimanche des Brandons as a result of the torches (*brandons*) used in the festivities. Some communities had bonfires with the torches, oth-ers just bonfires, and accompanying all types was the consumption of alcohol, including a type of mead in the diocese of Autun.[88] The end of Lent did not signal the end of occasions for communal drinking. In one London parish on Easter Monday, the wives played a game of barley-break with the parish priest and then adjourned to a tavern for drinking and feasting.[89] In England the second Monday and Tuesday after Easter formed a holiday known as Hock-tide that featured contests between men and women. The most common was for the women of a parish to chase the men and tie them up on Monday, the reverse occurring on Tuesday, but variations included the men keeping a pole erect on the top of a hill while the women tried to pull it down. No matter what the variation, the activities ended with the consumption of ale, some-times provided by the parish, sometimes sold to finance the parish.[90]

Anthropologists tend to interpret the celebrations of spring and early summer, beginning on May Day with its phallic Maypole, as fertility festivals. Given the drinking that accompanied the celebrations and the sexual activity that resulted, such an interpretation seems appropriate, except for those cases in which men were too overcome by alcohol to participate. Rather than focus on coupling, however, the festivals were communal celebrations of the arrival of summer with an emphasis on solidarity and socialization. Getting a head start on 28 April was the Feast of the Bottle at Evreux. Although the festival honored the memory of a thirteenth-century cathedral canon and was held on the feast day of the town's patron saint, Vital of Ravenna, the most notable

---

[85] Valenti, "Taverna comunale," 452.

[86] Lottin, *Chavatte, ouvrier lillois*, 321. See Grinberg, "Carnaval et société," 226.

[87] Hutton, *Stations of the Sun*, 152; Lardin, "Rôle du vin," 212; and Clark, *English Alehouse*, 23.

[88] Vaultier, *Folklore pendant la Guerre*, 47.

[89] Capp, "Separate Domains?" 130.

[90] French, "To Free Them," 387–412; Hindle, "Sense of Place?" 106–7; and MacLean, "Hocktide," 233–41.

features of it were plentiful wine, drinking binges, and merry drunkenness, so much so that drunken troops of men, youths, and children paraded through the streets.[91] A more traditional May Day festival occurred in the village of Buchy in Caux in 1405; the young men collected "May branches" that they then presented, after spending the night drinking beer, to the young women.[92] May Day celebrations in England also featured the collection of May branches but also May games, performances, and the Maypole. Henry Machyn described the festivities that accompanied the erection of a Maypole by the butchers and fishermen in London in 1562: "and they made great cheer, for there were two firkins of fresh sturgeon, and great conger [a species of eel], and great flounders, and great plenty of wine."[93] Frequently occurring also in May were the Rogationtide perambulations associated with Ascension Day, forty days after Easter. Members of each parish joined together in walking its boundaries as a means of maintaining their integrity. In 1604 sixty-eight-year-old John Shonke fondly remembered how he had attended every perambulation at Haverling since he was a boy, recalling at which places the walkers had stopped for a drink, sometimes with cheese and cakes.[94] Most parish officials provided rewards to ensure a good turnout, and the rewards usually included wine or beer, even for the children, that permitted a communal drinking.[95]

Other occasions for drinking sponsored by parish officials were church ales, which had many local variations in character and timing, but most had some form of entertainment and occurred around Pentecost—the English Whitsunday, fifty days after Easter—and all shared the same function of earning money by selling ale for either recurrent or special parish expenses. In the succinct words of Katherine French, "People who worshipped together drank together."[96] French also points out that the custom was not unique to England, for the Tyrol also had it.[97] Like carnival, church ales have attracted much attention from historians, partly because of the intense hostility of the puritans towards the practice and the resulting struggles over its continued existence.[98] In 1685 John Aubrey defended church ales in his *Natural History*

---

[91] Heers, *Fêtes des fous*, 96–101.

[92] Vaultier, *Folklore pendant la Guerre*, 66.

[93] Machyn, *Diary of Henry Machyn*, ed. Nichols, 283.

[94] McIntosh, *Community Transformed*, 202.

[95] Hutton, *Rise and Fall*, 35, 176, 247.

[96] French, "Parochial Fund-Raising," 129.

[97] French, *People of the Parish*, 262n158.

[98] See for example Barnes, "County Politics," 103–22.

of Wiltshire by describing what transpired in the days of his grandfather: "In every parish is (or was) a church-house to which belonged spits, crocks, etc., utensils for dressing provisions. Here the housekeepers met, and were merry, and gave their charity. The young people were there too, and had dancing, bowling, shootings at butts, etc., the ancients sitting gravely by and looking on. All things were civil, and without scandal."[99]

Festive drinking associated with Pentecost occurred in France as well, as it also did on the Feast of the Holy Trinity, the Sunday after Pentecost. Like the celebrations in England, those in France promoted socialization by providing opportunities for groups of bachelors, villagers, or parishioners to drink together, sometimes with drinks provided by their lords, sometimes over meals at taverns or churches.[100] The last of the spring and early summer festivals was Midsummer, 24 June, which coincided with the feast day of St. John the Baptist. John Stow described the Midsummer festivities that occurred in London in the early sixteenth century: "there were usually made bonfires in the streets, every man bestowing wood or labor towards them: the wealthier sort also before their doors near to the said bonfires would set out tables, … furnished with sweet bread, and good drink, and on the festival days with meat and drinks plentifully, whereunto they would invite their neighbors and passengers also to sit, and be merry with them."[101]

Come harvest time lords, like the wealthier sort in London, were expected to provide hospitality for their workers and peasants, as suggested by Thomas Tusser:

> In harvest time, harvest folk, servants and all,
>
> Should make, all together, good cheer in the hall;
>
> And fill out the black bowl of [joy] to their song,
>
> And let them be merry all harvest-time long.[102]

Although Tusser's poem was prescriptive, the practice of lords' providing food and drink for their peasants to celebrate harvest had a long tradition in England, and the custom went beyond the mere provision of food and drink as a wage or as an incentive to harvest the crops. Around 1400 mowers on an estate

---

[99] Hackwood, *Inns, Ales*, 52. See also Underdown, *Revel, Riot*, 62

[100] Pellegrin, *Bachelleries*, 83; Vaultier, *Folklore pendant la Guerre*, 71, 120; and Gauvard, "De Grace Especial," 449.

[101] Hutton, *Stations of the Sun*, 313.

[102] Tusser, *Five Hundred Points*, ed. Mavor, 187.

in Nottinghamshire who finished cutting the lord's meadow celebrated with a feast in the lord's hall that ended with a drinking ritual that required them to leave, return, and drink three times and then stagger home with a bucket of ale on their shoulders.[103] Similar traditions continued into the seventeenth century, as illustrated by *The Farming Book* written by Henry Best in 1642, containing instructions on the feast prepared for "pease pullers" that ended with hotcakes and ale.[104] In Italy and France vintage festivals could likewise be merry affairs, with young men smearing the faces of young women with grapes, but they were not occasions for massive consumption of wine simply because the cellars were likely to be empty or nearly so. Liquid celebrations would have to await the arrival of the new wine. In the Veneto, people celebrated the new wine with a pudding made from a mixture of wine, flour, and pine nuts, comparable to the modern *sugoli*, and the poor always received a free supply of *mezzo vino*.[105] Fifteenth-century Florentines celebrated the arrival of new wine by inviting their neighbors to taste it, but the *popolo minuto* celebrated with a public festival on 1 November, All Saints' Day.[106] Another agricultural activity that was part work, part ritual, and part celebration was the pig slaughter at the beginning of winter. In France relatives and neighbors could join the labor-intensive process and drink, eat, sing, gossip, and dance as they worked.[107]

Christmas rivaled carnival in popularity. It came at an opportune time when bitter winter weather made outdoor work virtually impossible so that people had little choice but to pass their time indoors in front of fire. In 1626, Nicholas Breton began his eloquent description of the festival in England with the words: "It is now Christmas, and not a cup of drink must pass without a carol."[108] And few carols could pass without a cup of drink. To cite just one of many examples, the 1695 edition of *Poor Robin's Almanac* contained a Christmas song whose opening lines were

> Now thrice welcome Christmas,
> Which brings us good cheer,
> Mince pies and plum porridge,

---

[103] Clark, *English Alehouse*, 25.

[104] Best, *Farming and Memorandum Books*, ed. Woodward, 98.

[105] Niero, *Tradizioni popolari*, 92.

[106] La Roncière, "Tuscan Notables," 245; and Balestracci, "Consumo del vino," 26.

[107] Goubert, *French Peasantry*, 92.

[108] Ashley, *Elizabethan Popular Culture*, 181.

Good ale and strong beer.[109]

The evidence indicates such songs were not just festive hyperbole; people consumed a large amount of alcoholic beverages during the Christmas season. One fourteenth-century household brewed 810 gallons of ale in February, but the amount in December was 3,500 gallons.[110] In both France and England, young men and women and in some places entire families spent much of the Christmas season in drinking establishments, drinking, eating, playing Christmas games, gossiping, and "frisking."[111] In England the focus of the drinking was the wassail bowl, which was passed not only among family members but also to neighbors and friends so that the entire village would become part of the celebration, jollification, and socialization.[112] Similarly, in France a custom on New Year's Eve was to visit friends and neighbors and collect money so that they could all drink together.[113] Thus, the year ended as it began, with people drinking with other people, not alone but celebrating the festive occasions as a community, whether it be friends, neighbors, or the entire village.

Interspersed throughout the year were yet more religious festivals that celebrated local feast days with festive drinking. So important was the festive drinking that the authorities in one Italian town exempted payment of taxes on wine sold on the local feast day of St. Bartholomew; another exempted the payment on its feast day in honor of St. Matthew and also for the two days before and after, while a third went even further by distributing free wine to the inhabitants of two rural communities on the feast day of its protector, St. Evasio.[114] The villages surrounding the French town of Grenoble celebrated their patron saints' day by attending a brief service in the church and spending the rest of the day dancing and drinking.[115] Winegrowers in France celebrated the feast day of their patron St. Vincent on 22 January by joining friends and fellow workers at taverns for wine and games.[116] Not everyone or

[109] Wright, *Specimens of Old Christmas Carols,* 69. See also Laroque, *Shakespeare's Festive World,* 149.

[110] Bennett, *Ale, Beer, and Brewsters,* 18.

[111] Goldberg, "Masters and Men," 67; Underdown, *Fire from Heaven,* 63; Denton, *Perambulation of Cumberland,* ed. Winchester and Wane, 255; and Vaultier, *Folklore pendant la Guerre,* 83, 86.

[112] Brears, "Wassail!" 106–41; Cressy, *Bonfires and Bells,* 16–17; Hutton, *Rise and Fall,* 13-14; Hutton, *Stations of the Sun,* 22; and Laroque, *Shakespeare's Festive World,* 150.

[113] Vaultier, *Folklore pendant la Guerre,* 93.

[114] Balestracci, "Consumo del vino," 26; and Patrone, *Cibo del ricco,* 468.

[115] Norberg, *Rich and Poor,* 37.

[116] Vaultier, *Folklore pendant la Guerre,* 164–65.

every place took part in all the festivals noted above, but everyone remembered the last one and looked forward to the next.

Rites of Passage

Birth, marriage, and death are not only the most notable stages in a person's life but also important social markers for families and communities and consequently imbued with meaning and ritual. Societies celebrate and commemorate these and other rites of passage with alcoholic beverages, and in traditional Europe these occasions joined those of the Christian and agricultural calendar in providing breaks from the routine. The number of breaks could be considerable, for even a small village could celebrate several rites of passage in a month. The demographic pattern of traditional Europe was characterized by high fertility and high mortality, both much higher than today. Infant and child mortality was tragically high, with about half of those born not reaching the age of five. As a result, half of the funerals could be for the very young. One of the few documented cases of a drinking at the funeral of an infant occurred in the small London parish of St. Bartholomew's Exchange in 1661 for the baby of a homeless woman; the parish spent seven shillings for bread and beer at a pauper's funeral.[117] In 1625 a Lincoln waterman paid for beer, bread, and other "victuals" at the funeral of his four-year-old son, while at the other end of the social ladder the very wealthy Blackett family of Newcastle spent large sums on the funerals of three infants who died in the 1690s.[118]

In great contrast to the sad drinkings at funerals of the very young were the joyous celebrations at their birth and subsequent baptism. In one area of France friends and relatives kidnapped the newly baptized infant and took it to a nearby tavern, where they held it until the parents came and ransomed it by purchasing drinks.[119] At the birth of her grandson in 1671, the Marchioness de Sévigné distributed money for drinks, resulting in toasts to his health for miles around her estate in Brittany.[120] In England parents and their friends, relatives, and neighbors celebrated the newborn's christening rather than its baptism. Henry Machyn recorded in his diary the wine served at the christenings he attended at London in the middle of the sixteenth century: hippocras

[117] Wear, *Health and Healing*, 8:48.

[118] Gittings, *Death, Burial*, 80; and Houlbrooke, *Death, Religion*, 281.

[119] Muchembled, *Société et mentalités*, 38.

[120] Sévigné, *Letters*, intro. Robinson, 2:121.

(spiced wine), muscatel, and French, Gascon, and Rhenish wine, always in "great plenty."[121] The "great plenty" probably did not match the amount consumed at a christening early in the seventeenth century, described by an indignant witness as "the greatest drinking and uncivil mirth that ever I knew."[122] Women quite often organized these celebrations and frequently did most of the drinking. The birth of a child also provided two other occasions for drinking. One was during the birth when female friends and neighbors assisted the mother and drank some of her caudle, a special drink made of warmed wine or ale with sugar and spices.[123] The other was the ceremony of churching, more formally the rite of Purification, Thanksgiving, and the Churching of Women that was required of women forty days after giving birth.[124] Women dominated these drinkings more than they did those of christening.

Marriages also provided several occasions for celebratory drinking. The first could occur at the time of engagement when the couple sealed the contract by drinking to each other in front of family and friends, often at a tavern or alehouse.[125] A woodcut from a seventeenth-century English ballad (fig. 3) depicts a woman drinking with four men in an alehouse; in front of the woman is a piece of paper that is probably a marriage contract. Other occasions might follow; Leonard Wheatcroft described in his *Courtship Narrative* that after his engagement he, his fiancée, and his and her brothers traveled to Snitterton to join her cousins at an inn, "and drinking verily merrily together, I did invite some of them to the wedding."[126] On the wedding day the drinking began at breakfast, sometimes held at an alehouse or tavern.[127] After the ceremony the drinking began in earnest, with massive amounts of wine recorded for the weddings of princes.[128] The record probably goes to Edward II, who ordered 1,000 *tonneaux* to celebrate his marriage to Isabella of France in 1308; according to the reckoning of one scholar this was the equivalent of 1,152,000 bottles.[129] Farther down the social ladder the amounts were more modest, but when a draper married the daughter of a

[121] Machyn, *Diary of Henry Machyn*, ed. Nichols, 198, 216, 264, 289.
[122] Oglander, *Royalist's Notebook*, ed. Bamford, 184.
[123] Wilson, "Ceremony of Childbirth," 70, 73, 76.
[124] Cressy, "Purification, Thanksgiving," 112.
[125] Vaultier, *Folklore pendant la Guerre*, 12; and Gowing, *Domestic Dangers*, 143.
[126] Wheatcroft, *Courtship Narrative*, ed. Parfitt and Houlbrooke, 77.
[127] Garrioch, *Neighbourhood and Community*, 26.
[128] Balestracci, "Consumo del vino," 25; Weiss, "Medieval and Renaissance Wedding," 159; and Austin, *Alcohol in Western Society*, 172.
[129] Penning-Rowsell, *Wines of Bordeaux*, 83–84.

Figure 3: Scene from *The Roxburghe Ballads* showing a woman with four male companions in a seventeenth-century English alehouse. On the table in front of the woman is a piece of paper, probably a marriage contract.

Reproduced from *The Roxburghe Ballads*, vol. 3, edited by William Chappell, 481. Hertford, UK: Stephen Austin and Sons, for the Ballad Society, 1881; reprint, New York: AM Press, 1966.

town clerk in London in 1559, Henry Machyn recorded the supply of hippocras and muscatel was "plenty to everybody."[130] The municipal officials in some towns of northern Italy ordered taverns to provide wine at cost during weddings.[131] Throughout Italy, moreover, sumptuary legislation designed to curb the excesses of wedding banquets did not place restrictions on the consumption of wine. The Venetian regulations of 1562, for example, limited the number of courses, forbade the consumption of wild animals and certain fish, and required fruits of the seasons and modest confections, but had nothing on wine.[132]

A widespread custom in France required the couple to supply wine to the youth of the village or to the youth of a neighboring village if the bride came from there to compensate them for the loss of a marriageable woman.[133] The English custom of bride ale had the opposite effect on the couple's

[130] Machyn, *Diary of Henry Machyn*, ed. Nichols, 199.

[131] Valenti, "Taverna comunale," 452.

[132] Chambers and Pullan, *Venice*, 178–79; and Redon, "Réglementation des banquets," 113–14.

[133] Vaultier, *Folklore pendant la Guerre*, 20–21; and Muchembled, "Jeunes, les jeux," 569.

finances. Just as church ales raised money for the parish church, bride ales provided financial assistance to the bride and groom that would help them meet the costs of establishing a new household. The couple could provide the ale, food, and entertainment, or the guests could provide them as an act of charity. As noted by Judith M. Bennett, the custom "provided regular occasions for the intermingling of conviviality and charity."[134] The final occasion for celebrating a wedding relates to the Yorkshire custom of the bride returning to her parents' house after the wedding, there to await her husband, as explained by Henry Best: "When the young man comes to fetch away his bride, some of his best friends, and young men his neighbors, come along with him, and others perhaps meet them in the way, and then is there the same jollity at his house, for they perhaps have ale or wine ready to give to the company."[135]

Among Catholics perhaps the most important purpose of supplying alcoholic beverages at funerals was to ensure a large gathering, especially of the poor, to pray for the soul of the deceased. The wealthy had an unfair advantage, for the largesse at their funerals could attract large crowds. Brewers used twenty-four quarters of malt for the funeral of Lady Margaret de Neville in 1319, enough to provide 1,440 gallons of ale.[136] When Christine de Lorraine, wife of Ferdinand I de' Medici, died in 1636, 5,000 flasks of wine were distributed at the cloister of San Lorenzo after the funeral.[137] The less wealthy did what they could; when Stephen Thomas of Essex made his will in 1417/1418, he asked that ten bushels of malt, enough for seventy-five gallons of ale, be brewed after his death to provide a gallon to every poor man of his parish.[138] The death of a Catholic could provide two other occasions for drinking. The first was the "month mind," celebrated one month after the death, and the other was the anniversary obit, one year after the death.[139]

The salvation of the deceased person's soul through prayer was not the sole reason for the provision of alcoholic beverages at funerals, even among Catholics. The funeral dinners and drinkings by friends, neighbors, and workmates awarded those who attended the service and celebrated the person's contribution to the community. They also injected lighthearted conviviality into

---

[134] Bennett, "Conviviality and Charity," 31–33.

[135] Best, *Farming and Memorandum Books,* ed. Woodward, 123.

[136] Kershaw, *Bolton Priory,* 139. Kershaw reckons 60 gallons a quarter, which is perhaps too low.

[137] Paronetto, *Chianti,* 143.

[138] Clark, *English Alehouse,* 25.

[139] Hanham, *Celys and their World,* 258; and Platt, *Medieval Southampton,* 187.

the somber proceedings, reaffirmed life over death, and confirmed the continuity of the community.[140] Rather than sell all of their wine or have the lord take it all, French peasants tried to keep some for themselves, the *vin d'honneur*, to serve to family and friends on special occasions. They also wanted it served at their funerals so the occasions would be joyous affairs, not sad and morose, and so the memory of the dead would be more intensely present.[141] Even without any *vin d'honneur*, the family and friends of the deceased gathered over a meal and some wine to remember the person.[142] In England puritans opposed the custom of funeral drinkings because of its association with Catholic prayers for the dead, but their opposition had little effect. Richard Hooker defended the practice by quoting wise King Solomon (Proverbs 31:6): "Give wine unto them that have grief of heart."[143] Rather than bequests to fund funeral sermons, as the puritans recommended, English wills contained instructions to pay for drinkings "for my neighbors" and for "them which go to church with me on the day of my burial," in short, for the old "good fellowship" rather than the new puritanism.[144]

Protestant funerals also provided several occasions for drinking. The first was the wake at which people watched over the corpse; in 1618 at Cambridge students watched over the body of a fellow student while consuming wine and beer.[145] Two other occasions were when the mourners came to fetch the corpse to carry it to its burial and then after the ceremonies when they gathered for a dinner. In the mid-seventeenth century Adam Martindale recorded both at the funeral of his father; all of those who came to fetch the corpse "were entertained with good meat, piping hot, and strong ale in great plenty," and then a dinner at a tavern for as many as the room could hold.[146] Death in the form of executions provided one final occasion for the consumption of alcohol. When James Yonge visited the gallows at Tyburn outside of London in 1681, he noted in his journal, "By it are two houses which have balconies and sell drink, and I believe do make great profit of them at execution time."[147]

---

[140] Houlbrooke, *Death, Religion,* 264; and Gittings, *Death, Burial,* 159.

[141] Garrier, *Histoire sociale,* 56; and Chiffoleau, *Comptabilité de l'au-delà,* 144.

[142] Vaultier, *Folklore pendant la Guerre,* 43.

[143] Houlbrooke, *Death, Religion,* 275.

[144] Collinson, "Cranbrook and the Fletchers," 187–88; and Schen, *Charity and Lay Piety,* 103.

[145] Gittings, *Death, Burial,* 106.

[146] Heal, *Hospitality in Early Modern England,* 371.

[147] Yonge, *Journal of James Yonge,* ed. Poynter, 176.

In addition to birth, marriage, and death, other rites of passage featured the consumption of alcohol, especially those related to the coming of age. Paul Griffiths, in his *Youth and Authority: Formative Experiences in England, 1560–1640*, suggests that drinking in an alehouse functioned as a rite of passage for young men, "providing a series of turning-points in which they forged alliances and constructed identities."[148] For young men more structured rituals than drinking at alehouses surrounded the completion of apprenticeship and university. When French apprentices completed four years of training and graduated to the ranks of journeymen, on the first Sunday after Epiphany they performed a ritual at the home of the grand master of the guild and then joined their fellow guild members at a dinner with wine, each member contributing to its cost.[149] English apprentices not only had to serve seven years before becoming journeymen, but they also had to pay for the drinks.[150] Students not only had to pay for drinks when they started their university degrees but also when they finished. At the University of Turin, the graduating student had to supply wine first at the solemn proclamation of his candidacy and then again when he had successfully defended his thesis.[151] Felix Platter described the ritual surrounding the awarding of a degree at Montpellier in 1555: the ceremony was conducted to the sound of an organ with great pomp, followed by a procession around the town to the sound of fifes, ending with a "grand repast" that featured sugared almonds. "The hippocras was delicious."[152]

Other Celebrations

Another type of recreational drinking occurred during parish, municipal, national, confraternal, and occupational festivals. Villages, towns, and cities organized public drinkings to celebrate local and national events; in addition to the functions of jollification and socialization, such occasions could help integrate the individual into the public body. The occupational and confraternal celebrations, which were often banquets accompanied by large amounts of alcoholic beverages, could likewise function to integrate members, but they also served to separate the membership from the rest of society and promote solidarity, the shared drinks reinforcing ties of obligation and

---

[148] Griffiths, *Youth and Authority*, 201.
[149] Faral, *Vie quotidienne*, 72–73.
[150] Heal, *Hospitality in Early Modern England*, 327; and Woodward, *Men at Work*, 33.
[151] Patrone, *Cibo del ricco*, 465–66.
[152] Platter, *Beloved Son Felix*, trans. Jennett, 94.

reciprocity. Similar drinkings helped establish solidarity among ruling elites in towns and cities. After completing their deliberations, the governing priors of Florence withdrew to drink wine together, while the merchant rulers of Saint-Omer followed an ancient ritual of meeting every year for two days of drinking together.[153] The officials of the Cornish village of Bodwin used public funds to purchase beer and cakes for themselves to celebrate a royal victory in Ireland in 1649 and to purchase wine, beer, and cakes for a victory over the Scots in the following year.[154] Magistrates throughout Europe probably regarded such drinkings as a well-deserved perquisite of office.

In a practice known as queening, craft guilds in France often celebrated their annual festival by selecting members to become their king and queen and others to become officials of the royal entourage with names such as chancellor, throne-bearer, goblet-filler, and wine-taster. The last two officials were probably the most important, because the primary activity of the brief reigns was to drink as much as possible and to encourage others to do the same.[155] In England, the association between excessive drinking and the annual guild festival was such that the occasion was called the *potatio*, "ye drynkyng," or the "time of drynk." Guild regulations governing conduct at the festival condemned those who refused to pass the cup, but the regulations of the Guild of St. Elene at Beverley perhaps tried to limit excessive drinking by stating members could "drink as much ale as is good for them."[156]

Religious associations, known variously as fraternities, confraternities, or companies, also celebrated their annual festivals with copious amounts of alcoholic beverages. A good illustration of the importance that drink had in these associations comes from the elaborate ritual enacted by the Fraternity of the Assumption, established at Lincoln in 1373. On drinking occasions its members opened three barrels of ale; on opening the first barrel one member read the regulations, on the second they prayed for the dead, and on the third they appealed to Virgin Mary on behalf of the living.[157] Members of other associations just did the drinking without paying too much attention to any rituals. In 1442 the Ascension Company at Florence provided six barrels of wine for about fifty people who attended its feast on the Wednesday before

---

[153] Trexler, *Public Life,* 229; and Duby, *Early Growth,* 243.

[154] Douch, *Old Cornish Inns,* 15.

[155] Bercé, *History of Peasant Revolts,* 27.

[156] Wallace, "Chaucer and the Absent City," 28.

[157] Rosser, "Going to the Fraternity Feast," 435.

Ascension Day.[158] The regulations of some French associations required members to drink together, while drinking during the religious functions of others had the potential to degenerate into binges.[159]

The poor also had an opportunity to drink during festivities celebrated by the erection of fountains that spouted wine, as described by Vespasiano da Bisticci when Emperor Frederic III visited Naples in the fifteenth century: "All about the place were set up fountains which spouted here Greek, here Muscat, and here red wine of every kind, and wines of luxury as well. At all the fountains were silver cups, and anyone who would might drink."[160] Similar fountains spewed wine at Avignon and Florence to celebrate the election of popes.[161] In France from the fourteenth to the seventeenth centuries, royal entries were occasions for fountains liberally dispensing wine at towns such as Lyon, Orléans, Brive, Paris, and Lille.[162] Similar celebrations in England did not feature fountains of wine, but conduits in London and elsewhere flowed with wine on royal occasions such as coronations, prompting John Milton's caustic comment, "the Conduit pisses Wine at Coronations."[163]

Although fountains and conduits pissing wine were spectacular, more often authorities dispensed drink in more conventional ways to celebrate special occasions. At Florence the return of the Medici from exile in 1512 resulted in the distribution of trebbiano and vermiglio wine, and the same occurred when Pope Leo X visited the city in 1515.[164] At Dijon in the sixteenth century, after annual mayoral elections the winner provided a traditional meal of bread, meat, cherries, and wine, while some candidates attempted to bribe voters by passing out wine before the election.[165] When the Maréchal de Vivonne defeated the combined fleets of Holland and Spain during a battle in 1676, his sister celebrated in Paris with fireworks in front of her gate and "set three hogsheads of wine running for the joy of this victory."[166] English towns and villages demonstrated their loyalty to the monarchy by celebrating royal

---

[158] Newbigin, "Cene and Cenacoli," 98.

[159] Heers, Fêtes, jeux et joutes, 86; and Venard, "Fraternité des banquets," 139.

[160] Vespasiano da Bisticci, Vespasiano Memoirs, trans. George and Waters, 77. See also Patrone, "Vini in Piemonte," 271.

[161] Garrier, Histoire sociale, 53; and Paronetto, Chianti, 98.

[162] Garrier, Histoire sociale, 63; and Lottin, Chavatte, ouvrier lillois, 309.

[163] "Upon the calling in of the Scots and thir comming," in Milton, Works of John Milton, ed. Patterson, 5:202; Hassall, They Saw It Happen, 23, 175; and Wood, Life and Times, ed. Powys, 276.

[164] Paronetto, Chianti, 97.

[165] Holt, "Wine, Life, and Death," 94.

[166] Sévigné, Letters, intro. Robinson, 5:35.

occasions: the accession of a new monarch, the anniversary of the accession, the coronation and its anniversary, the monarch's birthday, royal visits, and royal births, as well as the occasional royal victory. At times, municipal magistrates even supplied the wine, beer, and ale for the festivities from public funds; for example, on Accession Day in 1576, magistrates in Liverpool, after first dining privately, passed out sack, white wine, and sugar to the public.[167] At other times, wealthy citizens in a show of hospitality provided drinks on tables set up in the streets; when Prince Charles returned from his journey to Spain in 1623, John Taylor wrote, "divers noblemen, gentlemen, and others … gave vessels of wine in the streets" in London. Taylor's comment, "Ten thousand men will go to bed scarce sober," was an indication of his approval, but Simon D'Ewes was more critical in his assessment of the celebration: "the only thing to be lamented was the great excess and drunkenness of this day, the two usual faults of Englishmen upon any good hap."[168]

People in traditional Europe had ample opportunity to indulge in binge drinking as they celebrated Christian holidays, harvests and vintages, births, marriages, and deaths, and events of local and national significance. In between these drinkings was the daily consumption of alcoholic beverages as part of a person's diet, except, that is, for the poor who had to be content with water. However, even the poor could take advantage of the free wine that flowed from fountains and conduits, and of the many other opportunities for a festive drink. If continuous exposure to alcoholic beverages increases a person's tolerance to the inebriating consequences of alcohol, then most people in the past would be unlikely to be a "cheap" or "easy" drunkard, yet enough alcohol flowed on some festive occasions to make some observers, like Simon D'Ewes, complain of the resulting drunkenness. Some of the drunkenness was undoubtedly ugly, but the festive occasions that resulted in recreational drinking were supposed to be merry affairs that reinforced those virtues of jollification, celebration, and socialization. These were the same merry affairs that led to the condemnations of the moralists for the violent, immoral, and disorderly conduct of the participants. Rather than curtail the drinking on these festive occasions, many governments assisted it by providing free drinks or by

---

[167] Heal, *Hospitality in Early Modern England*, 334.
[168] Cressy, *Bonfires and Bells*, 95, 98–99.

decreeing that alcoholic beverages were not subject to the customary taxes. In other words, despite the concern about disorder and violence that could border on paranoia, officials chose to support the celebration, jollification, and socialization. 🍇

Chapter 5

Disorder: Places

Wine is treacherous.
—Habakkuk 2:5

Drinking is a social act, and people gather to share drinks as well as each other's company. In the past, the alehouse and tavern increasingly became the focal point of such gatherings, as drinking establishments replaced the church as the third place and zealous reformers opposed the disorder of celebrations in the public space of village greens and town squares. Two seventeenth-century critics of this trend, Richard Rawlidge and Claude de Rubys, believed drinking in public was more conducive to order than drinking in the privacy of alehouses and taverns, which could lead to drunkenness, whoring, and sedition. Even some clergy argued that when men were deprived of public celebrations and "their honest and lawful recreation," they would congregate in alehouses and there discuss matters of church and state.[1] In other words, the drinking was not as treacherous or as disorderly as the drinking establishments. Other authors likewise drew attention to the disorder inherent in drinking establishments. Late in the seventeenth century, Tom Brown described a disorderly London tavern in his *Amusements Serious and Comical*: "A tavern is a little Sodom, where as many vices are daily practiced as ever were known in the great one. Thither libertines repair to drink away their brains, and piss away their estates; aldermen to talk treason, and bewail the loss of trade; saints to elevate the spirit, hatch calumnies, coin false news, and reproach the Church; gamesters to shake their elbows, and pick the pockets of cullies [simpletons]; ... maids to be made

[1] Addy, *Sin and Society*, 105.

otherwise; married women to cuckold their husbands; and spendthrifts to be made miserable by a ridiculous consumption of their own fortunes."[2]

Tom Brown's account suggested tavern space was disordered space with a disorderly clientele. Some alehouses and taverns earned such notorious reputations for disorder that, rather than prosecute the customers who perpetrated the disorder, the authorities prosecuted the keepers for permitting it. Similarly, some alehouse and tavern keepers, often those who were proprietors of disorderly drinking establishments, had their own notorious reputations for disorder—the keepers from hell or anti-priests according to the condemnations of the moralists, priests of Bacchus according to Tom Brown.[3] Another factor in creating the image of the disorderly drinking establishment was a disorderly clientele that included thieves, gangs of criminals, prostitutes and their pimps, gamblers, vagabonds, and other denizens of the underworld. Religious and political dissidents formed another group of "disorderly" customers who, according to some clergymen, congregated in alehouses and there discussed matters of church and state. In other words, the potential for disorder in taverns and alehouses existed independently of the drunkard.

Defining Disorder, Interpreting Sources

Before examining disorderly drinking establishments, it is necessary to discuss the meaning of disorder and some problems in interpreting the sources. In the 1570s a puritan preacher in northeast Dorset condemned drinking and dancing as disorders and accordingly attempted to ban all church ales. The local people, however, had a different view of what constituted disorder and considered such activities to be orderly as long as no violence occurred.[4] Authorities at Dartmouth took a lenient stand by permitting ales and revels as long as they did not become disorderly, but their definition of disorderly included the youths at a Maypole dance in 1634 who drank "till they could not stand so steady as the pole did."[5] Other types of disorder apparently went unpunished, as did the drinkers in a tavern at Rennes in 1475 who pissed through the windows on the workers repairing a building below.[6]

[2] Brown, *Amusements Serious*, ed. Hayward, 83–84.

[3] Brown, *Amusements Serious*, ed. Hayward, 85.

[4] Hutton, *Stations of the Sun*, 254.

[5] Hutton, *Rise and Fall*, 198.

[6] Leguay, *Rue au Moyen Age*, 12.

In other words, the study of drunken disorder is difficult to separate from what the authorities considered to be orderly and disorderly behavior, and court records reflect the concerns of the authorities as well as the concerns of aggrieved citizens who complained of such things as noisy alehouses and domestic disturbances. The court records often report the indictment of a "disorderly" drunken person or a keeper of a "disorderly" alehouse or tavern without explaining the nature of the disorder. The court records also do not always provide a reliable indicator of the level of disorder. As noted by Paul Seaver, "The appearance of a court record is an indication of concern about certain behaviors but cannot be taken as a measure of the occurrence of that behavior."[7] Moreover, as argued by Alexandra Shepard, definitions of disorder were often class-related if not class-specific. The examples used by Shepard to illustrate this point are the drunken excesses of poor cottagers versus the debauchery of wealthy students, the former earning censure and appearing in court records and the latter treated with indulgence and usually not appearing in court records except in cases of violence.[8]

David Underdown, in his study of seventeenth-century Dorchester, calculated that 35 percent of the offenses recorded in the town's book of offenders between 1632 and 1637 were related to drink—drunkenness, selling ale, and entertaining drinkers.[9] Claude Gauvard likewise attempts to provide statistical evidence on the proportion of crimes related to drink and taverns in late medieval France and in the process provides a veritable cornucopia of statistics based on letters seeking remission for crimes. According to Gauvard's reckoning, 9.9 percent of crime, including crimes of violence, took place under the influence of alcohol.[10] Given Seaver and Shepard's comments, the interpretation of such statistics requires caution. Underdown's statistics reveal percentages in the book of offenders but not the level of drinking disorders in Dorchester, while Gauvard's statistics might conceal efforts by the rich and powerful to gain remission by pleading drunkenness at the time of the offense.

Chapter 8 examines the reaction of the authorities to drunken disorder and violence, but the distinction between their reaction and especially disorder is to a great extent an artificial one because of their role in defining disorder. Some forms of drunken disorder, such as vandalism, left

---

[7] Seaver, "Introduction, Symposium: Controlling (Mis)Behavior," 237.

[8] Shepard, "Manhood, Credit," 105.

[9] Underdown, *Fire from Heaven*, 72.

[10] Gauvard, *De Grace Especial*, 430.

more tangible results than did others, such as drinking in time of religious services on the Sabbath. Similarly, and, using the same examples, Sunday drinking was victimless, unless the parson preaching to empty pews could be considered a victim, while destroying gates and fences was not. In some areas and at some times authorities could prosecute people for drunkenness or for haunting drinking establishments, both "disorders" in the eyes of the arresting magistrates but not even remotely disorderly to the people of northeast Dorset. Magistrates probably had little difficulty in adding "and disorderly" whenever a drunkard faced prosecution. Sometimes the sources are vague on the precise nature of the charge. For example, in 1611 William Brown appeared as a witness in the Burgess Court of Westminster; when the judge discovered Brown "was so drunk that he could not deliver his mind," he fined him five shillings, but when Brown proved unable to pay the fine, he was committed to the stocks for six hours.[11] The punishment might have been solely for Brown's drunkenness, but it might have been compounded by his inability to cooperate with the court. Another example is the indictment of John Templer of Timsbury for selling beer at the "revel feast" in 1656. According to the charges, "a great concourse of people, 300 or 400 strangers, came to see the cudgel match, and diverse disorders and abuses were committed, chiefly ... by the sale of the said beer."[12] The actual nature of these "divers disorders and abuses" is not explained.

Another difficulty in interpreting the sources concerns the nature of court records, which represent what was stated in court rather than what happened in reality, and both plaintiffs and defendants could use the charge of drunkenness to blacken their opponent's reputation. In 1609 William Clayton of Blackburn, Lancashire, claimed in court he had an intimate relationship with Beatrice Bolton, the wife of Lancellot: "these three years done I have had my will and pleasure of her in every room in the house and at every apple and plum tree in the orchard." In defense of her honor, Beatrice counterclaimed that Clayton was "a common haunter and frequenter of alehouses and a common drunkard, a quarreler, a brawler, and a fighter." As noted by Richard Adair, "both these statements could have been true, but clearly it would be unwise to rely on either as a disinterested objective account."[13]

---

[11] Manchée, *Westminster City Fathers*, 100–101.

[12] Bretherton, "Country Inns," 199.

[13] Adair, *Courtship, Illegitimacy*, 175.

Disorderly Alehouses and Taverns

Keith Wrightson argues that for local communities in seventeenth-century England "the struggle over the alehouses was one of the most significant social dramas of the age," and he reckons for the Essex village of Terling between 1590 and 1660, 39 percent of court cases involved alehouses.[14] An examination of court records from the counties of Warwickshire, Kent, and Middlesex reveals a somewhat less dramatic situation, with the number of prosecutions relatively low and the nature of the transgressions relatively innocuous. An analysis of the Quarter Sessions Court records from the county of Warwickshire for the years 1625 to 1696 indicates the magistrates suppressed 112 alehouses for disorder in 72 years, about one and a half suppressions a year. The suppressions form no significant chronological patterns; a small increase resulting in two suppressions a year in the 1640s and 1650s might reflect the influence of the puritans, but that is the same rate for the 1670s and 1680s. Most of the "disorder" must have been relatively benign, because the records indicate only one act of violence in an alehouse in the 72 years covered by the records; in 1639, Robert Pettitt became drunk in the alehouse of Edmund Tibbottes at Rowington and "in the time of his drunkenness there did lately kill one William Benyon."

At first the standard complaint against an alehouse keeper in these records from Warwickshire was that he kept "very ill order and rule," which offended, wronged, disturbed, disquieted, or prejudiced his neighbors, and it frequently included precise charges, such as he "suffered diverse lewd and disorderly persons to be tippling and drinking in his house in the time of divine service on the Sabbath day." Over time the complaints became less revealing, and the most frequent charge was simply keeping a disorderly alehouse. Perhaps an indication of what constituted a disorderly alehouse comes from a seventeenth-century depiction (fig. 4); one patron urinates on the barrel, while the two men on the far side of the table fight over a hat, with one spilling his drink. When the legal charge did include a precise offense, the most frequent was selling drinks on the Sabbath; the most forceful expression of this occurred in 1661 when John Tasker of Charlecott faced the court for suffering "men to tipple and drink in his [ale]house upon the Lord's day to the high displeasure of Almighty God and the evil example of others." One of the longest charges was in 1633 against John Dunckley of Brandone who "often kept and harbored in his house wandering and suspected people

---

[14] Wrightson, *English Society,* 167; and Wrightson, "Alehouses, Order," 13.

Figure 4: A disorderly alehouse from *The Roxburghe Ballads*. One patron urinates on the barrel, while the two men on the far side of the table fight over a hat, with one spilling his drink. Illustration from "The Wine-Cooper's Delight," woodcut from *The Roxburghe Ballads*, English, seventeenth century [*Roxburghe Collection*, 3:244–45].

Reproduced from *The Roxburghe Ballads*, vol. 4, pt. 1, edited by J. Woodfall Ebsworth, 53. Hertford, UK: Stephen Austin and Sons, for the Ballad Society, 1881; reprint, New York: AMS Press, 1966.

and others of evil name and fame and suffered many to continue drinking in his said house until they be drunken, contrary to the laws of this realm, and many other misdemeanors to be committed in his said house, whereby his neighbors are much wronged and disquieted." Other charges included permitting games, violating curfew, and entertaining rogues, vagabonds, and wandering beggars. One keeper faced charges for keeping a bowling alley and another for suffering a mutiny in his house.[15]

The *Calendar of Assize Records* for the county of Kent shows a pattern similar to that of the Quarter Sessions records for Warwickshire. For roughly the same period, the number of indictments for disorderly alehouses averaged about two and a half a year, but that figure masks a large number of indictments in the 1670s and 1680s, when the average was almost six per year. The records for Kent reveal even less about the nature of disorderly alehouses than do those from Warwickshire. Until 1665 most indictments charged the keepers with "allowing ill rule"; then the standard complaint for the next ten years became allowing "riotous and ill-disposed" or "ill-affected" persons to

---

[15] *Warwick County Records*, ed. Ratcliff, Johnson, and Williams, 1:21, 181, 2:49, 4:108, 148, 7:235.

frequent the alehouse, and after that it was "keeping an ill-governed and disorderly" house. The number of indictments for gaming, such as that of Hugh
Hunt in 1670 "for keeping unlawful games and tables in his house at Crayford
and allowing several persons to play ninepins," was marginally higher than
those for selling drinks in time of divine service, which in turn was higher
than those for violating the curfew. As in Warwickshire, the indictments
reveal concerns about the character of the customers; in 1661 George Romney of Tonbridge was charged with "allowing persons of evil name, fame, and
conversation to congregate in his tippling house," and John Cropp of Offham
was indicted for "harboring Henry Cockerill, knowing him to have stolen a
gold watch in a gold-studded case (£20) from William Selbey, on 10 February 1683." As in Warwickshire most of the "disorder" was relatively benign
because only two cases of violence occurred, and on both occasions the perpetrators rather than the keepers faced the charges; in 1627 four laborers
from Lynsted were indicted "for quarreling and fighting in the alehouse of
Thomas Pollard," and in 1653 the violent behavior of Stephen Keeler at an
alehouse in Elmsted resulted in his conviction for manslaughter.[16]

The *Calendar to the Sessions Records* for the county of Middlesex covering the years 1612 to 1618 continues the patterns established in the records
from Warwickshire and Kent, despite covering part of London with its large
population and social dislocation. An average of four and a half indictments
a year, mainly for "keeping ill rule" or for keeping a "disordered" or "disorderly" alehouse, is the highest of the three counties, but that does not match
Kent's peak of six in the 1670s and 1680s. The number of indictments for
infringing the regulations on Sunday equaled those condemning the character of the customers, as keepers were prosecuted for entertaining, receiving,
harboring, lodging, or keeping common cozeners, cheaters, felons, whores,
and lewd, disordered, idle, or evil people. What is different for Middlesex
are the three indictments for bawdry, that is, for maintaining a brothel in an
alehouse. For example, in 1617 Elizabeth Gunter was charged with keeping
a disorderly alehouse after her neighbors accused her of being a common
disturber of the peace and suspected her of keeping a house of bawdry. What
is not different for Middlesex is the infrequency of violence; the only case
involved Robert Riccard who was charged with "permitting diverse men to
drink and to disorder themselves in his house on the Sabbath, when they

---

[16] *Calendar of Assize Records: Kent*, ed. Cockburn, 1:55, 2:150, 3:25, 237, 4:172.

quarreled and a man was then wounded."[17] To put the records from these three counties in context, according to the government survey of alehouses in 1577, Warwickshire had 447 alehouses, Kent 645, and Middlesex 720.[18] The numbers no doubt increased during the seventeenth century, as did the number of prosecutions in the 1670s and 1680s for the first two counties, but the number of prosecutions remained relatively low. Even when keeping in mind Paul Seaver's warning about the use of court records to determine the occurrence of certain behaviors, the records do not give the impression of a court system being swamped with indictments for disorderly alehouses.

What Keith Wrightson calls "the struggle over the alehouses" probably peaked in the seventeenth century, but the phenomenon had a long history. One of the earliest cases involved Juliana Fox of Thornbury, Gloucestershire, who was prosecuted in 1379 for receiving "priests and others into her house at illegal times, viz. around the middle of the night."[19] At Havering in the fifteenth century a keeper twice faced the courts for violations of the curfew, while the second occasion also included the charge of permitting evil rule by allowing his customers to brawl and fight.[20] Two cases from 1567 are notable for the breadth of the charges; George Blacklocke of Chelmsford kept a brothel, permitted servants and children to play dice and cards, violated the curfew, remained open during divine service, "and will not be reformed by any gentle persuasion," and Richard Strutt of Little Maplestead kept an unlicensed alehouse, harbored vagabonds, one of whom committed a robbery, "and also upon Saint Stephen's day last there was a bloodshed drawn in his house, viz. of one which had a broken head."[21] Some keepers faced charges for their role in the economic hardships endured by their customers. John Aldridge, a keeper at Terling in Essex, was indicted for permitting "poor men to sit tippling and drinking in his house for the space of half a day and all night together."[22] Worse was the case of Nathaniel Smith and his wife, Mary, who not only encouraged the poor to spend their money but also encouraged them to pawn something to pay for their drinks.[23] Worst was Robert Pennell of Islington, accused in 1657 of getting his poor customers so drunk that he

[17] *County of Middlesex*, ed. Hardy, 3:179–80, 4:126.

[18] Clark, *English Alehouse*, 42.

[19] McIntosh, *Controlling Misbehavior*, 76.

[20] McIntosh, *Autonomy and Community*, 257.

[21] Emmison, *Elizabethan Life*, 26, 34.

[22] Abbott, *Life Cycles*, 120–21.

[23] Sharpe, *Crime in Seventeenth-Century England*, 53.

could increase their reckonings.[24]

Although not as well documented as the English cases, French and Italian courts also dealt with cases of disorderly inns and taverns. At Paris in 1376, the neighbors of Agnès Piedelou complained to the authorities that loose-living men and women visited her inn both day and night and accused her of keeping a brothel, and neighbors lodged similar complaints against other women.[25] When a police official entered a tavern in Nantes on a Sunday in 1641 to determine if it was breaking the law by selling wine during divine services, its female keeper told him he should be in church rather than visiting taverns. Those officials who spent their Sundays visiting taverns could usually find many open taverns and fine many tavern keepers, as they did in Nantes and Paris.[26] In fourteenth-century Florence, authorities had difficulty imposing curfews on taverns, especially those close to brothels, and had to rely on heavy fines, such as the one imposed in 1431 on Giovanni di Francesco, keeper of La Vacca.[27] Rather than prosecute the tavern keeper, in 1492 Florentine officials convicted three cooks who worked at a tavern for procuring boy prostitutes there.[28]

One of the cases from 1567 cited above included the charge of permitting servants and children to play dice and cards. Just as many keepers faced charges for the unsavory character of their clientele, so also they faced charges for corrupting the young, including children, apprentices, servants, and students. In 1574 the authorities in Norwich put a widow in stocks for maintaining "apprentices in the house contrary to order."[29] In Florence in 1588, taverns came under concerted attack from a wide sector of the population for their role in the ruin of young men and boys.[30] One possible factor in the attack was the reputation of taverns as haunts for homosexuals.[31] French authorities similarly waged a campaign against cabarets for corrupting the youth. At Faye near La Rochelle, one cabaret entertained the youth of the town on Sundays, when they became drunk, took part in insolent and excessive behavior, quarreled, and swore; and in 1550 a cabaret in Arras had to

[24] Amussen, *Ordered Society,* 169.

[25] Geremek, *Margins of Society,* 236–37, n145.

[26] Collins, *Classes, Estates,* 101, 257, n29; and Nicolas, "Tavernier, le juge," 22.

[27] Mazzi, *Prostitute e lenoni,* 271, n48. *Vacca* means cow, but it is slang for a whore or a slut.

[28] Rocke, *Forbidden Friendships,* 160.

[29] McClendon, *Quiet Reformation,* 233.

[30] Weissman, *Ritual Brotherhood,* 203–5.

[31] Rocke, *Forbidden Friendships,* 33, 153–54, 159–61.

close for fifteen days because it had entertained youths and prostitutes on Good Friday during divine services.[32]

The indictments of keepers in England reveal several concerns about the behavior of youth. The first was the potential for corruption when disreputable alehouses attracted impressionable students, apprentices, and servants. Of specific concern was the potential for sexual license in licentious alehouses. A Hull alehouse keeper was imprisoned for forty-eight hours in 1576 "because he had allowed a young unmarried couple to lodge for the night and commit fornication."[33] In 1621 an Exeter court charged William Westlake and his wife for being the "principal agents" in permitting young people to use their alehouse for "dancing, drinking, and such other pastimes all the night," so much so that it was responsible for four bastard children born in the parish.[34] Another concern was the young were drinking during divine service on Sundays. A Springfield, Essex, tailor who also kept an alehouse was indicted in 1571 for using minstrels to attract the parish youth on Sundays and other holy days, "rioting and reveling," although in this case the charge did not mention the neglect of divine service but the neglect of archery practice.[35]

In addition to neglecting divine service and archery practice, young people were neglecting their responsibilities towards their parents and masters by spending too much time in alehouses. For example, another Essex keeper was charged with permitting servants to continue drinking "'til night, half the night and sometimes the whole, there misspending their time and neglecting their own and their master's business."[36] The authorities at Brinkloe, Warwickshire, believed the seven local alehouses caused children and servants to "neglect their callings," so in 1646 they suppressed six of them.[37] Also of concern to the authorities was the gambling and gaming at alehouses that were obvious attractions to the young. As a result, many keepers were indicted for keeping cards and other games that attracted the young, such as the two servants who played cards and "other ancient and unlawful games" at an unlicensed alehouse in 1565 at Great Bardfield, Essex.[38] The final concern is connected to the others, namely, the

[32] Pellegrin, *Bachelleries,* 277; and Muchembled, *Popular Culture,* 172.
[33] Woodward, *Men at Work,* 238.
[34] Helmholz, "Harboring Sexual Offenders," 267n48.
[35] Emmison, *Elizabethan Life,* 209–10.
[36] Wrightson, "Alehouses, Order," 8.
[37] *Warwick County Records,* ed. Ratcliff, Johnson, and Williams, 2:136.
[38] Emmison, *Elizabethan Life,* 220.

attractions of the alehouse could loosen the ties of social discipline by offering the young a third place for their leisure pursuits where they could be subject to temptations. To cite two examples, one young man spent the money he stole from his father getting drunk at an alehouse on Easter Sunday in 1627, and an apprentice went to an alehouse after evening prayer on a Sunday in 1634 and received an invitation from the keeper's wife to return when her husband was not there.[39]

Disorderly Keepers

As already noted, occasionally the disorderly tavern or alehouse keeper was himself disorderly, the antipriest of the moralists. In 1661 the curé of Frétigny complained that Macé Blot, a local "hostelier," had not attended the compulsory Easter services. Blot and his children were moreover hardened sinners who sold wine during church services despite promising not to do it year after year for twenty years, and their tavern was a place of "blasphemies, swearing, hatreds, and drunkenness."[40] The curé of Claveisolles, Jean de Vitry, made a similar complaint against Louis Bellet in 1682. Despite efforts to persuade him and court injunctions against him, Bellet continued to open his tavern during divine services, even hosting games of ninepins and *boules* so that their noise disrupted the services. When Vitry attempted to read the injunctions against games and taverns, Bellet stood at the back of the church and demonstrated his contempt by shouting Vitry should climb the steeple "to make himself better understood."[41] The English examples suggest the profession of alehouse or tavern keeper attracted men of unsavory character or perhaps produced them. In 1602 the inhabitants of East Tilbury claimed John Nicolson had "of his own evil mind procured and by force compelled diverse [people] to commit that horrible vice of drunkenness, whereby his good neighbors are greatly grieved, the Sabbath day profaned, God dishonored and the Kingdom of Satan erected, and the wicked vice of drunkenness increased."[42] John Ayly, keeper of the Unicorn in the Essex village of Kelvedon Easterford, faced court charges between 1613 and his death in 1636 for selling drink on the Sabbath, permitting ill

---

[39] Sharpe, "Crime and Delinquency," 102; and Sharpe, *Crime in Seventeenth-Century England*, 53.

[40] Gutton, *Sociabilité villageoise*, 248.

[41] Hoffman, *Church and Community*, 131.

[42] Emmison, *Elizabethan Life*, 205, 224.

rule, failing to attend church services, being drunk during sermons, swearing, cohabitating with a servant, and committing adultery with the wife of John Francis.[43]

Late in the sixteenth century both Edward Harvye and his wife, who kept an alehouse at Berwick-upon-Tweed, Northumberland, not only faced the typical charges of harboring "disordered and unlawful company" (including Scots), permitting games and cards, and violating the Sabbath but also that Harvye's wife had "been always wonderfully suspect to be a privy harlot."[44] The inclusion of Harvye's wife in the indictment illustrates women could also be disorderly keepers. Probably the most famous of these female keepers was the fictional Elynour Rummyng from John Skelton's poem "The Tunnyng [Brewing] of Elynour Rummyng," supposedly based on an actual alewife who kept an alehouse near Henry VIII's palace Nonsuch.[45] Elynour was the archetypal keeper from hell—Skelton even called her the devil's sibling—whose ale contained chicken droppings, but who nonetheless had a huge crowd of disorderly female customers eager to buy it. A good example of a disorderly female keeper is Jeanne de Baugie of Paris; she confessed in 1400 to the attempted abduction of a young girl, keeping a disorderly house, procuring, and the theft of a piece of fur from a merchant who had stopped for a drink of wine.[46] Many cases of disorderly female keepers focused on their sexual behavior, as they faced court for attracting "lecherous and suspicious" men and for being "most notorious" harlots.[47] An engraving by Jacques Lagniet from *Recueil des plus illustres proverbes,* published at Paris between 1657 and 1663 (fig. 5), shows a lecherous female keeper kissing a baker while her husband is "doing the laundry," that is, diluting his wine with water. Other cases illustrate sexual behavior had no role in the disorder of female keepers. In Northamptonshire, Anne Harris and her daughter proclaimed they would refuse to obey the regulations regarding the Sabbath "in despite of any justice in England," and their clients concurred by shouting they "would drink and sing and roar all night in despite of any man and so they did."[48]

---

[43] Sharpe, "Crime and Delinquency," 98, 102. See also *County of Middlesex,* ed. Hardy, 3:265.

[44] McIntosh, *Controlling Misbehavior,* 77–78.

[45] Skelton, "Sixteenth-Century English Alewife," ed. Jellinek, 102–10.

[46] Geremek, *Margins of Society,* 236, n141.

[47] Bailey, *Marginal Economy?* 169; and Capp, *When Gossips Meet,* 97.

[48] Clark, *English Alehouse,* 238. For other examples, see Goldberg, *Women, Work,* 116; and Capp, *When Gossips Meet,* 265.

Figure 5: *Il est bien sage, il met de l'eau dans son vin.* Engraving by Jacques Lagniet (French, 1620–72). The writing on the bucket states, "Wine from the big barrel. While he is downstairs doing his laundry by mixing water with his wine, the baker and his lecherous wife are taking other pleasures than those of the tavern." While kissing the baker the wife raises her two fingers, the cuckold's horns, to her husband. Other proverbs included are "Where the hostess is beautiful the wine is good" and "A beautiful hostess is hard on the purse."

Book 2, plate 14 in *Recueil des plus illustres proverbes.* Paris: J. Lagniet, 1657–63.

Disorderly Clientele

In a scene from Jean Bodel's early thirteenth-century farce entitled *Le jeu de Saint Nicholas,* three thieves planned their next heist while guzzling wine at a tavern.[49] Nearly four hundred years later, Robert Greene created a similar scene in *The Second Part of Cony-Catching* (1591). At the Three Tuns in Newgate Market two thieves sat drinking wine in a room with a view onto the street; when they observed a miller with a large bag by his side, they planned to steal it.[50] The association of drinking establishments with thieves, gangs of criminals, prostitutes, vagabonds, and other denizens of the underworld has a long history, and taverns and alehouses have had a reputation for being havens for a disorderly clientele. This was one of the significant charges in the indictments and suppressions of disorderly alehouses in the court records of the counties of Warwickshire, Kent, and Middlesex, and it was also a feature of taverns in France and Italy. Alehouses and taverns could function as the third place for poor men, but for vagabonds they also served as the first place—home—by offering cheap, perhaps free, accommodation, food and drink, companionship, and entertainment. The vagabonds of Paris knew which taverns in the surrounding villages and towns would welcome their visit.[51] Similar intelligence circulated among vagabonds in England. In 1572 the widow Jone Hailie managed to travel from London to Rye by taking advantage of accommodation at alehouses, while another vagabond managed a considerable journey by doing the same:

> First night, the Saracen's Head in Farringdon;
>
> Second night, the Star in Abingdon;
>
> Third night, an unnamed alehouse in Wallingford;
>
> Fourth night, the Hand in Reading;
>
> Fifth night, the Shoemaker's Last in Newbury;
>
> Sixth night, the Black Boys in Andover;
>
> Eighth night, an unnamed alehouse in Amesbury;
>
> Ninth night, a barn five miles from Amesbury;
>
> Tenth night, the White Horse in Fisherton Anger.[52]

---

[49] Bodel, *Jeu de Saint Nicholas,* trans. Mandel, 58–59.

[50] Greene, *Second Part of Cony-Catching,* ed. Judges, 166–76.

[51] Cohen, "Vagabondage à Paris," 304.

[52] Mayhew, *Tudor Rye,* 227; and Beier, *Masterless Men,* 80.

Rather than regard alehouses and taverns as providing a valuable social service for vagabonds, authorities viewed the situation with alarm. Because vagabonds traveled they escaped parochial discipline; because they were masterless they avoided social control, all leading to disorder. From around 1500,
magistrates increasingly prosecuted both the offending keepers by suppress-
ing their drinking establishments and the wandering vagabonds by whipping
them out of town. The charges against two early sixteenth-century keepers
were for offering hospitality to vagabonds to the harm of neighbors, while in
1675 the neighbors of Edward Humerstone's alehouse in Amwell, Hertfordshire, had even more cause for concern, since he harbored "vagabonds and
thieves in his house night and day to the prejudice of the neighborhood, suffering them to have fire and candle in a thatched barn day and night to the
great danger of the houses of the neighbors."[53]

Partly as a result of the patronage of vagabonds, alehouses and taverns
became centers for the exchange of stolen property. The vagabonds of Paris
who committed thefts in the surrounding villages and towns brought their
booty to Parisian taverns.[54] Similarly, in 1346 Giovanni di Benintendi, called
Capestro, traded his stolen goods with a Florentine tavern keeper for food
and drink.[55] Two English cases from the second half of the seventeenth century reveal the role of alehouse keepers in the exchange of stolen property. In
one, a stolen blanket was found in the possession of an alehouse keeper, and
in the other the constable searching for two stolen Cheshire cheeses found
one of them in a chest at an alehouse.[56] In addition to selling stolen property
to the keepers, thieves could hawk their goods to other customers, as possibly
occurred at Rye in 1592 when Charles Flahowe claimed he obtained the stolen canvas in his possession at the Sign of the Three Mariners.[57]

Some thieves apparently drank together at taverns to screw up their
courage before setting out at night in search of victims, and in 1576 five
thieves planned an assault on a gentleman at an alehouse in Southampton.[58]
Less clear is whether taverns and alehouses functioned as focal points of a

[53] McIntosh, *Controlling Misbehavior*, 76–77; and *Hertford Country Records*, ed. Hardy, 1:255–56.
[54] Cohen, "Vagabondage à Paris," 302.
[55] Caduff, "Publici latrones," 516, n59.
[56] Doughty, *Notebook of Robert Doughty*, ed. Rosnheim, 54–55; and *Portsmouth Record Series*, comp. Willis and ed. Hoad, 114–15.
[57] Mayhew, *Tudor Rye*, 226.
[58] Cherubini, "Taverna nel basso medioevo," 208; and Clark, "Alehouse and the Alternative Society," 57.

well-organized underworld of criminal activity or merely provided occasional safe havens for criminals to meet, exchange information, and perhaps hatch opportunistic plots.[59] An example of the opportunistic plot occurred when Felix Platter was traveling through the mountains of Savoy in 1552 and had to take shelter in a miserable inn at Mézières. Also staying at the inn was a group of peasants and beggars, "eating roasted chestnuts and black bread," who plotted to kill Platter and his traveling companions but became too drunk on the cheap wine to succeed.[60] Two cases from fifteenth-century Paris reveal criminal activity that was more professional. In 1417 three thieves formed an association with a goldsmith at a tavern by swearing on the bread and wine they would always work together and always bring their stolen property to the goldsmith. In 1481 Jean Augot, called Paris, sought royal remission for his robberies that began with an encounter at an inn with a group of rogues, including a priest, who first encouraged him to burgle the house of a prostitute and then provided him with a fence for his subsequent robberies.[61] In rural England, gangs of poachers and highway robbers used alehouses as staging posts, but most of the criminal use of drinking establishments centered on London, where different groups of professional thieves such as cutpurses congregated at particular alehouses and taverns.[62] Although thieves might have congregated in drinking establishments, few thefts occurred there.[63] A rare example is the theft of a wallet at a Parisian tavern in 1488; when a customer pulled out his wallet to pay for drinks, one of the men with whom he had been drinking hit him, took the wallet, and fled.[64] Another occurred in 1397 at the Cock in Westminster; when the keeper Alice atte Hethe enticed the vicar Simon Helgey to enter the inn, her associates pulled daggers rather than drinks and robbed him.[65]

The good vicar might have thought Alice's enticements would lead to more intimate activity, because many of Westminster's alewives and female keepers were also prostitutes, including those who sold ale at the three houses

---

[59] See the discussions by Clark, "Alehouse and the Alternative Society," 57; and Griffiths, "Overlapping Circles," 121.

[60] Platter, *Beloved Son Felix*, trans. Jennett, 32–33.

[61] Geremek, *Margins of Society*, 110–11. See also Misraki, "Criminalité et pauvreté," 540, n27.

[62] Clark, *English Alehouse*, 130, 146; Bailey, *Marginal Economy*, 170; and McMullan, *Canting Crew*, 57, 67.

[63] Brennan, *Public Drinking*, 27; and Gauvard, *"De Grace Especial,"* 284–85.

[64] Cohen, "Hundred Years' War," 118.

[65] Rosser, *Medieval Westminster*, 132.

known as Paradise, Purgatory, and Hell.[66] The vicar was fortunate because
not only did he get his money back, but also he could have lost his life; the
prostitute Agnes de Houdan met a client in a London tavern and lured him
back to her house, where her accomplices murdered him.[67] The connection
of drinking establishments with prostitution is even stronger than that with
gangs of thieves. Throughout Europe, prostitutes searched for clients at alehouses and taverns, while men in search of prostitutes knew their best chance
of finding them would be in alehouses and taverns. In the fifteenth century,
Venetian prostitutes congregated in those areas of the city, including the Piazza
di San Marco, which had the most taverns, and Florentine taverns were frequent haunts of pimps and prostitutes.[68] Court records from sixteenth-century
Southwark indicate alehouses were the most common venues for prostitution
and procuring.[69] Some whores and pimps mingled with customers without
the consent or knowledge of the keepers; for example, Lucy Francis and Mary
Hodges worked together while making a circuit of the inns and alehouses in
seventeenth-century Somerset.[70] Some keepers supplemented the income from
selling drinks by renting rooms, although during summer the prostitutes of
Grenoble had no need of rooms because after meeting their clients at cabarets
on the outskirts of town they moved to the neighboring vineyards and fields.[71]
Finally, some keepers simply combined the functions of alehouse or tavern with
that of brothel. Many of these brothels relied on amateur staff, quite often the
wife of the keeper, sometimes his daughter, or maids and tapsters. For example,
in 1379 Niccolò di Giunta was convicted of persuading a married woman to
sell wine and herself at his tavern in Florence.[72]

Not only prostitutes used alehouses and taverns for sexual engage-
ments, and the many couples who copulated in drinking establishments,
such as the man and woman who used a private chamber at the Crown in
Glaston, Somerset, while her husband searched the town for her, contributed to their reputation for disorder.[73] In 1663 Robert Sydebottom, a married

---

[66] Rosser, *Medieval Westminster,* 144, n121.

[67] Hanawalt, *Of Good and Ill Repute,* 113.

[68] Pavan, "Police des moeurs," 253–54; and Mazzi, *Prostitute e lenoni,* 270.

[69] Carlin, *Medieval Southwark,* 225.

[70] Quaife, *Wanton Wenches,* 146–47.

[71] Norberg, *Rich and Poor,* 49.

[72] Brucker, *Society of Renaissance Florence,* 196–98.

[73] Thompson, *Wives, Widows,* 57; Mendelson and Crawford, *Women in Early Modern England,* 295;
Clark, *English Alehouse,* 150; and Quaife, *Wanton Wenches,* 130.

man, and Isabella Ashcroft were charged with committing adultery at an ale-house in Bredbury, Stockport. According to the testimony of a witness, he had seen Robert with his breeches down "driving at" Ashcroft with her dress up; when they realized they had been seen Robert exclaimed, "God's wounds, I will fuck out my fucking if the king come."[74] For young unmarried couples, alehouses and taverns offered the possibility of private space for amorous adventures. When Joan Lower fell in love with an apprentice, they made love at alehouses in Salisbury, and in 1693 Agnes Lumman and Peter Randell had sex at an alehouse in Shillingford, Devon.[75] Such encounters often ended in pregnancy, and the resulting births of illegitimate children appeared in court records as the authorities attempted to determine paternity. Not all the sexual play in drinking establishments resulted in fornication. The exposure of private members was another manifestation of a disorderly clientele, such as when Jane Cook "did pull William Holt's prick out" at a Chester alehouse in 1677 and then pulled her dress up when he appeared angry, or when a fellow drinker pulled out the "privy members" of a sleeping Thomas Lane and "put it upon a child's shoe."[76]

Just as lovers and adulterers utilized alehouses and taverns, so too did gamblers. Legal records from late medieval France indicate the tavern was the most common location for games and gambling. Many keepers attempted to attract customers by providing cards and dice, and some taverns and ale-houses even had special tables, private rooms, and more elaborate equipment and facilities such as tennis, quoits, *boules,* shovelboard, and bowling alleys. Some keepers likewise provided credit for gamblers, as occurred in 1376 at Amiens when Jehan Bonnet lost more than he had while playing dice at a tavern.[77] On other occasions taverns and alehouses merely provided the venues for gamblers, professional or otherwise, to play for high stakes or just for drinks. A court in Orvieto convicted some people from Arezzo for gambling in the communal tavern in 1277.[78] In 1440 a group of Florentines organized games with loaded dice at several taverns and managed to cheat foreigners, soldiers, Jews, a priest, and servants of a cardinal.[79] As already indicated, especially by the court records from the county of Kent, keepers faced prosecution when

---

[74] Addy, *Sin and Society,* 136.

[75] Clark, "Alehouse and the Alternative Society," 60; and Thompson, *Wives, Widows,* 57.

[76] Addy, *Sin and Society,* 134; and Quaife, *Wanton Wenches,* 166.

[77] Mehl, *Jeux au royaume,* 249–50.

[78] Riccetti, "Naso di Simone," 154.

[79] Cherubini, "Taverna nel basso medioevo," 209.

they promoted gambling, but they could also be indicted when they permitted it on their premises. For example, a keeper at Moreton was fined in 1636 for allowing people to play cards at his alehouse, according to the testimony of witnesses, twenty people at one time.[80]

The stakes for much of the gambling in drinking establishments were the drinks themselves, a convivial means of combining the pleasures of companionship, games, and alcohol, almost like taking turns buying rounds. For example, four master artisans at a Parisian tavern in 1691 first ate a fried chicken paid for by the loser and then played a game of *boules* to determine who would pay for the wine.[81] On occasion the conviviality became strained as a result of disputes, as it did in 1476 in Vitry when Watier Baudessan complained of the losses he incurred while playing games of tennis.[82] Just as Robert Greene described a fictional case of thieves planning their next job in a tavern, he also described, this time in *A Notable Discovery of Cozenage,* how professional card sharks cheated their unsuspecting victims in taverns by first playing for a pint of wine.[83] Similarly, John Smyth of Somerset complained to authorities in 1623 that he began playing dice for a pot of beer and eventually lost ten shillings. One of the attractions of drinking establishments for the professional gambler would be the possibility of easy pickings against opponents whose brains might be befuddled by drink, and court records reveal many gamblers, like the Florentines with loaded dice, who cheated in taverns and alehouses. For example, a group playing a card game in an alehouse at Ribchester in Lancashire caught a player "pulling cards forth of his sleeve with intent to play foul play."[84] Other games that produced cheaters were Cross and Pile, Hide under Hat, and My Card before Thy Card.[85] Rather than cheat at cards, Peter Welden cheated with the stakes at a game in an alehouse in Rye in 1555 by playing with counterfeit money; their brains might have been befuddled with drink, but the other players still informed him that his coins looked "very evil."[86]

The public space of drinking establishments made them ideal venues to discredit rivals and enemies, and the insults exchanged in a tavern or

---

[80] Sharpe, *Crime in Seventeenth-Century England,* 53.

[81] Brennan, *Public Drinking,* 252.

[82] Mehl, *Jeux au royaume,* 281.

[83] Greene, *Notable Discovery,* ed. Judges, 125–56.

[84] Clark, *English Alehouse,* 155.

[85] Sharpe, *Crime in Seventeenth-Century England,* 53.

[86] Mayhew, *Tudor Rye,* 226.

an alehouse and the resulting possibility of violence furthered their disorderly atmosphere. In 1691 a Parisian cabaret was the scene for a confrontation between a master locksmith and a master carpenter. According to the locksmith's suit, the carpenter followed him into the cabaret for the purpose of insulting and slandering him in front of others, the carpenter repeatedly calling the locksmith a "dishonest man, a rogue, a thief."[87] Sexual or scatological insults were also frequent. A journeyman at a Dijon tavern in 1642 combined both when the keeper insisted he pay for a broken jug; the journeyman refused, called the keeper a cuckold, and when fleeing managed to stop long enough to fart and shout, "That's for you and yours!"[88] Women were usually subject to sexual insult, slander, or innuendo. Michael Richards, for example, defamed Luce Birch at an alehouse in London in 1630 by claiming she had offered herself to a sailor "and then took up her clothes and showed him all her nakedness." More typical were those cases when women defamed or insulted other women, as was the case when Elizabeth Fryer told Margaret Yard what she thought of her at a London tavern in 1611: "Thou art a whore, an arrant whore, and a filthy whore."[89] Had similar insults occurred between men, violence was a likely outcome, but women were more likely to redeem their honor in a court of law.

Religious and Political Dissidents

Just as vagabonds and prostitutes utilized taverns and alehouses, so also did religious dissidents and heretics who faced persecution for their views. Early in the fourteenth century, Cathar heretics such as Bérenger Escoulan visited the taverns in towns to gather and to distribute news, which would then be relayed to villages in the mountains where it contributed to protests against persecution and the collection of tithes.[90] Later in the century, the Lollard heretic William Ramsbury openly preached in the taverns of Wiltshire, a practice still occurring in 1481 when Richard Lillyngston preached in the taverns of Devizes and Marlborough.[91] The tradition continued into the sixteenth century although reduced in scale; in 1511 an archbishop's investigations uncovered the case of a Tenterden weaver who sought conversions

---

[87] Brennan, *Public Drinking*, 73.

[88] Farr, *Artisans in Europe*, 264.

[89] Gowing, *Domestic Dangers*, 67–68, 92. See also Karras, "Sharing Wine," 194.

[90] Le Roy Ladurie, *Montaillou*, 265.

[91] Brown, *Popular Piety*, 16, 219.

through discussions with one or two customers at alehouses.[92] During the fourteenth and fifteenth centuries, heretics in Italy likewise utilized taverns as convenient meeting places, which offered a certain degree of anonymity and where travelers did not immediately come under suspicion.[93] Come the sixteenth century and the increased supervision by authorities as a result of the religious controversies, alehouses and taverns were even more useful than they were in the Middle Ages for the exchange of information and the recruitment of followers. The records of the inquisition in Italy reveal many cases of people circulating heretical opinions at taverns and inns. In 1548, when several artisans from Belluno stopped at an *osteria* in Cadore, one of them claimed, "the true body of Christ is not in the consecrated host," and in 1555 a boatman testified that at a tavern in Brianza a coalporter had questioned the validity of religious ceremonies. Venetian authorities kept a nervous eye on two inns near the Rialto that had a reputation for spreading heretical ideas because of their German clientele, and a tavern in Modena proved a convenient place for heretics to meet and discuss religion.[94]

Peter Clark doubts English alehouses continued to perform similar functions for English heretics during this period,[95] but scattered incidents reveal they remained places for dissidents to discuss religion and to meet with those who had similar views. An early example occurred at the Sign of the Bell in Northampton in 1538 when a former friar engaged in disputes with other customers over the sacrament of communion.[96] When Mary's reign signaled the reintroduction of Catholicism, disgruntled Protestants held secret meetings at an alehouse in London, while others made their own personal feelings known at alehouses, usually by criticism of the Catholic mass.[97] Alehouses became prominent meeting places for religious dissidents once again during the political and religious ferment accompanying the English Civil War. As early as 1641, an anonymous pamphlet complained, "Religion is now become the common discourse and table talk in every tavern and alehouse."[98] In 1651 a hostile witness reported on a meeting of Ranters at a tavern, where they sang blasphemous songs and ate a communal feast, and in Royston a group

[92] Collinson, "Cranbrook and the Fletchers," 176.
[93] Patrone, *Cibo del ricco*, 420.
[94] Martin, *Venice's Hidden Enemies*, 170–71.
[95] Clark, *English Alehouse*, 157.
[96] Spufford, "Puritanism and Social Control," 44–45.
[97] Spufford, "Puritanism and Social Control," 45; and Clark, *English Alehouse*, 157.
[98] *Religions Enemies*, cited in Hill, *World Turned Upside Down*, 198.

of religious dissidents rented a private room at an alehouse for their meetings, "where without interruption, they might talk freely of the things of God."[99] God revealed to John Reeve and Lodowick Muggleton in February 1652 that they were the Two Last Witnesses of the Spirit and commissioned them to announce the coming of the Day of Judgment, to proclaim the true faith, to bless the true followers, and to curse the reprobate, all of which they performed at taverns in London and the provinces.[100] Just as significant as the use of drinking establishments by religious dissidents was their role in voicing and disseminating popular resentment against the reforming efforts of puritans. A good example is the ballad composed at a Rymes alehouse in 1632 that libeled two of the town's leading puritans by implying adultery between them; one customer liked it so much that he paid a quart of wine to obtain a copy.[101] People likewise could demonstrate their disapproval of puritanical preachers by going to the alehouse during divine service and where they could pass the time criticizing and abusing them.[102]

Political dissidents found drinking establishments to have the same advantages religious dissidents found in them: a venue to meet like-minded people, propagate views, exchange information, and perhaps plot against the authorities. The goals of the plotting could include strikes, an illegal practice at the time. At Nantes in 1650, journeymen tailors secretly met at the tavern of the Croix Blanche to plan their strike, and the silk workers of Paris did the same at cabarets in 1691.[103] Earlier, in the fourteenth and fifteenth centuries, Italian taverns had been the birthplaces and nurseries of many small local revolts.[104] English alehouses and taverns had a long history of similar activities. In the wake of the Peasants' Revolt of 1381, a wandering vagabond named John Shirley addressed the men assembled at a tavern on Bridge Street in Cambridge. He praised the itinerant preacher John Ball, condemned those who had executed him for his role in the Revolt, and prophesied Ball's death would not go unpunished.[105] The trend continued in the next century, when seditious speech was so commonplace at alehouses that the government paid

---

[99] Hill, *World Turned Upside Down*, 200; and Spufford, "Puritanism and Social Control," 45.

[100] Reay, "Muggletonians," 23.

[101] Watt, *Cheap Print*, 71.

[102] Clark, *English Alehouse*, 158.

[103] Collins, *Classes, Estates*, 20, 101; and Brennan, *Public Drinking*, 273.

[104] Patrone, *Cibo del ricco*, 420.

[105] Hanna, "Pilate's Voice," 794–95.

spies to visit them and report on the conversations.[106] A fine line separated seditious speech from rumor, and alehouses were ideal venues for the spread of rumors; in 1537, when many Englishmen were left wondering about the king's next step on religion, Nicholas Holte heard rumors about the king's intentions as he went on a pub crawl in Shrewsbury.[107]

The role of English taverns and alehouses in promoting radical political movements in the last half of the sixteenth century and the first half of the seventeenth is subject to disagreement. Just as he doubted the significance of alehouses for heretical movements, Peter Clark cautions, "The radical dimension of the alehouse must not be overstated," and "The alehouse's contribution to political resistance to the ruling class also tended to be small."[108] Buchanan Sharp, on the other hand, argues that for the common people alehouses functioned as a disseminator of news, rumors, and plots. An example he gives in his local study is the rising in Hampshire in 1586, which was planned in alehouses and obtained its participants in alehouses near Selborne.[109] Because his work is national in scope, Clark actually provides more examples than does Sharp—agitation against enclosures in York in the 1530s, action against corrupt officials at Maldon in 1594, upheavals in the Kentish Weald in 1595, seditious rumors of treason in Kent in 1619—all with the involvement of alehouses. As for the Levellers, they met in taverns rather than alehouses. Instead of providing a focus for radical political movements, Clark argues, in the 1650s alehouses were centers for royalists, as they tried to maintain their spirits by singing loyalist songs and drinking healths to the exiled king.[110]

Whatever the precise role of the English alehouse in fomenting and sustaining political and religious dissidents, drinking establishments in England as well as in France and Italy had reputations for fomenting and sustaining a disorderly clientele. When the disorderly clientele congregated at disorderly alehouses and taverns run by disorderly keepers, the result could give the consumption of alcohol a bad name. To state the obvious, alehouses and taverns

---

[106] Harvey, "Was There Popular Politics?" 160, 162.

[107] Shagan, "Rumours and Popular Politics," 37.

[108] Clark, *English Alehouse*, 159; and Clark, "Alehouse and the Alternative Society," 66.

[109] Sharp, *In Contempt of All Authority*, 41.

[110] Clark, *English Alehouse*, 158–59; and Clark, "Alehouse and the Alternative Society," 66–67. Kümin's conclusion, *Drinking Matters*, 138–39, for Central Europe is that "public houses facilitated popular protest."

functioned as dispensers of drink, too much of which led to drunkenness, but both the drink and the drunkenness seldom figured in the depiction of disordered places and clientele, and the actual role of drinking in all of this disorder is unclear. Indeed, although many of the indictments of disorderly drinking establishments were imprecise about the nature and character of the disorder, only few actually cited drunkenness. Many of the imprecise charges of "keeping ill rule" or "keeping a disorderly alehouse" no doubt hid cases of drunken misbehavior, but aside from the very few cases of violence the sources give little indication of the nature of that misbehavior. The consumption of alcohol was an obvious factor when keepers faced charges of permitting drinking on the Sabbath and after curfew, but it was absent when the charges included allowing games or harboring undesirable customers. Professional gamblers might have sought drunkards at taverns and alehouses to gain unscrupulous advantages, and prostitutes and pimps might have had similar motives in their selection of possible clients at drinking establishments. For other types of disorderly customers, drunkenness would have been anathema. Thieves planning their next job required a clear head, and they did not need one of their co-conspirators to become so intoxicated that drunken mumblings would compromise their plans. Likewise, both political and religious dissidents sought sober adherents to the cause, and their need for secrecy could be as great as that of the thieves.

In short, the evidence does not present a clear picture of the role of alcohol, drinking, and drunkenness in the making of a disorderly alehouse or tavern. On the other hand, the evidence indicates drinking establishments had the potential to become disorderly space, much more so than village greens, town squares, and private homes, where the consumption of alcohol was not as much a threat to public order. Nonetheless, the quantitative data from the three English counties demonstrate a low level of disorder, while much of the qualitative evidence illustrates the importance of alehouses and taverns as the third place in traditional society. They constituted a relatively secure public space where people could gather, talk, relax, and socialize as well as gamble, fornicate, plot, and scheme. The advantages of drinking establishments as a third place were particularly valuable for the young, the students, apprentices, and servants who often chafed under strict discipline and who consequently longed for the liberating atmosphere of taverns and alehouses. As already noted, a tavern or an alehouse could also be the first place—home— for vagabonds, while for some of the disorderly clientele, notably prostitutes, drinking establishments could be all three places as home, workplace, and center of relaxation. To make their third place orderly rather than disorderly space, keepers first and foremost had to manage their clientele by refusing service to vagabonds and other suspicious persons and by limiting service to servants, students, and apprentices. They had to observe the curfew, close during divine services on Sundays and other holy days, and prohibit games and gambling. Finally, they had to prevent drunkenness either by ceasing service to customers who were drinking too much or by evicting them from the premises.

Legal records contain evidence of disorderly alehouses, taverns, keepers, and clientele, but they say nothing about the hundreds and thousands of drinking establishments that posed little threat to public order. One source that does provide this evidence is the diary kept between 1663 and 1674 by Roger Lowe, the previously mentioned mercer's apprentice of Ashton-in-Makerfield, Lancashire. Lowe's third place was the alehouse, so much so that a customer warned him to stop drinking so much. His frequent trips to the local alehouses and those in the surrounding towns and villages reveal a benign institution without a single case of drunkenness, so benign in fact that women were frequent customers. The only alehouse violence Lowe described was perpetrated by Lowe himself when cold sober after someone defamed him by telling his girlfriend he was illegitimate. Lowe never once mentioned a disorderly alehouse, a disorderly keeper, or a disorderly clientele; instead the most frequent word used by Lowe to describe his drinking sessions was "merry." What made them merry was primarily the companionship, both male and female. He sometimes engaged in religious disputes, and, although he had strong religious feelings, even these disputes were not acrimonious. As noted in chapter 4, one ended in "love and peace."[111] To argue the prevailing mood at alehouses and taverns was love and peace would be naïve, as would the counterargument that it was treachery and disorder, but perhaps merry would be appropriate. 🍇

[111] Martin, "Drinking and Alehouses," 93–105.

Chapter 6

Disorder: Persons

Wine and new wine take away the understanding.
—Hosea 4:11

The role of alcohol in producing court indictments of drunken and disorderly persons might at first glance seem unambiguous, but like its role in creating prosecutions of disorderly drinking establishments, alcohol's role was ambiguous. Before modern blood tests and Breathalyzers, judgments on drunkenness were subjective, despite efforts to define the condition. As noted in chapter 2, according to a seventeenth-century definition, drunkenness was "where the same legs which carry a man into the house, cannot bring him out again," and according to a medieval penitential, "This is drunkenness, when it changes the state of the mind, and the tongue babbles and the eyes are wild and there is dizziness and distension of the stomach and pain follows." Neither definition would be of much help to a night watch that encountered an old man disturbing the peace by singing in the early hours of the morning. Significantly, the churchwardens at King's Sutton, Northamptonshire, who were responsible for prosecuting drunkards, admitted in 1619, "We cannot define a ... drunkard."[1] Even if an indictment for drunkenness was valid, the next difficulty is ascertaining the relationship between inebriation and the accompanying charges. To cite one example, at Chester in 1618, John Bolland was indicted for drunkenness; the accompanying charges were horrible blasphemy, abusing the head constable, bear-baiting, and being a wandering rogue.[2] Notwithstanding these problems,

[1] Ingram, "Reformation of Manners," 76.
[2] Hindle, "Custom, Festival," 165.

many cases demonstrate that under the influence of alcohol, people acted as if they had lost their understanding and the result was behavior that anyone would classify as disorderly. Some of the disorderly persons prosecuted in the courts would nowadays be diagnosed as alcoholics. Although the concept of alcoholism developed in the nineteenth century, several contemporary writers described the typical characteristics associated with alcoholics. One of the best descriptions is from the fourteenth-century set of instructions written by a citizen of Paris for his young wife. The husband compared the sin of gluttony to a woman who had trouble rising in the morning in time for church as a result of a hangover. "When she has with some difficulty risen, know you what be her hours? Her matins are: 'Ha! what shall we drink? Is there nought left over from last night?' Then she says her lauds, thus: 'Ha! we drank good wine yesterday evening.' Afterwards she says her orisons, thus: 'My head aches; I shall not be at ease until I have had a drink.'"[3]

Disorderly Persons

Despite the problem of objectivity in court records as discussed in chapter 5, an examination of those from the counties of Warwickshire, Kent, and Middlesex at least helps establish the extent and nature of drunken and disorderly persons in court indictments. The nine volumes of Quarter Sessions Court records from the county of Warwickshire for the years 1625 to 1696 indicate only two cases of people prosecuted for drunkenness; in 1685 Richard Malt of Wootton was fined five shillings for being drunk, and in 1690 Richard Smith of Atherstone was indicted for being "a drunken, disorderly person." Three other cases involved drunkenness either as cause, effect, or accompanying factor. In 1650 six men from Solihull faced charges of riotous assembly that led to drunkenness and disorder, four years later the overseers of the poor at Hatton objected to paying Thomas Stocke a pension because he was "a man of lewd behavior given up to drunkenness, disorder and abuse of neighbors," and in 1656 Thomas West was imprisoned for six days and then whipped out of town for pretending to be a minister, "abusing himself and others by drunkenness, swearing, and other profanities."[4] The very small number of cases in Warwickshire might be cause for surprise if not amazement, but other courts and especially church courts probably heard cases regarding disorderly people.

---

[3] *Goodman of Paris,* trans. Power, 84. See Warner, "Before There Was 'Alcoholism.'"

[4] *Warwick County Records,* ed. Ratcliff, Johnson, and Williams, 3:2, 204, 316, 8:155, 9:2.

The *Calendar of Assize Records* for the county of Kent for the years 1625 to 1688 documents many more indictments of persons for drinking offenses than do the records from Warwickshire, but the total of seventy-four averages only a bit more than one prosecution per year, and 30 percent of these occurred in two years, 1642 and 1653. The most common charge was for drunkenness or being a drunkard, which accounted for 60 percent of the indictments, while 28 percent of the indictments charged individuals with haunting alehouses or spending much time there, and only three persons answered charges for drinking during divine service on Sunday. Four of the indictments for drunkenness included the charge of disturbing the peace. Aside from the two cases of violence mentioned in chapter 5, the worst offender was Martin Clarke of Ruckinge, indicted in 1632 as "a common alehouse-haunter, swearer and brawler and stirrer of discords."[5]

The *Calendar to the Sessions Records* for the county of Middlesex covering the years 1612 to 1618 documents a larger number of cases per year (about ten) and a wider range of charges than do the records for Warwickshire and Kent. Unlike the large percentage of indictments just for drunkenness or being a drunkard in Kent, only 19 percent of those for Middlesex cited no other charges in the indictments. More prevalent, with 32 percent, were the charges for drunkenness and various forms of misdemeanors, misbehaviors, or breaches of the peace, such as that for Joan Daniell, the wife of a chimney sweeper, who faced court in 1614 for being "drunk and very disordered." Drunken violations of the curfew and incidents of violence each accounted for 13 percent of the cases. Many individuals compounded the charge of drunkenness by abusing the arresting officials. In 1613 a drunken gentleman assaulted and abused a headborough, and in 1615 another drunkard called a constable a "shit pot." When Richard Godson abused a constable in 1617, the sentence against him stated, "He is to be set in the stocks at Ruislip before the alehouse door where he was drunk and did the abuse, to sit there from the beginning of morning prayer until the end of evening prayer upon Sunday."[6]

The use of a woman in the fourteenth-century *Goodman of Paris* to illustrate a heavy drinker is not remarkable, because women faced courts on charges of drunken and disorderly behavior, as indicated by the wife of the chimney sweeper. The drinking wife posed a number of problems. First, she threatened

[5] *Calendar of Assize Records: Kent,* ed. Cockburn, 1:171.

[6] *County of Middlesex,* ed. Hardy, 1:30, 2:7, 52, 346, 4:248.

the domestic economy; not only was she spending money on alcohol, but by spending time that way she was unproductive. Second, she endangered marital bonds, because drunken women were considered sexually permeable. Third, she challenged patriarchal authority. Two similar cases from seventeenth-century England reveal the disorderly conduct of women possibly addicted to drink. In 1625 Thomas Case of Chester petitioned for a divorce from his wife, Elizabeth, on the grounds of drunkenness and adultery. The court heard witnesses describe the many times she drank with men at alehouses and taverns, the reports of adultery with some of these men, and the occasions she was drunk. Two witnesses stated they had seen Elizabeth "very much distempered with drink," and another who saw her "foully distempered with drink" later found the room in which she had slept covered with vomit. One man found her "distempered in drink" at a tavern, where she had fallen and hurt her face, a member of the night watch reported that when they had encountered her at about eleven at night "she had drunk too much and did talk idly," and another man had heard others claim they had met Elizabeth at an alehouse and "did then make her foul drunk." Thomas Case got his divorce.[7] In 1635 the archdeaconry court in London heard a case against a married midwife named Elizabeth Wyatt and Abraham Brand, whose wife was petitioning the court for a warrant to keep the two apart. According to the complaint, Elizabeth was Brand's constant drinking companion at taverns and alehouses for over three years, leading to the dissipation of Brand's family resources and the ruin of his household. Testifying in support of Brand's wife, other women accused Elizabeth of being "a great frequenter of taverns and alehouses" at all times of the day and at unlawful times of the night, "overtaken by" and "very much overcome with" drink, and so drunk on occasion that others feared she would fall in the street. Brand's wife got the warrant.[8]

Many other cases against drunken and disorderly women involved accusations of sexual misbehavior. One of the most famous cases involved Mary Frith, known as Moll Cutpurse, who became the subject of a play written by Thomas Dekker and Thomas Middleton in 1611. Mary admitted she was a cross-dresser, a blasphemer, and a drunkard who mixed with bad company in London's alehouses, but she vehemently denied the accusation she was a whore or a lewd example for other women.[9] Another woman who faced

[7] Addy, *Sin and Society*, 189–95.

[8] Cressy, *Travesties and Transgressions*, 84–85.

[9] Fletcher, *Gender, Sex, and Subordination*, 8–9.

charges of adultery was Isabel Collins of Halstead, Essex, accused in 1620 of being often drunk and once "so distempered with drink that she pissed as she sat."[10] Not all the women charged with drunken and disorderly conduct faced accusations of sexual misbehavior, even though their husbands refused to live with them. When accused in 1640 of not living with his wife, a Wapping man explained his wife was so often drunk and so often overcome with drink that he dared not keep her at home, but he paid for her to live elsewhere.[11]

Disorderly men likewise gave indications they were addicted to drink. In 1656 the seamen from the frigate *Basing* made the following complaints against their captain, Alexander Farly, at a court in Portsmouth: He was so drunk or drank so much that at Milford when he came aboard he asked what ship he was on, that at a house in Popton he laid on a chest and vomited and had to be led back to the boat, that at Kinsale in Ireland he quarreled with two other captains, that at a tavern in Plymouth he could not eat the meal he had ordered but vomited in bed with his boots and spurs on, that when returning to the boat from Tenby he fell on the sand, and that at Pembroke he fell in the street.[12] None of the seamen accused Captain Farly of sexual misconduct—he might have been too drunk for that—but other drunken and disorderly men faced such charges. Nicholas Marshall, a schoolmaster at Urswick, faced a series of charges over several years, beginning in 1621, that he neglected his duties primarily as a result of his fondness for drinking and gambling, sometimes being so drunk that he had no recollection of what he had said or done or with whom he had fought. According to one witness, Marshall fell asleep in John Fleming's alehouse and pissed in his pants, and another produced evidence of Marshall's adultery.[13] More common were the charges that linked drunkenness with different combinations of blasphemy, disturbing the peace, swearing, slander, and quarreling.[14] The behavior of Robert Cole, a Romford, Essex, shoemaker, included many of these offenses, for he was indicted "for a most notorious and common drunkard, infamous and offensive to the whole parish, who in his drunken fits walks about the streets with his naked sword breaking the windows, quarreling and railing, braving and cursing after a fearful manner."[15]

[10] Martin Ingram, "Sexual Manners," 105–6. See also Addy, *Sin and Society,* 111.

[11] Capp, *When Gossips Meet,* 83–84. For another example, see Hair, *Before the Bawdy Court,* 77.

[12] *Portsmouth Record Series,* comp. Willis and ed. Hoad, 170–71.

[13] Addy, *Sin and Society,* 84–85. For another example, see Shoemaker, *Prosecution and Punishment,* 101.

[14] For some examples, see Higgs, *Godliness and Governance,* 276–77.

[15] Sharpe, *Crime in Seventeenth-Century England,* 54–55.

A special category of drunken and disorderly men was the clergy, whose privileged position in society secured access to a large and usually superior supply of alcohol.[16] Catholic clergy could excuse their drinking by claiming the stresses of celibacy required the occasional liquid alleviation, but the excuse was not valid when their drunken deportment included sexual misbehavior. Some French priests who had reputations for frequenting taverns and drunkenness also faced punishment for keeping a concubine, having a suspect woman in the house, fathering children, and visiting "suspicious incontinent women." In 1673 at Gonesse near Paris a drunken priest chased after the young girls of his parish and lost his hood in the process; "a great scandal" then erupted when some peasants found it and offered it for sale in the market.[17] One of the more notorious cases concerned Charles Lavery, priest at Avalon, accused in 1668 of divulging confessions when he was drunk at the tavern and charged with failing to teach the catechism, withholding the sacraments of baptism and extreme unction, botching the celebration of the mass, soliciting women, and sticking a hot poker iron under the skirt of a young woman who resisted his advances. Unclear is how many of these other offenses were connected to his drinking.[18] The deportment of drunken English clergy was no better than that of their French counterparts. A catalogue of the drunken charges against them includes being unable to stand at a christening, to read the prayers at a wedding, and to walk home, reading the morning service instead of the afternoon service, preaching a sermon in an alehouse, keeping an alehouse, sending children to the alehouse for drinks but never paying for them, offering a book in exchange for a drink, dancing with young women in the alehouse, making indecent comments to a female keeper, threatening a man with a gun, being addicted to quarreling and fighting, throwing a pot at someone's head in an alehouse, spending Holy Week in fights and brawls with parishioners, playing football, and wrestling.[19]

Many of these and similar charges formed part of the indictment of William Storrs, rector at Hawkswell, who was one of the worst clerical offenders. In 1639 he pleaded guilty to ten charges presented by the High Commission at York. As an excessive drinker, Storrs had often "reeled, staggered, and fallen to the ground." He was frequently so drunk that he could not read

[16] See Martin, "Alcohol and the Clergy," 23–39.

[17] Taveneaux, *Catholicisme dans la France classique*, 1:139.

[18] Farr, *Authority and Sexuality*, 79.

[19] Addy, *Sin and Society*, 29–33; Hair, *Before the Bawdy Court*, 91; and *Acts of the High Commission Court*, 5, 105.

prayers or celebrate Holy Communion, a situation that was especially evident during the Christmas season, and when he was drunk he became so violent and aggressive that his parishioners fled at his approach, but even then he succeeded in wounding "Thomas Dickenson with a thick short staff, John Glasse with a long pole, William Rudd with a great stone, John Maisterman with a hand hammer, Thomas Wynne with a stone, [and] Anne Barker with a battledore [a small racket]." The High Commission removed Storrs from his office.[20] The drunken and disorderly individual threatened civil society, but the drunken and disorderly cleric formed a worse category because of the clergy's role as moral exemplars and teachers. If the tavern/alehouse was the antichurch and the keeper an antipriest, clergy who blurred the distinction set a very bad example indeed.

One form of drunken disorderly conduct that received attention from the authorities was verbal abuse or scolding; the drunkard who continually ranted and raved at neighbors created tensions in the close-knit rural communities and urban parishes, and produced demands for authorities to punish the perpetrator. In folklore a scold was usually a poor old woman, but the drunken scold could just as easily be a man. For example, Harrington Bickley of North Mynes, Hertfordshire, was a persistent drunkard and abuser of neighbors who called two respectable women whores and a leading citizen an "old fat-backed rogue."[21] Bickley's abuse pales in comparison to that of Robert Simpson, a scrivener who faced nine charges at a court in Nottingham. The general charges were he was a common alehouse-haunter and drunkard and "a common railer and reviler of honest and sober-minded people" who "used in the alehouse among his companions base and contemptuous terms against the magistrates and many others." As for the particulars, he called Thomas Barnes the elder an old drunkard and his wife a whore, Thomas Barnes the younger a thief, rogue, and rascal and his wife an old whore, and Robert Wood a lame rogue and rascal, villain, dissembling puritan, and hypocrite, and said of Master Maior, "let him kiss my ass, even the very nock of my ass."[22] As for the women scolds, according to the testimony of two witnesses at a court in Chester in 1684, Mary Mooreton was a common drunkard who "abuses one neighbor or other, calling them whores and thieves" whenever she was drunk, and "sets a great deal of dissension among her neighbors."[23]

[20] Addy, *Sin and Society,* 22–23.

[21] Wrightson, "Two Concepts of Order," 29–30.

[22] *Records of the Borough of Nottingham,* ed. Stevenson and Raine, 367–68.

[23] Curtis, "Quarter Sessions Appearances," 139.

Marguine la Faucharde from the small village of Lesches near Meaux was such a scold when drunk that on one occasion in 1354 she left her sleeping husband and shouted abuse and attempted to start a quarrel in the street even though no one was there.[24]

One of the sad consequences for many drunkards was economic ruin, a disorder that had disastrous effects on their families and as a result became a concern for the authorities. As illustrated by the large number of good fellow ballads of the seventeenth century, this was a fault most often associated with men. The ballads described usually tradesmen or craftsmen who wasted their time and resources drinking at alehouses and taverns under the spell of a female keeper or tapster despite the complaints and warnings of their long-suffering wives. When the inevitable occurred and they found themselves ruined, the keeper/tapster no longer tolerated them, and they returned to their wise wives.[25] Thomas Hoccleve, an early fifteenth-century official of the Privy Seal, bared his similar experiences in *La male regle de T. Hoccleve*. Although his salary was small, he spent twenty years of his life drinking too much and eating too well at London taverns, where female company proved a great temptation. Ultimately, his money ran out, and his health was ruined, so just as the good fellows returned to their wives, Hoccleve turned to marriage as a means of putting his life in order.[26]

Men of property could lose their estates through drunken dissipation. In *The History of Myddle*, Richard Gough told the story of Thomas Hayward, a successful farmer who had the misfortune to marry a woman "shrewd with tongue, so that they lived unquietly and uncomfortably." Thomas found solace in the alehouse, where he spent much of his time and much of his money, neglecting his business as his debts mounted. Eventually he had to sell his land, and although his brother cared for him after his wife died, his ultimate fate was a pauper's funeral.[27] An unfortunate fate also happened in the mid-sixteenth century to Jean Foucart of Coucy in Picardy, who dissipated his goods and made poor bargains while drinking in taverns. What was worse for his wife was he wasted the goods and property she had brought to the marriage. On one occasion when she complained, he attacked her with a knife, so she killed him in self-defense.[28] For

---

[24] Murray, *Violent against Themselves*, 210–11.

[25] See the analysis in Martin, *Alcohol, Sex, and Gender*, 120–24.

[26] Bennett, *Six Medieval Men*, 87–89.

[27] Gough, *History of Myddle*, ed. Hey, 195, 278–79.

[28] Davis, *Fiction in the Archives*, 94.

tradesmen and craftsmen without property, often the most grievous aspect of their drinking was the time spent in an alehouse or tavern rather than at work. At a court hearing in 1626, the neighbors of the tailor James Browning declared he was "an idle and loose fellow" who misspent his time in alehouses; and in 1691 a merchant dyer of Paris went to cabarets daily, "giving no order to his business or his commerce, which he neglect[ed] entirely."[29]

A seventeenth-century ballad entitled "John and Joan" told the story of a married couple who copied each other, even drink for drink at the alehouse. Eventually they had to pawn their clothes to pay for the drinks, and

> after a year or more
> this couple mad
> all wasted had
> and were grown very poor.[30]

According to Richard Gough, an actual married couple, William and Judith Crosse, had a similar experience. William had "a good estate in lands and a fair house in Yorton" and Judith a considerable marriage portion, but they were "both overmuch addicted to drunkenness." Husband and wife went daily to the alehouse, "and soon after the cows went thither also"; they consumed his estate and her portion and died poor.[31] Although the many cases of drunken and disorderly women indicate they could spend much money on drinks, few women were actually accused of dissipating family resources or property. Anglebert Théodore Berg complained to the Parisian police that his drunken wife had consumed all the profits from their business as wine merchants, but such a business provided enormous temptations to those addicted to alcohol.[32]

Disorderly Youth

The antiquarian Anthony à Wood was a master at Oxford University during the second half of the seventeenth century until his death in 1695. His diary provides glimpses of disorderly student drinking, something that

[29] Shepard, "Manhood, Credit," 85; and Brennan, *Public Drinking,* 211. For another example, see Clark, "Migrant in Kentish Towns," 141.

[30] *Roxburghe Ballads,* ed. Chappell, 1:504–8.

[31] Gough, *History of Myddle,* ed. Hey, 130.

[32] Fairchilds, *Domestic Enemies,* 94.

legal records did not always document as a result of the privileged position of students, the exceptions being on occasions of violence. In the diary entry for 6 June 1681, Wood recorded that after drinking at the Crown Tavern, three gentlemen and four students, all of Christ Church College, pulled Lady Lovelace from her coach and called her "old protesting bitch"; they continued their rampage by breaking windows and committing "many misdemeanors." In January of the following year, Wood reported the fighting "occasioned by drunkenness" that occurred in St. John's College and used the occasion to comment on the state of the "most debauched college": "They come drunk into the chapel and vomit in their hats or caps there. They'll come into an alehouse and ask for 'a room that is private, where God almighty shall not see them.'" Wood continued by claiming New College also needed a thorough reformation, "much given to drinking and gaming, and vain brutish pleasure." The next atrocity, in December 1683, was nonetheless committed by three students from All Souls College; after getting drunk at the Mermaid, they came to the Miter although it was closed and demanded something to eat. When Mistress Lazenby refused to get out of bed to serve them, they called her "popish bitch" and "old popish whore" and claimed "she deserved to have her throat cut." Poor Mistress Lazenby became so frightened she fell into a fit and died. The students' turn came in 1687 when a drunken encounter with soldiers left the students with broken heads.[33] A book published at Strasbourg about 1489 (fig. 6) contained an illustration of a student drinking bout, revealing that continental students could be just as rowdy as their English counterparts.

Drunken disorderly behavior by servants and apprentices frequently appears in court records, indicating a high level of either misbehavior or supervision, or perhaps both. Apprentices no doubt chafed under the restraints imposed by their contracts, which forbade them to haunt alehouses; they could easily succumb to the attractions of drink, both male and female companionship, and competitive games that made alehouses such an appealing third place. Many of the young who were not apprentices were servants in rural or urban households and faced similar constraints and temptations, as did those who were neither apprentices nor servants. All of these contracts, restrictions, and constraints had the effect of lengthening the adolescence of young men, who sought greater freedom than the authorities were prepared to give them. In 1576 authorities in London acted with alarm when groups of apprentices

---

[33] Wood, *Life and Times*, ed. Powys, 255–56, 260–61, 268, 297–98.

Figure 6: A students' drinking bout. One student lies on the floor, one sprawls on a bench, while another pours drink into the mouth of a student lying on the table. Their money bags are unattended on the floor.

Woodcut from *Directorium statuum, seu tribulatio seculi.* Strasbourg: Johann Prüss for Peter Attendorn, ca. 1489.

faced the court at Bridewell for banqueting, gambling, and whoring at the Bell tavern, thereby violating key provisions of their contracts.[34] The authorities would have been equally concerned with the threat made by two apprentices when caught haunting alehouses: they would kill anyone who tried "to call them into question for their lewd courses."[35]

The prosecutions of apprentices and servants reflect the concerns about the behavior of the young evident in indictments of keepers, discussed in the previous chapter. Foremost among the concerns was the neglect of their obligations towards their masters. The specific charges against apprentices who were notable drunkards included "absenting himself from his master's service night by night," "abusing his master many ways, offering him violence and beating him, and absenting himself from his service," and pilfering of his master's goods and running to alehouses whenever sent on a task.[36] Accompanying such behavior was the prodigious consumption of alcohol. In 1632 a barber-surgeon complained of the habits of one servant: "in his drinking he is most unreasonable and insatiable. Sometimes to show his valor in that wickedness he has set a can of three pints to his head and drank it off."[37] Constables as well as masters frequently had to deal with violations of the curfew, as servants and apprentices returned home late from a night of drinking and upset the household, and the good Reverend Henry Newcome complained in his diary in the early 1660s that his sleep was always interrupted every Saturday night by "the villainous carriage of the servants that were all out at the time of the night."[38] The late Saturday night reveling by the servants made it difficult for them to attend church services on Sunday morning, and attendance at Sunday and holy day services was another concern of the authorities that influenced their attitudes towards the drinking of young people. The attraction of minstrels playing at an alehouse in Bethersden on a Sunday in August 1578 was the reason the young people of the community failed to attend evening prayer.[39] Also of concern were other types of misbehavior such as vandalism, gambling, and whoring that could result from drinking sessions and the haunting of alehouses.[40]

[34] Archer, "Material Londoners?" 185.

[35] Griffiths, *Youth and Authority*, 202.

[36] Griffiths, *Youth and Authority*, 202, 204.

[37] Shepard, "Manhood, Credit," 103.

[38] Earle, *Making of the English Middle Class*, 102–3; and Griffiths, *Youth and Authority*, 201–2.

[39] Collinson, *Religion of Protestants*, 206.

[40] Griffiths, *Youth and Authority*, 201, 204, 213–15.

Drunken servants and apprentices could pose the same threats to ordered society and hierarchical authority that masterless vagabonds posed, and just as vagabonds could be whipped out of town the same fate awaited incorrigible servants. At Rye in 1576, the servant Drew Cornish was ordered to leave town or face whipping and having a notice nailed to his ear as a result of his "drunkenness and evil demeanor." Similarly, in 1593 Richard Starne was so drunk and disorderly that he was ordered to leave the service of a widow and find a master who could control him.[41] At the bottom of the social scale of drunken youth was the masterless person, male or female, such as Thomas Carr of Billericay, who was charged in 1600 with "living idly, following no trade to live by, being a lusty young man that goes from alehouse to alehouse spending his time."[42] Masterless young women also faced charges of alehouse haunting and were often suspected of sexual license; Dorothy Merry was arrested in 1619 at the Fountain Tavern in Fleet Street, "where many gallons of wine were drunk."[43] The French youth were no different from their English counterparts in resenting the restrictions placed on them and seeking freedom to enjoy the anarchic atmosphere of taverns. Taking part in drinking contests and getting drunk were both a right and a duty in their opinion. As a result young men took the lead in protesting the efforts by the authorities to curtail festive drinking by closing taverns on Sundays and other feast days.[44] As noted by Alexandra Shepard, the drunken behavior of young men was "a deliberate inversion of prescribed norms" and a rejection of society's "expectations of frugality, order, and control." They embraced what their elders considered disorderly, scandalous, and improvident and believed their heavy drinking, rather than sobriety, provided a route to adulthood. In short, the drinking culture of the young created a subversive model of manhood.[45]

Sunday, Sacrilege, and Sedition

One of the frequent charges against disorderly alehouses and taverns, as discussed in chapter 5, was selling drinks on Sundays and on other holy days during divine service. Individuals likewise faced prosecution for drinking at these times, especially during the sixteenth and seventeenth centuries when

[41] Mayhew, *Tudor Rye*, 229.

[42] Salgãdo, *Elizabethan Underworld*, 132.

[43] Griffiths, "Masterless Young People," 170; and Capp, *When Gossips Meet*, 335.

[44] Collins, *Classes, Estates*, 72; Bercé, *Fête et révolte*, 164; and Hoffman, *Church and Community*, 142.

[45] Shepard, *Meanings of Manhood*, 105, 111, 113, 248–49.

both Catholic and Protestant authorities promoted the sanctification of the Sabbath as a day to be spent in worship and not in frivolous activities. The popularity of drinking on Sundays, the one day of rest, has a long history. When Saint Vincent Ferrier traveled across France in the early fifteenth century, he observed crowds of people drinking in taverns during the celebration of the mass on Sundays; at the sound of the elevation of the host they rushed from the tavern to the church "like a herd of swine in a pigsty." Parishioners at Nantes in 1385 persuaded their chaplain to celebrate an early mass so they could spend the rest of the day at the tavern in drunken revelry.[46] Normally, however, the Sunday drinkers did not bother to pay their respects to the body of Christ, and church officials fought a losing battle against people flocking to taverns during divine services. On a Sunday in March 1634, a frustrated provost found the taverns of Nantes were full of people as if it were a working day; twenty-five people were at a tavern near the port, more than thirty at another. Records of episcopal visitations indicate the situation was similar in rural areas as well, and efforts to enforce closure of taverns during divine service met with enterprising resistance, including the use of back doors if the front doors were closed.[47]

Drinking during divine service was just as popular in England as in France, if not more so. Vagabonds, who escaped parish discipline, and the poor, whose clothes often were unfit for churches and whose means prevented the payment of parish dues, preferred the convivial environment of alehouses to the somber sermons of the church. Even the middling and better sort could succumb to the temptations of traditional sports, fiddling, and dancing that were on offer at many alehouses. At Cranbrook in 1606, twenty people gathered at the house of James Rich during the time of divine service to enjoy fiddling, piping, dancing, and a firkin of beer.[48] Some incorrigible drunkards were just as incorrigible in their failure to attend church services. Robert Sampson, a Dorchester shoemaker who was frequently charged with drunkenness, missed services on Christmas Eve in 1629 because he was drinking with a friend until the early hours of the morning. He celebrated Christmas Day by drinking as soon as he got up and so missed morning prayer, and he then missed afternoon prayer because he was sleeping it off.[49]

Drunkenness sometimes resulted in the religious offenses of sacrilege,

[46] Adam, *Vie paroissiale en France*, 249–50.

[47] Collins, *Classes, Estates*, 257, n29; and Goubert, *French Peasantry*, 136.

[48] Collinson, *Religion of Protestants*, 207.

[49] Underdown, *Fire from Heaven*, 62–63.

profanation, and blasphemy. One such offense was to attend divine services in a state of inebriation. In some cases the inebriation resulted in behavior no more offensive than sleeping through the service, but others came into church stumbling and reeling, occasionally disturbing fellow worshippers.[50] The worst type of offender disturbed the services. According to one complaint, in 1624 the potter William Munnery of Graffham, Sussex, "was so exceedingly drunk that he spewed in our church most beastly, in the time of divine service, at evening prayer, before all the congregation," and in 1627 Edmund Saurer of Leeds vomited on the communion table at morning prayer.[51] Other drunkards spewed words instead of vomit; James Mills of Duncton, Sussex, was indicted in 1623 for coming to chapel on Whit Sunday and swearing "most horribly in the churchyard at the very time of ministering the Holy Communion," and witnesses before the diocesan court of Durham in 1629 accused William Hixon of being drunk and disturbing divine service with his "roaring or crying in very barbarous manner."[52] Such drunken profanation of divine services attracted the attention of the authorities because of their belief that not only such actions were immoral but also they could bring ill fortune to the community that permitted them.

Drunkards profaned divine services in other ways. John Prowse of Brixham, Devon, was drunk when he rode his horse into church in 1618 and asked to have it christened, and two years later a group of drunkards at the Red Lion in East Brent, Somerset, christened a dog "to the great profanation of the holy sacrament of baptism." They gave the dog a drink, christened it Cutty Hill "in derision of the minister, Mr. Hill," poured more drink on its head, made the sign of the cross, and appointed two godfathers.[53] Sermons were targets of similar mockery, such as the one given by a drunken Richard Hutchins of Stanton Bernard, Wiltshire, at the church of All Cannings on Guy Fawkes Day in 1613. He ascended the pulpit and preached to his companions: "The twenty-first chapter of Maud Butcher and the seventh verse. Man love thy wife and thy wife will love thee, and if she will not do as thou wilt have her, take a staff and break her arms and her legs and she will forgive thee."[54] A more notorious drunken sermon was delivered by Sir Charles Sedley, a close companion of Charles II, in 1663: together with some drunken

---

[50] *Portsmouth Record Series,* comp. Willis and ed. Hoad, 77; and Marcombe, *English Small Town Life,* 252.

[51] Hair, *Before the Bawdy Court,* 104; and Addy, *Sin and Society,* 108.

[52] Hair, *Before the Bawdy Court,* 74–75; and *Acts of the High Commission Court,* 16–17.

[53] Cressy, *Travesties and Transgressions,* 178.

[54] Amussen, "Gendering of Popular Culture," 64–65.

friends he caused a riot at Covent Gardens when they appeared on a balcony; "putting down their breeches they excrementized into the street; which being done, Sedley stripped himself naked, and with eloquence preached blasphemy to the people."[55]

Most of the drunkards indicted for blasphemy, profanation, or sacrilege were charged with verbal offenses. Relatively rare was the case of Rosso Adolfo, a guard at a Venetian flour warehouse, accused in 1388 of attacking a picture of the Virgin Mary with his sword, "shamefully blaspheming God and his mother."[56] More usual were the cases of blasphemy and swearing, such as that of Jean Le Naire of Sailly-Laurette (Amiens), encumbered with the burdens of old age, widowhood, and habitual drunkenness, who was charged in 1400 of profaning the name of God over a period of ten years on different days and in different places.[57] While under the influence of alcohol, some people uttered things they probably regretted upon sober reflection. A witness accused John Edwards of drinking "a health to the Devil or to Beelzebub the prince of the Devils" at an alehouse in Chester in 1640, and another drinker at a Stratford alehouse proclaimed Christ was a bastard and the Virgin Mary a whore.[58] A cobbler was fined one hundred livres for his blasphemy in a tavern in Grenoble in 1676. While cobblers and tailors were drinking together, someone suggested toasts to the patron saints of their professions, Saint Crespin and Saint Luce; the cobbler asserted that because Saint Luce was Saint Crespin's pimp the toasts were appropriate.[59]

In the period following the restoration of Charles II, royalists defended their reputation for hard drinking by claiming in prose and verse that drunkards were unlikely political plotters. For example, the undated and anonymous ballad entitled *The Loyal Subject (as it is reason) Drinks good sack and is free from Treason* proclaimed,

> We that drink good sack in plate
> To make us blithe and jolly
> Never plot against the state
> To be punished for such folly.[60]

[55] Bristow, *Vice and Vigilance*, 15.

[56] Crouzet-Pavan, *Sopra le acque salse*, 623.

[57] Gauvard, *"De Grace Especial,"* 372.

[58] Addy, *Sin and Society*, 107; and Clark, *English Alehouse*, 158.

[59] Norberg, *Rich and Poor*, 57–58.

[60] McShane Jones, "Roaring Royalists," 80.

Even if true, drinkers in their cups were notorious for their drunken slander of the government, including the king. Both Margaret Chanseler and Margery Cowpland pleaded drunkenness to excuse their comments about the marital policies of Henry VIII in 1535; according to Margaret the queen was "a goggle-eyed whore," to Margery "a strong harlot," and the king's servant was "the devil's turd." The investigating magistrate reported Margery was "a marvelous drunken woman" and "somewhat straight out of her wits."[61] Henry Crompton likewise pleaded drunkenness early in the seventeenth century when he stated that the king's crown would be "pulled about his head"; Crompton got off with a fine of five shillings paid to the poor of the parish of St. Giles-in-the-Fields.[62] During the Civil War and the Protectorate, the drunken seditious slander turned from the king to the Parliament and Oliver Cromwell. A Devon merchant and the wife of a tailor were indicted in 1647 for comments about the Parliament made while "in drink." The merchant stated, "Some of the Parliament men had the pox and were whoremasters, and some of them were rogues and rebels," and the wife bid "a pox of God take the Parliament." The Restoration resulted not only in the return of the king but also in the drunken slander against him; William Sparkes, being "distempered with drink," stated that "the King was a poor and beggarly King," and Anthony Dereew, a Whitechapel weaver, drank a health "to the King and all whores."[63]

A couple of cases demonstrate the way drunken alehouse banter could lead to seditious comments. In September 1595 Thomas Byndar, a blacksmith of Danbury, Essex, became involved in an argument at Widow Glascock's alehouse over the price of horsenails. Byndar claimed everything was too expensive and asserted that the poor would seek redress before Christmas by moving against those merchant victuallers who were responsible for the high prices, that twenty of the victuallers "would be hanged at their gates before Christmas," and that since he did not have a wife or children he would join the poor in their action. One of the witnesses told the investigating justice of the peace, "I think he were drunk when he spoke these words."[64] A similar case occurred in 1668 at the time of the bawdy-house riots in London; John Lilley, a Southwark waterman, was arrested for claiming he would join the 40,000 others who were ready to riot on 1 May. According to a witness, Lilley spoke these words

---

[61] Jansen, *Dangerous Talk*, 88–89.

[62] *Middlesex County Records*, ed. Jeaffreson, 2:76.

[63] *Middlesex County Records*, ed. Jeaffreson, 3:98, 183–84, 207–8, 211–12, 224–25, 250, 284, 305, 339.

[64] Emmison, *Elizabethan Life*, 61–62.

when he was "horribly overladen with drink."[65] Unclear in all of these verbal slanders and blasphemies is the drunkenness of the speakers, who might have attempted to excuse their statements by claiming they were drunk at the time. Favorable witnesses might have also supported such claims and thereby mitigated the punishment. The defilement of sacred space by vomiting on the communion table is less excusable, unless the perpetrator could claim illness, which would mean some people pleaded drunkenness to excuse their behavior while others pleaded illness to excuse their drunkenness.

Disorderly Conduct

Drunken violations of the curfew produced some weird and wonderful disorderly conduct that disturbed sleeping inhabitants. In 1488 sergeants arrested four companions for making noise by crying and singing on a Parisian street between ten and eleven at night; two of the companions had been previously arrested for the same offense and had been ordered not to frequent each other's company.[66] Cuthbert Foster confessed to a Westminster court in 1613 he had been "drunk and disorderly in the night by raising people and crying 'murder' to the great disturbance of the inhabitants there in Tuttle Street."[67] The noise from yet other incidents probably led officials to the discovery of the perpetrators. A Middlesex headborough reported in 1656 he found Elizabeth Wight "in an uncivil posture, dancing upon the knee of a deboist [debauched] man that was among others ranting and singing in a disorderly and suspicious alehouse at an unseasonable hour in the night." He also charged four men "for being of the same ranting, singing, disorderly, and riotous company in the suspicious alehouse."[68]

The Middlesex headborough who reported Elizabeth Wight also complained her companions "threatened and abused" him and the other members of the night watch and "the house raised against them." The incident reveals the enforcement of the curfew on drunkards could become a dangerous activity. The night watch at Dunmow, Essex, encountered two men fetching beer from an alehouse late a night. The two men quarreled with the watchmen, who called for help from the neighbors, but one of the neighbors

---

[65] Harris, "Bawdy House Riots," 550–51.

[66] Gauvard, *De Grace Especial,* 872n92.

[67] Manchée, *Westminster City Fathers,* 101. For another example, see Durston, "Puritan Rule," 230.

[68] *Middlesex County Records,* ed. Jeaffreson, 3:256. For another example, see *Records of Early English Drama,* ed. Hays, McGee, Joyce, and Newlyn, 282.

took the offenders' side and tried to provoke further resistance by urging them to prick the watchmen with pins.[69] Other encounters ended peacefully when the night watch succumbed to the revelers. The night watch at Dorchester heard drunken singing coming from the Antelope late one night in 1637. Two men from the watch investigated the disturbance and found the noise came from a group of men from Sherbourne, who promptly offered them a jug of beer. Word quickly spread to the rest of the watch, and they came seeking their share of the beer, in exchange for which they promised not to inform the constables.[70]

On occasion, the night watch encountered cases of vandalism. Many cases of drunken vandalism were relatively mindless acts, although some demonstrated more inventiveness than others. One drunkard knocked down alehouse signs, a group of drunken villagers of Bayton, Worcestershire, rolled timber onto the roads and pulled up fences, and another group broke a fish pond after getting drunk.[71] A group of six men went on a drunken, mindless rampage through the town of Rye on the night of 26 September 1575. They threw property over a cliff, upset a cask in one street and a tan vat in another, broke a window, knocked down the wall of a kitchen, and pulled a lattice from a window, which they then threw into the yard of the vicarage.[72] On the other hand, some cases of vandalism were not mindless but directed at specific persons and targets. In 1665 Martha Nichols, a spinster of Sustead, Norfolk, broke the window of William Grice, a local cordwainer who also kept an alehouse. Nichols had been drinking in the alehouse but was ejected after becoming abusive, so she retaliated.[73]

According to the statistics compiled by Thomas Brennan for his book on public drinking in Paris, theft accounted for only 13 percent of the incidents in taverns that were reported to authorities,[74] and similar statistics would probably apply to English alehouses. Aside from other customers, the modest furnishings of most alehouses and taverns had little value to thieves, except for the drink itself. If the statutes concerning poor people drinking more than they could afford are an indication, tavern keepers in

[69] Emmison, *Elizabethan Life,* 178.

[70] Underdown, *Fire from Heaven,* 96. For a similar example, see Durston, "Puritan Rule," 221.

[71] Bailey, "Rural Society," 166; Clark, "Alehouse and the Alternative Society," 58; and Sharpe, "Crime and Delinquency," 103.

[72] Mayhew, *Tudor Rye,* 224–25.

[73] Doughty, *Notebook of Robert Doughty,* ed. Rosenheim, 20, 52, 81n241.

[74] Brennan, *Public Drinking,* 27.

Italy frequently encountered customers who did not have the money to pay for the drinks already consumed.[75] Court cases of thefts while under the influence of alcohol were relatively rare, although a drunken thief could be more easily caught than a sober one. An example of this might be Perrin Le Normant, who stole two bridles in 1393 after becoming drunk while drinking with friends in several Parisian taverns; he was caught after offering to sell them to the craftsman who made them.[76] Several cases of drunken thefts give the distinct impression the criminal claimed inebriation as an extenuating circumstance to mitigate the punishment. Such a claim did not help Samuel Wheeler; when caught with two stolen hogs, he pretended to be drunk, but the judge sent him to prison. Another culprit, when accused of housebreaking, claimed he had consumed three quarts of beer and entered the house to sleep it off.[77] Similarly, in 1426 a baker claimed in a letter seeking remission for a theft that the crime resulted from a long day of drinking to celebrate the feast day of St. Bartholomew at Senlis.[78] Some thefts while under the influence of alcohol were not mindless acts but directed at specific victims; such was the case in Libourne when men of means stole from their enemies.[79] Finally, some cases were obvious examples of drunken exuberance gone wrong, as when Will Porter stole a horse in 1617; the enraged owner had him imprisoned for five weeks, during which Porter nearly committed suicide as a result of his shame and embarrassment.[80]

Another form of drunken disorderly conduct was sexual. Unlike the use of alehouses and taverns for sexual rendezvous discussed in the previous chapter, this behavior involved people fornicating or exposing themselves while under the influence of alcohol. Court cases to determine the paternity of illegitimate children often discovered single women succumbed while drunk, as uncovered by G. R. Quaife's research into seventeenth-century Somerset, with cases of drunken women deflowered in a stable, succumbing to two men, seduced by a soldier, and yielding to the master of the household "two or three times" in a single night.[81] In 1608 a London consistory court heard a case against Thomas Creede for fornication and bastardy. The

---

[75] Patrone, *Cibo del ricco*, 416–17.

[76] Geremek, *Margins of Society*, 97n9.

[77] Sharpe, *Crime in Seventeenth-Century England*, 55.

[78] Vaultier, *Folklore pendant la Guerre*, 98–99.

[79] Ruff, *Crime, Justice*, 119.

[80] MacDonald and Murphy, *Sleepless Souls*, 284.

[81] Quaife, *Wanton Wenches*, 67.

main witness was Suzan More, a twenty-five-year-old servant, who testified Creede often invited her to drink with him. On one occasion he gave her so much wine to drink at the Sun Tavern that she became drunk, whereupon he brought her to Widow Grime's alehouse and had sex with her in an upper chamber.[82] Other cases indicate other ways men took advantage of drunken women. Rowland Wood of Horsham bragged to his neighbors in 1612 that when Joan Sammeway had become drunk he was able to "put his hands into her clothes and feel her privities."[83] Another case was so extraordinary that Thomas Dekker used it for the basis of a play entitled *Keep the Widow Waking,* although Dekker was just as shameful in his perversion of the facts in the case as the perpetrators were in their treatment of the widow. After the death of her husband in 1624, the sixty-two-year-old Anne Elsdon was "courted" by Tobias Audley, with assistance from some unscrupulous friends, by going from one tavern to another for the space of three days until Anne was well and truly befuddled by drink and unaware that she and Tobias were now man and wife.[84]

On the occasions when the men got drunk the sexual misconduct had several permutations. In 1664 Henry Byare testified he had seen Mary Darwin leave her husband, who was sleeping off his drunken stupor on the floor, and go with another man to another room at an alehouse in Clayton-le-Moors, where he heard "much puffing and blowing."[85] A drunken escapade in London landed a yeoman and two tailors in court in 1615; the three visited the brothel of the widow Joan Wood and frightened her with their demeanor, and the yeoman as well as perhaps the two tailors had sex with Joan Graunt.[86] The most typical behavior of drunken men seems to be exposure, although some were falsely accused of displaying their private parts when all they were doing was relieving themselves after a drinking bout. A Somerset clergyman was more open in his intentions after he became "much overcrowded with drink" by riding his horse up and down the street of Wridlington and attempting to kiss all the women, especially one Katherine Weaver, who knocked him into a ditch after he "showed his privy parts unto her."[87] Another example of exposure ended in a court case at Dorchester in

---

[82] Crawford and Gowing, *Women's Worlds,* 142–44.

[83] Capp, *When Gossips Meet,* 225.

[84] Carlton, "Widow's Tale," 118.

[85] Addy, *Sin and Society,* 110.

[86] *County of Middlesex,* ed. Hardy, II, 264.

[87] Quaife, *Wanton Wenches,* 166.

1634. Roger Buck, a young man from Fordington, had joined a group of men and women for a night of food, drink, and revelry. When drunk, Buck was first offered money if he would dance and then if he would expose himself, which he did. When the women complained the room was too dark for them to see, a candle was brought closer, so close that it burned him so badly that he died a few weeks later.[88] The incident would have provided a puritan moralist with an ideal example of how God could punish drunkenness.

Much of the material on disorderly persons mirrors similar material from the previous chapter on disorderly places. This is most obvious in the sections devoted to young people; the concerns about the behavior of youth that prompted authorities to prosecute keepers of drinking establishments were almost identical to the drunken disorderly conduct of students, apprentices, and servants. This is not at all surprising, but the point that needs emphasizing is the disorder inherent in many alehouses and taverns regardless of the inebriation of their customers. Even in this chapter on drunken disorder alehouses and taverns had major roles, and if all the incidents involving them were removed, the chapter would be very short indeed. In other words, drunkenness per se seems much less a cause of disorder than its venues. In addition to this point is the ambiguous role of drunkenness in causing disorder. When giving testimony at a court case, a constable who raided an alehouse could be certain of the venue of a particular offense, but his judgment on the inebriation of the offender could elude such certainty. Defendants could plead drunkenness in an attempt to mitigate punishments, and plaintiffs could charge them with drunkenness in an attempt to blacken their reputations. If all the incidents involving false pleadings and false allegations were removed from this chapter, how long would it be?

Similarly if all the material concerning England were removed from these two chapters, the remaining material on France and especially Italy would not make even a short chapter. This is mainly a function of the sources; English historians have given considerable attention to legal sources to document their work on various aspects of English social history, so the anecdotal and qualitative evidence from English sources is valuable in establishing trends and patterns. One such pattern involves those who could be considered alco-

---

[88] Underdown, *Fire from Heaven*, 61–62.

holics; many of those prosecuted in courts suffered from alcohol dependency. Hidden among many of these were probably cases of what anthropologists term "despair drinking," or what Jerome Blum describes as the hopeless and desperate drinking by the oppressed masses. Above all else the trends and patterns demonstrate the concerns of the political, religious, and economic elite. One of the foremost of these concerns was the disorderly conduct of apprentices and servants due to fears about the loosening ties of social discipline. Scolds could interrupt the social harmony of neighborhoods, parishes, and villages, while the profanation of the Sabbath and instances of sacrilege could threaten the entire community with divine wrath. The patriarchal ideology of this elite is evident from the fears about drinking women. Despite the valuable anecdotal evidence from English sources, the quantitative data for the three English counties demonstrate, as they do in the previous chapter, that the level of drunken disorder was low. Nonetheless, the problems of disorderly places and disorderly persons seem more acute in England than in the other countries. If this was actually the case, the reason might be found among the attitudes of the elite who were the ones defining disorder and prosecuting disorderly offenders. 🍇

Chapter 7

Violence

Wine is a mocker, strong drink a brawler.
—Proverbs 20:1

Before the advent of modern medicine, relatives and neighbors took seriously injured persons home, put them to bed, and awaited their death. Wounds that could easily be treated in modern hospitals were life threatening, and traditional medical techniques were as likely to harm as to help a patient; Richard Wiseman's standard book on surgical procedures, printed in 1676, was popularly known as *Wiseman's Book of Martyrs.*[1] Nonetheless, many of those killed in drunken brawls had such serious wounds that modern medicine might not have helped them, especially if the combatants forsook fisticuffs and pulled out swords, as they are doing in a depiction of a tavern brawl from late seventeenth-century London (fig. 7). A group of Venetian cobblers was drinking at an inn when a dispute erupted between them over rival factions in the squads that held public fights on the city's bridges. "One of the most ardent among them (maybe also incited by the anger of Bacchus) punched a companion in the face. Another, seeing his friend offended, knocked [the attacker] off his bench onto the ground.... Another pulled out one of the wide knives they carry, cutting in a blow two fingers off [that one's] left hand ... until [finally] everyone had pulled out daggers, knives, cleavers, swords, boathooks, harpoons, and [even] skewers from the kitchen." When the fight was over three were dead and eleven badly wounded.[2] Ellis Morgan

[1] Thomas, *Religion and the Decline of Magic,* 10.
[2] Davis, *War of the Fists,* 37–38, 181–82n80.

Figure 7: A tavern brawl, English, seventeenth century, from Tom Brown, *Amusements Serious and Comical.* The man on the far right tries to restrain the man pulling the arm of his protagonist across the table and raising his tankard either to hit him or to protect himself from the raised sword. Two other drinkers have joined the brawl with their swords. While the dog seems interested, the man on the far left looks on impassively. Outside two constables arrive to restore order.

Reproduced from Tom Brown, *Amusements Serious and Comical* (1700?), edited with notes by Arthur L. Hayward. New York: Dodd Mead & Co., 1927.

was the victim of a stabbing by a fellow soldier who was also a relative when a drunken brawl erupted one night in London in June 1640. According to the surgeon who examined him, Morgan "received four several punctures ... one in the middle of the sternum, one in the upper side of the left breast ..., one near to the left shoulder ..., one a little above the right armpit going towards the end of the clavicle."[3] The brawls resulting from drinking sessions could be very serious indeed.

An examination of violence has fewer problems of definition than those associated with disorder. According to the authorities, some forms of disorder were class specific, but even powerful lords could face court indictments for violence. Nonetheless, the nature of court records results in the same problems of analysis for violence as it does for disorder; the records are not representations of reality but of legal processes, as both plaintiffs and defendants engaged in fabrications of events, intentions, and words to gain favorable verdicts. One of the best examples of this is the complaint made by Jacques Le François in 1709 that the owner of a cabaret at Pîtres attempted without reason or warning to force him to leave, and when he refused to do so he was assaulted by the owner's family and cut by a tankard. However, the owner of the cabaret told a different version: Le François and several companions had forced their way into the cabaret, assaulted a customer, beat the owner when he intervened, and then damaged his apple trees. Yet a third perspective came from a landowner, who testified that he had transferred a lease of land to the owner of the cabaret and to the assaulted customer from the family of Le François, who reacted by repeatedly harassing the new tenants.[4] As a result of such conflicting testimonies, the level of drunkenness in acts of violence is uncertain, since defendants could claim they were drunk in an attempt to mitigate punishment, and plaintiffs could accuse an attacker of drunkenness to convince the court they were blameless. An analysis of violence shares another similarity with an analysis of disorder, and that is the important role of drinking establishments. Much of the disorder associated with drinking occurred in taverns and alehouses; most of the drunken violence and much violence that was not drunken occurred there, so much so that here again taverns and alehouses gave drinking and drunkenness a bad name.

[3] Beier, *Sufferers and Healers*, 65. For another example, see Norberg, *Rich and Poor*, 93.
[4] Dewald, *Pont-St-Pierre*, 132.

Places and Persons

As noted in chapter 1, modern studies of violence indicate alcohol is a factor in about half of violent crimes. In traditional Europe the figure was much less. Given the complaints and the claims of the moralists, given the large amounts of alcohol consumed as part of a person's daily diet, given all the occasions for recreational drinking, and given the important role of drinking establishments as the third place, that statement is remarkable and deserves reiteration. The level of violence caused by drinking and drunkenness was low. Precisely how low is of course difficult to ascertain, but many historians have produced statistics that quantify the level of crimes, violence, and/or murders connected to drunkenness and/or drinking establishments. The statistics are based on analyses of legal records, which suffer from the distortions mentioned above, and must therefore be viewed with caution. Additional difficulties result from attempts to quantify violence.[5] Despite their limitations, the statistics provide a useful impression. In her analysis of violent deaths documented in coroners' rolls in fourteenth- and early fifteenth-century England, Barbara Hanawalt reckons drink was involved in 6 percent of 112 homicides in London and 4.3 percent of 347 homicides in rural Northamptonshire.[6] Claude Gauvard's sources are letters seeking remission for crimes from late medieval France, and he calculates 9.9 percent of all crimes and 15 percent of murders occurred while under the influence of alcohol.[7] An analysis of 400 criminal cases involving rural offenses, morals, theft, and nonfatal violence heard by the courts of Angoulême and Lectoure between 1643 and 1644 indicates drunkenness was the cause of 8.1 percent of these crimes.[8]

None of these examples provides the precise statistics required to compare traditional Europe with the modern situation—that is, the percentage of violent cases involving drink. My analysis of two sets of legal documents provides such statistics, even though the sample in both of them is relatively small. The first is the casebook of Sir Francis Ashley, recorder of Dorchester from 1614 until 1635, which contains 76 cases of violence. Seven of these, or 9 percent, were committed by a person who had been drinking. On three occasions drunkards assaulted officials who had come to arrest them, one drunkard attacked someone for refusing to drink with him, a man killed

---

[5] See the discussion in Walker, *Crime, Gender,* 25; and Shepard, *Meanings of Manhood,* 130.

[6] Hanawalt, "Violent Death," 320.

[7] Gauvard, *"De Grace Especial,"* 430, 450–51.

[8] Bercé, "Aspects de la criminalité," 38–39.

another in a duel that resulted from a quarrel while drinking beer in an ale-house, and one servant rose from his drink to attack another who tried to take a lit candle into a barn. An example of class antagonism occurred when two tinkers objected to the preferential treatment received by two gentlemen at an alehouse, whereupon one of the gentlemen "threw a glass of beer that he had in his hand in one of their faces, upon which they all fell together by the ears."[9] The other legal document is the notebook of Robert Doughty, a Norfolk justice of the peace in the 1660s. For the years 1662 to 1665, Doughty's notebooks mentioned 71 cases of violence, only one of which was committed by a drunkard. Even this case is not clear-cut; on 13 July 1665 Doughty recorded "a general warrant against John Oakely of North Walsham, laborer, for beating Thomas Mautby and his wife, being drunk and swearing."[10] A possible reading of this passage is the "beating" and "being drunk and swearing" were two separate incidents. Be that as it may, the statistics indicate a small correlation between drinking and acts of violence, and they complement the impressions that emerge from the analysis of the court records of the counties of Warwickshire, Kent, and Middlesex.

With some exceptions, the statistics demonstrate a greater correlation between drinking establishments and acts of violence than between drinking and acts of violence. The earliest statistics come from James Buchanan Given's analysis of homicides in thirteenth-century England; of 1,368 cases in which the sources mention the location, only 26, or 1.9 percent, occurred in a tavern.[11] This extremely low figure might be a function of the small number of drinking establishments at that time. Although he cites no statistics, Jacques Chiffoleau claims alcohol was seldom a factor in the frequent tavern brawls in fourteenth-century Avignon.[12] Hanawalt produces figures of 7 percent for homicides in both London and rural Northamptonshire, which are slightly higher than her figures for homicides connected to drink.[13] Gauvard, on the other hand, calculates 10.5 percent of crimes occurred in taverns but only 11.5 percent of murders, down from the 15 percent associated with drinking.[14] Much higher are the figures from J. A. Sharpe's study of seventeenth-century Essex; 21 of 64 homicides, or 32.8 percent, occurred

---

[9] Ashley, *Casebook of Sir Francis Ashley*, ed. Bettey, 29, 31, 48, 51–52, 56, 81–82, 91.

[10] Doughty, *Notebook of Robert Doughty*, ed. Rosenheim, 60.

[11] Given, *Society and Homicide*, 195.

[12] Chiffoleau, *Justices du pape*, 142.

[13] Hanawalt, "Violent Death," 320.

[14] Gauvard, *De Grace Especial*, 516, 737.

during or after drinking in an alehouse.[15] The highest statistic, as high as those from modern studies, comes from the region of Artois; from the fifteenth to the seventeenth century, 55 percent of violent acts whose perpetrators received pardons occurred in taverns.[16] Some French studies conflate the cases of drinking with cases in taverns; in late medieval Touraine this represented 35 percent of violent crimes, 26 percent in Libourne, and 8.8 percent in Pont-Saint-Pierre.[17] Finally, a study of fourteenth-century England points to a correlation between homicide and both nighttime and weekends, which were occasions for haunting drinking establishments. According to Carl I. Hammer, "If one were a young adult male with university connections living in eastern Oxford and likely to haunt taverns at night on weekends, especially in the suburbs, the chances of being involved in a homicide as assailant, accomplice, or victim were high indeed."[18]

In 1702 George Hilton of Westmorland knocked out a man's eye in a drunken brawl at Appleby; he subsequently recorded in his diary his resolution to spend less time and money on drink: "I have often lost my reason by my immoderate drinking and am then too provoked to passion."[19] Just as Hilton blamed drink for his violent behavior, some scholars attempt to explain drunken violence or the violence that occurs in drinking establishments by pointing to, among other factors, the drink itself.[20] However, given the low level of violence and the high level of consumption, it might be more appropriate to point to drink as an agent that mitigated violence rather than caused it. Perhaps the violence occurred in spite of the drunkenness of the protagonists rather than because of it. Rather than seek causes for violence in the drink, the role of alehouses and taverns in much of the violence requires explanation. One feature of drinking establishments that was an obvious contributor to violence was the nature of their clientele. As discussed in chapter 5, alehouses and taverns attracted a disorderly clientele that included thieves, gangs of criminals, prostitutes and their pimps, gamblers, vagabonds, and other denizens of the underworld. Into this volatile mix came transients such

[15] Sharpe, *Crime in Seventeenth-Century England*, 131.

[16] Ruff, *Violence in Early Modern Europe*, 126. The figures provided by Kümin in *Drinking Matters*, 134, are higher, but they are inflated by the inclusion of cases of defamation.

[17] Leguay, *Rue au Moyen Age*, 155; Ruff, *Crime, Justice*, 81; and Dewald, *Pont-St-Pierre*, 133.

[18] Hammer, "Patterns of Homicide," 22. Hanawalt, "Violent Death," 305, notices the same correlation.

[19] Foyster, *Manhood in Early Modern England*, 41.

[20] For example, Amussen, "Gendering of Popular Culture," 63; Hanlon, "Rituels de l'agression," 252; and Lascombes, "Fortunes de l'*ale*," 133.

as soldiers and sailors, whose vocations had accustomed them to violence, and young men intent on demonstrating through macho drinking and posturing that they were no longer boys.[21] Such an environment weakened the social rituals, rules, and responsibilities that could help prevent outbreaks of violence.[22]

Another feature of drinking establishments that contributed to their potential for violence was the public nature of their space. The public space of alehouses and taverns made them not only ideal venues in which to discredit an enemy or a rival but also dangerous venues as a result of the obsession with honor that characterized all levels of society in traditional Europe. One effect of this obsession was that people attempted to appear more important than permitted by their social status. As a result, honor was an externalized value dependent on what others thought of a person, and in consequence social convention required people to defend any affronts to their honor. If the affront occurred in the public space of drinking establishments, violence could result. Contemporary notions of manhood that fostered competitive interaction could exacerbate such confrontations and legitimize the consequent violence.[23] Compounding the possibility of this type of violence were the multiple loyalties of family, neighborhood, social status, and occupation that required defense from the threats, slanders, and insults of the "other," as civilians confronted soldiers, the gown fought the town, and village youths skirmished with those from neighboring villages.[24] According to Maria Serena Mazzi, a subterranean climate of violence reigned in fifteenth-century Florentine taverns as a result of "the little rivalries among work companions, the disagreements of neighbors, the antagonisms of nationalities, and the hidden resentment against the well-being of the rich."[25]

One feature of tavern and alehouse brawls that made them particularly dangerous was that the disputes begun inside over a pot of wine or jug of ale could end outside on the streets.[26] In 1643 three young workers shared drinks

---

[21] Foyster, *Manhood in Early Modern England,* 40.

[22] Taylor, *Drinking, Homicide,* 66. I disagree with the historians who argue the violence in drinking establishments conformed to social rituals and rules; Tlusty, *Bacchus and Civic Order,* 129–33; and Crouzet-Pavan, *Sopra le acque salse,* 821. The authors provide no empirical evidence of such behavior but base their argument on sociological models.

[23] Shepard, *Meanings of Manhood,* 150.

[24] Brennan, *Public Drinking,* 25–26; Fouret, "Violence en fête," 378; Hanlon, "Rituels de l'agression," 244–45; and Ruff, *Violence in Early Modern Europe,* 75–77.

[25] Mazzi, *Prostitute e lenoni,* 270.

[26] Crouzet-Pavan, *Sopra le acque salse,* 819; and Gauvard, *De Grace Especial,* 285.

at a tavern in Dijon but began fighting when they stumbled into the street, and when a young man was wounded after leaving a Lille tavern in 1684, he was brought back to the tavern where he received the last rites.[27] What increased the danger of such brawls was the propensity for others to join the engagement, especially if they sensed any of their multiple loyalties of family, neighborhood, social status, and occupation were at stake.[28] A brawl between two drinkers in an alehouse in Malpas in 1615 suddenly developed into a widespread disturbance that ended with "most of the town ... disquieted," and another in 1610 that began with a dozen customers at an alehouse in Walsall resulted in over one hundred people fighting in the street.[29]

Despite the volatile clientele, the public space of the tavern, and the role of honor in causing violence, some outbursts of violence remain inexplicable. An example of gratuitous drunken murder occurred at Bromholm in 1272; four men accosted the son of the vicar in front of the village church, demanded to know who he was, and when he replied, "A man; who are you?" one of them struck him on the head with an axe. According to the testimony of the locals, the four men "were waiting to do injury to someone else there."[30] John Aubrey recalled an occasion when "I was in great danger of being killed by a drunkard in the street opposite Grays-Inn—a gentleman whom I never saw before, but (*Deo gratias*) one of his companions hindered his thrust."[31] More disconcerting than threats from a complete stranger were those from people who had received treatment for which they should have been grateful. A master engraver encountered a journeyman clockmaker who was "entirely drunk" on a Paris street in 1701; in an act of compassion the engraver brought the clockmaker home, whereupon the clockmaker wounded him with a sword.[32]

Violent Persons

Thomas Jevon's comedy *The Devil of a Wife* (1686) depicted a cobbler's wife begging her husband not to go drinking without her since he would spend his money, come home drunk, and beat her. The husband interpreted the plea

[27] Brackett, *Criminal Justice,* 106; Farr, *Hands of Honor,* 173; and Lottin, *Chavatte, ouvrier lillois,* 352.

[28] Lorcin, "Paysans et la justice," 284.

[29] Clark, "Alehouse and the Alternative Society," 58; and Clark, *English Alehouse,* 147.

[30] Given, *Society and Homicide,* 162.

[31] Aubrey, *Brief Lives,* ed. Clark, 1:48.

[32] Brennan, *Public Drinking,* 50.

as a threat to his authority: "How now brazen-face," he replied, "do you speak
ill of the government? I am king in my own house, and this is treason against
my Majesty."[33] The husband's assertion was an expression of accepted views
of patriarchal authority, which permitted men to slake their thirst and to seek
recreation in drinking establishments and to exercise authority over their
wives, children, and servants, even to dispense physical discipline if necessary. William Miller of Dorchester expressed a rather extreme form of this
attitude: "He would go to the alehouse ... and have his cup and a pot of sack
and a whore, and ... his wife should stand by and see it, and ... if she would
dare to speak he would beat her to pieces."[34] However, men who dissipated
their wealth and time at alehouses and taverns were subject to condemnation, as were men who beat their wives, children, and servants too much, beyond what was necessary for reasons of discipline.[35] Many men exceeded the
permissible limits, for the most frequent form of drunken violence that did
not occur in drinking establishments was domestic; men came home drunk
from a night of drinking and beat their wives, as expressed by one poet:

> Drunk, at midnight, home the knave doth creep,
> And beats his wife, and spews, and falls asleep.[36]

The severity of some of the beatings indicates the husband's drunkenness was not enough to incapacitate him. When John Barnes of Ely came
home drunk one day in 1652, his wife called him a rogue and said, "There
was many a truer man hanged"; he reacted by beating and kicking her so
violently that she later died.[37] Not just women received severe beatings; when
the wife of William Ixworth sent their servant boy to a Norfolk alehouse
in 1665 to fetch him after a long drinking binge, William beat him with a
cudgel, breaking his head and leaving twenty black and blue bruises.[38] The
husband of Jeanne Bourdon not only beat his wife and servants when he
was drunk but also his children, and drove them all from the house.[39] Even
officials could be on the receiving end if they intervened in a domestic dispute, as occurred to a constable in Worcestershire when he rushed into a

---

[33] Capp, *When Gossips Meet,* 87.

[34] Underdown, *Fire from Heaven,* 71–72.

[35] See the discussion in Fletcher, "Manhood, the Male Body," 419–36.

[36] W. Fennor, *Pasquils Palinodia* (1619), quoted in Capp, *When Gossips Meet,* 104.

[37] Fletcher, *Gender, Sex,* 197.

[38] Doughty, *Notebook of Robert Doughty,* ed. Rosenheim, 56.

[39] Hufton, *Prospect Before Her,* 1:282.

Figure 8: A woman confronts her husband at an alehouse. Illustration from "The Courtier's Health; or, The Merry Boyes of the Times," woodcut from *The Roxburghe Ballads,* English, seventeenth century [*Roxburghe Collection,* 2:88. 3:395, 4:38].
Reproduced from *The Roxburghe Ballads,* vol. 3, pt. 1, edited by Wm. Chappell, 632. Hertford, UK: Stephen Austin and Sons, for the Ballad Society, 1875; reprint, New York: AMS Press, 1966.

drunkard's house.[40] On occasion the wives turned the tables. In 1677 Sarah Elston of Southwark killed her drunken husband, stabbing him with a pair of scissors, and claimed she only intended "to do him some slight mischief in revenge of his cruelty in beating her."[41]

When Eleanor Sackville learned her brick-maker husband had sold one of her pails to pay for his drinking, she rushed to an alehouse in Clerkenwell to berate him in a scene comparable to a seventeenth-century depiction from the *Roxburghe Ballads* (fig. 8). Confronting a husband in the public space of

[40] Wrightson, "Two Concepts of Order," 31.
[41] Capp, *When Gossips Meet,* 88.

a drinking establishment was a dangerous tactic, condemned by ministers, pamphleteers, and popular ballads. On returning home, Eleanor was probably fortunate to escape with a black eye, but this injury increased both her fury and her abuse, so he hit her with a shovel and killed her. Given the prevailing patriarchal values, her husband was probably unfortunate to swing on the gallows, for other cases demonstrate the strength of patriarchal ideology.[42] When the wheelwright John Dilworth of Lincolnshire came home drunk one night in 1607, his wife used the occasion to tell him "his great and gross faults." At the subsequent coroner's inquest, Dilworth freely confessed he had become enraged and killed her and claimed he had "done God and the world good service in sending so unquiet a creature out of it."[43]

The wife of a Parisian basket maker complained to authorities in 1701 about the conduct of her husband, almost always coming home drunk late at night and beating her, but of greater concern than the beatings was the dissipation of his time and their resources. Her gentle protests only provoked further angry beatings.[44] If some wives were too frightened to challenge their husbands' authority directly, they did so indirectly by complaining, as did the wife of the basket maker, to the authorities. In 1581 Helen Frotier received a certificate from the magistrates at Rye permitting her to escape from her husband, John Frotier, locksmith, "a very drunken and beastly person" who "has from time to time continually beaten and marvelously evilly treated the said Helen."[45] Similarly, in 1610 Paola da Venezia petitioned a Venetian court to grant her separation from her husband, Jacobo Furlano, fuller, who continually became drunk in taverns and then beat her when he came home.[46] On occasion the neighbors rather than the long-suffering wives complained to the authorities. In March 1613 a Westminster waterman was sentenced to four hours in the stocks if he was found drunk again after his neighbors complained that while drunk he had slandered them and beat his wife.[47] Since modern cases of domestic violence are often unreported, it is likely many cases of wife beating by drunken husbands never reached the ears of authorities, even if they did reach the ears of neighbors, especially because of contemporary views on the rights of husbands. As the case of

[42] Capp, *When Gossips Meet,* 89.

[43] Sharpe, "Domestic Homicide," 43.

[44] Brennan, *Public Drinking,* 207–8.

[45] Mayhew, *Tudor Rye,* 203.

[46] Ferraro, *Marriage Wars,* 125.

[47] Manchée, *Westminster City Fathers,* 101. See also Amussen, *Ordered Society,* 168.

Eleanor Sackville demonstrates, even if wives confronted husbands in the public space of drinking establishments, the violence occurred later in the private space of homes.

Rape is another form of violence usually associated with private space, but many rapes occurred in drinking establishments. A London case in 1689 involved the female keeper herself; a customer raped Ruth Turner and then offered to spend 20 shillings in the alehouse to placate her, but she was determined to have her justice.[48] Other cases involve women raped while in a drunken stupor, although the evidence indicates some single women falsely claimed they had been drunk when authorities later questioned them about the paternity of the subsequent children.[49] At Portsmouth in 1654, Dorothy Hayter testified "she had drunk too much wine; otherwise she would not have yielded" to John Sanders, but she was still sober enough to ask him to admit paternity if she became pregnant. Sanders agreed and promised to marry her, but during the following court case Dorothy claimed that "if he had kept his promise she would not have complained." In this case Sanders confirmed both her story and his promise.[50] Early in the eighteenth century, Martha Vose, a servant in the house of a substantial merchant, was raped by her master after he plied her with "strong waters."[51] Rape, like domestic violence, is underreported in modern societies and was probably more so in traditional Europe as a result of the patriarchal values, and especially if alcohol had befuddled the victim's brain. The cases of Dorothy Hayter and Martha Vose probably represent only a small portion of the total.

Another case of rape was the result of festive celebrations. As part of the festivities marking the Feast of the Holy Sacrament in 1393, members of a confraternity gathered at the home of a priest in Houville and made "great cheer." The celebrations ended on a less cheerful note when one of the members became drunk and raped the priest's sister. As illustrated by the rape, much of the violence that resulted from festive celebrations was committed by a drunken individual rather than by a group of drunken revelers. In a case remarkably similar to the confraternal celebrations of the Feast of the Holy Sacrament, Jehan Ragnault joined other members of a confraternity to celebrate a feast day in the rectory of the parish of Pont-Farcy in Normandy. As was customary for the occasion, those gathered "made very good cheer" with

[48] Capp, "Double Standard," 94.

[49] Quaife, *Wanton Wenches*, 65–66.

[50] *Portsmouth Record Series,* comp. Willis and ed. Hoad, 4.

[51] Meldrum, "London Domestic Servants," 54.

the wine and some, including Ragnault, drank more than reasonable and became dizzy. In 1427 Ragnault received a royal letter of remission for killing a priest on the occasion. Much more festive in its atmosphere than the rape of a priest's sister and the murder of a priest was the case involving a group of merry companions celebrating Carnival at Saint-Sever, near Caen, with a late supper of wine and cheese. They all began throwing pieces of cheese at each other, except a monk who objected to the high-spirited antics of the others, so they asked him to leave; he drew his sword and was killed in the ensuing fight.[52]

Festive celebrations often featured ritualized communal violence, which has attracted much attention from anthropologists and historians, who have variously interpreted the phenomenon as a safety valve, as a cohesive force, as an expression of communal solidarity, and/or as a world turned upside down, that is, an inversion of the social order. However, festive drinking occasionally produced incidents of actual, as opposed to ritualized, violent behavior that do not neatly fit these interpretations.[53] Some festive occasions had a tradition of violent disorder; the custom on All Saints' Day in Florence was to drink new wine from the autumn's vintage, and also according to custom the drinking led to disturbances of the public order.[54] Another festival that had a history of drunken violent conduct was the *fête de l'epinette* on Saint Michael's Day in the village of Somain, where brawls and murders occurred in 1531.[55] Other drunken brawls occurred when festive customs were breached, as happened at a wedding in the village of Pargny-les-Reims in 1428; when a group of young drunken revelers asked for the two pots of wine that, according to tradition, they should receive for accompanying the newlyweds to their quarters, they started a fight when they did not get any.[56] Another breach of custom was to refuse to drink on festive occasions, as Jean le Prévost did on the feast day of the *bailliage* of Caux in 1400 because it was late and he did not want to return home alone at night; his refusal so enraged another drinker that he threw a torch at his legs and shouted, "You will die tonight!"[57]

Some of the violence had no connection to customs or traditions and appeared to be opportunistic, spur of the moment, just for the hell of it.

[52] Vaultier, *Folklore pendant la Guerre*, 51, 172–73.

[53] Ruff, *Violence in Early Modern Europe*, 178.

[54] Balestracci, "Consumo del vino," 25–26.

[55] Muchembled, *Popular Culture*, 98–99.

[56] Vaultier, *Folklore pendant la Guerre*, 22.

[57] Gauvard, "*De Grace Especial*," 449.

For example, a group celebrating the Christmas season at Frome in 1657 by "drinking, playing cards, and fiddling all day in disguised habits" beat up a man who reported the attack to the authorities.[58] In 1335 students at the university in Toulouse celebrated Easter by drinking and then disturbed Easter services by beating pots and pans; when a magistrate attempted to arrest the ringleader another student pulled out a dagger and cut off his nose, lips, and part of his chin.[59]

One frequent form of festive violence involved attacks on the "other." On the first day of March in 1662, the Dutch artist William Schellinks observed the St. David's Day celebrations in London. The Welsh celebrated the day of their patron saint by wearing leeks in their hats, a custom mimicked by the English. "With heavy boozing," wrote Schellinks, "both sides, from the ale, strong beer, sack and claret, become short-tempered, obstinate, and wild, so it is not often that this day goes by without mishaps, and without one or the other getting into an argument or a blood fight." Schellinks continued by describing a wild brawl that erupted when an English cook insulted a Welsh lord and his servants.[60] When the inhabitants of Rocquigny were celebrating the Feast of the Assumption at a tavern, one of them idly stated the inhabitants of the neighboring village of Mainbressy were ready to quarrel with those of Rocquigny; the statement provoked the drinkers to attack Mainbressy.[61]

In France the village youth usually took the lead in festive brawls with neighboring villages and parishes. To return to the anthropological interpretations of ritualized communal violence, these incidents of actual communal violence could function as a cohesive force and promote communal solidarity. On occasion, specific incidents precipitated the brawls, as occurred in 1396 at a wedding banquet in Hondevilliers attended by a young man from the neighboring village of Verdelot. When the young man broke a glass, the locals armed themselves with clubs and not only sought retribution from his village but also from all the other neighboring villages, and in the ensuing battle one was killed.[62] In 1537 a woman from La Gorgue (Lalleu) married a man from the neighboring parish of Lestrem. Such a marriage always had the potential to make the youth of the village that had lost a marriageable woman resentful of the successful suitor and his village, and the large amount of

---

[58] Hutton, *Stations of the Sun*, 21.

[59] Lacroix, *France in the Middle Ages*, 37–38.

[60] Schellinks, *Journal of William Schellinks*, trans. and ed. Exwood and Lehmann, 75.

[61] Gauvard, "De Grace Especial," 518. For another example, see Quaife, *Wanton Wenches*, 25.

[62] Gauvard, "De Grace Especial," 515–16.

drinking that followed the wedding fueled the resentment. When a quarrel broke out between the two groups, the youth from La Gorgue attacked with pikes, whereupon some of the wounded youth from Lestrem took refuge in the house of the newlyweds, but their pursuers threw pikes and spears at them. One died immediately and another two weeks later.[63] Some brawls between villages on festive occasions required no precipitating incidents but were as traditional as the festivals themselves. A custom among the youth of Billy in the late fifteenth century was to spend the night before May Day drinking and collecting "the May" along the river, while a custom for the youth of nearby La Roche de Chizay was to prevent them from doing so. In 1491 a confrontation occurred resulting in several mortal blows, "without anyone knowing who or how, because of the night and the drink."[64]

Authorities in Valenciennes outlawed a festival in 1547 because women with "wine in the head" had started quarrels that turned into riots.[65] Such local riots had the potential to erupt into more widespread and longer-lasting rebellions and revolts. According to the French historian of revolts and revolution, Yves-Marie Bercé, drunkenness characterized the festive element present in many popular revolts.[66] Nonetheless, contemporary accounts of riots, rebellions, and revolts only occasionally claimed drunken mobs precipitated the violence. In the 1660s riots against the inspectors of wine duties developed among drinkers in taverns at Nantes, often with the connivance of the keepers, and in 1669 a large crowd killed an inspector when he was investigating the wine duties of a tavern.[67] The accounts of drink in popular riots and rebellions in England provide comic relief rather than violent tragedy. According to a sixteen-year-old lad arrested in 1536 during the Pilgrimage of Grace, his role in it had been a drunken teenage prank.[68] After government forces put down Kett's Rebellion in 1549, one of the leaders of the rebellion sued for the return of the hops he had given to a brewer to make beer for the rebels from Melton.[69] During the Midland Revolt of 1607, rioters in Blunham, Bedfordshire, marched behind a

---

[63] Muchembled, "Jeunes, les jeux," 568.

[64] Pellegrin, *Bachelleries*, 155. For another example, see Hoffman, *Church and Community*, 218–19n8.

[65] Bercé, *Fête et révolte*, 34–35.

[66] Bercé, *Revolt and Revolution*, 116.

[67] Collins, *Classes, Estates*, 101, 256.

[68] Davies, "Popular Religion," 66.

[69] MacCulloch, "Kett's Rebellion," 49.

drunken peddler, while the real leader marched alongside the others.[70] The evidence indicates drunken revelers were involved in the Fleet Street Riots in London in 1628 because a constable tried to rescue a drunken offender being led to prison by other officers.[71] All of this, to say the least, is petty stuff. More serious were the occasions when drunken soldiers or sailors mutinied, as they did before the Battle of Falkirk in 1298.[72]

Many of the violent political disputes between the Whigs and Tories in England during the early 1680s took place in or around taverns. In April 1682 a group of Whigs confronted a group of their opponents drinking at the Queen's Head Tavern, and in the following month the Tories attacked the Whigs at the King's Head Tavern.[73] Similarly, in the following year a tavern brawl between Whigs and Tories at Oxford turned into a large riot between townsmen and students.[74] Another violent confrontation had occurred in London during the celebrations marking Gunpowder Treason Day in November 1682, but rather than drink being a possible cause it was a consequence. Young Whig apprentices fought off groups of Tories intent on dousing the bonfires lit for the occasion, marched through the streets breaking the windows of their opponents and beating any Tory who got in their way, made a huge bonfire of the household effects of one opponent, and drank toasts to the destruction of their enemies with drinks provided by supporters. When the authorities finally attempted to move against them, they met with drunken defiance, but the important point to note is the drunkenness was the result of the victory over their opponents and not the cause of the violence.[75]

Alcohol's role in other riots, rebellions, and revolutions was more consequence than cause, and in this sense the evidence supports Yves-Marie Bercé's statement that drunkenness characterized the festive element present in many popular revolts. During the Peasants' Revolt of 1381, a group of rebels attacked a manor in Essex; on finding it well stocked with wine they drank three casks and then proceeded to destroy the manor, and when another group captured a manor in Kent, they drank as much wine as they could, poured the rest on the floor, and ransacked the place to shouts of "A

---

[70] Manning, *Village Revolts*, 83.

[71] Lindley, "Riot Prevention," 118–19.

[72] Prestwich, *Armies and Warfare*, 247. See also Higgs, "Research into the History."

[73] Harris, *London Crowds*, 179–80.

[74] Crossley, "City and University," 118.

[75] Cressy, *Bonfires and Bells*, 183.

revel! A revel!"[76] In London, the destruction continued as the rebels targeted the houses of hated officials, but after drinking the wine from the cellar of the bishop of Chester they left without causing further damage, while on another occasion after they had drunk, in the words of the hostile chronicler, "various wines and expensive drinks at will and so had become less drunk than mad," they set out to destroy the residence of the Duke of Lancaster.[77] Wine had a similar celebratory function for those involved in the many riots and rebellions that plagued authorities in seventeenth-century France. Winemakers led the great revolt of Lanturelu at Dijon in 1630 against new tax policies; they attacked the mansion of a royal official, made a bonfire of its furnishings, and consumed the wine from its cellar.[78] Similar revolts against taxes occurred at Bordeaux and Périgueux in 1635 and at Rouen in 1639, likewise accompanied by festive drinking in the streets.[79] A grain riot at Vannes, Brittany, in 1643 followed a similar pattern; the unruly crowd sacked the house of a merchant considered responsible for the shortage of grain and became drunk on the wine it found there. The rioters nonetheless demanded the authorities bring them more wine and threatened to "burn and pillage everything."[80] In short, when drinking accompanied riots, revolts, and rebellions, it did so more as a means of festive jollification and celebration than as a cause of violent destruction—more revel than rampage.

Drinking Establishments and Honor: The Devil's Knife

The tavern was called "the devil's knife" in thirteenth-century England. However, the very small number of murders that took place in taverns then indicates the epithet was not entirely appropriate. A better candidate for "the devil's knife" is honor because of its important role in causing much of the violence that occurred in drinking establishments as well as some of the drunken violence that occurred outside them. Honor was a factor in much of the violence discussed above, as drunken husbands reacted to challenges to their authority, and village youths fought to demonstrate their superiority over the youths from neighboring villages. The public space of drinking establishments made them ideal venues in which to impugn an opponent's

---

[76] Dobson, *Peasants' Revolt*, 125; and *Westminster Chronicle*, ed. and trans. Hector and Harvey, 3.

[77] Dobson, *Peasants' Revolt*, 157, 169.

[78] Farr, *Hands of Honor*, 203; and Holt, "Wine, Life," 94.

[79] Bercé, *Fête et révolte*, 87.

[80] Beik, *Urban Protest*, 52–53.

honor, as illustrated by the criminal charges laid by Mathieu Robert against a man who insulted and slapped him at a cabaret: "that which aggravates this action, which is as contemptible as it is reprehensible, is the publicity; it was in a cabaret that the blows were struck."[81] When the insults and slaps occurred to someone who preferred immediate retribution rather than relying on legal processes, the violence could escalate. According to Richard Gough's *History of Myddle*, Richard Evans was one who preferred immediate retribution; he was "too much given to drinking, and being a stout man of his hands, he would not take an affront, especially when he was in drink, which caused him to be engaged in many frivolous affrays and quarrels in which he commonly had the better."[82]

Sometimes neither side was willing to back down, as witnessed by Samuel Pepys at Covent Gardens in 1667. Two of his friends, Henry Belasyse and Tom Parker, were drinking together in a tavern, when someone asked them if they were quarreling. Belasyse responded, "No ... I never quarrel but I strike." Parker replied he would like to see anyone in England dare to strike him, so Belasyse hit him, an action that resulted in a duel.[83] Many of these violent confrontations were the result of spontaneous actions and statements without forethought, but on occasion the insults were nourished by ancient hatreds, feuds, and debts, particularly among the old.[84] A sixty-year-old man from Saint-Crépin-aux-Bois exchanged bitter comments with an old enemy at a tavern in 1388; the old man followed him from the tavern and killed him.[85]

The typical pattern was an exchange of insults in a drinking establishment leading to an exchange of blows, such as occurred at La Baldacca in Florence in 1431 between Marco di Giovanni from Piacenza and a certain Besso. If one of the belligerents was armed, death or serious injury could result; in 1427 a man from Prato mocked a German weaver at the tavern of Vinegia in Florence and wounded him with a knife.[86] On many occasions, the issues leading to confrontations would be laughable were it not for their tragic consequences. A group of Venetian workers spent an evening drinking in 1394 and became involved in an argument over who was the drunkest

[81] Ruff, *Crime, Justice*, 81.

[82] Gough, *History of Myddle*, ed. Hey, 286.

[83] Shoemaker, "Male Honour," 195.

[84] Shoemaker, "Male Honour," 198; and Knafla, *Kent at Law*, 21.

[85] Gauvard, "*De Grace Especial*," 372.

[86] Mazzi, *Prostitute e lenoni*, 270n.

and who had drunk the most—result: one dead drunkard.[87] On Christmas Eve in 1409 the members of a confraternity gathered at a tavern in Tournai became involved in a heated discussion on the suitability of a candidate for membership—result: one dead member.[88] Finally, two fiddlers playing at a tavern in Paris in 1691 attracted the neighbors, including wives and children, so that everyone in the tavern was dancing, but the drinkers who paid for the music objected—result: a brawl.[89] These and many of the following incidents might seem foolish, senseless acts, but the healing of wounded pride, the prevention of public humiliation, the preservation of rights, and the defense of space were integral to everyone's sense of honor.

Nicholas Holmes became involved in a quarrel with William Jackson at an alehouse in Leeds in 1642. The keeper noticed Holmes was drunk and asked him to go home; as he left, Jackson stopped him, saying, "If you will not come in and drink a cup I will not be friends to you," so Holmes returned. The keeper later heard the fall of a bench and discovered Jackson had fatally wounded Holmes with a dagger.[90] Holmes had complied with the social convention of accepting a drink; to refuse to do so was an insult that could lead to violence. More likely than Holmes's unfortunate death was the incident that occurred in the small village of Thillois near Reims. In 1380 two men were drinking at a tavern before going to work in the vineyards. They returned to the tavern about midday and asked a friend to join them for a drink, but he refused since he had been drinking all day. Insulted by his refusal, the two men chased him down and beat him with a spade.[91] Just as bad a breach of social convention as refusing a drink was failing to pay for a drink. A group of young men played a game of tennis for drinks at Chevannes (Sens) in 1406; when the loser refused to pay for the drinks, his companions beat him.[92] Another brawl occurred when a latecomer objected to the arrangement for the payment of drinks at a tavern because it favored those who had arrived first.[93]

Some of the insults that resulted in violence were simple name-calling. In 1301 a drunken Alice Quernbetere started a brawl that resulted in the

[87] Ruggiero, *Violence in Early Renaissance Venice,* 179.

[88] Gauvard, "*De Grace Especial,*" 259n55.

[89] Brennan, *Public Drinking,* 262.

[90] Amussen, "Gendering of Popular Culture," 63–64.

[91] Gauvard, "*De Grace Especial,*" 266.

[92] Gauvard, "*De Grace Especial,*" 286.

[93] Gauvard, "*De Grace Especial,*" 714.

death of one man when she called two workmen "tredekeiles," meaning they had sex with chickens.[94] When Joan Williamson called Ellen Peake "a whore" and "my husband's whore" at an alehouse in Cheshire in 1667, Ellen slapped her, Joan retaliated, Ellen's daughter came to her assistance, and Joan fought them both until two men managed to separate them.[95] Scatological insults might not require any words at all; knives were drawn at a tavern in Laon (Vermandois) in 1400 after a drinker objected to the farting and burping of a companion.[96] Rather than object to such behavior, it was safer to remain quiet; in seventeenth-century Somerset, a man who complained about the language used by a group of drinkers was beaten, stabbed, and nearly killed.[97]

Ties of kinship and friendship contributed to the violence, especially since the public arena of an alehouse or a tavern could publicize the vengeance expected in family feuds. When Hennequin Have came to the aid of a cousin in a fight, he received serious wounds on his arm, side, and thigh from Jaquot Tavier. Have and his cousins later gained their revenge when they cornered Tavier at a tavern in 1385.[98] Guillebert Motte brutally killed Martin Marlière at a tavern in 1508 because Marlière had a short time earlier mortally wounded his wife's cousin.[99] Other violent incidents in defense of kin or friends were spontaneous acts rather than the calculated revenge that operated in those cases. On an evening in April 1412 near Lyon, a young man came to the tavern to ask his father to come home only to see him knocked to the floor with a punch; the son seized a large rock and broke the assailant's skull.[100] Bernard Yvain was drinking with some young people at a tavern in Floringhem in 1575; when one of them fell asleep, Yvain poured a glass of beer on his head. A friend of the sleeper asked Yvain why he had done that; he responded at first it was a joke but then so as not to lose face added, "Do you want to talk about it?" The exchange of words became heated and ended in a duel in the village square, where Yvain died from a wound in the stomach.[101]

Rivalry, rather than ties of kinship and friendship, was responsible for some of the violence. In 1611 William Maphew took a new pair of boots to an

[94] Getz, *Medicine in the English Middle Ages*, 73.
[95] Walker, "Expanding the Boundaries," 237.
[96] Gauvard, *"De Grace Especial,"* 724n68.
[97] Quaife, *Wanton Wenches*, 25.
[98] Gauvard, *"De Grace Especial,"* 773–74.
[99] Mehl, *Jeux au royaume*, 306.
[100] Lorcin, "Paysans et la justice," 294.
[101] Muchembled, "Jeunes, les jeux," 567.

alehouse to show to his fellow shoemakers, but one of them, John Humbletoft, made fun of them, stating he "would be ashamed to bring up such fashions," and derisively threw one on the ground. Maphew returned like with like and apparently got the better of the verbal battle because a frustrated Humbletoft "gave him a box on the ear with his hand," which started the physical battle.[102] Roof makers competing for work became involved in a vicious assault at a cabaret in Paris in 1691. Two of them were jealous of the work secured by one Delaville on the Invalides, but the confrontation began with one offering him a glass of wine. Quickly following this act of friendship were first abusive insults directed at Delaville and his "bugger of a master" and then such a ferocious beating that Delaville could not work for three weeks.[103]

In one of the ballads celebrating the deeds of Robin Hood, three of King Henry's foresters challenged Robin and his merry men to a fight in Sherwood Forest. The foresters gained the upper hand, so Robin called a halt to the fight and challenged them to a drinking contest:

> Come and go with me to Nottingham,
> And there we will fight it out.
> With a butt of sack we will bang it out,
> To see who wins the day.[104]

The ballad inverted the normal sequence; usually contests, games, and gambling led to violence. Such was the sequence at widow Cooke's alehouse in Over in 1676. Jonathon Robinson challenged Abraham Smith to drink a quart or flagon of ale. Smith, who was already "full of ale," could not manage it, and in the resulting quarrel Smith grabbed Robinson's hat and "turned it round his head and with his fist gave him a blow on the ears."[105] Challenges to drink "whole pots" could frequently result in brawls among young men, as the winners, losers, and those who refused to participate competed for manhood.[106]

Gambling could also provoke much violence as the public loss of face combined with the private shame of defeat, and as the possibility of winning heightened the competitive atmosphere. One of the earliest recorded cases

---

[102] Shepard, "Manhood, Credit," 104.

[103] Brennan, *Public Drinking*, 58.

[104] *Robin Hood's Delight*, quoted in Holt, *Robin Hood*, 167.

[105] Addy, *Sin and Society*, 32.

[106] Shepard, *Meanings of Manhood*, 105.

resulted in the death of Agnes, wife of Robert, after a quarrel erupted while she was drinking and gaming with other men and women in London in 1276.[107] William Neald of Tarvin was fortunate to escape with a punch after he provoked two other card players at an alehouse in 1680—lucky because a dispute during a game of shovelboard between two men at an alehouse in Hertfordshire resulted in the death of one.[108] Breaches of rules could be precipitating factors in the violence. In 1642 a group of bakers at Dijon drained a jug of wine before a game of ninepins, but the convivial atmosphere quickly ended when one of the players stepped over the line; in the ensuing quarrel one of them received a cracked skull with one of the balls.[109] Another breach of the rules was to win too much—so much that others assume the winner had been cheating—as discovered by the Florentine Buonaccorso Pitti when he played dice in Paris in 1395 with a group of French lords. A viscount who "had drunk a lot of wine" called Pitti "a damned cheat" after he had won twelve games in a row and after the thirteenth, grabbed his hat and tried to hit him.[110]

An especially dangerous thing for gamblers to do was to leave with the winnings before giving fellow players a chance to regain their losses, and some successful gamblers met their deaths on the streets after leaving the tavern or the alehouse.[111] Pierre Martin, a Norman who had sworn not to gamble, was nonetheless persuaded to play dice at a tavern in 1381. When he won and started to leave, his fellow player refused to let him go.[112] Violence could result even when the contestants were playing for a convivial round of drinks. In 1380 after a quiet evening of drinking wine in a tavern at Thin-le-Moutier (Vermandois), the arrival of the bill led one drinker to propose to his two companions they play dice to determine who paid the bill. When the two companions lost, they felt they had been hustled, so on the way home they started a quarrel that resulted in the death of the winner.[113] A similar incident occurred in Dijon in 1556: when three men played tennis to determine who paid for the wine, they afterwards fought each other with stones and knives.[114] Just as a loss of face could result from losing a game, so could

[107] Carter, *Medieval Games*, 84.

[108] Curtis, "Quarter Sessions Appearances," 136; and Clark, *English Alehouse*, 147.

[109] Farr, *Hands of Honor*, 173.

[110] Pitti and Dati, *Two Memoirs*, trans. Martines and ed. Brucker, 51–52.

[111] Hanawalt, *Of Good and Ill Repute*, 112.

[112] Mehl, *Jeux au royaume*, 280. For another example see Fairchilds, *Poverty and Charity*, 125.

[113] Gauvard, "De Grace Especial," 294.

[114] Farr, *Hands of Honor*, 173.

it result when a person was not permitted to play. A schoolmaster discovered a game of dice in progress when he entered a tavern in Orléans in 1388 and asked if he could join, but the players were unanimous in their opposition under the pretext that a game of dice was not an appropriate game for a schoolmaster. The refusal and the pretext so infuriated him that he started a fight that cost him his life.[115]

William Hornby's poem entitled "The Scourge of Drunkenness" (1614?) warned gentlemen of the dangers of mingling with the poor in alehouses:

> There every upstart, base-conditioned slave,
>
> If that he have but money in his bag,
>
> A gentleman unto his teeth will brave.[116]

Nonetheless, the sources contain only a few incidents of the poor attacking their superiors in alehouses and taverns. Cited above is the brawl that started when two tinkers objected to the preferential treatment of two gentlemen at an alehouse, but one of the gentlemen precipitated the violence. At a Cheshire tavern in 1665, Jack Hunt insulted a gentleman, calling him thief, and then assaulted him so vehemently that it required the female keeper, Hunt's own wife, and the other drinkers to restrain him.[117] A possible case of class antagonism occurred in the Venetian suburb of Murano in 1415, when six young noblemen from important Venetian families were drinking with prostitutes at the tavern of San Matteo late at night and fought with the night watch who had come to arrest them, with members of the night watch perhaps relishing the opportunity to thump nobles, who in turn might have warmed to the prospect of stabbing a Muranese.[118]

Another case might reveal either class rivalry or antagonism towards the "other." On the evening of 1 September 1654, the notary Hugues Navarre brutally attacked Jean Tourdes in the countryside near Aurillac, a beating so severe that Tourdes had to be carried home by his father, probably a prosperous peasant, and could not speak for ten days. He then made a submission under oath that Navarre had abused him, swore at him, and threatened to kill him when they ate together at a tavern in Aurillac. Navarre told a different story: When he had stopped at the tavern Tourdes was drunk and

---

[115] Mehl, *Jeux au royaume*, 212.

[116] Leinwand, "Spongy Plebs," 162.

[117] Walker, *Crime, Gender*, 41.

[118] Crouzet-Pavan, *Sopra le acque salse*, 703–4. See also Neveux, "Déclin et reprise," 157.

began insulting him by attacking his profession, shouting "that all notaries were forgers and that they were worthless." Navarre responded by comparing Tourdes to a well-known drunkard.[119] An obvious example of a confrontation between two contrasting vocations involved a resident and a soldier at Meltham, Yorkshire, in 1648. John Oldfield resented the presence of soldiers in the community since the residents had to house and maintain them, so when he encountered the soldier John Probart in an alehouse, he called him a rogue and a rascal. He nonetheless asked Probart to drink with him, but compounded the insults by then refusing to give him anything to drink. They began fighting, and Probart killed him with his sword.[120]

The Dangers of Keeping

Keeping an alehouse or a tavern was a dangerous occupation; many keepers as well as their staff became involved in the violence that occurred in their establishments, and some lost their lives in consequence. To a certain extent this was a result of the keeper's own actions or language; as discussed in chapter 5, the keepers of some disorderly places had their own notorious reputations for disorder. However, most of the violent episodes involving keepers were the result of the actions and language of the customers, with some keepers losing their lives when they attempted to act as peacemakers. The keeper was, after all, the paterfamilias of the establishment, which often was also his home and used the labor of his wife and children. Just as husbands enjoyed patriarchal authority over their households, so did a keeper over his drinking establishment, and customers generally recognized it. Perhaps the best illustration of this occurred at an alehouse in Whitechapel in 1698. The keeper, John Ballard, heard four customers in a heated argument agree to fight the next morning; he immediately expelled two of them and prevented the other two from leaving for three quarters of an hour in an attempt to cool their anger.[121]

Most of the violence involving keepers demonstrated the same characteristics of the violence discussed above—the same inexplicable causes, the same festive outbursts, the same preoccupation with honor, and the same aggression towards "the other." Just as violence could occur when someone

[119] Greenshields, *Economy of Violence*, 80–83.
[120] Amussen, "Punishment, Discipline," 25.
[121] Shoemaker, "Male Honour," 201.

was refused a drink at, for example, a wedding, a keeper's refusal to serve a customer could also produce a violent confrontation. After dinner a group of drunken gentlemen led by a drummer went noisily through the streets of Limerzel in 1551 and spent the night laying siege to a tavern whose keeper refused to serve such "debauched rogues, thieves, and brigands." They finally gained access through a window, but one was killed in the process.[122] Christmas Eve celebrations in 1638 at an alehouse in Norfolk came to an end with the refusal to sell any more ale to a group of people including William Metcalf and his wife. Mrs. Metcalf hit the keeper's wife and broke a jug on his son's head, and the following all-in brawl included both Metcalfs and the keeper's entire household.[123]

On occasion violence resulted from disputes over the bill, but whether this was a result of the keeper's chicanery or the customer's niggardliness is difficult to say. According to the account by Matthew of Paris around 1230, students at the University of Paris balked at the size of the bill for sweet wine at a tavern. The students' objections resulted in "the pulling of ears and the tearing of hair," so the keeper sought reinforcements from his neighbors, who gave the students a good beating and drove them out. The students returned the next day with their own reinforcements, armed with sticks and swords, gained revenge for their beating, and celebrated their victory by drinking more wine and letting the rest run onto the floor.[124] When Anne Guion asked Bernard de Conquans to pay his account, he went berserk, called her a whore and an impudent slut, threatened to kill her, and left the inn only when other drinkers intervened. Once outside he continued to shout insults, drew his sword, and attempted to reenter, only to face the intervention of the others once again, so he turned his attention and his sword to one of the inn's servants and cut her so severely that she was left a cripple.[125]

Keepers of drinking establishments were just as likely as their contemporaries to react to insults, and they had their own honor to protect with force if necessary. On 10 February 1355 the St. Scholastica's Day riot erupted at Oxford after a dispute between the keeper of Swyndlestock Tavern and some clerks from the university. The clerks complained about the quality of

---

[122] Vaissière, *Gentilshommes campagnards,* 129–30. For another example, see Gauvard, *"De Grace Especial,"* 644.

[123] Amussen, "Gendering of Popular Culture," 64. This incident is also discussed in Amussen, "Punishment, Discipline," 24, with slightly different details.

[124] Daly, *Medieval University,* 191–92.

[125] Greenshields, *Economy of Violence,* 83. For another example, see Emmison, *Elizabethan Life,* 150.

the wine served to them, which led to a verbal confrontation and an exchange of insults. This led in turn to the clerks throwing the wine and its vessel at the keeper's head. The keeper withdrew, but his family and neighbors told him not to endure such abuse and promised their support. The result was a battle between town and gown that resulted in the townspeople sacking five student hostels and killing about forty students.[126] For many of the violent incidents, the finger of blame points at the keepers or at their staff, although the evidence sometimes prevents a clear conclusion. Thibaut Berart, a tavern keeper in Sens, became involved in 1391 in a nasty dispute with Robin Blondeau, who sought to protect himself from future attacks by obtaining an *asseurement,* a legal document comparable to the modern restraining order. Nonetheless, when Blondeau visited Berart's tavern on Christmas Eve to play dice with friends, Berart reignited the dispute and tried to evict him from the tavern, without success.[127] For other incidents, the keepers and their staffs appear to be the injured parties. In 1260 a married couple attacked a woman named Guirauda who sold wine at her uncle's tavern in Manosque, north of Marseille, with the wife slapping her face and the husband calling her a whore.[128] A Somerset alehouse was the scene for a confrontation between a gang of drunkards and the keeper's family in the 1660s; when they attacked, the wife and son protected the property by arming themselves with a pike and standing at the top of the stairs.[129]

The peacekeeping attempts by keepers could result in customers involved in disputes redirecting their blows to the keeper, as occurred at an alehouse in Pleshey in 1583. The keeper, John Wilkinson, intervened after Nicholas Eve accused a customer of theft. "Thou dost misuse my guests," said the keeper. Eve reacted by striking Wilkinson.[130] The keepers' wives could also be victims of the violence; the men fighting in William Hawarden's tavern in Chester in 1393 damaged the furnishings and assaulted his wife, and in 1680 the wife of a keeper was knocked "several times upon the stones" by William Littler of Budworth, whom she had told to leave for quarreling with

---

[126] King, *Beer Has a History,* 26.

[127] Cohen, "Violence Control," 111. See also *Portsmouth Record Series,* comp. Willis and ed. Hoad, 94–95; Thompson, *Wives, Widows,* 57; and Shoemaker, "Male Honour," 198.

[128] Gosselin, "Honneur et violence," 46.

[129] Clark, *English Alehouse,* 207. See also Hanawalt, *Growing up in Medieval London,* 77–78; and *Portsmouth Record Series,* comp. Willis and ed. Hoad, 122.

[130] Emmison, *Elizabethan Life,* 174.

the other customers.[131] Many of these peacekeeping efforts resulted in the death of either a customer or the keeper. At a cabaret in Saint-Hilaire near Cambrai in 1536, Jean Lempereur grabbed a customer's hat. When the customer reacted by reaching for his sword, Lempereur struck him so hard with his staff that he had to be taken to another room to recover. Not satisfied with this, Lempereur tried to force the door, but the keeper intervened and drew his sword, only to receive a blow that knocked him down. At this juncture, the keeper's brother-in-law came to his rescue by hitting Lempereur in the eye with a pike, a wound that resulted in his death five or six hours later.[132] On the feast day of St. Mary Magdalen in 1626 at a cabaret in La Peyrousse (Haute Auvergne), two men continued to play cards into the night long after the keeper and his household had gone to bed. The keeper's wife woke up at midnight to the sound of the two men fighting; she shouted at her husband to wake up and stop the fight. When he stepped between the two combatants, he was struck by a sword and subsequently died.[133] The ballad entitled *The Industrious Smith* (1635) told the story of a poor smith who decided to improve his situation by having his wife keep an alehouse. Things went from bad to worse as he first found his wife flirting with customers and then in bed with one. Her reply on each occasion was, "These things must be if we sell ale."[134] So it was with alehouse keepers, as they had to cope with customers who on occasion fought with each other and with their host. One unfortunate female keeper even faced charges of keeping a disorderly house as a result of a customer striking her twice with a pair of tongs when disputing a bill.[135]

To end with a happy outcome, in 1637 at an alehouse in Dorchester, Thomas Pouncey insulted Richard Paty, so they went outside for a fistfight before returning to the alehouse "all bloody with fighting" to drink together.[136] In assessing the blame for all the violence documented in this chapter, three "culprits" stand out—alcohol, the drinking establishment, and honor. All three were present in the bloody fistfight with the happy outcome, but in this

[131] Laughton, "Alewives of Later Medieval Chester," 146.

[132] Neveux, "Déclin et reprise," 156.

[133] Greenshields, *Economy of Violence*, 83–85.

[134] Farmer, *Merry Songs*, 3:45–50.

[135] Walker, *Crime, Gender*, 81.

[136] Foyster, *Manhood in Early Modern England*, 179.

case the violence was limited, and alcohol's role in promoting jollification and camaraderie made a belated appearance. Drunkenness was a factor in many of the incidents that had a more tragic outcome, as many of the perpetrators and/or their victims had consumed too much wine or ale, as did George Hilton, quoted above, who blamed immoderate drinking for his loss of reason and for provoking his passion. Precision in determining how many incidents resulted from drinking is impossible. Drunkenness in the absence of scientific measurements is often in the eye of the beholder, while those who drank themselves into a stupor were by and large incapable of perpetrating violence and were only victims. Since much of the violence occurred in drinking establishments, a safe assumption is many of those involved in fighting were at least doing some drinking even if they were not completely drunk. Nonetheless, some men became violent immediately on entering an alehouse or a tavern, as if the violence was preplanned or the sight of an enemy was too great a provocation. To return to the *asseurement* obtained by Robin Blondeau against Thibaut Berart, some of these legal documents prohibited a person from going into a tavern if his enemy was present.[137] This was an excellent precaution, and had it become a widespread practice, many brawls would have been avoided and many lives would have been saved.

The drinking establishments could not, however, be separated from alcohol. The reverse is true; alcohol could be separated from drinking establishments during festive celebrations such as church ales, whose purpose was to raise funds by selling ale, the more ale sold the better. Moralists condemned church ales for their disorder and violence, but Thomas G. Barnes's examination of church ales in Somerset presents a different picture: "After consulting every information and examination involving crime sent to Somerset quarter sessions for trial, 1625–1640, I have found only one church ale disturbance among them.... These documents are complete for the period." Barnes admits the records for cases of murder and manslaughter do not exist, but the extant records would include cases of fights, brawls, and riots.[138] In other words, at least in the case of church ales, drinking was not a cause of disturbances when it occurred outside a drinking establishment. A more dangerous mix than alcohol and drinking establishments was the mix of honor and the drinking establishments. Exacerbating this volatile mixture was the competitive nature of contemporary notions of manhood that could prevent

---

[137] Hanlon, "Rituels de l'agression," 257.
[138] Barnes, "County Politics," 107n2.

compromise and conciliation. Nonetheless, the violent defense of honor was not just a masculine preoccupation, because women also reacted violently if their honor was besmirched in the public space of the alehouse. In the final analysis, the role of alcohol in jollification, celebration, and socialization leads to the conclusion that violence occurred despite the drinking.

Chapter 8

Regulations

He is a glutton and a drunkard. Then all the men of the city shall stone him to death.

—Deuteronomy 21:20–21

No, authorities did not condone capital punishment for drunkards in traditional Europe, even though many moralists believed drunkards deserved more punishment than governments were willing to dispense. On the other hand, authorities did attempt to regulate drinking and drinking establishments, but the nature of the regulations and their lack of severity provide support for the argument of the previous three chapters that the role of alcohol in causing violence and disorder was at best ambivalent. Given all governments' concerns with the preservation of order, and given the condemnations of the moralists, a harsh regimen of restrictions would seem likely; their leniency indicates that officials appreciated the role of alcoholic beverages in providing sustenance and as social lubricant. Government regulation has a long history dating back to ancient times; the first written code of laws, the Babylonian Code of Hammurabi (died ca. 1750 BCE), included regulations on the clientele of taverns and provisions to protect the consumer. An extreme form of regulation has been prohibition, inevitably a failure, while the various components of many regulatory regimes, including taxation, licenses for production and distribution, consumer protection, restrictions on hours of sale, age, and gender, and locations and types of vendors, have been complex to say the least, controlling who drank, how much, when, and where. Adding to the complexity were the often-conflicting purposes of the regulations, with fiscal interests of governments competing with their concerns for public order.[1] Not only is the topic of regulations complex, it also requires delving into political, institutional, and legal history. Fortunately, the tangled history of English regulations of drinking and drinking establishments has been the subject of several studies, so this discussion can utilize them as well as dispense with repeating some of the material in them.[2]

Many moralists favored not only heavy punishments for drunkards but also increased government intervention against drinking and drinking establishments. A rather sobering indication of their program was the introduction of fifty-one bills to the English Parliament between 1576 and 1628 dealing with drunkenness, alehouses, taverns, vintners, and brewers, including the following:

1584: Against excessive and common drunkenness.

1601: Against excessive and common drunkenness.

1601: Against drunkards and common haunters of alehouses and taverns.

1604: Against haunting of alehouses.

1604: To restrain the inordinate haunting and tippling in inns, alehouses, and other victualling houses.

1606: Against the loathsome sin of drunkenness.

1606–1607: For repressing the odious and loathsome sin of drunkenness.

1614: For repressing the odious and loathsome sin of drunkenness and for repressing the consuming of corn.

1621: For repressing the odious and loathsome sin of drunkenness and for preventing the inordinate consuming of corn.

1621: For better repressing drunkenness and restraining the inordinate haunting of inns, alehouses, and other victualling houses.

1624: For repressing drunkenness and restraining the inordinate haunting of inns and alehouses.[3]

---

[1] Heath and Rosovsky, "Community Reactions," 205–18; and Baird, "Alcohol Problem and the Law: I," 535.

[2] Iles, "Early Stages"; Bretherton, "Country Inns"; Hudson, *Study of Social Regulations*; Baird, "Alcohol Problem and the Law: I"; Baird, "Alcohol Problem and the Law: II"; Roberts, "Alehouses, Brewing," 45–71; Clark, *English Alehouse*, chap. 8, Clark, "The Rise of Regulation, 1500–1700," 166–94; and Hunter, "English Inns," 65–82. Two studies that provide excellent analyses of the local administration of the regulations are the section on "Alehouse regulation," 229–53, in Fletcher, *Reform in the Provinces*; and King, "Regulation of Alehouses," 31–46. For the regulations in central Europe, see Kümin, *Drinking Matters*, 74–81.

[3] Kent, "Attitudes of Members," 64–68.

The repetitive nature of many bills reveals the difficulty experienced by the moral reformers in gaining parliamentary approval for their program. Most of the fifty-one bills were not passed, but English regulations were still more restrictive than those in France and Italy.

Protecting the Consumer

The best indication that governments did not succumb to the righteous pleadings of the moralists and demonize the consumption of alcoholic beverages was the protection of consumer rights by establishing regulatory machinery to ensure people obtained a good drink at the right price in correct measures. Indeed, even English magistrates were more likely to prosecute alehouse keepers for selling poor ale at high prices in illegal pots than for suffering disorder in their establishments. In England, France, and Italy, these laws developed in the Middle Ages and continued to be enforced in the sixteenth and seventeenth centuries. Like the comparable regulations on the supply of bread, their purpose was the preservation of order; bread and alcoholic beverages—wine, beer, or ale—were the two dietary staples whose availability was crucial for political and civic stability.[4] In other words, governments considered the occasional drunkenness resulting from the trade in drink less of a threat to public order than the disruption of that trade or the unscrupulous behavior of its purveyors. Another reason for the regulations, particularly for price controls, was to prevent public pressure for higher wages.[5] Of course, many governments, especially during the Middle Ages, lacked the administrative machinery to enforce the regulations, and some communities in England made a mockery of the regulations by merely fining all brewers on the assumption they had violated the regulations, thereby transforming the fines into a lucrative system of licensing.[6] Other communities, however, were far more vigilant, as was medieval London. The twelve volumes of the *Letter Books* of the City of London, dating from 1275 to 1485, reveal a continuing concern to guarantee that Londoners would receive good and wholesome ale at the correct price in approved measures. The city's officials were just as diligent on behalf of the wine drinkers, as illustrated by the punishment of John Penrose, convicted in 1364 of selling unwholesome

[4] Bennett, *Ale, Beer, and Brewsters*, 9.
[5] Hilton, "Pain et cervoise," 222.
[6] Britnell, *Growth and Decline*, 89; and Britton, *Community of the Vill*, 25.

wine; he was "condemned to drink a draught of his own wine, the remainder to be poured on his head."[7] Officials who did not act as diligently as those in London could face pressure to do so. In 1524 the citizens of Nottingham petitioned the mayor "to be a good master to us and to see a remedy to the brewers, for we find us grieved with their ale," and in 1556 constables even prosecuted the mayor for not upholding the regulations.[8]

Governments in Italy demonstrated their determination to provide their citizens with a reliable and inexpensive supply of wine by passing laws and enforcing them. In fourteenth-century Siena, both bread and wine came under price and quality controls that were supervised by commissions which could prosecute violations in the communal courts.[9] During the same period, the government of Chioggia appointed an inspector to visit the three taverns in the town every day, checking on the quality of the wine and the fairness of the measures.[10] To protect the quality of the wine, a common regulation was to prohibit the mixing of wines or putting water in them; in fact, some communities even prohibited containers of water in taverns to prevent the water being sold as wine, no doubt to inebriated customers.[11] Much worse than adding water to wine was the addition of other things expressly prohibited by the statutes: honey, alum, mustard, rue, chalk, garlic, and onion.[12] To ensure their supplies, towns such as Bologna, Ferrara, and Florence adopted various measures such as promoting viticulture, banning exports, preventing hoarding, and punishing the theft of grapes from vineyards, which apparently was a serious problem.[13] Many communities also set prices for wine; for example, in 1344 the small town of Garessio in Piedmont decreed no tavern should charge more than 6 Genoan denari for a pint of wine.[14] Offenders were prosecuted, as were Donna Clara, wife of Bernardino, who sold wine at twice the permitted price at Orvieto in 1277 and the tavern keeper in Rome who overcharged a clown's apprentice in 1641.[15] Finally, communities imposed standard measures for the sale of wine; for example, in 1447 authorities in Rome

[7] Sharpe, *Calendar of Letter-Books*, vol. G, 178.

[8] Hewitt, "Malting and Brewing," 2:364.

[9] Bowsky, *Medieval Italian Commune*, 208.

[10] Goy, *Chioggia and the Villages*, 43–44.

[11] Patrone, *Cibo del ricco*, 410.

[12] Soriga, "Vite e il vino," 139.

[13] Cattini, "Individualismo agrario," 213–14; Paronetto, *Chianti*, 128; and Pini, *Vite e vino*, 100–101, 106–7.

[14] Greci, "Commercio del vino," 267.

[15] Riccetti, "Naso di Simone," 153; and Nussdorfer, *Civic Politics,* 122.

required tavern keepers "to make and give the full and just measures."[16] The authorities at Florence discovered "full and just measures" were difficult to obtain, for they tried in 1579, 1636, and 1639 to create a uniform measurement for flasks of 2.28 modern liters as a means to protect the consumer.[17]

French authorities enacted similar measures. In the fourteenth century, officials at Avignon controlled the price and quality of wine in addition to bread, meat, and fish, and in the sixteenth century, the municipal government at Paris closely supervised the sale of wine arriving at the port of Grève to ensure the quality of the wine and the stability of its price.[18] An ingenious edict of King John the Good in 1351 helped customers overcome cheating tavern keepers who drew cheap wine from the barrels in their cellars; customers had the right to see the keeper drawing their wine. At the same time the good King John established a corps of eighty officers known as "vendors of wine" whose principal function was the prevention of fraudulent practices, and some communities passed laws prohibiting the addition of water, lime, eggs, and other substances to wine.[19] Because France produced enough wine to engage in a large export market, measures to protect local supplies were not as necessary as they were in Italy, and towns such as Reims, Beaune, and Bordeaux appointed official wine brokers whose function was to facilitate trade by ensuring quality.[20] Nonetheless, as in Italy, theft of grapes was a serious problem, forcing many wine-producing communities to hire guards to patrol their vineyards.[21] French authorities likewise fixed the price of wine, and in the seventeenth century officials at Nancy fixed the price of beer, making a pot of good wine worth four times more than a pot of good beer.[22] Finally, as in Italy, officials struggled to regulate measures; in fourteenth-century Avignon, courts handled many cases of tavern keepers using pots that had not received approval by the authorities.[23]

English regulations governing the provision of ale date as far back as the Domesday Book, but the assize of ale, enacted in 1266, provided the legislative framework that would continue until the end of the seventeenth

[16] Cortonesi, "Vini e commercio," 140n47.

[17] Paronetto, *Chianti,* 128, 138.

[18] Chiffoleau, *Justices du pape,* 107; and Babelon, *Nouvelle histoire,* 312.

[19] Dion, *Histoire de la vigne,* 484, 495–96; and Stouff, *Ravitaillement et alimentation,* 91, n6.

[20] Brennan, "Anatomy of Inter-regional Markets," 584–85; and Brennan, *Burgundy to Champagne,* 78–80.

[21] Jacquart, *Crise rurale,* 309.

[22] Desportes, *Reims et les rémois,* 393; and Cabourdin, *Terre et hommes,* 691.

[23] Chiffoleau, *Justices du pape,* 107.

century. Its main provision was a mechanism for determining the price of
ale by fixing it to the price of barley, and it also included provisions regarding quality and measures. As already noted, enforcement of the regulations
varied because it was in the hands of local authorities, who were supposed to
appoint ale-tasters, also known as aleconners, to check the quality of the ale
by tasting it, as well as to examine prices and measures.[24] Local authorities
set their own punishments; at York in 1301 brewers who violated the assize
were fined for the first two offenses, but the third resulted in the cucking
stool.[25] In the sixteenth century, the mayor of Bristol visited the town brewers on every Wednesday and Saturday morning "to oversee them in serving
of their ale to the poor commons of the town, and that they have their true
measures; and his aleconner with him, to taste and understand that the ale be
good, able, and sufficient."[26] To ensure the quality of the brew, local authorities issued detailed regulations on every aspect of the trade, including the
purity of the water, the quality of the malt and the hops (for the production
of beer), and the brewing process itself.[27] In 1676 the chancellor of Oxford
University, which had the authority to regulate the brewers of Oxford, noted
the ale and beer were unwholesome and not as good as formerly, and accordingly issued instructions that the brewers "well and sufficiently boil or cause
to have so boiled all their several worts for the making of double beer, middle
beer, and ale, and that they also take particular care that the said sorts of beer
and ale in all other respects be made good and wholesome and agreeable."[28]
Brewers who made bad ale faced prosecution; in 1365 a manorial court at
Durham fined Agnes Postell and Alice of Belasis 12 pence for brewing bad
ale, and Alice was fined an additional 2 shillings because her ale "was of no
strength."[29]

    The chancellor of Oxford University also set the price of ale and beer in
1579 and again in 1615, to the chagrin of some brewers, who refused to brew
at such prices.[30] Punishment for selling ale and beer above the set price could
be quite severe; in 1337 London authorities set the penalty at three days in
prison and a substantial fine for the first offense, six days and a bigger fine

[24] Bennett, *Ale, Beer, and Brewsters,* 100; Hilton, "Pain et cervoise," 221; and Wilson, *Food and Drink,* 372.

[25] Goldberg, *Women in England,* 185.

[26] Ricart, *Maire of Bristowe,* ed. Smith, 83.

[27] Brears, "Food Guilds," 88; and Salzman, *English Industries,* 291–92, 296–97.

[28] Jeffery, "Malting and Brewing," 2:263.

[29] Amt, *Women's Lives,* 185. See also Crick, "Brewing," 2:366.

[30] Jeffery, "Malting and Brewing," 2:262–63.

Figure 9: "The Ale-Wife's End." Drawing of a fourteenth-century carved wood misericord from Ludlow Church, England, showing an alewife, still clutching her fraudulent measure, being carried to the entrance of Hell by a headless demon. A demon on the left reads her long list of sins.

From Thomas Wright, *A History of Domestic Manners and Sentiments in England during the Middle Ages*, with illustrations... by F. W. Fairholt. London: Chapman and Hill, 1862 (no. 226, p. 337). Reproduced from Frank A. King, *Beer Has a History* (redrawn by George Horton), 33. London: Hutchinson, 1947.

for the second, and expulsion from the city for the third.[31] As in Italy, officials had difficulty imposing a system of correct measures on brewers and alehouse keepers, as examples from the fifteenth to the seventeenth century indicate. To cite one, the manorial court at Abbots Ripton decreed in 1492 that brewers and keepers could not sell ale "in pots, cups, dishes, or bowls, but only in true measures that have been properly marked as the law requires."[32] A fourteenth-century carved wood misericord from Ludlow Church (fig. 9) shows an ale-wife clutching her fraudulent measure, while a headless demon carries her to the entrance of Hell. As a result of the combined pressures of producing their

[31] Hammond, *Food and Feast*, 55.

[32] Raftis, *Tenure and Mobility*, 126–27. For other examples, see *Records of the Borough of Nottingham*, ed. Stevenson and Raine, 193; Couth, *Grantham during the Interregnum*, 100; and *Liverpool Town Books*, ed. Power, 204.

product at a set price, of selling it by official measures, and of facing prosecution if it was bad, some brewers unsurprisingly refused to brew. However, local governments were just as determined to have a reliable and adequate supply, so they forced brewers to brew. In 1434 officials at Oxford summoned the local brewers to the Church of the Blessed Mary the Virgin and ordered them to supply malt for the production of ale and required several of them to offer their ale for sale two or three times a week. Five years later, when Alice Everarde refused to brew because it did not suit her, officials suspended her from practicing the trade.[33] The manorial court at Abbots Ripton recognized in 1492 that the local brewers were producing their ale on the same days, leaving some periods without sufficient supply, which resulted in the suffering of the villagers, so it ordered them to take turns brewing and "provide in season and out of season an adequate service."[34]

One of the extraordinary features of these measures was the special concern for the drink of the poor at a time when officials were expressing alarm that the drinking poor, the wandering poor, and the idle poor were passing their time in drinking establishments. Governments in both Italy and France attempted to decrease the cost of wine consumed by the poor. In Italy a distinction was made between "wine of the vine" made from grapes and "wine of the tree" made from blackberries, wild brambles, and elder berries, which was drunk by the poor and not taxed.[35] Similarly, *mezzo vino,* the cheap wine made from watered marc, often escaped taxation.[36] In France in 1421, a royal decree fixed the price for the so-called *petit vin* that was consumed by the laboring poor.[37] In England the focus was to secure a supply of small ale or beer that the poor could afford, and to this end the government issued a *Book of Orders* in 1586 and reissued or revised it in 1597, 1608, 1622, and 1630.[38] In 1608, for example, the king ordered brewers to "make their beer and ale not too strong" so they could sell it "at low and reasonable prices, that the poorer sort may have the greater proportion for their money."[39] Local authorities enacted similar ordinances; at Leicester in the fifteenth century brewers had to make small

---

[33] Jeffery, "Malting and Brewing," II, 260.

[34] Raftis, *Tenure and Mobility,* 126–27.

[35] Allocco, "Criminalità in Savigliano,"124n79.

[36] Patrone, *Cibo del ricco,* 429.

[37] Dion, *Histoire de la vigne,* 494.

[38] Hunter, "English Inns," 68.

[39] "A Proclamation touching Maultsters, Common-Brewers and Alehouse-Keepers," in Larkin and Hughes, *Stuart Royal Proclamations,* 1:201.

ale that the poor could purchase for a half penny a gallon, and in 1549 the town of Witney ordered its brewers to produce "good and wholesome" small drink "for the comfort of the poor people."[40] As noted previously, all of these regulatory measures designed to protect the consumer by providing a good drink at reasonable prices in the correct measures had a long history and were official policy during the late medieval and the early modern periods. In England this regulatory regime ceased operating after 1700. The reasons for this were complex and include the large varieties of drink, making standardized prices and processes unworkable; the increase in excise duty after the accession of William III; and the rise of the economic and political power of brewers, who favored an end to the traditional controls.[41]

Licensing Taverns and Alehouses

In contrast to the regulations protecting the consumers of alcoholic beverages were those controlling drinking establishments. Governments required purveyors of drink to purchase licenses; not only would this promote public order, but it would also increase revenues through licensing fees as well as by ensuring the drink sold had not escaped any excise taxes. Authorities in Italy could vacillate between very strict and very permissive policies, as illustrated by the examples of Siena and Florence. In its constitutions of 1262 through 1270, Siena forbade any taverns to operate, and innkeepers could only sell wine to bona fide travelers and to guests of those travelers. By the fourteenth century, however, this severe policy had given way to one that permitted all inhabitants to sell wine provided they purchased a license.[42] Florence had a similarly permissive policy; anyone could sell wine provided the purchaser did not consume it while sitting down, which in effect would create a tavern and require a license.[43] Moral fervor overcame fiscal advantage in 1528, when the government closed all taverns, believing the sins committed in them angered God, but they eventually reopened only to be the subject of moral indignation again in 1588.[44] Chioggia steered towards moderation by permitting only three taverns to operate, while Venice waged a long struggle against

---

[40] Salzman, *English Industries*, 293; and Jeffery, "Malting and Brewing," 2:261. See also Brears, "Food Guilds," 88.

[41] Clark, *English Alehouse*, 182.

[42] Heywood, *"Ensamples" of Fra Filippo*, 192.

[43] Balestracci, "Produzione e la vendità," 51.

[44] Trexler, *Public Life*, 350; and Weissman, *Ritual Brotherhood*, 203–5.

against illegal taverns that operated without licenses from boats—the *fura-tole*—with punishments including fines and the confiscation and destruction of property.[45] An indication of the futility of these measures is the claim by a visitor in 1668 that over two hundred illegal taverns operated in the area near the Arsenal.[46] At Faenza the punishment for selling wine without a license was a flogging through the town for the indigent; those not indigent were bound for a day with their hands tied behind their backs next to the Palazzo del Podestà.[47] Often accompanying the regulations on licenses were restrictions on tavern keepers. At Siena women and children could not sell wine, in 1337 the authorities at Montepulciano forbade women to keep taverns, and Venice prohibited brothels to sell wine.[48] More sensibly, many communities in Piedmont established strict guidelines to ensure the honesty of the keepers and the safety of the customers.[49]

The French government likewise licensed taverns and cabarets. According to a law passed in 1577, they had to display their legitimacy with a sign indicating "par permission du Roy."[50] French regulations distinguished between a tavern and a cabaret; a tavern sold wine that was consumed off the premises, while the wine purchased in a cabaret could be drunk there, although the distinction disappeared after 1680 when the proprietors of taverns agreed to pay a higher tax.[51] Even more so than in Italy the revenue earned from wine guided the government's policies, for as noted by Jean-Baptiste Colbert, finance minister to Louis XIV, the wines of France were the "mines of the kingdom."[52] Old legislation limited the sale of wine in cabarets to travelers, while locals had to purchase their wine from taverns and take it home; if strictly enforced this would reduce the royal revenues. As a result, royal edicts in 1587 and 1613 attempted to eliminate this restriction and thereby increase revenues, but the definitive end to the policy did not come until 1670 when the royal council decreed the prohibition of selling wine to locals applied only during hours of

---

[45] Goy, *Chioggia and the Villages*, 25; Crouzet-Pavan, *Sopra le acque salse*, 309, 861–62; and Mackenney, *Tradesmen and Traders*, 147–48.

[46] Davis, "Venetian Shipbuilders," 70n42.

[47] Soriga, "Vite e il vino," 139.

[48] Heywood, *"Ensamples" of Fra Filippo*, 194; Balestracci, "Consumo del vino," 29; Cherubini, "Taverna nel basso medioevo," 198; and Brundage, *Law, Sex*, 525.

[49] Patrone, *Cibo del ricco*, 414.

[50] Franklin, *Moeurs et coutumes*, 91–92.

[51] Brennan, *Public Drinking*, 78–80; and Thibault, "Parisiens et le vin," 239–40.

[52] Dion, *Histoire de la vigne*, 30.

divine service on Sundays and other holy days.[53] As in Italy, French authorities placed restrictions on the keepers, the most notable enacted by the city of Toulouse in 1205 to protect pilgrims from the rapacity of innkeepers. The restrictions prohibited a keeper from forcing pilgrims to enter his inn by seizing their clothes or horses, from locking pilgrims in the inn once they had entered, and from compelling them to purchase food and wine at the inn.[54] Probably just as effective in controlling the behavior of keepers was the understated policy at Apt in Provence: keepers who annoyed the authorities lost their license.[55] A Parisian ordinance issued in 1698 revealed a greater concern for the behavior of customers than the rapacity of keepers; all keepers had to inform the local police of any "brawls, quarrels, disputes, and differences" that occurred in their taverns.[56]

Notwithstanding sporadic and ineffective local efforts, the English government did not address the control and licensing of drinking establishments until much later than the French and Italian governments, and then it compensated for its tardiness by the creation of comprehensive legislation. The first legislative attempt to regulate alehouses occurred during the reign of Henry VII in 1495, when according to the terms of the Beggars Act, justices of the peace could suppress "common ale selling" and require keepers to provide bonds for good behavior. Partly as a result of its voluntary nature, few communities took advantage of the act to control local alehouses.[57] The Act of 1552 required justices to make alehouse licensing compulsory rather than voluntary and formed the basis of the later legislation enacted in the early seventeenth century. The act obliged local justices to require keepers to purchase a license and agree to a bond for their good behavior; the punishment for those selling without a license was three days in jail.[58] Officials in Middlesex responded immediately to the new act and issued 312 licenses in 1553, binding the keepers for the "maintenance of good order and rule," but other communities were slow off the mark; Colchester, for example, did not enforce it until 1577.[59] One of the causes of ineffective enforcement was local

[53] Dion, *Histoire de la vigne,* 488–89; and Sournia, *History of Alcoholism,* 18.

[54] Cowell, *At Play in the Tavern,* 16.

[55] Stouff, *Ravitaillement et alimentation,* 91.

[56] Brennan, *Public Drinking,* 43n49.

[57] Clark, *English Alehouse,* 48, 169; Bretherton, "Country Inns," 148–49; and Earnshaw, *Pub in Literature,* 45–46.

[58] Clark, *English Alehouse,* 169, 172; and Bretherton, "Country Inns," 149. The text of the act is in Tanner, *Tudor Constitutional Documents,* 501.

[59] *Middlesex County Records,* ed. Jeaffreson, 1:10–11; and Higgs, *Godliness and Governance,* 258, 274–75.

rivalry among families of the gentry and between town and country justices; in 1562 the government learned, "if one or two justices be ready to put [alehouses] down that be too bad, by and by other justices be ready to set them up again." As noted in chapter 4, a 1577 government survey of alehouses in thirty counties revealed the extent of the problem. The survey counted over 15,000 alehouses, but, as reckoned by Peter Clark, the total number was more than 24,000, and before 1600 less than half the alehouses were operating legally.[60]

The twenty-five years following the accession of James I in 1603 produced a flurry of legislative activity that complemented the act of 1552 and attempted to overcome its shortcomings. According to an act of 1604, alehouse keepers faced punishment if they allowed drinking by anyone except travelers, while local workers could only drink for one hour around dinnertime. The preamble to the act noted the ancient use of inns and alehouses was for "the receipt, relief, and lodging of wayfaring people traveling from place to place, ... and not meant for the entertainment and harboring of lewd and idle people to spend and consume their money and times in lewd and drunken manner." While inns were necessary conveniences, alehouses were nuisances and should be subject to suppression or strict control.[61] The legislative assault against alehouses continued, and later acts and proclamations forbade keepers to permit games, to remain open during divine service and after nine o'clock at night, or to harbor "any rogues, vagabonds, sturdy beggars, masterless men, or other notorious offenders whatsoever," required that only honest, trustworthy, and honorable men should obtain alehouse licenses, ordered punishment for brewers who delivered ale to unlicensed alehouses, for constables who did not uphold the law, and for anyone who haunted alehouses or became drunk, and, finally, decreed that some of the fines collected should go to the parish.[62]

The purpose of the last measure was to garner local support for the regulations, which had no chance of success without that support, as indicated by a comparison of indictments in Kent and Warwickshire. In the twenty-five years between 1625 and 1659, courts in Kent heard 936 indictments for unlicensed alehouses—an average of twenty-six a year—while during roughly the same period, courts in Warwickshire were only handling an average of five

---

[60] Clark, *English Alehouse*, 42–43, 169–71.

[61] Bretherton, "Country Inns," 150–52.

[62] Roberts, "Alehouses, Brewing," 57–59. The Proclamation of 1619 is in Larkin and Hughes, *Stuart Royal Proclamations,* 1:409–13.

cases a year. Although Kent had a much higher population and more alehouses than Warwickshire, indications are that local officials in Kent were zealous in their pursuit of unlicensed alehouses, while those in Warwickshire were lax. Other figures likewise indicate the crucial role of local authorities. Because a committee of magistrates in Cheshire refused to cooperate with the courts in the prosecution of unlicensed alehouses in 1609 and 1610, the courts had no choice but to find over 1,000 unlicensed alehouse keepers not guilty.[63] On the other hand, surveys taken in Westminster, Southwark, Kentish Town, and Finsbury during the famine of 1629 to 1631 found 1,085 alehouses, and local justices suppressed 391 of them.[64] Another survey of thirty townships in Lancashire in 1647 revealed 83 licensed and 143 unlicensed alehouses, meaning one alehouse for every twelve households.[65] Local officials sometimes reacted to government pressure with periodic drives against unlicensed alehouses, as apparently happened at Durham in 1602 and again in 1607, when the courts charged 101 keepers with the offense.[66] Some local officials found it preferable to profit from illegal alehouses than to suppress them, which was an attitude that could affect an entire community if the alehouses in question were paying local taxes or if their keepers were so poor that they would become a charge to the parish should they no longer be able to sell ale.[67] Added to these concerns were the antipuritan feelings in many towns and villages, and the increasingly important role of alehouses in popular recreation and culture and the services they provided for the community.[68]

Integral to the control and licensing of alehouses were measures to monitor their keepers. Before the Act of 1552, these measures concentrated, as in Italy, on the age and gender of the keepers; for example, in 1540 the mayor of Chester issued orders that no woman between the ages of fourteen and forty could keep an alehouse or a tavern.[69] After the Act of 1552 required keepers to agree to a bond or recognizance of good behavior, the actual wording of the bond was left to local justices, so the conditions imposed on keepers varied

---

[63] Hindle, *State and Social Change*, 152; and Curtis, "Quarter Sessions Appearances," 151, which puts the number at approximately 1,300.

[64] Iles, "Early Stages," 259.

[65] Wrightson, *English Society*, 168.

[66] *Durham Quarter Sessions Rolls*, ed. Fraser, 30–31, 154–55.

[67] King, "Regulation of Alehouses," 37; Fletcher, *Reform in the Provinces*, 233–34; and Hindle, *State and Social Change*, 152.

[68] Bretherton, "Country Inns," 174–75; and King, "Regulation of Alehouses" 40–41.

[69] Bennett, *Ale, Beer, and Brewsters*, 142.

from place to place.[70] Over time the conditions became more and more complex. An early example from Essex, dated 1556–1557, required the keeper to refuse hospitality to vagabonds and other suspicious or disorderly people, to prohibit games and gambling, and to close during hours of divine service.[71] The Royal Proclamation of 1618 established guidelines for the bonds, but even before then, the conditions imposed on keepers had increased considerably, so that the bonds became substantial documents with as many as ten articles.[72] According to the papers of Nathaniel Bacon, a Norfolk justice of peace in the late sixteenth and early seventeenth centuries, the process of obtaining an alehouse license could be complicated. First a person had to obtain letters of recommendation from members of the community, next people had to agree to stand as guarantors of his/her conduct, then the putative keeper had to pay the fee for the license and to agree to the bond, and all of this just for a temporary license.[73] Of course, not all local officials enforced these procedures or the bonds that accompanied them, and many areas had large numbers of unlicensed alehouses that escaped control. Nonetheless, as noted by Anthony Fletcher, as the seventeenth century progressed the overall picture was "one of slow and painful realization of control," and local courts were "groping rather haphazardly towards a national program of alehouse control."[74]

Regulating Who, How, When, and Where

Intimately connected with the efforts to regulate alehouses and taverns were restrictions placed on their clientele, their activities, their hours and days of operation, and their location. As already noted, authorities decreed that only travelers could drink at taverns and alehouses. In France this policy dated from a royal edict of 1256, and its enforcement relied on local governments, which could issue their own regulations forbidding locals to patronize taverns, as occurred at Rouen in 1556.[75] At Lyon officials forbade taverns to allow residents to consume wine on their premises; they had to bring their pots to the tavern,

---

[70] Bretherton, "Country Inns," 149.

[71] Emmison, *Elizabethan Life*, 5.

[72] Bretherton, "Country Inns," 149. For examples, see *Hertford Country Records*, ed. Hardy, 1:24–25 (1597), 154 (1663); Douch, *Old Cornish Inns*, 19; Bacon, *Official Papers*, ed. Saunders, 54–55 (1608); and Thompson, *Wives, Widows*, 51 (1671).

[73] Bacon, *Official Papers*, ed. Saunders, xxiii–xxiv.

[74] Fletcher, *Reform in the Provinces*, 243, 245.

[75] Benedict, *Rouen during the Wars*, 16n3.

purchase their wine, and take it home, which was a simple, effective means of preventing taverns from becoming centers of popular disorder. The frequent renewals of this regulation by both national and local governments indicate the difficulties of its enforcement, and in 1398 Parisian officials had to enact another ordinance specifically directed at workers and the poor who haunted taverns.[76] Compounding the difficulty of enforcement were those travelers whom officials wished to ban from drinking establishments, namely, vagabonds. Governments at every level in Italy, France, and England required keepers to banish vagabonds and suspicious men from their premises, but enforcement of this regulation was just as difficult as was the enforcement of laws forbidding residents to drink at taverns and alehouses. In 1526 an edict of Francis I required Parisian officials to seize the vagabonds congregating in taverns, and in 1690, after centuries of decrees and efforts to rid vagabonds from English alehouses, officials still feared that alehouses harbored "all sorts of wandering and traveling rogues, vagabonds and suspicious persons."[77] Authorities in small communities could conflate the traveler, vagabond, and suspicious person, as they evidently did at Halesowen in 1573 by forbidding keepers to offer hospitality to "any traveling people from outside beyond the space of one day and one night unless there is cause due to sickness."[78] Such a regulation begs the question: If only travelers could drink at alehouses, and if they could only remain there overnight, who were the regular customers?

Obviously, the regulations privileging travelers were unworkable, and cracks began to appear in the legislation. In 1587 authorities at Ipswich ordered that no inhabitant of the town should eat or drink in alehouses and taverns but added as a qualifying clause, "without reasonable cause," but the ordinance did not state if hunger or thirst could be a reasonable cause.[79] The English act of 1603, while affirming that the main function of inns and alehouses was for the relief and lodging of travelers, also noted their role in supplying food and drink for the poor,[80] and the act of 1604, cited above, permitted local workers to drink for an hour around dinnertime. Local ordinances could further dilute the regulations by permitting residents to use alehouses when attending markets, visiting travelers, or on "urgent and

---

[76] Lachiver, *Vins, vignes et vignerons: Histoire,* 156, 312–13; and Dion, *Histoire de la vigne,* 487, 493.

[77] Brennan, *Public Drinking,* 275; Amussen, *Ordered Society,* 169, n96; and Patrone, *Cibo del ricco,* 416.

[78] McIntosh, *Controlling Misbehavior,* 76.

[79] Iles, "Early Stages," 255.

[80] Emmison, *Elizabethan Life,* 202.

necessary occasions," which is as vague as Ipswich's "reasonable cause."[81] As residents gained the right to patronize drinking establishments, authorities tried to make the best of the situation by paying more attention to the young, including students, servants, and apprentices. As indicated by the discussions in chapters 5 and 6, officials prosecuted keepers for the disorderly conduct of the young, and they prosecuted young offenders, but no laws prohibited children from drinking. In the thirteenth century, Siena forbade children under the age of fifteen to go to taverns, but this was the only instance of such a law.[82] Other Italian towns attempted to protect young drinkers by banning keepers from extending credit to those under eighteen or twenty years of age.[83] English regulations regarding children were usually fused with those governing servants and/or apprentices, especially when dealing with curfews. For example, in 1577 officials in Manchester ordered "that no man's children or servants shall go abroad in the streets nor come in any alehouse having no lawful business after eight o'clock in winter and after nine o'clock in summer."[84]

The attempts by governments to curtail drinking by the young deserve high marks for effort but low marks for effect. To reform the notorious drinking behavior of students, university authorities at Oxford and Cambridge undertook periodic efforts, such as those initiated by a new chancellor at Oxford early in the seventeenth century and those ordered by Charles I at Cambridge in 1630, with little apparent results.[85] Despite indenture contracts that prohibited apprentices from haunting alehouses and taverns, despite centuries of legislation banning keepers from serving servants and apprentices, and despite severe punishments including imprisonment and whipping for young offenders, the youth of England would have their pint at an alehouse. Tellingly, whenever authorities in London feared an outbreak of rioting or other types of violence, their first precaution was to declare a curfew for servants and apprentices and to order the closure of all alehouses.[86] As residents gained the right to patronize alehouses and taverns, so too did servants and apprentices. By the time Roger Lowe started his diary in 1663, this Lancashire apprentice encountered no restrictions on his recreational drinking at ale-

---

[81] Amussen, *Ordered Society,* 168–69.

[82] Balestracci, "Consumo del vino," 29; and Heywood, *"Ensamples" of Fra Filippo,* 194.

[83] Patrone, *Cibo del ricco,* 416; and Riccetti, "Naso di Simone," 154.

[84] Iles, "Early Stages," 255.

[85] Fincham, "Oxford and the Early Stuart Policy," 188; Abbott, *Life Cycles,* 94–95; and Shepard, *Meanings of Manhood,* 104–5.

[86] Brigden, "Youth and the English Reformation," 62.

houses, which played an obviously important role in the popular culture of the area.[87] Although Anthony Fletcher may be correct in his assessment that authorities won the battle to achieve a national program of alehouse control, they ultimately lost the war as taverns and alehouses became the focus of popular recreation and popular culture.

The diary of Roger Lowe also makes it abundantly clear that women used alehouses for their recreational drinking. Thirteenth-century and seventeenth-century ordinances in Siena and Lille banned women from taverns,[88] but these were isolated attempts to prevent women of ill repute from exercising their trade at drinking establishments by restricting clientele to men. Much more common were the laws against prostitutes. "To eschew the stinking and horrible sin of lechery," officials in London issued ordinances preventing prostitutes from entering taverns and alehouses in the fourteenth, fifteenth, and sixteenth centuries.[89] Venetian authorities similarly waged a long and losing battle with prostitutes, beginning in 1266 with an edict banning them from the city, followed by another fifty years later in 1316 that merely banned them from taverns. In the following century, even this restriction was relaxed, with officials then trying to prevent them from congregating at taverns in Piazza San Marco. Sodomy was another major concern of the Venetian government, so much so that the night watch received instructions to search taverns for evidence of homosexual activity, including men who drank with those much younger or with those of an inferior social status.[90] In 1339 the government of Florence demonstrated general concerns over the disorder associated with taverns when it banned them from operating within a mile outside the city's wall, claiming "many people of different manners come there day and night and gamble, and beyond this they do many disgusting and illegal things, and these taverns ... are dens of thieves, gamblers, and dishonest and evil men."[91]

In their efforts to prevent taverns and alehouses from becoming centers of popular recreation, governments attempted various measures over the years, such as restricting both the hours of consumption and the amount consumed, prohibiting the sale of food, and forbidding customers to sit while

[87] Martin, "Drinking and Alehouses," 93–105.

[88] Balestracci, "Consumo del vino," 29; Heywood, *"Ensamples" of Fra Filippo*, 194; and Lottin, *Chavatte, ouvrier lillois*, 347.

[89] Karras, *Common Women*, 15–16, 72.

[90] Pavan, "Police des moeurs," 243–54, 270–71.

[91] Balestracci, "Consumo del vino," 21.

drinking.[92] Another measure was the prohibition of gambling, but the prohibition was neither universal nor complete. Some governments took a hard stand, possibly because of the propensity of gambling to lead to disorder and violence, possibly because of concerns about the debauchment of young men.[93] For example, when gambling dens proliferated throughout Venice in the early fourteenth century with proprietors luring young men with wine, officials banned games of dice in the city, in the duchy, and in the entire Venetian empire, and Rome similarly forbade gambling in taverns as well as in private houses.[94] At Monte Cassino in the thirteenth century, however, customers could gamble for drinks, and at Montepulciano in the fourteenth century they could use the gambling tables provided the tavern keeper paid a monthly tax of 5 scudi.[95] Similarly, in France the prohibition of gambling in taverns was not absolute. Officials in fourteenth-century Avignon hedged their condemnations of gambling at taverns by stating it was banned only at night and then did not apply the ban to the nobility.[96] Other bans were also class- as well as age-specific: in 1397 the provost of Paris prohibited workers from playing "tennis, boules, dice, cards, and ninepins and other games in…taverns" but only on "workable days," and in 1577 the government ordered tavern keepers to ban youth, children, and other debauched people from playing dice and cards and to stop giving them credit to do so.[97] The English government's disapproval of gambling extended to most games and dated from an act in 1388 during the reign of Richard II; the cause of such disapproval was probably the desire to encourage archery as a national pastime that could promote the defense of the realm. Henry VIII renewed the legislation in 1541 and added other games so that the list of those forbidden included backgammon, cards, dice, football, tennis, quoits, ninepins, shuffleboard, and casting the stone—so much for Merry England![98] The Beggars Act of 1495, cited above, had specified that alehouse keepers should not permit unlawful games, but local governments had previously issued similar orders, and their continued issuing of such orders is an indication that in gaming

[92] Benedict, *Rouen during the Wars*, 39; Heywood, *"Ensamples" of Fra Filippo*, 194; Gascon, *Grand commerce*, 385, 738; and Brears, "Food Guilds," 89.

[93] Patrone, *Cibo del ricco*, 415–16.

[94] Crouzet-Pavan, *Sopra le acque salse*, 857. See also Chambers and Pullan, *Venice*, 129; and Cortonesi, "Vini e commercio," 142n56.

[95] Cherubini, "Taverna nel basso medioevo," 214; and Balestracci, "Consumo del vino," 20–21.

[96] Chiffoleau, *Justices du pape*, 267.

[97] Farr, *Artisans in Europe*, 270; and Franklin, *Moeurs et coutumes*, 92.

[98] Emmison, *Elizabethan Life*, 218.

and gambling, as in other matters, government efforts to prevent alehouses from becoming centers of popular recreation were not successful.[99]

In addition to regulations governing the clientele and activities of drinking establishments, governments also attempted to control their opening hours. Curfews were an effective means of ensuring that late-night drinking parties would not become disorderly and that drunkards heading home in the dead of the night would not disturb their neighbors or worse. Indeed, curfews had long been a widespread practice; in England they dated to 1068 when William the Conqueror set eight o'clock as the time to cover fires (curfew derives from the French *couvre-feu*, meaning "cover-fire") as a means of preventing fires and discouraging conspiracies.[100] What is not clear is whether the regulations specifically citing taverns and alehouses were more restrictive than the general curfew. Many Italian governments stipulated that taverns had to close at the sound of the last bell, and fifteenth-century Roman taverns had to close at the sound of the bell for the night watch, indications that they observed the general curfew.[101] Likewise in London, as stipulated in statutes promulgated by Edward I in 1285, when the bells sounded the curfew at nine o'clock all drinking establishments as well as other businesses closed their doors until six o'clock the next morning. According to the statutes, the curfew was necessary because armed men who wandered the streets at night "commonly resort and have their meetings and hold their evil talk in taverns more than elsewhere, and there do seek for shelter, lying in wait, and watching their time to do mischief."[102] Some English towns required closure at eight o'clock, some at nine o'clock, and others varied the time depending on the season; a royal proclamation in 1618 established nine o'clock as the uniform time for the nation regardless of season.[103] Authorities in Paris were at first vague about the precise hour of curfew for taverns, with "late" sufficing in the fifteenth and sixteenth centuries. Come the seventeenth century, they abandoned vagueness for precision and gradually permitted a later closure; at first the closing hour was seven o'clock in winter and eight o'clock in summer, then six o'clock and nine o'clock, and finally eight o'clock and ten o'clock.[104]

---

[99] Hunter, "English Inns," 66; and Iles, "Early Stages," 255.

[100] Ekirch, *At Day's Close*, 63–66.

[101] Allocco, "Criminalità in Savigliano," 129; Patrone, *Cibo del ricco*, 414–15; and Cortonesi, "Vini e commercio," 141n53.

[102] Hanawalt, *Of Good and Ill Repute*, 111, 113–14; and Crawford, *History of the Vintners' Company*, 32.

[103] Bailey, "Rural Society," 165–66; Brears, "Food Guilds," 89; Goldberg, *Women, Work*, 116; Brown, *Popular Piety*, 15; Mayhew, *Tudor Rye*, 49; and Bretherton, "Country Inns," 150.

[104] Brennan, *Public Drinking*, 277–78.

Just as widespread as the regulations on curfews were those requiring ale-houses and taverns to close during divine services on Sundays and other holy days. Religious authorities had long forbade the selling of drinks at this time, and political authorities increasingly legislated against the practice, so that by 1670 the French royal council declared that the rules prohibiting residents from drinking at taverns only applied to the hours of divine service on Sundays and holy days.[105] Provincial parlements had previously required closure during divine services, and local officials visited taverns to ensure they were closed and levied substantial fines on offending keepers.[106] Religious authorities continued to issue decrees, as did the bishop of Troyes in 1640, excommunicating those who sold drink during divine services as well those who were heretics, witches, and poisoners.[107] Italian authorities likewise forbade taverns to open during divine services on Sundays, and they issued similar regulations for certain holy days. For the small community of Mazzorbo in the Venetian lagoon, this meant the days of Christmas, Easter, Ascension, Pentecost, and the Feasts of the Virgin and of the Apostles, while at Florence, taverns could not open during Lent and on Good Friday, and they had to remain closed on every Friday until the reading of the gospel and on the Feast of St. Martin until the offering to the saint.[108] Italian statutes likewise forbade taverns to operate near churches or other sacred sites; in fourteenth-century Florence, authorities stipulated a distance of 300 *braccia* or "arms."[109]

Because of the role of English religious authorities in policing closures during divine service, local officials belatedly issued regulations on it; the first legislation in the *Letter Books* of the city of London was dated 1484.[110] Thereafter local authorities increasingly backed the ecclesiastical injunctions against opening during the hours of divine service, a development that accelerated in the second half of the sixteenth century as a result of puritan influence.[111] In 1590 the corporation of the city of York appointed four men to search alehouses and taverns during divine services, and, according to the orders issued by the justices of the peace for Lancashire in 1616, "if any be

[105] Adam, *Vie paroissiale*, 248; and Dion, *Histoire de la vigne*, 489.

[106] Norberg, *Rich and Poor*, 36; and Collins, *Classes, Estates*, 100–101, 257, n29.

[107] Babeau, *Village sous l'ancien régime*, 127.

[108] Balestracci, "Produzione e la vendita," 52; Balestracci, "Consumo del vino," 20; Cherubini, "Taverna nel basso medioevo," 193; and Paronetto, *Chianti*, 37–38.

[109] Balestracci, "Produzione e la vendita," 52; and Paronetto, *Chianti*, 26, 31.

[110] Sharpe, *Calendar of Letter-Books*, L, 217.

[111] Phythian-Adams, *Desolation of a City*, 79; Dennison, *Market Day*, 2, 142–43; Carlin, *Medieval Southwark*, 208; and Marchant, *Church under the Law*, 225.

found in any alehouse in time of divine service the said alehouse [is] to be put down and henceforth not to be licensed again."[112] In some places the reforming zeal of the puritans succeeded in closing down taverns and alehouses not just during divine services but all day on Sundays and holy days.[113] Even when not ordered to close all day, alehouse and tavern keepers could find few windows of opportunity to exercise their trade; the visitation articles of the archbishop of York in 1607, for example, required closure "on Sundays in time of morning and evening prayers, sermons, lectures, and catechizing."[114] The puritan push to sanctify the Sabbath not only required the closure of alehouses and taverns but also the elimination of other forms of recreation. Not everyone, including the government, approved of such zealotry, and in 1618 King James I issued The Book (or Declaration) of Sports supporting traditional Sunday recreations after divine service. When Charles I renewed the declaration in 1633, it listed recreations "such as dancing, either men or women; archery for men, leaping, vaulting, or any other such harmless recreation, … having of May-games, Whitsun ales, and morris dances; and the setting up of Maypoles," and it noted, somewhat ironically, that the deprivation of recreation led men into "filthy tippling and drunkenness" and bred "a number of idle and discontented speeches in their alehouses."[115]

Authorities directed the vast majority of their regulations at alehouses and taverns and only occasionally at the potential disorder of festive occasions. In 1540 the mayor of Chester, for example, ordered limitations on the traditional celebrations of childbirth and the subsequent churching of women, limitations that included the amount of drink consumed in celebrations, and officials in Kendal and Leicester issued similar regulations later in the century.[116] The drinking festivities surrounding weddings likewise received the disapproving attention of officials. Medieval ecclesiastical synods in England and France forbade couples from marrying in taverns and condemned the drunkenness that often attended the holy sacrament of matrimony.[117] In the sixteenth century the municipal governments of Chester, Halesowen, Manchester, and Wakefield placed restrictions on bridales and

---

[112] Palliser, *Tudor York*, 255; and Harrison and Royston, *How They Lived*, 239.

[113] Bretherton, "Country Inns," 150; Brushfield, "Church Ales," 346–47; Crawford, *History of the Vintners' Company*, 106–7; *Middlesex County Records*, ed. Jeaffreson, 3:190; and Mayhew, *Tudor Rye*, 201.

[114] Fincham, *Visitation Articles*, 1:59.

[115] Gardiner, *Constitutional Documents*, 31–35.

[116] Bennett, *Ale, Beer, and Brewsters*, 142–43; and Heal, *Hospitality in Early Modern England*, 366.

[117] Brundage, *Law, Sex*, 440, n122; and Bennett, *Life on the English Manor*, 264.

weddings, usually by limiting the amount of ale brewed and the number of people at the wedding dinner. The authorities at Kendal went further; in 1575 they decreed that no public or private drinking should accompany weddings and later forbade drinking before and after the wedding.[118]

While the primary concern of political authorities was order, for religious authorities it was sanctity and the separation of the sacred and the profane.[119] On occasion the two concerns could merge, as they obviously did on English regulations governing excessive drinking at weddings; religious authorities objected to the profanation of the sacrament of marriage, but for the local governments the drunken wedding party could result in disorder. The decrees of synods and bishops promoted pious behavior on religious occasions and on religious property, be it church, cemetery, or churchyard. A diocesan synod at Ferrara in 1612 prohibited drunkenness as well as gluttony, dancing, and obscenity on feast days, and in 1670 the bishop of Alet refused to grant absolution to those who became drunk or danced on the feast day of their patron saint.[120] Religious authorities increasingly acted to end the centuries-old traditions of drinking in churches; a synod at Bologna in 1566, for example, forbade any drinking in churches or cemeteries, while in England they legislated against customary church ales, bride ales, and funeral wakes in churches.[121]

As in the case of celebratory drinks at weddings, the concerns of religious and political authorities could merge in the suppression of church ales. As discussed in chapter 4, church ales were primarily an English phenomenon whose function was to raise money for the parish church by selling ale. They increasingly drew the ire of religious authorities, who objected to the use of church property for the ales, as well as the concern of political authorities, who feared the potential for disorder whenever large groups of people drank large amounts of ale on festive occasions. The first concerted move against them occurred in the reign of Edward VI as a result of the policies of Protector Somerset; of the eighteen parishes that held well-documented regular church ales in the early 1540s, sixteen had abandoned them during

---

[118] Bennett, "Conviviality and Charity," 32; Heal, *Hospitality in Early Modern England*, 370–71; and Carrington, "Ancient Ales," 203.

[119] Hutton, *Rise and Fall*, 70.

[120] Camporesi, *Bread of Dreams*, 136; and Bercé, *Fête et révolte*, 151.

[121] Camporesi, *Bread of Dreams*, 136; Fincham, *Visitation Articles*, 1:11, 2:26, 35, 132; French, *Nineteen Centuries of Drink*, 123; and Gittings, *Death, Burial*, 156.

the period from 1547 to 1549.[122] The rise of puritanism in the second half of the century threatened the rest, even those that occurred irregularly. Officials at Devon banned church ales held on Sundays in 1595, in 1600 they banned them altogether and repeated the ban in 1615, while neighboring Somerset prohibited them in 1594 and continued issuing such decrees over the next thirty years.[123] Nonetheless, in 1632 a Somerset judge, acting on a petition from clergymen, ordered pastors to read an injunction against church ales to their parishioners once a year on the first Sunday in February. This secular interference in the affairs of the church so angered William Laud, bishop of London, that he convinced King Charles I to revoke all orders forbidding church ales and to reissue his father's Declaration of Sports.[124] Ultimately, however, church ales were a lost cause, and after the Restoration the only record of a revival was in Williton, Somerset, and that revival only lasted until 1689.[125]

Drunkenness

The church considered drunkenness a mortal sin. As indicated by the instructions to confessors from the Doctors in Theology of the Faculty in Paris in 1721, the sin applied to various states of inebriation from the minor to the unmanageable.[126] In support of the opinion of theologians, medieval handbooks of penance had imposed penalties ranging from three to forty days on bread and water, but increasing to three years for the habitual drunkard.[127] Similarly, ecclesiastical courts in England had a long history of hearing cases of drunkenness, and their efforts to enforce not only sobriety but also other forms of morality on an unruly population continued after the Reformation and into the seventeenth century.[128] Punishments for drunkenness included admonishments to reform, imposition of penances, and excommunication for the recalcitrant, with some courts exercising greater severity than others.[129] The case of Richard Elsmere at Maidstone, Kent, in 1557 is an example

---

[122] Hutton, *Rise and Fall*, 87.

[123] Hutton, *Rise and Fall*, 139; Hutton, *Stations of the Sun*, 254; and Litzenberger, *English Reformation*, 140–41.

[124] Barnes, "County Politics," 108–11, 119.

[125] Hutton, *Stations of the Sun*, 257.

[126] Brennan, *Public Drinking*, 198.

[127] *Medieval Handbooks*, trans. McNeill and Gamer, 101, 158, 184, 230, 292.

[128] Hair, *Before the Bawdy Court*, 33; and Addy, *Sin and Society*, 199.

[129] Marchant, *Church under the Law*, 138.

of a mild punishment; when presented for a "drunker" he was "admonished to refrain from the same vice and to behave himself honestly hereafter."[130] An Essex villager who "was so drunken that he was not able to go of his legs" on New Year's Day received one of the more interesting penances: "to sit on his knees in the church porch with three empty (ale) pots before him till the Second Lesson with a white wand in his hand and then to come into church to the minister and there to speak…words of penitence."[131] Such outlandish penances might have been responsible for the contempt that many felt for the proceedings, and some men openly defied the courts and their judgments, as occurred in 1584 at Romford when William Hampshire proclaimed that he would "continue still in his drunkenness."[132] The contempt in turn might have contributed to the low level of presentments of drunkards in church courts; for example, presentments for drunkenness at the archdeacon's court of Colchester between 1600 and 1642 numbered thirteen of 756 total cases, slightly less than two percent.[133]

While church courts at least in England were hearing cases of drunkenness, criminal courts in France and Italy paid little or no attention to drunkards, as drunkenness remained a religious sin and not a criminal offense. Only Venice of all the communal governments in Italy apparently made it a crime, at least according to one historian who asserts, "Those who wassailed in taverns or went on a rowdy tour of the bars could be condemned to the galleys."[134] However, Venetians never "wassailed," and they never went to "bars," and the sources contain no other evidence of this regulation or any cases of prosecution. At first glance the situation in France seems clear; when Nicolas Delamare compiled the *Traité de la Police* for King Louis XIV early in the eighteenth century, his search of edicts issued since the thirteenth century uncovered no laws against drunkenness.[135] Nonetheless, an edict issued in 1536 condemned drunkenness and ordered imprisonment for the first offense and whipping for recurrences.[136] Not only did Delamare's

[130] Hair, *Before the Bawdy Court*, 222.

[131] Emmison, *Elizabethan Life*, 214.

[132] McIntosh, *Community Transformed*, 248.

[133] Sharpe, "Crime and Delinquency," 109. See also Brinkworth and Gilkes, *Bawdy Court*, 35; Ingram, *Church Courts*, 100; Marchant, *Church under the Law*, 219; and McIntosh, *Community Transformed*, 65n136.

[134] Mackenney, *Tradesmen and Traders*, 148. Mackenney cites manuscripts from the Biblioteca Marciana in Venice, dated 1571, 1348–1801, and 1348–1795, but this reference is inclusive of other regulations on taverns.

[135] Dion, *Histoire de la vigne*, 488; and Nahoum-Grappe, "Histoire du vin," 301.

[136] Brennan, *Public Drinking*, 199; and Franklin, *Moeurs et coutumes*, 58–59.

survey miss this edict, but also the jurist Jean Papon failed to acknowledge it when he published his legal treatise in 1575.[137] No evidence exists that the edict was reissued or even ever enforced.[138] Local authorities could issue their own ordinances against drunkenness, but even drunkards who violated the curfew in Paris during the fifteenth century did not face prosecution.[139] The sources reveal only one case of a prosecution of a drunkard in France during this period, and that occurred at Cambrai in 1692 when the accused responded in disbelief, "Where could you find a man who has never gone to a cabaret?"[140]

English authorities, unlike those in France and Italy, made drunkenness a criminal offense. In 1699 the author of *An Account of the Societies for Reformation of Manners* listed six statutes against drunkenness, the first of which was the "Act to repress the odious and loathsome sin of drunkenness," dated 1606.[141] Even before 1606, many local authorities had issued ordinances criminalizing the offense. In the sixteenth century, London officials punished drunkards with imprisonment and whippings, while a Manchester ordinance in 1577 set the punishment for public drunkenness as a night in the dungeon plus a payment on release of 6 pence to the poor.[142] Officials at Colchester took a leaf from the church courts by requiring drunkards to confess their sins at church on Sundays. Another similarity between the church courts and secular courts at Colchester was the small number of offenders; between 1510 and 1564 the secular courts only dealt with nine cases of drunkenness, and elsewhere the cases heard as a result of these local ordinances were small in number.[143] Despite the prosecution of drunkenness by religious courts and by some local courts, moral reformers pressed for Parliament to make drunkenness a crime, and the result was the legislative program outlined at the beginning of this chapter. The reform agenda achieved a significant success in 1606 when Parliament passed a law against drunkenness and excessive drinking, setting a fine of 5 shillings or, for those who could not or would not pay, six hours in the stocks. As a means of ensuring enforcement, the act empowered all

---

[137] Davis, *Fiction in the Archives*, 12, n.

[138] Brennan, *Public Drinking*, 199–200.

[139] Cohen, "Hundred Years' War," 118.

[140] Watts, *Social History*, 85.

[141] Bahlman, *Moral Revolution*, 14.

[142] Archer, *Pursuit of Stability*, 218; and Iles, "Early Stages," 255.

[143] Higgs, *Godliness and Governance*, 275–76; Mayhew, *Tudor Rye*, 214–15; and Archer, *Pursuit of Stability*, 239.

common-law and assize courts, justices of the peace, mayors, and local courts to punish offenders.[144] Aside from any questions of morality, the purposes of the legislation were to limit idleness and the accompanying demands on parish poor relief, to maintain good order, and to divert grain from the brewing of beer to the baking of bread.[145] Significantly, the economic aspects of these purposes reemerge from the patterns of prosecution, for the number of cases increased during periods of economic hardship such as the mid-1620s.[146]

In 1655 Oliver Cromwell sent his newly appointed major generals throughout England with instructions to "encourage and promote godliness, and discourage and discountenance all profaneness and ungodliness," including of course drunkenness. The major generals' efforts to enforce the laws against drunkards, as well as other aspects of the puritan reform program, proved a failure as did other efforts to promote the puritan moral vision.[147] Shortly after ascending the throne, in 1689 King William ordered all the clergy to preach frequently against prevailing sins and vices, including drunkenness of course, and to read to their congregations the appropriate statutes, such as the law passed in 1606.[148] William's order would have been welcomed by a new reform movement, the Societies for Reformation of Manners. However, a successful campaign against drunkenness would once again elude the reformers, for the annual reports of the societies indicate that in the closing years of the seventeenth century they did not succeed in bringing a single drunkard to justice.[149] The difficulty in achieving a significant number of prosecutions against drunkards, as it was for the legislation concerning alehouses, was the reliance on local authorities. In recognition of this and in an effort to gain their support, the act of 1606 stipulated that the fines collected from drunkards go to relief of the parish poor, which in turn would provide relief to the ratepayers of the parish.[150] Nonetheless, the enforcement of the legislation faced several problems. The first was the widespread contempt for it as well as for other aspects of moralizing reform. Adding to the contempt was the view that the law against drunkenness was class specific and focused on those too poor even to pay the fine. In the debates preceding

[144] Baird, "Alcohol Problem and the Law: II," 143, 145.

[145] Hudson, *Study of Social Regulations,* 9.

[146] Ingram, "Religion, Communities," 187–88.

[147] Durston, "Puritan Rule," 218, 222.

[148] Bahlman, *Moral Revolution,* 15.

[149] Hunt, *Governing Morals,* 35–37.

[150] Baird, "Alcohol Problem and the Law: II," 145–46.

the passage of the legislation, the Parliamentarian Edward Glascock claimed a bill against drunkenness introduced in 1601 was "a mere cobweb to catch poor flies in."[151] John Taylor, in a poem entitled "Partiality," contrasted the reaction to the drunken gentleman and the drunken porter; people would say that the gentleman was sick, but the porter would be hauled to the stocks "and there endure a world of flouts and mocks."[152]

Another problem with the enforcement of the legislation was the burden it imposed on local justices. Part of the burden resulted from the necessity of a formal indictment before prosecution could proceed, and local constables required instruction on the form of oath needed for an indictment: "You shall swear that A B of C in the county of Norfolk, blacksmith, on Monday now last past in C aforesaid was drunk, and so God help you."[153] Probably even a larger impediment to prosecution was the possibility of disagreement over what constituted drunkenness. According to two seventeenth-century definitions, it was "where the same legs which carry a man into the house, cannot bring him out again" and "the privation of orderly motion and understanding." In 1624 a Maldon man used a similar definition to protest when authorities placed a friend in the stocks: "He was not drunk, for he that was drunk could not stand nor go."[154] The problems with the enforcement of the legislation were probably one of the reasons villagers, townspeople, and even local officials were reluctant to appear in court and support accusations that their neighbors were drunkards. Either that or seventeenth-century English men and women were extremely sober, because the presentments for drunkenness after the passage of the act of 1606 were, as they were in local courts prior to 1606 and in ecclesiastical courts, extremely low. For example, a study of the quarter sessions courts in Lancashire and Warwickshire in the seventeenth century reveals that only twenty-two of 7,959 offenses were for drunkenness or for committing another crime while drunk.[155]

Committing a crime while drunk has been a vexed problem for legal systems: Is the drunkenness a mitigating or an aggravating factor? And does a person who commits a crime while under the influence of alcohol receive a reduced punishment? According to medieval commentators on canon law,

[151] Kent, "Attitudes of Members," 61.

[152] Manley, *London in the Age,* 247.

[153] Bretherton, "Country Inns," 150, 168; and Doughty, *Notebook of Robert Doughty,* ed. Rosenheim, 16.

[154] Sharpe, *Crime in Seventeenth-Century England,* 54.

[155] King, "Regulation of Alehouses," 34. See also Hindle, *State and Social Change,* 182; and Herrup, *Common Peace,* 33–34.

drunkenness could be a mitigating factor in the sin of adultery and pre-
sumably other sins, which means the commission of one sin—drunkenness—could reduce the penalties imposed for the commission of another.[156]
Criminal courts in Germany recognized the same principle, that drunkenness was both an offense and a legal defense in the commission of criminal
acts.[157] In 1538 the distinguished Frankfort jurist Johann Fichard argued that
the crimes of a madman and a drunkard were similar, since both were committed without intent and should therefore receive a reduced punishment if
any punishment at all.[158] The situation in France was not as clear-cut. French
jurists tended to agree with their German counterparts, but a complicating
factor was the above-mentioned edict of 1536, which not only criminalized
drunkenness but also declared that people who committed a crime under
the influence of drink should not receive a pardon. Their punishment should
be the same as if they had been sober and even increased due to the aggravating factor of drunkenness.[159] The previously mentioned jurist Jean Papon
ignored this edict when he argued in 1575 that the crimes of a drunkard were
pardonable because they occurred without the intent of fraud or malice. As
a result of this legal principle, a textile worker who killed his master in a
drunken brawl at Amiens received a pardon on the payment of a fine. The
principle apparently did not apply to women, for an inebriated woman who
committed incest with her father was hanged while her father was burned at
the stake.[160] Unlike the French, the English position was unambiguous. All
the notable jurists concurred that drunkenness was not a mitigating factor
when committing a crime. Both Richard Hooker in his *Laws of the Ecclesiastical Polity* and Francis Bacon in *Elements of the Common Laws of England*
argued that drunkards could not claim diminished responsibility since they
were responsible for their own drunkenness. In a judgment supported by
Edward Coke, the judge of a case in 1603 claimed that, while the drunkard was *non compos mentis* when committing the crime, rather than dimin-
ish the offense, the drunkenness aggravated it.[161] As the moralists declared,
"Woe to drunkards!"

[156] Brundage, *Law, Sex*, 301.

[157] Tlusty, *Bacchus and Civic Order*, 80–81.

[158] Midelfort, *History of Madness*, 196.

[159] Brennan, *Public Drinking*, 49; and Franklin, *Moeurs et coutumes*, 59.

[160] Davis, *Fiction in the Archives*, 12, n92, 155, n19.

[161] Singh, "History of the Defence," 530–31.

———— 🍇 ————

The legal position of drunkards in England was unique. Drunkenness was a criminal offense in England as a result of laws enacted early in the seventeenth century. Despite the Venetian law against "wassailing" and "touring bars" and the French edict of 1536, the policy in France and Italy was one of laissez-faire. Similarly, England was unique in making drunkenness an aggravating factor in the commission of crimes, while elsewhere a drunken murderer could expect leniency from the courts. The reasons for these differences are hard to explain, especially since in many aspects of regulation and punishment, England, France, and Italy shared common values. Governments in all three countries passed legislation protecting the rights of consumers by regulating the quality, quantity, and price of alcoholic beverages. They issued ordinances overseeing drinking establishments and their proprietors, and with varying degrees of commitment they attempted to control who drank what, where, when, and how. The English criminalization of drunkenness might have been a function of the severity of the problem; perhaps English towns and villages suffered drunkards in plague proportions, much more than in France and Italy. So, one could argue, English governments had to take a stand. The problem with this argument is that the evidence from all the courts indicates very low levels of presentment and prosecution for drunkenness. An opposing argument might consider the legislation to be a function not of a high rate of drunkenness but of a vocal moralizing reform movement—puritanism—that tried to impose the views of a minority on the rest of the nation. After securing the puritan legislative programs, these moral do-gooders would then have been ready to swear in court against their neighbors that A B of C in the county of Norfolk, blacksmith, on Monday now last past in C aforesaid was drunk. The low levels of presentment and prosecution indicate that very few of them did so.

The low levels of presentment and prosecution along with the French and Italian refusal to make drunkenness a crime show that alcohol-fueled violence and disorder were not as serious a problem in traditional Europe as the moralists would have people believe. In other words, if the moralists had been right, the levels would be higher and French and Italian governments would have legislated against drunkenness. Similarly, fears of the drunken poor were not strong enough to prevent the enactment of regulations that attempted to secure them a supply of good drink at a reasonable price. The condemnations of the moralists give a misleading picture of the role of alcoholic beverages in traditional Europe. They fail to illustrate the role of alcohol in people's sustenance and recreation, they likewise fail to demonstrate the positive attributes of celebration, jollification, and socialization, and they overemphasize the role of drink in disorder and violence. The regulations enacted by governments are indications of the failures and the overemphasis. 🍇

Chapter 9

Alcohol, Violence, & Disorder

ETOH, alias Ethanol, Alcohol, C_2H_5OH
food, complement to food, and poison.
stimulant to appetite and aid to digestion,
tonic, medicine, and harmful drug,
elixir, potion, or "a tool of the devil,"
energizer or soporific,
sacrament or abomination,
aphrodisiac or turn-off,
euphoriant, and depressant,
adjunct to sociability or means of retreat,
stimulant or relaxant,
tasty nectar or godawful stuff,
exculpatory, or aggravating, with respect to blame,
god's gift or a curse,
analgesic and anesthetic, disinhibitor or knock-out,
etc., etc.[1]

This book is similar to a jigsaw puzzle whose pieces do not fit together, and, like the conflicting attributes of alcohol itself, it demonstrates conflicting aspects of the consumption of alcohol in traditional Europe. The first piece of the puzzle is the link between alcohol and both violent crime and antisocial behavior documented by studies of modern Western societies. Next are the high levels of violence in traditional Europe and the preoccupation of authorities with maintaining order. The condemnations of

---

[1] Heath, *Drinking Occasions*, dedication page.

the moralists form another piece, as they demonstrate concern about the effects of drunkenness and drinking establishments on violence and disorder, greatly so in England, significantly so in France, and moderately so in Italy. So far the pieces seem to fit, but evidence on the consumption of alcohol indicates that Italians consumed the most, and consumption in England and France declined in the early modern period just as the moralists were becoming more vociferous in their condemnations. Consumption in all three countries was higher than in their modern counterparts. Recreational drinking produces an awkward piece, for the effects of the jollification, celebration, and socialization that accompanied it would, on the one hand, mitigate any violent and disorderly behavior, but the resultant binge drinking could, on the other hand, exacerbate such behavior. Many moralists, in fact, condemned festive drinking for causing violence and disorder. They also pointed their indignant fingers at drinking establishments, but alehouses and taverns functioned as a third place where people could relax and socialize with friends and neighbors. Even more awkward are the pieces involving disorderly places and persons. The role of drinking and drunkenness in producing the disorder was ambivalent, and although most of the disorder centered on drinking establishments, whenever statistical evidence is available, as it is for seventeenth-century England, it demonstrates that the vast majority of alehouse keepers did not face prosecution for running disorderly premises. The piece representing violence does not fit at all. To be sure, the sources document many cases of violence associated with drinking and drinking establishments, but when statistical evidence is available, it demonstrates much lower levels of violence than occurs in modern societies. Only half of the final piece fits, as government regulations attempted to guarantee supplies of alcoholic beverages, while at the same time placing restrictions on taverns and alehouses. Aside from an apparently disregarded and forgotten French royal edict early in the sixteenth century, drunkenness became a crime only in England, but here prosecution was sporadic; either that or inebriation was rare.

Unfortunately for those who like neat and tidy solutions to historical puzzles, no theories or explanations can be completely successful in resolving the role of alcohol in violent and disorderly behavior in traditional Europe. Even scholars of modern behavior, as noted in chapter 1, are at a loss to explain the link. To repeat the statement of Alan R. Lang, "Drinking can cause increases in aggressive behavior, at least in certain doses, in certain persons, and under certain circumstances. In many ways, however, this is really all we know. It is not clear which of the many potentially important aspects of the agent, the host, and the environment are critical to the inter-action that produces increased aggression." In addition to the three impor-tant aspects of the agent, the host, and the environment, a fourth, that of the observer, is necessary to understand the situation in traditional Europe. An examination of each of these in turn might help put at least some of the pieces of the puzzle together.

The Agent

The alcoholic beverages were overwhelmingly ale, beer, and wine. If the strength of these beverages were weak, then drunkenness would have been less widespread. However, the evidence indicates that their strength was roughly comparable to modern drinks, except for the French *piquette*, the Italian *mezzo vino*, and the English small ale and beer, all drinks of the la-boring poor. Probably the best indicator that the alcoholic drinks, be they wine, ale, or beer, were not exceptionally weak is the chorus of complaints about drunkenness. The complaints focused on recreational drinking. No one condemned the daily consumption of alcohol that formed an essential part of people's diet. Governments throughout Europe recognized the im-portance of alcoholic beverages for the sustenance of their citizens by enact-ing laws that attempted to guarantee a reliable supply of ale, beer, or wine of reasonable quality and price in honest measures, and even the English legislation on alehouses acknowledged their role in providing drink for the poor. As a result of the daily drinking of alcoholic beverages as part of meals, England, France, and Italy had what anthropologists call a wet rather than a dry drinking culture. Even when the consumption of alcohol was beyond people's financial means, an expectation existed that it should be part of their meals. In modern dry drinking cultures, most of the drinking is recreational, often resulting in binge drinking and leading in turn to an increase in alco-hol-related problems. One of the deficiencies in the large amount of statistical evidence introduced in chapter 3 is that it does not differentiate between the amount of alcohol consumed with meals and the amount for recreational drinking. However, since most people were accustomed to regular encoun-ters with alcohol, they were less likely to become cheap and easy drunkards as a result of binge drinking, and their recreational drinking in turn was less likely to lead to alcohol-related problems.

Despite popular belief to the contrary, alcohol does not produce a pharmacological trigger for violence, and most of the drinking in modern societies does not produce violence. People in traditional Europe consumed much more alcohol than is consumed in modern Europe, and the levels of violence were similarly higher in traditional Europe than they are today, but the statistical evidence demonstrates a lower correlation between alcohol and violence than does the evidence for modern societies. Perhaps a different perspective is necessary for understanding the relationship between alcohol and violence in traditional Europe. Given the violent tenor of the period, the consumption of alcohol might have inhibited the propensity to attack friend, stranger, or foe. Rather than being a cause of violence, alcohol decreased the likelihood of its occurring.

The Host

The usual hosts in modern societies are young adult males, who consume the most alcohol and commit the most acts of violence. Age-specific statistics for alcohol consumption and acts of violence do not exist for traditional Europe, although some evidence suggests that young men comprised the largest clientele in taverns and alehouses. James B. Collins, for example, argues that the drinkers in Brittany's taverns were predominantly unmarried men between the ages of fifteen and thirty.[2] Peter Clark believes that the clientele in English alehouses formed two major groups. The first included young unmarried men who were apprentices, journeymen, and servants; the second group comprised young and middle-aged married men.[3] Much of the violence perpetrated by young men originated in drinking establishments, as village youth planned their battles with those from neighboring villages, student encounters with keepers led to town-gown clashes, and young men with rape on their minds plied maidens with drink. Nonetheless, the available evidence does not permit a definitive conclusion on whether young males were responsible for most of the violence. Whether young men were involved in most of the drunken disorder is similarly unclear. Servants, apprentices, and students were guilty of haunting drinking establishments, violating curfews, missing church services, idleness, gambling, playing cards, sexual license, dancing, singing, banqueting, vomiting, swearing, brawling, vandalism, and stealing, but so were their elders.

Although young men were responsible for a considerable amount of

[2] Collins, *Classes, Estates,* 20, 62, 72.
[3] Clark, *English Alehouse,* 127.

drunken disorder, most people in traditional Europe had the capacity for disorderly behavior while engaged in recreational drinking. The functions of recreational drinking were jollification, celebration, and socialization, which would result in a break from daily constraints, hierarchy, and order in favor of carnival license. The carnival side in Peter Bruegel's *Combat between Carnival and Lent* depicts many of the disorderly behaviors of young men listed above: haunting drinking establishments, missing church services, idleness, gambling, playing cards, sexual license, dancing, singing, banqueting, vomiting, and brawling. People engaged in recreational drinking did not exhibit the Lenten values of decency, diligence, gravity, modesty, orderliness, prudence, reason, self-control, sobriety, and thrift. In other words, recreational drinking created a propensity for disorder, so much so that the low number of prosecutions for disorderly alehouses in seventeenth-century England is surprising.

While the license of carnival led to disorder, the obsession with honor led to violence. Men could nourish ancient hatreds and recent affronts in taverns and alehouses, screwing up their courage with drink after drink while waiting for the appearance of their enemy. Not alcohol, but the appearance of the enemy, was the trigger for violence in such situations. The drinks could have fuddled the protagonist's mind, giving him a false sense of security or causing him to take dangerous risks that he would have avoided had he been sober, but the devil's knife was the obsession with honor that provoked such intense emotions in traditional Europe. The weakness of the premodern state and especially its system of justice left aggrieved men and women, but especially men, to seek their own retribution and vengeance, sometimes resulting in murderous vendettas that endured for generations.

The Environment

The microenvironment for most of the violence and the disorder was the drinking establishment and, to a lesser extent, the festive occasion. Authorities feared the potential for disorder and violence whenever large groups of people gathered for festive drinking, but commentators such as John Aubrey, Richard Rawlidge, and Claude de Rubys commended the public festivals and complained that their demise led to worse behavior in alehouses and taverns. Studies of modern drinking establishments have demonstrated their role in violence; as summarized by Dwight B. Heath, "Evidence is increasing that aggressive people tend to be more aggressive in a setting where alcohol ... gives an excuse for asocial or antisocial behavior."[4] Several features of traditional European taverns and alehouses presented an excuse for asocial or antisocial behavior. The first was their disorderly clientele that included young men determined to assert their manhood, criminal elements such as thieves, prostitutes, and gamblers, and the transient population of vagabonds and soldiers. The second was their public space that made them an ideal venue to blacken an enemy's reputation through insults, slander, or gossip. As a result of these features, drinking establishments could give drinking a bad name, and governments accordingly tried to restrict the clientele to travelers.

The efforts of the governments failed, and alehouses and taverns increasingly became the third place where people could meet for jollification, celebration, and socialization. They similarly became the centers of popular recreation and popular culture, a place for courtship and weddings, music, songs and dances, gambling and games, stories and news, debates and discussions, and reconciliation with foes and enemies. The reconciliation illustrates that if drinking establishments could be settings for asocial and antisocial behavior, they could also be settings for convivial companionship and hospitality. To complete Heath's statement, evidence is also increasing that alcohol "does nothing to foster violence on the part of nonaggressive people." While authorities feared the potential for disorder and violence whenever large groups of people gathered for festive drinking, they also feared gatherings in private space. At least taverns and alehouses represented public space, where keepers could notice the arrival of strangers and report suspicious activity to the government, as their licenses often obliged them to do.[5] As patresfamilias of their households, keepers were also responsible for what happened in their establishments, and they had the authority to maintain control, although the indictments of keepers for permitting disorder and of the antipriest keepers from hell indicate that they were not always responsible and did not always exercise their authority.

The macroenvironment was the wider society. According to the anthropological perspective, society teaches what alcohol does, and drunken comportment is learned. *Alcohol, Sex, and Gender* argued that traditional European society taught the consumption of alcohol led to sexual activity, and the prevailing cultural script linked drinking with intimate contact. The prevailing cultural script also linked drinking with jollification, celebration, socialization, and the related functions of sociability, conviviality, hospitality, and com-

---

[4] Heath, *Drinking Occasions,* 132.
[5] Tlusty, *Bacchus and Civic Order,* 158–59.

panionship. The carnival license implicit in these functions linked drinking to disorder, but it did not link it to violence. The moralists' demonization of alcohol attempted to change the cultural script by linking drinking to murder and mayhem. The low correlation between alcohol and violence and between drinking establishments and violence indicates that the efforts to demonize alcohol were not successful. In other words, traditional European society taught that alcohol did not lead to violent behavior. Perhaps the high correlation that exists in modern societies is an indication that subsequent moralists were successful in changing the cultural script.

In between the micro and the macro is the national environment. Of the three countries examined, England was unique for several reasons: it paid homage to Ceres rather than to Bacchus, that is, it was a beer-drinking rather than a wine-drinking country; it was Protestant from the middle of the sixteenth century; its moralists were more vehement than those from France and Italy in attacking the perceived dangers of alcohol; it made drunkenness a crime; and its legal system did not consider drunkenness an extenuating circumstance in the commission of a crime. Nowadays a popular perception distinguishes between the chardonnay-sipping wine culture and the jug-chugging beer culture, but it would be anachronistic to apply this distinction to traditional Europe. Nonetheless, the beverage of choice in modern dry drinking cultures is beer and, to a lesser extent, spirits, while it is wine in wet drinking cultures, indicating that wine is somehow easier than beer to integrate into sustained daily consumption that avoids binge drinking. If wine works as a way of separating dry and wet drinking cultures, Catholicism does not, as the examples of Ireland and Poland demonstrate.

England's Protestants and especially its puritans demonized alcohol, and, as already suggested, this might have been responsible for turning England from a wet drinking culture to a dry drinking culture. The puritan assault on drunkenness and drinking establishments had many of the characteristics of a moral panic, and the movement was at least partly responsible for the criminalization of drunkenness as a result of the act of Parliament in 1606. Much of the anecdotal material for the two chapters on disorder comes from English sources, but all the quantitative data from England—prosecutions of disorderly alehouses and persons, violence associated with drinking establishments or drinking assailants, presentations of people charged with drunkenness—indicate that the moralists were guilty of exaggeration. While Italian moralists condemned drinking establishments, they showed little concern for the problems associated with drunkenness, which leads to the possible conclusion that Italy had far fewer drinking problems than England and to a lesser extent France, although more research is necessary to prove it.

The Observer

Just as important as the agent, the host, and the environment in understanding the relationship of alcohol with violence and disorder in traditional Europe is the observer. Perceptions of violence were the least likely to vary according to the observer, but drunkenness was, like Shakespeare's beauty, in the eye of the beholder, despite efforts to define it. A good illustration of this comes from the Norman nobleman, the Sire de Gouberville; when his friends drank too much they were "bons campagnons," but when others did so they were drunkards.[6] More important were varying perceptions of disorder. The people of northeast Dorset, mentioned on several occasions, equated disorder with violence; if no violence took place during their drinking revels then no disorder took place. They were not alone in their opinions, and several incidents indicate that other observers not only disagreed with the views of the authorities on the matter but also were prepared to take action against them. When a magistrate attempted to suppress the St. Peter's Day wakes at Little Budworth in 1596, the people went ahead with them anyway and had their customary drinking, dancing, and entertainment, including a bearbaiting organized by the local alewives. When the magistrate's servants attempted to disperse the crowd, they were assaulted and threatened, and even the local constables apparently sided with the crowd and enjoyed the entertainment.[7] A similar incident involved William Baxter, who traveled from alehouse to alehouse, entertaining people with his pet bear. When he came to Wilmslow in April 1629, the magistrates arrested him for drunkenness, "diverse misdemeanors and outcries," and for swearing "six terrible oaths." His placement in the stocks nearly caused a riot among his numerous supporters in the town, who threatened the magistrates and challenged them to a fight, attempted to destroy the stocks, supplied Baxter with ale, and bolstered his spirits with drums and music. The supporters made two telling comments; the local butcher claimed, "We will not be restrained; we will have our pastimes in this town," and another pleaded with the constable to let Baxter go

---

[6] Fedden, *Manor Life*, 78

[7] Hindle, "Custom, Festival," 167.

by reminding him, "You are our constable."[8]

When arrested for drunkenness, a blacksmith from Milbourne St. Andrew asked, "What had any justice to do with [my] drinking?"[9] According to Joseph Gusfield's paper on "Benevolent Repression: Popular Culture, Social Structure, and the Control of Drinking," the answer to the blacksmith's question lies in the attitudes of the elites. As Gusfield argues, "Elites institute drinking controls that benefit themselves and do so in the name of helping others."[10] The elites, including moralists, local officials and notables, and religious and political authorities, sought a stable, diligent, and hardworking supply of labor, and they also sought a devout and orderly society. Instead of the license of carnival they wanted to see more of the values of Lent. However, Gusfield's answer is incomplete. The elites were not the only ones who objected to the disorder resulting from drinking and drinking establishments, for the indictments of disorderly drinkers and keepers indicate fellow parishioners and workers, neighbors, and relatives, especially husbands and wives, complained of the disorder. Not only were they observers of the license of carnival, but they were also its victims.

When I began writing this book I envisaged one much different than this one. In my *Alcohol, Sex, and Gender,* I argued that the connection between alcohol and sexual activity encapsulated by Ogden Nash's witticism, "Candy is dandy, but liquor is quicker," was similar in modern Western societies and traditional Europe. I anticipated that in this book, I would make the same argument regarding the connection between alcohol and violence. The evidence forced me to reach a different conclusion. Alcohol's primary role in jollification, celebration, and socialization in the past meant that its consumption did not lead to violent behavior. Oddly enough, in modern societies alcohol has a similar role, but its consumption sometimes leads to violent and antisocial behavior. That is another of its many conflicting attributes.

---

[8] Hindle, *State and Social Change,* 200.

[9] Underdown, *Revel, Riot,* 93–94.

[10] Gusfield, "Benevolent Repression," 406.

Bibliography

Primary Sources

Acts of the High Commission Court within the Diocese of Durham. London: George Andrews, 1858.

Alberti, Leon Battista. *The Family in Renaissance Florence [I libri della famiglia].* Translated by Renée Neu Watkins. Columbia: University of South Carolina Press, 1969.

Amt, Emilie, ed. *Women's Lives in Medieval Europe: A Sourcebook.* New York: Routledge, 1993.

Apperson, G. L., ed. *English Proverbs and Proverbial Phrases: A Historical Dictionary.* London: J. M. Dent and Sons, 1929.

Ashley, Francis. *The Casebook of Sir Francis Ashley JP, Recorder of Dorchester, 1614–35.* Edited by J. H. Bettey. Dorset: Dorset Record Society, 1981.

Ashley, Leonard R. N., ed. *Elizabethan Popular Culture.* Bowling Green, OH: Bowling Green State University Popular Press, 1988.

Aubrey, John. *"Brief Lives," Chiefly of Contemporaries, Set Down by John Aubrey, between the Years 1669 and 1696.* Edited by Andrew Clark. 2 vols. Oxford: Clarendon Press, 1898.

Bacon, Nathaniel. *The Official Papers of Sir Nathaniel Bacon of Stiffkey, Norfolk, as Justice of the Peace, 1580–1620.* Edited by H. W. Saunders. London: Royal Historical Society, 1915.

Bandello, Matteo. *Twelve Stories.* Translated and edited by Percy Pinkerton. London: John C. Nimmo, 1895.

Barclay, Alexander. *The Eclogues of Alexander Barclay.* Edited by Beatrice White. London: Oxford University Press, 1928.

Basile, Giambattista. *The Pentameron of Giambattista Basile.* Translated by Richard Burton and introduction by E. R. Vincent. London: Spring Books, n.d.

Best, Henry. *The Farming and Memorandum Books of Henry Best of Elmswell, 1642.* Edited by Donald Woodward. London: Oxford University Press, 1984.

Bodel, Jean. *Le jeu de Saint Nicholas.* In *Five Comedies of Medieval France,* translated by Oscar Mandel, 35–75. New York: E. P. Dutton, 1970.

Boorde, Andrew. *A Compendyous Regyment or a Dyetary of Helth (1542).* Edited by F. J. Furnivall. London: Early English Text Society, 1870.

Bradwell, Stephen. *Physick for the Sicknesse, Commonly Called the Plague.* London: Benjamin

Fisher, 1636.

Brereton, Geoffrey, ed. *Sixteenth to Eighteenth Centuries*. Vol. 2 of *The Penguin Book of French Verse*. Harmondsworth: Penguin, 1958.

Brinkworth, E. R. C., and R. K. Gilkes, eds. *The "Bawdy Court" of Banbury: The Act Book of the Peculiar Court of Banbury, Oxfordshire and Northamptonshire, 1625–1638*. Banbury: Banbury Historical Society, 1997.

Brown, Tom. *Amusements Serious and Comical and Other Works*. Edited by Arthur L. Hayward. London: George Routledge and Sons, 1927.

Brucker, Gene, ed. *The Society of Renaissance Florence: A Documentary Study*. New York: Harper and Row, 1971.

Calendar of Assize Records: Kent Indictments, edited by J. S. Cockburn. 4 vols. London: Her Majesty's Stationery Office, 1989–97.

Cellini, Benvenuto. *The Autobiography of Benvenuto Cellini*. Translated by George Bull. Harmondsworth: Penguin, 1956.

Certaldo, Paolo da. *Libro di buoni costumi*. Edited by Alfredo Schiaffini. Florence: Felice Le Monnier, 1945.

Chambers, David, and Brian Pullan, eds. *Venice: A Documentary History, 1450–1630*. Oxford: Blackwell, 1992.

Chandos, John, ed. *In God's Name: Examples of Preaching in England from the Act of Supremacy to the Act of Uniformity, 1534–1662*. London: Hutchinson, 1971.

Chaucer, Geoffrey. *The Canterbury Tales*. Translated by Nevill Coghill. Baltimore: Penguin, 1958.

Clifford, Anne. *The Diary of the Lady Anne Clifford*. Edited by V. Sackville-West. London: William Heinemann, 1923.

Cohen, Thomas V., and Elizabeth S. Cohen, eds. *Words and Deeds in Renaissance Rome: Trials before the Papal Magistrates*. Toronto: University of Toronto Press, 1993.

Collier, J. Payne, ed. *Illustrations of Early English Popular Literature*. 2 vols. New York: Benjamin Bloom, 1966.

Conversini da Ravenna, Giovanni. *Dialogue between Giovanni and a Letter*. Edited and translated by Helen Lanneau Eaker. Binghamton: Medieval and Renaissance Texts and Studies, 1989.

Copland, Robert. *The Highway to the Spital-House*. In *The Elizabethan Underworld*, edited by A. V. Judges, 1–25. London: Routledge and Kegan Paul, 1965.

Coulton, G. G., trans. and ed. *Life in the Middle Ages*. 4 vols. Cambridge: Cambridge University Press, 1967.

———, trans. and ed. *Social Life in Britain from the Conquest to the Reformation*. Cambridge: Cambridge University Press, 1918.

County of Middlesex: Calendar to the Sessions Records. Edited by William Le Hardy. New series, 4 vols. London: Guildhall, Westminster, 1935–41.

Couth, Bill, ed. *Grantham during the Interregnum: The Hall Book of Grantham, 1641–1649*. Woodbridge: Lincoln Record Society, 1995.

Crawford, Patricia, and Laura Gowing, eds. *Women's Worlds in Seventeenth-Century England*. London: Routledge, 2000.

Le Débat des hérauts d'armes de France et d'Angleterre, suivi de The Debate between the Heralds of England and France by John Coke. Edited by Léopold Pannier and Paul Meyer. Paris: Firmin-Didot, 1877.

The Debate of the Carpenter's Tools. In *Remains of the Early Popular Poetry of England*, edited by William Carew Hazlitt, 1:79–90. London: John Russell Smith, 1864.

[Defoe, Daniel]. *The Complete English Tradesman in Familiar Letters*. 2 vols. in 3 parts. New York: Augustus M. Kelley, 1969.

Dekker, Thomas. *The Dead Tearme*. In *The Non-Dramatic Works of Thomas Dekker*, edited by Alexander B. Grosart, 4:1–84. London: Huth, 1885.

————. *English Villainies Discoverd by Lantern and Candlelight*. In *Thomas Dekker: The Wonderful Year; The Gull's Horn-Book; Penny-Wise, Pound Foolish; English Villainies Discovered by Lantern and Candlelight; and Selected Writings*, edited by E. D. Pendry, 169–308. London: Edward Arnold, 1967.

————. *O Per Se O*. In *The Elizabethan Underworld*, edited by A. V. Judges, 366–82. London: Routledge and Kegan Paul, 1965.

————. *The Seven Deadly Sinnes*. In *The Non-Dramatic Works of Thomas Dekker*, edited by Alexander B. Grosart, 2:1–81. London: Huth, 1885.

Denton, Thomas. *A Perambulation of Cumberland, 1687–1688, Including Descriptions of Westmorland, the Isle of Man and Ireland*. Edited by Angus J. L. Winchester and Mary Wane. Woodbridge: Boydell, 2003.

Dixon, James Henry, ed. *Ancient Poems, Ballads, and Songs of the Peasantry of England*. Early English Poetry, Ballads, and Popular Literature of the Middle Ages 17. London: Percy Society, 1846.

Dobson, R. B., ed. *The Peasants' Revolt of 1381*. London: Macmillan, 1970.

Doughty, Robert. *The Notebook of Robert Doughty, 1662–1665*. Edited by James M. Rosenheim. Norwich: Norfolk Record Society, 1989.

Durham Quarter Sessions Rolls, 1471–1625. Edited by C. M. Fraser. Newcastle: Athenaeum, 1991.

Earle, John. *Microcosmography, or, A Piece of the World Discovered in Essays and Characters*. Edited by Harold Osborne. London: University Tutorial, 1933.

Edgeworth, Roger. *Sermons Very Fruitfull, Godly and Learned: Preaching in the Reformation, c. 1535–c. 1553*. Edited by Janet Wilson. Cambridge: D. S. Brewer, 1993.

Elyot, Thomas. *The Castel of Helth (1541)*. New York: Scholars' Facsimiles and Reprints, 1937.

Farmer, John S., ed. *Merry Songs and Ballads Prior to the Year A.D. 1800*. 5 vols. New York: Cooper Square, 1964.

Fincham, Kenneth, ed. *Visitation Articles and Injunctions of the Early Stuart Church*. 2 vols. Woodbridge: Boydell, 1994–98.

Franklin, Benjamin. *The Autobiography of Benjamin Franklin: A Genetic Text*. Edited by J. A. Leo Lemay and P. M. Zall. Knoxville: University of Tennessee Press, 1981.

Fuller, Thomas. *The History of the Worthies of England*. Edited by P. Austin Nuttall. 3 vols. London: Thomas Tegg, 1840.

Gammer Gurtons Nedle. Edited by H. F. B. Brett-Smith. Oxford: Basil Blackwell, 1920.

Gardiner, Samuel Rawson, ed. *The Constitutional Documents of the Puritan Revolution, 1628–1660*. Oxford: Clarendon Press, 1889.

Gascoigne, George. *A Delicate Diet, for Daintiemouthde Droonkardes*. In *The Complete Works of George Gascoigne*, edited by John W. Cunliffe, 2:451–71. Cambridge: Cambridge University Press, 1910.

Goldberg, P. J. P., trans. and ed. *Women in England, c. 1275–1525: Documentary Sources.* Manchester: Manchester University Press, 1995.

The Goodman of Paris (Le Ménagier de Paris): A Treatise on Moral and Domestic Economy by a Citizen of Paris (c. 1393). Translated and edited by Eileen Power. London: George Routledge and Sons, 1928.

Gough, Richard. *The History of Myddle*. Edited by David Hey. Harmondsworth: Penguin, 1981.

Gray, Todd, ed. *Devon Household Accounts, 1627–59*. 2 vols. Exeter: Devon and Cornwall Record Society, 1995–96.

Greban, Arnould. *Le mystère de la passion*. Edited by Gaston Paris and Gaston Raynaud. Geneva: Slatkine, 1970.

Greene, Robert. *A Notable Discovery of Cozenage*. In *The Elizabethan Underworld*, edited by A. V. Judges, 119–48. London: Routledge and Kegan Paul, 1965.

———. *The Second Part of Cony-Catching*. In *The Elizabethan Underworld*, edited by A. V. Judges, 149–78. London: Routledge and Kegan Paul, 1965.

Hair, Paul, ed. *Before the Bawdy Court: Selections from Church Court and Other Records Relating to the Correction of Moral Offences in England, Scotland and New England, 1300–1800*. London: Elek, 1970.

Harman, Thomas. *A Caveat or Warning for Common Cursitors, Vulgarly Called Vagabonds.* In *The Elizabethan Underworld*, edited by A. V. Judges, 61–118. London: Routledge and Kegan Paul, 1965.

Harrison, Molly, and O. M. Royston, eds. *How They Lived: An Anthology of Original Accounts Written Between 1485 and 1700*. Oxford: Basil Blackwell, 1963.

Harrison, William. *The Description of England*. Edited by Georges Edelen. Ithaca: Cornell University Press, 1968.

Hassall, W. O., ed. *They Saw It Happen: An Anthology of Eye-witnesses' Accounts of Events in British History, 55 B.C.–A.D. 1485*. Oxford: Basil Blackwell, 1957.

Hertford Country Records: Notes and Extracts from the Session Rolls. Edited by W. J. Hardy. 2 vols. Hertford: C. E. Longmore, 1905.

Howell, James. *Epistolae Ho-Elianae: The Familiar Letters of James Howell, Historiographer Royal to Charles II*. Edited by Joseph Jacobs. 2 vols. London: David Nutt, 1892.

Jacob's Well: An English Treatise on the Cleansing of Man's Conscience. Edited by Arthur Brandeis. London: Early English Text Society, 1900.

Josselin, Ralph. *The Diary of Ralph Josselin, 1616–1683*. Edited by Alan Macfarlane. London: Oxford University Press, 1976.

Knafla, Louis A., ed. *Kent at Law, 1602, The County Jurisdiction: Assizes and Sessions of the Peace*. London: Her Majesty's Stationery Office, 1994.

La Chesnaye, Nicolas de. *La condamnation de Banquet*. Edited by Jelle Koopmans and Paul Verhuyck. Geneva: Droz, 1991.

Lambarde, William. *William Lambarde and Local Government: His "Ephemeris" and Twenty-nine Charges to Juries and Commissions*. Edited by Conyers Read. Ithaca: Cornell University Press, 1962.

Landucci, Luca. *A Florentine Diary from 1450 to 1516*. Translated by Alice de Rosen Jervis.

Freeport, NY: Books for Libraries Press, 1971.

Langland, William. *The Vision of Piers Plowman*. Translated and edited by Terence Tiller. London: British Broadcasting Corporation, 1981.

Lanza, Antonio, ed. *Lirici toscani del quattrocento*. 2 vols. Rome: Bulzoni, 1973–75.

Larkin, James F., and Paul L. Hughes, eds. *Stuart Royal Proclamations*. Vol. 1 of *Royal Proclamations of King James I, 1603–1625*. Oxford: Clarendon Press, 1973.

Latini, Brunetto. *Il tesoretto (The Little Treasure)*. Translated and edited by Julia Bolton Holloway. New York: Garland, 1981.

Liverpool Town Books, 1649–1671. Edited by Michael Power. Dorchester: Record Society of Lancashire and Cheshire, 1999.

Locke, John. *Locke's Travels in France, 1675–1679*. Edited by John Lough. Cambridge: Cambridge University Press, 1953.

Lowe, Roger. *The Diary of Roger Lowe of Ashton-in-Makerfield, Lancashire, 1663–74*. Edited by William L. Sachse. New Haven: Yale University Press, 1938.

Machyn, Henry. *The Diary of Henry Machyn, Citizen and Merchant-Taylor of London, From A.D. 1550 to A.D. 1563*. Edited by John Gough Nichols. London: J. B. Nichols and Son, 1848.

The Man in the Moone Telling Strange Fortunes; or, The English Fortune Teller. Edited by James Orchard Halliwall. Early English Poetry, Ballads, and Popular Literature of the Middle Ages 29. London: Percy Society, 1851.

Manley, Lawrence, ed. *London in the Age of Shakespeare: An Anthology*. London: Croom Helm, 1986.

Mannyng of Brunne, Robert. *Handlyng Synne*. Edited by Idelle Sullens. Binghamton, NY: Medieval and Renaissance Texts and Sources, 1983.

Matarasso, Pauline, trans. and ed. *The Cistercian World: Monastic Writings of the Twelfth Century*. Harmondsworth: Penguin, 1993.

Medieval Handbooks of Penance: A Translation of the Principal Libri Poenitentiales and Selections from Related Documents. Translated by John T. McNeill and Helena M. Gamer. New York: Octagon, 1965.

Middlesex County Records. Edited by John Cordy Jeaffreson. 3 vols. London: Middlesex County Records Society, 1886–88.

Milton, John. *The Works of John Milton*. Edited by Frank Allen Patterson. 18 vols. New York: Columbia University Press, 1931–38.

Montaigne, Michel de. *Travel Journal*. Translated by Donald M. Frame. San Francisco: North Point, 1983.

Morawski, Joseph, ed. *Proverbes français antérieurs au XVe siècle*. Paris: Edouard Champion, 1925.

Morgan, R. B., ed. *Readings in English Social History from Pre-Roman Days to A.D. 1837*. Cambridge: Cambridge University Press, 1928.

Morris, Richard, ed. *Old English Homilies and Homiletic Treatises (Sawles Ward, and the Wohunge of Ure Lauerd: Ureisuns of Ure Lauerd and of Ure Lefdi, etc.) of the Twelfth and Thirteenth Centuries*. London: Early English Text Society, 1868.

———, ed. *Old English Homilies of the Twelfth Century, From the Unique Ms. B.14.52 in the Library of Trinity College, Cambridge*. London: Early English Text Society, 1873.

Moryson, Fynes. *An Itinerary*. London: John Beale, 1617.

Le Mystère de la résurrection: Angers (1456). Edited by Pierre Servet. 2 vols. Geneva: Droz, 1993.

Oglander, John. *A Royalist's Notebook: The Commonplace Book of Sir John Oglander Kt. of Nunwell, Born 1585, Died 1655*. Edited by Francis Bamford. New York: Benjamin Blom, 1971.

A Parisian Journal, 1405–1449 [Journal d'un Bourgeois de Paris]. Translated by Janet Shirley. Oxford: Clarendon Press, 1968.

Petrarca, Francesco. *Petrarch's Remedies for Fortune Fair and Foul [De remediis utriusque Fortune]*. Translated and edited by Conrad H. Rawski. 5 vols. Bloomington: Indiana University Press, 1991.

Pisan, Christine de. *A Medieval Woman's Mirror of Honor: The Treasury of the City of Ladies*. Translated and introduced by Charity Cannon Willard and edited and introduced by Madeleine Pelner Cosman. New York: Bard Hall, 1989.

Pitti, Buonaccorso, and Gregorio Dati. *Two Memoirs of Renaissance Florence*. Translated by Julia Martines and edited by Gene Brucker. New York: Harper, 1967.

Pius II. *Memoirs of a Renaissance Pope: The Commentaries of Pius II*. Translated by Florence A. Gragg and edited by Leona C. Gabel. New York: Capricorn, 1962.

Platter, Felix. *Beloved Son Felix: The Journal of Felix Platter a Medical Student in Montpellier in the Sixteenth Century*. Translated by Seán Jennett. London: Frederick Muller, 1961.

Portsmouth Record Series: Borough Sessions Papers, 1653–1688. Compiled by Arthur J. Willis and edited by Margaret J. Hoad. London: Phillimore, 1971.

Price, Rebecca. *The Compleat Cook or the Secrets of a Seventeenth-Century Housewife*. Edited by Madeleine Masson. London: Routledge and Kegan Paul, 1974.

Rabelais, François. *The Portable Rabelais*. Translated and edited by Samuel Putnam. New York: Viking, 1946.

Records of Early English Drama: Dorset and Cornwall. Edited by Rosalind Conklin Hays, C. E. McGee, Sally L. Joyce, and Evelyn S. Newlyn. Toronto: University of Toronto Press, 1999.

Records of the Borough of Nottingham, Being a Series of Extracts from the Archives of the Corporation of Nottingham. Edited by W. H. Stevenson and James Raine. London: Bernard Quaritch, 1889.

Ricart, Robert. *The Maire of Bristowe Is Kalendar*. Edited by Lucy Toulmin Smith. London: Camden Society, 1872.

Rich, Barnaby. *The Honestie of This Age: Proving by Good Circumstance That the World Was Never Honest Till Now*. Edited by Peter Cunningham. Early English Poetry, Ballads, and Popular Literature of the Middle Ages 11. London: Percy Society, 1844.

Ronsard, Pierre de. *Oeuvres complètes*. Edited by Paul Laumonier, I. Silver, and R. Lebègue. 20 vols. Paris: Droz, 1931–75.

Ross, James Bruce, and Mary Martin McLaughlin, eds. *The Portable Renaissance Reader*. New York: Viking, 1953.

Routh, C. R. N., ed. *They Saw It Happen: An Anthology of Eye-witnesses' Accounts of Events in British History, 1485–1688*. Oxford: Basil Blackwell, 1956.

Rowlands, Samuel. *The Four Knaves: Series of Satirical Tracts, by Samuel Rowlands*. Edited by E. F. Rimbault. Early English Poetry, Ballads, and Popular Literature of the Middle Ages 9. London: Percy Society, 1844.

The Roxburghe Ballads. Edited by William Chappell. 7 vols. Hertford: Ballad Society by Stephen Austin and Sons, 1880–90.

Rye, William Brenchley, ed. *England as Seen by Foreigners in the Days of Elizabeth and James the First*. New York: Benjamin Blom, 1967.

Salimbene. *From St. Francis to Dante: Translations from the Chronicle of the Franciscan Salimbene (1221–1288)*. Translated by G. G. Coulton. Philadelphia: University of Pennsylvania Press, 1972.

Schellinks, William. *The Journal of William Schellinks' Travels in England, 1661–1663*. Translated and edited by Maurice Exwood and H. L. Lehmann. Camden Fifth Series 1. London: Royal Historical Society, 1993.

Sermons or Homilies Appointed to Be Read in Churches in the Time of Queen Elizabeth of Famous Memory. London: Society for Promoting Christian Knowledge, 1839.

Sévigné, Marchioness de. *Letters from the Marchioness de Sévigné to Her Daughter the Countess of Grignan*. Introduction by A. Mary F. Robinson. 10 vols. London: Spurr and Swift, 1927.

Shakespeare, William. *The Complete Works of William Shakespeare*. New York: Walter J. Black, n.d.

Sharpe, Reginald R., ed. *Calendar of Letter-Books Preserved among the Archives of the Corporation of the City of London at the Guildhall*. 12 vols. London: John Edward Francis, 1899–1912.

Skelton, John. "A Sixteenth-Century English Alewife and Her Customers: Skelton's *Tunnyng of Elynour Rummyng*." Edited by E. M. Jellinek. *Quarterly Journal of Studies on Alcohol* 6 (1945): 102–10.

Speroni, Charles, ed. *Wit and Wisdom of the Italian Renaissance*. Berkeley: University of California Press, 1964.

S. T. "An Appendix Shewing the Chiefe Cause of Wandering Poor in England, and the Remedies Thereof." In *Common Good; or The Improvement of Commons, Forests and Chases by Enclosure*. In *Country Life in England*, edited by E. W. Martin, 38–44. London: MacDonald, 1966.

Stubbes, Phillip. *The Anatomie of Abuses*. London: R. Iones, 1583. Reprint, Amsterdam: Theatrum Orbis Terrarum, 1972.

Taillevent [Guillaume Tirel]. *The Viandier of Taillevent*. Edited by Terence Scully. Ottawa: University of Ottawa Press, 1988.

Tanner, J. R., ed. *Tudor Constitutional Documents, A.D. 1485–1603: With an Historical Commentary*, 2nd ed. 1930. Reprint, Cambridge: Cambridge University Press, 1951.

Tawney, R. H., and Eileen Power, eds. *Tudor Economic Documents*. 3 vols. London: Longmans, Green, 1924.

Thirsk, Joan, and J. P. Cooper, eds. *Seventeenth-Century Economic Documents*. Oxford: Clarendon Press, 1972.

Tusser, Thomas. *Five Hundred Points of Good Husbandry, As Well for the Champion or Open Country, as for the Woodland or Several; Together with a Book of Huswifery, Being a Calendar of Rural and Domestic Economy, for Every Month in the Year; and Exhibiting a Picture of the Agriculture, Customs, and Manners of England, in the Sixteenth Century*. Edited by William Mavor. London: Lackington, Allen, 1812.

Vasari, Georgio. *The Lives of the Artists*. Translated by George Bull. Harmondsworth:

Penguin, 1971.

Vespasiano da Bisticci. *The Vespasiano Memoirs: Lives of Illustrious Men of the XVth Century*. Translated by William George and Emily Waters. London: George Routledge and Sons, 1926.

The Vivendier: Chy commenche un vivendier et ordonnance pour appariller plusieurs manierez de viandes. Edited and translated by Terence Scully. London: Prospect, 1998.

Ward, Ned. *The London Spy: The Vanities and Vices of the Town Exposed to View*. Edited by Arthur L. Hayward. London: Cassell, 1927.

Ward, Samuel. *Woe to Drunkards*. In *In God's Name: Examples of Preaching in England from the Act of Supremacy to the Act of Uniformity, 1534–1662*, edited by John Chandos, 232–40. London: Hutchinson, 1971.

Warwick County Records. Edited by S. C. Ratcliff, H. C. Johnson, and N. J. Williams. 9 vols. Warwick: L. Edgar Stephens, 1935–64.

The Westminster Chronicle, 1381–1394. Edited and translated by L. C. Hector and Barbara F. Harvey. Oxford: Clarendon Press, 1982.

Weyer, Johann. *Witches, Devils, and Doctors in the Renaissance: Johann Weyer, De praestigiis daemonum*. Edited by George Mora and Benjamin Kohl and translated by John Shea. Binghamton, NY: Medieval and Renaissance Texts and Studies, 1991.

Wheatcroft, Leonard. *The Courtship Narrative of Leonard Wheatcroft, Derbyshire Yeoman*. Edited by George Parfitt and Ralph Houlbrooke. Reading, UK: Whiteknights Press, 1986.

Williams, C. H., ed. *English Historical Documents, 1485–1558*. London: Eyre and Spottiswoode, 1967.

Wood, Anthony à. *The Life and Times of Anthony à Wood*. Edited by Llewelyn Powys. London: Oxford University Press, 1961.

Wright, Thomas, ed. *Specimens of Old Christmas Carols Selected from Manuscripts and Printed Books*. Early English Poetry, Ballads, and Popular Literature of the Middle Ages 4. London: Percy Society, 1841.

Wyclif, John. *Select English Works*. Edited by Thomas Arnold. 3 vols. Oxford: Clarendon Press, 1869–71.

Yonge, James. *The Journal of James Yonge (1647–1721), Plymouth Surgeon*. Edited by F. N. L. Poynter. London: Longmans, 1963.

Secondary Sources

Abbott, Mary. *Life Cycles in England, 1560–1720: Cradle to Grave*. London: Routledge, 1996.

Achilleos, Stella. "The *Anacreontea* and a Tradition of Refined Male Sociability." In *A Pleasing Sinne: Drink and Conviviality in Seventeenth-Century England*, edited by Adam Smyth, 21–35. Cambridge: D. S. Brewer, 2004.

Adair, Richard. *Courtship, Illegitimacy and Marriage in Early Modern England*. Manchester: Manchester University Press, 1996.

Adam, Paul. *La vie paroissiale en France au XIVe siècle*. Paris: Sirey, 1964.

Addy, John. *Sin and Society in the Seventeenth Century*. London: Routledge, 1989.

Adler, Marianna. "From Symbolic Exchange to Commodity Consumption: Anthropological Notes on Drinking as a Symbolic Practice." In *Drinking Behavior and Belief in Modern*

History, edited by Susanna Barrows and Robin Room, 376–98. Berkeley: University of California Press, 1991.

Ait, Ivana. "Il commercio delle derrate alimentari nella Roma del '400.'" *Archeologia medievale: Cultura materiale, insediamenti, territorio* 8 (1981): 155–72.

Allocco, Mirella. "La criminalità in Savigliano attraverso i conti della castellania dal 1428 al 1438." *Bolletino della Società per gli Studi Storici, Archeologici ed Artistici della Provincia di Cune* (1984): 109–36.

Amussen, Susan Dwyer. "The Gendering of Popular Culture in Early Modern England." In *Popular Culture in England, c. 1500–1850*, edited by Tim Harris, 48–68. London: Macmillan, 1995.

————. *An Ordered Society: Gender and Class in Early Modern England*. Oxford: Basil Blackwell, 1988.

————. "Punishment, Discipline, and Power: The Social Meanings of Violence in Early Modern England." *Journal of British Studies* 34 (1995): 1–34.

Archer, Ian W. "Material Londoners?" In *Material London, ca. 1600*, edited by Lena Cowen Orlin, 174–92. Philadelphia: University of Pennsylvania Press, 2000.

————. *The Pursuit of Stability: Social Relations in Elizabethan London*. Cambridge: Cambridge University Press, 1991.

Ashton, Robert. "Popular Entertainment and Social Control in Later Elizabethan and Early Stuart London." *London Journal* 9 (Summer 1983): 3–19.

Austin, Gregory A. *Alcohol in Western Society from Antiquity to 1800: A Chronological History*. Santa Barbara, CA: ABC-CLIO, 1985.

Babeau, Albert. *Le village sous l'ancien régime*. Paris: Didier, 1882.

Babelon, Jean-Pierre. *Nouvelle histoire de Paris: Paris au XVIe siècle*. Paris: Association pour la publication d'une Histoire de Paris, 1986.

Bacon, Selden D. "Alcohol and Complex Society." In *Society, Culture, and Drinking Patterns*, edited by David J. Pittman and Charles R. Snyder, 78–93. New York: John Wiley and Sons, 1962.

Bahlman, Dudley W. R. *The Moral Revolution of 1688*. New Haven: Yale University Press, 1957.

Bailey, Mark. *A Marginal Economy? East Anglian Breckland in the Later Middle Ages*. Cambridge: Cambridge University Press, 1989.

————. "Rural Society." In *Fifteenth-Century Attitudes: Perceptions of Society in Late Medieval England*, edited by Rosemary Horrow, 150–68. Cambridge: Cambridge University Press, 1994.

Baird, Edward G. "The Alcohol Problem and the Law: I; The Ancient Laws and Customs." *Quarterly Journal of Studies on Alcohol* 4 (1944): 535–56.

————. "The Alcohol Problem and the Law: II; The Common-Law Bases of Modern Liquor Controls." *Quarterly Journal of Studies on Alcohol* 5 (1944): 126–61.

Balestracci, Duccio, "Il consumo del vino nella Toscana bassomedievale." In *Il vino nell'economia e nella società italiana medioevale e moderna*, 1:13–29. Florence: Accademia economico-agraria dei Georgofili, 1988.

————. "La produzione e la vendità del vino nella Toscana medievale." In *Vino y viñedo en la Europa medieval*, edited by Fermín Miranda García, 39–54. Pamplona: Alfonso

López de Corella, 1996.

———. *The Renaissance in the Fields: Family Memoirs of a Fifteenth-Century Tuscan Peasant*. University Park: Pennsylvania State University Press, 1999.

Barnes, Thomas G. "County Politics and a Puritan Cause Célèbre: Somerset Churchales, 1633." *Transactions of the Royal Historical Society*, 5th ser., 9 (1959): 103–22.

Barr, Andrew. *Drink*. London: Bantam, 1995.

Barthes, Roland. *Mythologies*. London: Jonathan Cape, 1972.

Barty-King, Hugh. *A Tradition of English Wine: The Story of Two Thousand Years of English Wine Made from English Grapes*. Oxford: Oxford Illustrated, 1977.

Bechmann, Roland. *Trees and Man: The Forest in the Middle Ages*. New York: Paragon House, 1990.

Beier, A. L. *Masterless Men: The Vagrancy Problem in England, 1560–1640*. London: Methuen, 1985.

Beier, Lucinda McCray. *Sufferers and Healers: The Experience of Illness in Seventeenth-Century England*. London: Routledge and Kegan Paul, 1987.

Beik, William. *Urban Protest in Seventeenth-Century France: The Culture of Retribution*. Cambridge: Cambridge University Press, 1997.

Bell, Rudolph M. *Holy Anorexia*. Chicago: University of Chicago Press, 1985.

Benedict, Philip. *Rouen during the Wars of Religion*. Cambridge: Cambridge University Press, 1981.

Bennassar, Bartolomé, and Joseph Goy. "Contribution à l'histoire de la consommation alimentaire du XIVe au XIXe siècle." *Annales, économies, sociétés, civilisations* 30 (1975): 402–30.

Bennett, H. S. *Life on the English Manor: A Study of Peasant Conditions, 1150–1400*. Cambridge: Cambridge University Press, 1969.

———. *Six Medieval Men and Women*. New York: Atheneum, 1970.

Bennett, Judith M. *Ale, Beer, and Brewsters in England: Women's Work in a Changing World, 1300–1600*. New York: Oxford University Press, 1996.

———. "Conviviality and Charity in Medieval and Early Modern England." *Past and Present* 134 (February 1992): 19–41.

Bercé, Yves-Marie. "Aspects de la criminalité au XVIIe siècle." *Revue historique* 139 (1968): 33–42.

———. *Fête et révolte: Des mentalités populaires du XVIe au XVIIIe siècle*. Paris: Hachette, 1976.

———. *History of Peasant Revolts: The Social Origins of Rebellion in Early Modern France*. Cambridge: Polity, 1990.

———. *Revolt and Revolution in Early Modern Europe: An Essay on the History of Political Violence*. Manchester: Manchester University Press, 1987.

Black, Maggie. "Survival Kit (16th-Century Seamen's Fare)." In *Oxford Symposium on Food and Cookery 1989, Staple Foods, Proceedings*, 57–60. London: Prospect, 1990.

Bloomfield, Morton W. *The Seven Deadly Sins: An Introduction to the History of a Religious Concept with Special Reference to Medieval English Literature*. East Lansing: Michigan State College Press, 1952.

Blum, Jerome. *The End of the Old Order in Rural Europe*. Princeton: Princeton University

Press, 1978.

Blunt, Wilfrid. *Sebastiano: The Adventures of an Italian Priest, Sebastiano Locatelli, during His Journey from Bologna to Paris and Back, 1664–1665*. London: James Barrie, 1956.

Bois, Guy. *The Crisis of Feudalism: Economy and Society in Eastern Normandy c. 1300–1550*. Cambridge: Cambridge University Press, 1984.

Boucher, Jacqueline. "L'alimentation en milieu de cour sous les derniers Valois." In *Pratiques et discours alimentaires à la Renaissance*, edited by Jean-Claude Margolin and Robert Sauzet, 161–76. Paris: G.-P. Maisonneuve et Larose, 1982.

Bowsky, William M. *A Medieval Italian Commune: Siena under the Nine, 1287–1355*. Berkeley: University of California Press, 1981.

Boyatzis, Richard E. "Drinking as a Manifestation of Power Concerns." In *Cross-Cultural Approaches to the Study of Alcohol: An Interdisciplinary Perspective*, edited by Michael W. Everett, Jack O. Waddell, and Dwight B. Heath, 265–86. The Hague: Mouton, 1976.

Brackett, John K. *Criminal Justice and Crime in Late Renaissance Florence, 1537–1609*. Cambridge: Cambridge University, 1992.

Brears, Peter. "The Food Guilds of York." In *Feeding a City: York, The Provision of Food from Roman Times to the Beginning of the Twentieth Century*, edited by Eileen White, 79–100. Blackawton, Totnes: Prospect Books, 2000.

———. "Wassail! Celebrations in Hot Ale." In *"Liquid Nourishment": Potable Foods and Stimulating Drinks*, edited by C. Anne Wilson, 106–41. Edinburgh: Edinburgh University Press, 1993.

Brennan, Thomas. "The Anatomy of Inter-regional Markets in the Early Modern French Wine Trade." *Journal of European Economic History* 23 (1994): 581–617.

———. *Burgundy to Champagne: The Wine Trade in Early Modern France*. Baltimore: Johns Hopkins University Press, 1997.

———. *Public Drinking and Popular Culture in Eighteenth-Century Paris*. Princeton: Princeton University Press, 1988.

———. "Towards the Cultural History of Alcohol in France." *Journal of Social History* 23 (1989): 71–92.

Bretherton, R. F. "Country Inns and Alehouses." In *Englishmen at Rest and Play: Some Phases of English Leisure, 1558–1714*, edited by Reginald Lennard, 145–201. Oxford: Clarendon Press, 1931.

Brigden, Susan. "Youth and the English Reformation." In *The Impact of the English Reformation, 1500–1640*, edited by Peter Marshall, 55–85. London: Arnold, 1997.

Briggs, Robin. *Communities of Belief: Cultural and Social Tension in Early Modern France*. Oxford: Clarendon Press, 1989.

Bristow, Edward J. *Vice and Vigilance: Purity Movements in Britain since 1700*. Dublin: Gill and Macmillan, 1977.

Britnell, R. H. *Growth and Decline in Colchester, 1300–1525*. Cambridge: Cambridge University Press, 1986.

Britton, Edward. *The Community of the Vill: A Study in the History of the Family and Village Life in Fourteenth-Century England*. Toronto: Macmillan, 1977.

Brown, Andrew D. *Popular Piety in Late Medieval England: The Diocese of Salisbury, 1250–1550*. Oxford: Clarendon Press, 1995.

Brundage, James A. *Law, Sex, and Christian Society in Medieval Europe*. Chicago: University of Chicago Press, 1987.

Brushfield, T. N. "Church Ales [The Church of All Saints, East Budleigh]." *Report and Transactions of the Devonshire Association* 24 (1892): 334–58.

Bruun, Kettil. "Drinking Practices and Their Social Function." In *Alcohol and Civilization*, edited by Salvatore Pablo Lucia, 218–28. New York: McGraw-Hill, 1963.

Buccellato, Rosa Maria Dentici. "Produzione, commercio e consumo del vino nella Sicilia medievale." In *Il vino nell'economia e nella società italiana medioevale e moderna*, 157–67. Florence: Accademia economico-agraria dei Georgofili, 1988.

Burke, Peter. *Popular Culture in Early Modern Europe*. New York: Harper, 1978.

Burnett, John. *Liquid Pleasures: A Social History of Drinks in Modern Britain*. London: Routledge, 1999.

Cabourdin, Guy. *Terre et hommes en Lorraine (1550–1635): Toulois et Comté de Vaudémont*. Nancy: L'Université de Nancy II, 1977.

Caduff, Claudia. "I 'publici latrones' nella città e nel contado di Firenze a metà trecento." *Ricerche storiche* 16 (1988): 497–521.

Camporesi, Piero. *Bread of Dreams: Food and Fantasy in Early Modern Europe*. Chicago: University of Chicago Press, 1989.

———. *The Incorruptible Flesh: Bodily Mutation and Mortification in Religion and Folklore*. Cambridge: Cambridge University Press, 1988.

Capp, Bernard. "The Double Standard Revisited: Plebeian Women and Male Sexual Reputation in Early Modern England." *Past and Present* 162 (February 1999): 70–100.

———. "Popular Literature." In *Popular Culture in Seventeenth-Century England*, edited by Barry Reay, 198–243. London: Croom Helm, 1985.

———. "Separate Domains? Women and Authority in Early Modern England." In *The Experience of Authority in Early Modern England*, edited by Paul Griffiths, Adam Fox, and Steve Hindle, 117–45. London: Macmillan, 1996.

———. *When Gossips Meet: Women, Family, and Neighbourhood in Early Modern England*. Oxford: Oxford University Press, 2003.

Carlin, Martha. *Medieval Southwark*. London: Hambledon, 1996.

Carlton, Charles. "The Widow's Tale: Male Myths and Female Reality in 16th and 17th Century England." *Albion* 10 (1978): 118–29.

Carrington, F. A. "Ancient Ales in the County of Wilts, and in the Diocese of Sarum." *Wiltshire Archaeological and Natural History Magazine* 2 (1855): 191–204.

Carter, John Marshall. *Medieval Games: Sports and Recreations in Feudal Society*. New York: Greenwood, 1992.

Cast, Andrea Snowden. "Women Drinking in Early Modern England." PhD diss., University of Adelaide, 2002.

Cattini, Marco. "Individualismo agrario, viticoltura e mercato del vino in Emilia nei secoli dell'età moderna." In *Il vino nell'economia e nella società italiana medioevale e moderna*, 203–22. Florence: Accademia economico-agraria dei Georgofili, 1988.

Charbonnier, Pierre. *Une autre France: La seigneurie rurale en Basse Auvergne du XIVe au XVIe siècle*, 2 vols. Clermont-Ferrand: Institut d'Etudes du Massif Central, 1980.

Chartres, John. "Food Consumption and Internal Trade." In *London, 1500–1700: The Making of the Metropolis*, edited by A. L. Beier and Roger Finlay, 168–96. London: Longman, 1986.

———. "No English Calvados? English Distillers and the Cider Industry in the Seventeenth and Eighteenth Centuries." In *English Rural Society, 1500–1800: Essays in Honour of Joan Thirsk*, edited by John Chartres and David Hey, 313–42. Cambridge: Cambridge University Press, 1990.

Chatelain, Emile. "Notes sur quelques tavernes fréquentées par l'Université de Paris aux XIVe et XVe siècles." *Bulletin de la Société de l'Histoire de Paris et de l'Ile de France* (1898): 87–109.

Chatellier, Louis. *The Europe of the Devout: The Catholic Reformation and the Formation of a New Society*. Cambridge: Cambridge University Press, 1989.

Cherubini, Giovanni. "La taverna nel basso medioevo." In *Il lavoro, la taverna, la strada: Scorci di medioevo*, 191–224. Naples: Liguori Editore, 1997.

Chevalier, Bernard. *Les bonnes villes de France du XIVe au XVIe siècle*. Paris: Aubier Montaigne, 1982.

Chiffoleau, Jacques. *La comptabilité de l'au-delà: Les hommes, la mort et la religion dans la région d'Avignon à la fin du Moyen Age (vers 1320–vers 1480)*. Rome: École française de Rome, 1980.

———. *Les justices du pape: Délinquance et criminalité dans la région d'Avignon au quatorzième siècle*. Paris: La Sorbonne, 1984.

Clark, Elaine. "The Quest for Security in Medieval England." In *Aging and the Aged in Medieval Europe*, edited by Michael M. Sheehan, 189–200. Toronto: Pontifical Institute of Mediaeval Studies, 1990.

———. "Some Aspects of Social Security in Medieval England." *Journal of Family History* 7 (1982): 307–20.

Clark, Peter. "The Alehouse and the Alternative Society." In *Puritans and Revolutionaries: Essays in Seventeenth-Century History Presented to Christopher Hill*, edited by Donald Pennington and Keith Thomas, 47–72. Oxford: Clarendon Press, 1978.

———. *British Clubs and Societies, 1580–1800: The Origins of an Associational World*. Oxford: Clarendon Press, 2000.

———. *The English Alehouse: A Social History, 1200–1830*. London: Longman, 1983.

———. "The Migrant in Kentish Towns, 1580–1640." In *Crisis and Order in English Towns, 1500–1700: Essays in Urban History*, edited by Peter Clark and Paul Slack, 117–63. London: Routledge and Kegan Paul, 1972.

Cohen, Esther. "The Hundred Years' War and Crime in Paris, 1332–1488." In *The Civilization of Crime: Violence in Town and Country since the Middle Ages*, edited by Eric A. Johnson and Eric H. Monkkonen, 109–24. Urbana: University of Illinois Press, 1996.

———. "Le vagabondage à Paris au XIVe siècle: Analyse conceptuelle." *Le Moyen Age: Revue d'histoire et de philologie* 88 (1982): 293–313.

———. "Violence Control in Late Medieval France: The Social Transformation of the Asseurement." *Revue d'histoire du droit* 51 (1983): 111–22.

Cohn, Samuel Kline, Jr. *The Laboring Classes in Renaissance Florence*. New York: Academic Press, 1980.

Collins, James B. *Classes, Estates, and Order in Early Modern Brittany*. Cambridge: Cambridge University Press, 1994.

Collins, James J. "Drinking and Violations of the Criminal Law." In *Society, Culture, and Drinking Patterns Reexamined*, edited by David J. Pittman and Helene Raskin White, 650–60. New Brunswick: Rutgers Center of Alcohol Studies, 1991.

———, and Pamela M. Messerschmidt. "Epidemiology of Alcohol-Related Violence." *Alcohol Health and Research World* 17 (1993): 93–100.

Collinson, Patrick. "Cranbrook and the Fletchers: Popular and Unpopular Religion in the Kentish Weald." In *Reformation Principle and Practice: Essays in Honour of Arthur Geoffrey Dickens*, edited by Peter Newman Brooks, 171–202. London: Scolar, 1980.

———. *The Religion of Protestants: The Church in English Society, 1559–1625*. Oxford: Clarendon Press, 1982.

Comet, Georges. "L'iconographie du vin au Moyen Age." In *Le vin des historiens*, edited by Gilbert Garrier, 119–34. Suze-la-Rousse: Université du Vin, 1990.

Contamine, Philippe. *La vie quotidienne pendant la Guerre de Cent Ans: France et Angleterre (XIVe siècle)*. Paris: Hachette, 1976.

Cortonesi, Alfio. "Vini e commercio vinicolo nel Lazio tardomedioevale." In *Il vino nell'economia e nella società italiana medioevale e moderna*, 129–45. Florence: Accademia economico-agraria dei Georgofili, 1988.

Coulton, G. G. *Medieval Village, Manor, and Monastery*. New York: Harper and Row, 1960.

Courtois, Martine. "Les ferments interdits dans la Bible." In *Le ferment divin*, edited by Dominique Fournier and Salvatore D'Onofrio, 63–75. Paris: Maison des sciences de l'homme, 1991.

Cowell, Andrew. *At Play in the Tavern: Signs, Coins, and Bodies in the Middle Ages*. Ann Arbor: University of Michigan Press, 1999.

Crawford, Anne. *A History of the Vintners' Company*. London: Constable, 1977.

Cressy, David. *Bonfires and Bells: National Memory and the Protestant Calendar in Elizabethan and Stuart England*. London: Weidenfeld and Nicolson, 1989.

———. "Purification, Thanksgiving and the Churching of Women in Post-Reformation England." *Past and Present* 141 (November 1993): 106–46.

———. *Travesties and Transgressions in Tudor and Stuart England: Tales of Discord and Dissension*. Oxford: Oxford University Press, 2000.

Crick, M. M. "Brewing." In *The Victoria History of the Counties of England: Dorset*, edited by William Page, II, 366–69. Folkestone: University of London, Institute of Historical Research, 1975.

Crossley, Alan. "City and University." In *Seventeenth-Century Oxford*, edited by Nicholas Tyacke, 105–34. History of the University of Oxford 4. Oxford: Clarendon Press, 1997.

Crouzet-Pavan, Elisabeth. *"Sopra le acque salse": Espaces, pouvoir et société à Venise à la fin du Moyen Age*. Rome: Ecole Française de Rome, 1992.

Curtis, T. C. "Quarter Sessions Appearances and Their Background: A Seventeenth-Century Regional Study." In *Crime in England, 1550–1800*, edited by J. S. Cockburn, 145–54. London: Methuen, 1977.

Daly, Lowrie J. *The Medieval University, 1200–1400*. New York: Sheed and Ward, 1961.

Davies, C. S. L. "Popular Religion and the Pilgrimage of Grace." In *Order and Disorder in Early Modern England*, edited by Anthony Fletcher and John Stevenson, 58–91. Cambridge: Cambridge University Press, 1985.

———. "Les rations alimentaires de l'armée et de la marine anglaises au XVIe siècle." In *Pour une histoire de l'alimentation*, edited by Jean-Jacques Hémardinquer, 93–95. Cahiers des annales 28. Paris: A. Colin, 1970.

Davies, Stuart. "'Vinetum Britannicum': Cider and Perry in the Seventeenth Century." In *"Liquid Nourishment": Potable Foods and Stimulating Drinks*, edited by C. Anne Wilson, 79–105. Edinburgh: Edinburgh University Press, 1993.

Davis, Natalie Zemon. *Fiction in the Archives: Pardon Tales and Their Tellers in Sixteenth-Century France*. Stanford: Stanford University Press, 1987.

———. *Society and Culture in Early Modern France*. Stanford: Stanford University Press, 1975.

Davis, Robert C. "Venetian Shipbuilders and the Fountain of Wine." *Past and Present* 156 (August 1997): 55–86.

———. *The War of the Fists: Popular Culture and Public Violence in Late Renaissance Venice*. New York: Oxford University Press, 1994.

Delumeau, Jean. *La mort des pays de cocagne: Comportement collectif de la Renaissance à l'âge classique*. Paris: La Sorbonne, 1976.

Dennison, James T., Jr. *The Market Day of the Soul: The Puritan Doctrine of the Sabbath in England, 1532–1700*. Lanham, MD: University Press of America, 1983.

Desportes, Pierre. *Reims et les rémois au XIIIe et XIVe siècles*. Paris: A. and J. Picard, 1979.

Dewald, Jonathan. *Pont-St.-Pierre, 1398–1789: Lordship, Community and Capitalism in Early Modern France*. Berkeley: University of California Press, 1987.

Dion, Roger. *Histoire de la vigne et du vin en France des origines au XIXe siècle*. Paris: Flammarion, 1977.

Douch, H. L. *Old Cornish Inns and Their Place in the Social History of the County*. Marazion: D. Bradford Barton, 1966.

Douglas, Mary. "A Distinctive Anthropological Perspective." In *Constructive Drinking: Perspectives on Drink from Anthropology*, edited by Mary Douglas, 3–15. Cambridge: Cambridge University Press, 1987.

Driessen, Henk. "Drinking on Masculinity: Alcohol and Gender in Andalusia." In *Alcohol, Gender and Culture*, edited by Dimitra Gefou-Madianou, 71–79. London: Routledge, 1992.

Drummond, J. C., and Anne Wilbraham. *The Englishman's Food: A History of Five Centuries of English Diet*. London: Jonathan Cape, 1939.

Duby, Georges. *The Early Growth of the European Economy: Warriors and Peasants from the Seventh to the Twelfth Century*. Ithaca: Cornell University Press, 1978.

Dupèbe, Jean. "La diététique et l'alimentation des pauvres selon Sylvius." In *Pratiques et discours alimentaires à la Renaissance*, edited by Jean-Claude Margolin and Robert Sauzet, 41–56. Paris: G.-P. Maisonneuve et Larose, 1982.

Durand, Georges. *Vin, vigne et vignerons en Lyonnais et Beaujolais (XVIe–XVIIIe siècles)*. Lyon: Presses Universitaires de Lyon, 1979.

Durston, Christopher. "Puritan Rule and the Failure of Cultural Revolution, 1645–1660." In *The Culture of English Puritanism, 1560–1700*, edited by Christopher Durston and Jacqueline Eales, 210–33. New York: St. Martin's, 1996.

———, and Jacqueline Eales. "Introduction: The Puritan Ethos, 1560–1700." In *The Culture of English Puritanism, 1560–1700*, edited by Christopher Durston and Jacqueline Eales, 1–31. New York: St. Martin's, 1996.

Dyer, Christopher. "Changes in Diet in the Late Middle Ages: The Case of Harvest Workers." *Agricultural History Review* 36 (1988): 21–37.

———. "English Diet in the Later Middle Ages." In *Social Relations and Ideas: Essays in Honour of R. H. Hilton*, edited by T. H. Aston, P. R. Coss, Christopher Dyer, and Joan Thirsk, 191–216. Cambridge: Cambridge University Press, 1983.

———. *Making a Living in the Middle Ages: The People of Britain, 850–1520*. New Haven: Yale University Press, 2002.

———. *Standards of Living in the Later Middle Ages: Social Change in England, c. 1200–1520*. Cambridge: Cambridge University Press, 1989.

Earle, Peter. *The Making of the English Middle Class: Business, Society and Family Life in London, 1660–1730*. London: Methuen, 1989.

Earnshaw, Steven. *The Pub in Literature: England's Altered State*. Manchester: Manchester University Press, 2000.

Ekirch, A. Roger. *At Day's Close: Night in Times Past*. New York: W. W. Norton, 2005.

Emerson, Edward R. *Beverages, Past and Present: An Historical Sketch of Their Production, together with a Study of the Customs Connected with Their Use*. 2 vols. New York: G. P. Putnam's Sons, 1908.

Emmison, F. G. *Elizabethan Life: Disorder, Mainly from Essex Sessions and Assize Records*. Chelmsford: Essex County Council, 1970.

———. *Tudor Food and Pastimes*. London: Ernest Benn, 1964.

Enjalbert, Henri. "Comment naissent les grands crus: Bordeaux, Porto, Cognac." *Annales: Economies, sociétés, civilisations* 8 (1977): 315–28, 457–74.

———. "La naissance des grands vins et la formation du vignoble moderne de Bordeaux, 1647–1767." In *Géographie historique des vignobles*, edited by A. Huetz de Lemps, R. Pijassou, and P. Roudié, 59–88. Paris: Centre National de la Recherche Scientifique, 1978.

Everitt, Alan. "The English Urban Inn, 1560–1760." In *Perspectives in English Urban History*, edited by Alan Everitt, 91–137. London: Macmillan, 1973.

Fairchilds, Cissie C. *Domestic Enemies: Servants and Their Masters in Old Regime France*. Baltimore: Johns Hopkins University Press, 1984.

———. *Poverty and Charity in Aix-en-Provence, 1640–1789*. Baltimore: Johns Hopkins University Press, 1976.

Faral, Edmond. *La vie quotidienne au temps de Saint Louis*. Paris: Hachette, 1938.

Farr, James R. *Artisans in Europe, 1300–1914*. Cambridge: Cambridge University Press, 2000.

———. *Authority and Sexuality in Early Modern Burgundy (1550–1730)*. Oxford: Oxford University Press, 1995.

———. *Hands of Honor: Artisans and Their World in Dijon, 1550–1650*. Ithaca: Cornell University Press, 1988.

Fedden, Katharine. *Manor Life in Old France: From the Journal of the Sire de Gouberville for the Years 1549–1562*. New York: Columbia University Press, 1933.

Ferraro, Joanne M. *Marriage Wars in Late Renaissance Venice*. Oxford: Oxford University Press, 2001.

Fincham, Kenneth. "Oxford and the Early Stuart Policy." In *Seventeenth-Century Oxford*, edited by Nicholas Tyacke, 179–210. History of the University of Oxford 4. Oxford: Clarendon Press, 1997.

Fissel, Mark Charles. *English Warfare, 1511–1642*. London: Routledge, 2001.

Fiumi, Enrico. "Economia e vita privata dei fiorentini nelle rilevazioni statistiche di Giovanni Villani." *Archivio Storico Italiano* 111 (1953): 207–41.

Flandrin, Jean-Louis. "Boissons et manières de boire en Europe du XVIe au XVIIIe siècle." In *L'imaginaire du vin*, edited by Max Milner and Martine Chatelain, 309–14. Marseille: Jeanne Laffitte, 1983.

———. "La diversité des goûts et des pratiques alimentaires en Europe du XVIe au XVIIIe siècle." *Revue d'histoire moderne et contemporaine* 30 (1983): 66–83.

Fletcher, Anthony. *Gender, Sex and Subordination in England, 1500–1800*. New Haven: Yale University Press, 1995.

———. "Manhood, the Male Body, Courtship and the Household in Early Modern England." *History* 84 (1999): 419–36.

———. *Reform in the Provinces: The Government of Stuart England*. New Haven: Yale University Press, 1986.

Fouret, Claude. "La violence en fête: La course de l'Epinette à Lille à la fin du Moyen Age." *Revue du Nord* 63 (1981): 377–90.

Foyster, Elizabeth A. *Manhood in Early Modern England: Honour, Sex and Marriage*. London: Longman, 1999.

Francis, A. D. *The Wine Trade*. London: Adam and Charles Black, 1972.

Franklin, Alfred. *Les moeurs et coutumes des parisiens au XVIe siècle*. Paris: Léon Willem, 1876.

Freeman, Joseph T. "Medical Perspectives in Aging (12th–19th Century)." *Gerontologist* 5 (1965): 1–24.

French, Katherine L. "Parochial Fund-Raising in Late Medieval Somerset." In *The Parish in English Life, 1400–1600*, edited by Katherine L. French, Gary G. Gibbs, and Beat A. Kümin, 115–32. Manchester: Manchester University Press, 1997.

———. *The People of the Parish: Community Life in a Late Medieval English Diocese*. Philadelphia: University of Pennsylvania Press, 2001.

———. "'To Free Them from Binding': Women in the Late Medieval English Parish." *Journal of Interdisciplinary History* 27 (1997): 387–412.

French, Richard Valpy. *Nineteen Centuries of Drink in England: A History*. London: National Temperance Publication Depôt, 1884.

Fumerton, Patricia. "Not Home: Alehouses, Ballads, and the Vagrant Husband in Early Modern England." *Journal of Medieval and Early Modern Studies* 32 (2002): 493–518.

Galloway, James A. "Driven by Drink? Ale Consumption and the Agrarian Economy of the London Region, c. 1300–1400." In *Food and Eating in Medieval Europe*, edited by Martha Carlin and Joel T. Rosenthal, 87–100. London: Hambledon, 1998.

Garrier, Gilbert. *Histoire sociale et culturelle du vin*. Paris: Bordas, 1995.

Garrioch, David. *Neighbourhood and Community in Paris, 1740–1790*. Cambridge: Cambridge University Press, 1986.

Gascon, Richard. *Grand commerce et vie urbaine au XVIe siècle: Lyon et ses marchands (environs de 1520–environs de 1580)*. Paris: Mouton, 1971.

———. "La France du mouvement: Les commerces et les villes." In *L'état et la ville (de 1450 à 1660)*, edited by Pierre Chaunu and Richard Gascon, 229–479. Vol. 1, pt. 1 of *Histoire économique et sociale de la France*. Paris: Presses Universitaires de France, 1977.

Gauvard, Claude. *"De Grace Especial"*: *Crime, état et société à la fin du Moyen Age*. Paris: La Sorbonne, 1991.

Gayre, G. R. *Wassail! In Mazers of Mead*. London: Phillimore, 1948.

Gefou-Madianou, Dimitra. "Introduction: Alcohol Commensality, Identity Transformations and Transcendence." In *Alcohol, Gender and Culture*, edited by Dimitra Gefou-Madianou, 1–34. London: Routledge, 1992.

Geremek, Bronislaw. *The Margins of Society in Late Medieval Paris*. Cambridge: Cambridge University Press, 1987.

Getz, Faye Marie. *Medicine in the English Middle Ages*. Princeton: Princeton University Press, 1998.

Gittings, Clare. *Death, Burial and the Individual in Early Modern England*. London: Croom Helm, 1984.

Given, James Buchanan. *Society and Homicide in Thirteenth-Century England*. Stanford: Stanford University Press, 1977.

Goldberg, P. J. P. "Masters and Men in Later Medieval England." In *Masculinity in Medieval Europe*, edited by D. M. Hadley, 56–70. London: Longman, 1999.

———. *Women, Work, and Life Cycle in a Medieval Economy: Women in York and Yorkshire, c. 1300–1520*. Oxford: Clarendon Press, 1992.

Goldthwaite, Richard A. *The Building of Renaissance Florence: An Economic and Social History*. Baltimore: Johns Hopkins University Press, 1982.

Gosselin, Ronald. "Honneur et violence à Manosque (1240–1260)." In *Vie privée et ordre public à la fin du Moyen-Age: Etudes sur Manosque, la Provence et le Piémont (1250–1450)*, edited by Michel Hébert, 45–63. Aix-en-Provence: Université de Provence, 1987.

Goubert, Pierre. *The French Peasantry in the Seventeenth Century*. Cambridge: Cambridge University Press, 1986.

Gouk, Penelope. *Music, Science and Natural Magic in Seventeenth-Century England*. New Haven: Yale University Press, 1999.

Gowing, Laura. *Domestic Dangers: Women, Words, and Sex in Early Modern London*. Oxford: Clarendon Press, 1996.

Goy, Richard J. *Chioggia and the Villages of the Venetian Lagoon: Studies in Urban History*. Cambridge: Cambridge University Press, 1985.

Gracia, Jorge J. E. "Rules and Regulations for Drinking Wine in Francesc Eiximenis' 'Terç del Crestià' (1384)." *Traditio: Studies in Ancient and Medieval History, Thought, and Religion* 32 (1976): 369–85.

Greci, Roberto. "Il commercio del vino negli statuti comunali di area piemontese." In *Vigne e vini nel Piemonte medievale*, edited by Rinaldo Comba, 245–80. Cuneo: L'Arciere, 1990.

Greenshields, Malcolm. *An Economy of Violence in Early Modern France: Crime and Justice in the Haute Auvergne, 1587–1664*. University Park: Pennsylvania State University Press, 1994.

Griffiths, Paul. "Masterless Young People in Norwich, 1560–1645." In *The Experience of Authority in Early Modern England*, edited by Paul Griffiths, Adam Fox, and Steve Hindle, 146–86. London: Macmillan, 1996.

———. "Overlapping Circles: Imagining Criminal Communities in London, 1545–1645." In *Communities in Early Modern England: Networks, Place, Rhetoric*, edited by Alexandra

Shepard and Phil Withington, 115–33. Manchester: Manchester University Press, 2000.

———. *Youth and Authority: Formative Experiences in England, 1560–1640*. Oxford: Clarendon Press, 1996.

Grinberg, Martine. "Carnaval et société urbaine XIVe–XVIe siècles: Le royaume dans la ville." *Ethnologie française* 4 (1974): 215–44.

Gusfield, Joseph. "Benevolent Repression: Popular Culture, Social Structure, and the Control of Drinking." In *Drinking Behavior and Belief in Modern History*, edited by Susanna Barrows and Robin Room, 399–424. Berkeley: University of California Press, 1991.

Gutton, Jean-Pierre. *La sociabilité villageoise dans l'ancienne France: Solidarités et voisinages du XVIe au XVIIIe siècle*. Paris: Hachette, 1979.

Hackwood, Frederick W. *Inns, Ales, and Drinking Customs of Old England*. London: T. Fisher Unwin, 1909.

Hallam, H. E., Edward Miller, and Joan Thirsk, eds. *The Agrarian History of England and Wales*, vols. 2–5. Cambridge: Cambridge University Press, 1967–88.

Hammer, Carl I. "Patterns of Homicide in a Medieval University Town: Fourteenth-Century Oxford." *Past and Present* 78 (February 1978): 3–23.

Hammond, P. W. *Food and Feast in Medieval England*. Phoenix Mill: Alan Sutton, 1995.

Hanawalt, Barbara A. *Growing up in Medieval London: The Experience of Childhood in History*. New York: Oxford University Press, 1993.

———. *"Of Good and Ill Repute": Gender and Social Control in Medieval England*. New York: Oxford University Press, 1998.

———. *The Ties That Bound: Peasant Families in Medieval England*. New York: Oxford University Press, 1986.

———. "Violent Death in Fourteenth- and Early Fifteenth-Century England." *Comparative Studies in Society and History* 18 (1976): 297–320.

Hanham, Alison. *The Celys and Their World: An English Merchant Family of the Fifteenth Century*. Cambridge: Cambridge University Press, 1985.

Hanlon, Gregory. "Les rituels de l'agression en Aquitaine au XVIIe siècle." *Annales: Economies, sociétés, civilisations* 40 (1985): 244–68.

Hanna, Ralph, III. "Pilate's Voice/Shirley's Case." *South Atlantic Quarterly* 91 (1992): 793–812.

Harper, Richard I. "A Note on Corrodies in the Fourteenth Century." *Albion* 15 (1983): 95–101.

Harrell, Stevan. "Normal and Deviant Drinking in Rural Taiwan." In *Normal and Abnormal Behavior in Chinese Culture*, edited by Arthur Kleinman and Tsung-Yi Lin, 49–59. Dordrecht: D. Reidel, 1981.

Harris, J. Rendel. "Origin and Meaning of Apple Cults." *Bulletin of the John Rylands Library Manchester* 5 (1918–20): 29–74.

Harris, Tim. "The Bawdy House Riots of 1668." *Historical Journal* 29 (1986): 537–56.

———. *London Crowds in the Reign of Charles II: Propaganda and Politics from the Restoration until the Exclusion Crisis*. Cambridge: Cambridge University Press, 1987.

Harvey, Barbara. *Living and Dying in England, 1100–1540: The Monastic Experience*. Oxford: Clarendon Press, 1995.

———. "Monastic Diet, XIIIth–XVIth Centuries: Problems and Perspectives." In *Alimentazione e nutrizione: Secc. XIII–XVIII*, edited by Simonetta Cavaciocchi, 611–41.

Florence: Le Monnier, 1997.

Harvey, I. M. W. "Was There Popular Politics in Fifteenth-Century England?" In *The McFarlane Legacy: Studies in Late Medieval Politics and Society*, edited by R. H. Britnell and A. J. Pollard, 155–74. Stroud: Alan Sutton, 1995.

Harwood, Audrey. "The Public Houses of Helmdon." In *Aspects of Helmdon*, edited by Ross Vicars, 54–70. Helmdon: Helmdon Branch W.E.A., 1998.

Heal, Felicity. *Hospitality in Early Modern England*. Oxford: Clarendon Press, 1990.

Heath, Dwight B. "A Decade of Development in the Anthropological Study of Alcohol Use: 1970–1980." In *Constructive Drinking: Perspectives on Drink from Anthropology*, edited by Mary Douglas, 16–69. Cambridge: Cambridge University Press, 1987.

———. *Drinking Occasions: Comparative Perspectives on Alcohol and Culture*. Philadelphia: Brunner/Mazel, 2000.

———, and Haydée Rosovsky. "Community Reactions to Alcohol Policies." In *Drinking Patterns and Their Consequences*, edited by Marcus Grant and Jorge Litvak, 205–18. Washington: Taylor and Francis, 1998.

Heers, Jacques. *Fêtes des fous et carnavals*. Paris: Fayard, 1983.

———. *Fêtes, jeux et joutes dans les sociétés d'Occident à la fin du Moyen Age*. Montréal: Institut d'Etudes Médiévales, 1971.

Helmholz, R. H. "Harboring Sexual Offenders: Ecclesiastical Courts and Controlling Misbehavior." *Journal of British Studies* 37 (1998): 258–68.

Hémardinquer, Jean-Jacques. "Sur les galères de Toscane au XVIe siècle." In *Pour une histoire de l'alimentation*, edited by Jean-Jacques Hémardinquer, 85–92. Cahiers des annales 28. Paris: A. Colin, 1970.

Herrup, Cynthia B. *The Common Peace: Participation and the Criminal Law in Seventeenth-Century England*. Cambridge: Cambridge University Press, 1987.

Hewitt, Ethel M. "Brewing." In *The Victoria History of the Counties of England: Somerset*, edited by William Page, 2:401–3. London: University of London Press, 1969.

———. "Malting and Brewing." In *The Victoria History of the Counties of England: Nottinghamshire*, edited by William Page, 2:363–66. London: University of London Press, 1910.

Heywood, William. *The "Ensamples" of Fra Filippo: A Study of Mediaeval Siena*. Siena: Enrico Torrini, 1901.

Higgs, E. J. "Research into the History of Alcohol Use and Control in England and Wales: The Available Sources in the Public Record Office." *British Journal of Addiction* 79 (1984): 41–47.

Higgs, Laquita M. *Godliness and Governance in Tudor Colchester*. Ann Arbor: University of Michigan Press, 1998.

Hill, Christopher. *Society and Puritanism in Pre-Revolutionary England*. London: Secker and Warburg, 1964.

———. *The World Turned Upside Down: Radical Ideas during the English Revolution*. Harmondsworth: Penguin, 1975.

Hilton, Rodney H. "Pain et cervoise dans les villes anglaises au Moyen Age." In *L'approvisionnement dans les villes de l'Europe occidentale*, 221–29. Auch: 5e Flaran Journées Internationales d'Histoire, 1985.

Hindle, Steve. "Custom, Festival and Protest in Early Modern England: The Little Budworth Wakes, St. Peter's Day, 1596." *Rural History* 6 (1995): 155–78.

———. "A Sense of Place? Becoming and Belonging in the Rural Parish, 1550–1650." In *Communities in Early Modern England: Networks, Place, Rhetoric*, edited by Alexandra Shepard and Phil Withington, 96–114. Manchester: Manchester University Press, 2000.

———. *The State and Social Change in Early Modern England, c. 1550–1640*. Basingstoke: Palgrave, 2000.

Hoffman, Philip T. *Church and Community in the Diocese of Lyon, 1500–1789*. New Haven: Yale University Press, 1984.

Holt, J. C. *Robin Hood*. New York: Thames and Hudson, 1983.

Holt, Mack P. "Wine, Community and Reformation in Sixteenth-Century Burgundy." *Past and Present* 138 (February 1993): 58–93.

———. "Wine, Life, and Death in Early Modern Burgundy." *Food and Foodways* 8 (1999): 73–98.

Houlbrooke, Ralph. *Death, Religion and the Family in England, 1480–1750*. Oxford: Clarendon Press, 1998.

Howell, Cicely. *Land, Family and Inheritance in Transition: Kibworth Harcourt, 1280–1700*. Cambridge: Cambridge University Press, 1983.

Hudson, H. G. *A Study of Social Regulations in England under James I and Charles I: Drink and Tobacco*. Chicago: Private edition, distributed by the University of Chicago Libraries, 1933.

Hufton, Olwen. *The Prospect Before Her: A History of Women in Western Europe*. Vol. 1. New York: Harper Collins, 1995.

Hunt, Alan. *Governing Morals: A Social History of Moral Regulation*. Cambridge: Cambridge University Press, 1999.

Hunter, Judith. "English Inns, Taverns, Alehouses and Brandy Shops: The Legislative Framework, 1495–1797." In *The World of the Tavern: Public Houses in Early Modern Europe*, edited by Beat Kümin and B. Ann Tlusty, 65–82. Burlington, VT: Ashgate, 2002.

Hutton, Ronald. *The Rise and Fall of Merry England: The Ritual Year, 1400–1700*. Oxford: Oxford University Press, 1994.

———. *The Stations of the Sun: A History of the Ritual Year in Britain*. Oxford: Oxford University Press, 1996.

Iles, C. M. "Early Stages of English Public House Regulations." *Economic Journal* 13 (1903): 251–62.

Imberciadori, Ildebrando. "Vite e vigna nell'alto medio evo." In *Agricoltura e mondo rurale in occidente nell'alto medioevo: 22–28 aprile 1965*, 307–42. Spoleto: Presso la Sede del Centro, 1966.

Ingram, Martin. *Church Courts, Sex and Marriage in England, 1570–1640*. Cambridge: Cambridge University Press, 1987.

———. "Reformation of Manners in Early Modern England." In *The Experience of Authority in Early Modern England*, edited by Paul Griffiths, Adam Fox, and Steve Hindle, 47–88. London: Macmillan, 1996.

———. "Religion, Communities and Moral Discipline in Late Sixteenth- and Early Seventeenth-Century England: Case Studies." In *Religion and Society in Early Modern*

Europe, 1500–1800, edited by Kaspar von Greyerz, 177–93. London: George Allen and Unwin, 1984.

―――. "Sexual Manners: The Other Face of Civility in Early Modern England." In *Civil Histories: Essays Presented to Sir Keith Thomas,* edited by Peter Burke, Brian Harrison, and Paul Slack, 87–109. Oxford: Oxford University Press, 2000.

Jacquart, Jean. *La crise rurale en Ile-de-France, 1550–1670.* Paris: Armand Colin, 1974.

Jansen, Sharon L. *Dangerous Talk and Strange Behavior: Women and Popular Resistance to the Reforms of Henry VIII.* New York: St. Martin's, 1996.

Jaritz, Gerhard. "The Material Culture of the Peasantry in the Late Middle Ages: 'Image' and 'Reality.'" In *Agriculture in the Middle Ages: Technology, Practice, and Representation,* edited by Del Sweney, 163–88. Philadelphia: University of Pennsylvania Press, 1995.

Jeffery, Reginald W. "Malting and Brewing." In *The Victoria History of the County of Oxford,* edited by William Page, 2:259–64. London: University of London Press, 1907.

Jéhanno, Christine. "Boire à Paris au XVe siècle: Le vin à l'Hôtel-Dieu." *Revue Historique* 276 (1986): 3–28.

Jellinek, E. M. "The Symbolism of Drinking: A Culture-Historical Approach." *Journal of Studies on Alcohol* 38 (1977): 849–66.

Karras, Ruth Mazo. *Common Women: Prostitution and Sexuality in Medieval England.* New York: Oxford University Press, 1996.

―――. "Sharing Wine, Women, and Song: Masculine Identity Formation in the Medieval European Universities." In *Becoming Male in the Middle Ages,* edited by Jeffrey Jerome Cohen and Bonnie Wheeler, 187–202. New York: Garland, 1997.

Kent, Joan. "Attitudes of Members of the House of Commons to the Regulation of 'Personal Conduct' in Late Elizabethan and Early Stuart England." *Bulletin of the Institute of Historical Research* 46 (May 1973): 41–71.

Kerr, Berenice M. *Religious Life for Women, c. 1100–c. 1350: Fontevraud in England.* Oxford: Clarendon Press, 1999.

Kershaw, Ian. *Bolton Priory: The Economy of a Northern Monastery, 1286–1325.* Oxford: Oxford University Press, 1973.

Kiernan, V. G. *The Duel in European History: Honour and the Reign of Aristocracy.* Oxford: Oxford University Press, 1988.

King, Frank A. *Beer Has a History.* London: Hutchinson, 1947.

King, Walter J. "Regulation of Alehouses in Stuart Lancashire: An Example of Discretionary Administration of the Law." *Transactions of the Historic Society of Lancashire and Cheshire* 129 (1979): 31–46.

Kümin, Beat. *Drinking Matters: Public Houses and Social Exchange in Early Modern Central Europe.* Basingstoke: Palgrave Macmillan, 2007.

Lachiver, Marcel. *Vins, vignes et vignerons en région parisienne du XVIIe au XIXe siècle.* Pontoise: Société Historique et Archéologique de Pontoise, du Val d'Oise et du Vexin, 1982.

―――. *Vins, vignes et vignerons: Histoire du vignoble français.* Poitiers: Fayard, 1988.

Lacroix, Paul. *France in the Middle Ages: Customs, Classes and Conditions.* New York: Frederick Ungar, 1963.

Lancaster, Henry Carrington. *A History of French Dramatic Literature in the Seventeenth Century.* 5 vols. in 9. Baltimore: Johns Hopkins University Press, 1936–42.

Lane, Frederic Chapin. *Venice and History: The Collected Papers of Frederic C. Lane.* Baltimore: Johns Hopkins University Press, 1966.

Lang, Alan R. "Alcohol-Related Violence: Psychological Perspectives." In *Alcohol and Interpersonal Violence: Fostering Multidisciplinary Perspectives*, edited by Susan E. Martin, 121–47. Rockville, MD: National Institutes of Health, 1993.

Lardin, Philippe. "Le rôle du vin et de la nourriture dans la rémunération des ouvriers du bâtiment à la fin du Moyen Age." In *La sociabilité à table*, 209–15. Rouen: Presses Universitaires de Rouen, 1992.

La Roncière, Charles de. "Alimentation et ravitaillement à Florence au XIV siècle." *Archeologia medievale: Cultura materiale, insediamenti, territorio* 8 (1981): 183–92.

———. "Tuscan Notables on the Eve of the Renaissance." In *Revelations of the Medieval World*, edited by Georges Duby, 157–309. Vol. 2 of *A History of Private Life*. Cambridge: Harvard University Press, 1988.

———. "Le vignoble florentin et ses transformations au XIVe siècle." In *Le vin au Moyen Age: Production et producteurs*, 125–59. Grenoble: Société des Historiens Médiévistes de l'Enseignement Supérieur Public, 1978.

Laroque, François. *Shakespeare's Festive World: Elizabethan Seasonal Entertainment and the Professional Stage.* Cambridge: Cambridge University Press, 1991.

Lascombes, André. "Fortunes de l'*ale*: A propos de Coventry, 1420–1555." In *Pratiques et discours alimentaires à la Renaissance*, edited by Jean-Claude Margolin and Robert Sauzet, 127–36. Paris: G.-P. Maisonneuve et Larose, 1982.

Laughton, Jane. "The Alewives of Later Medieval Chester." In *Crown, Government and People in the Fifteenth Century*, edited by Rowena A. Archer, 191–208. Stroud: Alan Sutton, 1995.

Legouis, Emile. "The Bacchic Element in Shakespeare's Plays." *Proceedings of the British Academy* 12 (1926): 115–32.

Leguay, Jean-Pierre. *La rue au Moyen Age.* Rennes: Ouest France, 1984.

Leinwand, Theodore B. "Spongy Plebs, Mighty Lords, and the Dynamics of the Alehouse." *Journal of Medieval and Renaissance Studies* 19 (1989): 159–84.

Le Roy Ladurie, Emmanuel. "Les masses profondes: La paysannerie." In *Paysannerie et croissance (de 1450 à 1660)*, edited by Emmanuel Le Roy Ladurie et Michel Morineau, 481–865. Vol. 1, pt. 2 of *Histoire économique et sociale de la France*. Paris: Presses Universitaires de France, 1977.

———. *Montaillou: Cathars and Catholics in a French Village, 1294–1324.* London: Scolar, 1978.

———. *The Peasants of Languedoc.* Urbana: University of Illinois Press, 1976.

Levi, Giovanni. *Inheriting Power: The Story of an Exorcist.* Chicago: University of Chicago Press, 1988.

Levine, Harry G. "Temperance Cultures: Concern about Alcohol Problems in Nordic and English-Speaking Cultures." In *The Nature of Alcohol and Drug Related Problems*, edited by Malcolm Lader, Griffith Edwards, and D. Colin Drummond, 15–36. Oxford: Oxford University Press, 1992.

Lindley, K. J. "Riot Prevention and Control in Early Stuart London." *Transactions of the Royal Historical Society*, 5th ser., 33 (1983): 109–26.

Little, A. G. "Corrodies at the Carmelite Friary of Lynn," edited by Eric Stone. *Journal of*

Ecclesiastical History 9 (1958): 8–29.

Litzenberger, Caroline. *The English Reformation and the Laity: Gloucestershire, 1540–1580.* Cambridge: Cambridge University Press, 1997.

Lorcin, Marie-Thérèse. *Les Campagnes de la région lyonnaise aux XIVe et XVe siècles.* Lyon: Bosc Frères, 1974.

———. "Les paysans et la justice dans la région lyonnaise aux XIVe et XVe siècles." *Le Moyen Age: Revue d'histoire et de philologie* 74 (1968): 269–300.

———. "Les usages du vin à la fin du Moyen Age (XIIIe–XVe siècles)." In *Le vin des historiens,* edited by Gilbert Garrier, 99–108. Suze-la-Rousse: Université du Vin, 1990.

Lottin, Alain. *Chavatte, ouvrier lillois: Un contemporain de Louis XIV.* Paris: Flammarion, 1979.

MacAndrew, Craig, and Robert B. Edgerton. *Drunken Comportment: A Social Explanation.* London: Nelson, 1970.

MacCulloch, Diarmaid. "Kett's Rebellion in Context." In *Rebellion, Popular Protest and the Social Order in Early Modern England,* edited by Paul Slack, 39–74. Cambridge: Cambridge University Press, 1984.

MacDonald, Michael, and Terence R. Murphy. *Sleepless Souls: Suicide in Early Modern England.* Oxford: Clarendon Press, 1990.

Macfarlane, Alan. *The Justice and the Mare's Ale: Law and Disorder in Seventeenth-Century England.* Cambridge: Cambridge University Press, 1981.

Mackenney, Richard. *Tradesmen and Traders: The World of the Guilds in Venice and Europe, c. 1250–c. 1650.* London: Croom Helm, 1987.

MacLean, Sally-Beth. "Hocktide: A Reassessment of a Popular Pre-Reformation Festival." In *Festive Drama,* edited by Meg Twycross, 233–41. Cambridge: D. S. Brewer, 1996.

Maddern, Philippa. *Violence and Social Order: East Anglia, 1422–1442.* Oxford: Clarendon Press, 1992.

Magennis, Hugh. *Anglo-Saxon Appetites: Food and Drink and Their Consumption in Old English and Related Literature.* Dublin: Four Courts, 1999.

Maguin, Martine. *La vigne et le vin en Lorraine: L'exemple de la Lorraine médiane à la fin du Moyen Age.* Nancy: Presses Universitaires de Nancy, 1982.

Manchée, W. H. *The Westminster City Fathers (The Burgess Court of Westminster), 1585–1901: Being Some Account of Their Powers and Domestic Rule of the City Prior to Its Incorporation in 1901.* London: John Lane The Bodley Head, 1924.

Mandelbaum, David G. "Alcohol and Culture." In *Beliefs, Behaviors, and Alcoholic Beverages: A Cross-Cultural Survey,* edited by Mac Marshall, 14–30. Ann Arbor: University of Michigan Press, 1979.

Manning, Roger B. *Village Revolts: Social Protest and Popular Disturbance in England, 1509–1640.* Oxford: Clarendon Press, 1988.

Marchant, Ronald A. *The Church under the Law: Justice, Administration and Discipline in the Diocese of York, 1560–1640.* Cambridge: Cambridge University Press, 1969.

Marchant, W. T. *In Praise of Ale, or Songs, Ballads, Epigrams, and Anecdotes Relating to Beer, Malt, and Hops.* London: George Redway, 1888.

Marcombe, David. *English Small Town Life: Retford, 1520–1642.* Nottingham: University of Nottingham Press, 1993.

Marquette, Jean-Barnard. "La vinification dans les domaines de l'archevêque de Bordeaux à la fin du Moyen Age." In *Géographie historique des vignobles*, edited by A. Huetz de Lemps, R. Pijassou, and P. Roudié, 123–47. Paris: Centre National de la Recherche Scientifique, 1978.

Marshall, Mac. "Introduction," and "Conclusions." In *Beliefs, Behaviors, and Alcoholic Beverages: A Cross-Cultural Survey*, edited by Mac Marshall, 1–11, 451–57. Ann Arbor: University of Michigan Press, 1979.

Martin, A. Lynn. "Alcohol and the Clergy in Traditional Europe." In *History Has Many Voices*, edited by Lee Palmer Wandel, 23–29. Kirksville, MO: Truman State University Press, 2003.

———. *Alcohol, Sex, and Gender in Late Medieval and Early Modern Europe.* Basingstoke: Palgrave, 2001.

———. "The Baptism of Wine in Traditional Europe." *Gastronomica: The Journal of Food and Culture* 3 (Fall 2003): 21–30.

———. "Drinking and Alehouses in the Diary of an English Mercer's Apprentice, 1663–1674." In *Alcohol: A Social and Cultural History*, edited by Mack P. Holt, 93–105. New York: Berg, 2006.

———. "National Reputations for Drinking in Traditional Europe." *Parergon: The Journal of the Australian and New Zealand Association for Medieval and Renaissance Studies* 16 (1999): 163–86.

Martin, John. *Venice's Hidden Enemies: Italian Heretics in a Renaissance City.* Berkeley: University of California Press, 1993.

Martin, Susan E. "The Epidemiology of Alcohol-Related Interpersonal Violence." *Alcohol Health and Research World* 16 (1992): 230–37.

Mayhew, Graham. *Tudor Rye.* Falmer: University of Sussex Press, 1987.

Mazzi, Maria Serena. "Note per una storia dell'alimentazione nell'Italia medievale." In *Studi di storia medievale e moderna per Ernesto Sestan*, 57–102. Florence: Olschki, 1980.

———. *Prostitute e lenoni nella Firenze del Quattrocento.* Milan: Il Saggiatore, 1991.

McClendon, Muriel C. *The Quiet Reformation: Magistrates and the Emergence of Protestantism in Tudor Norwich.* Stanford: Stanford University Press, 1999.

McIntosh, Marjorie Keniston. *Autonomy and Community: The Royal Manor of Havering, 1200–1500.* Cambridge: Cambridge University Press, 1986.

———. *A Community Transformed: The Manor and Liberty of Havering, 1500–1620.* Cambridge: Cambridge University Press, 1991.

———. *Controlling Misbehavior in England, 1370–1600.* Cambridge: Cambridge University Press, 1998.

McMullan, John L. *The Canting Crew: London's Criminal Underworld, 1550–1700.* Rutgers: Rutgers University Press, 1984.

McShane Jones, Angela. "Roaring Royalists and Ranting Brewers: The Politicisation of Drink and Drunkenness in Political Broadside Ballads from 1640 to 1689." In *A Pleasing Sinne: Drink and Conviviality in Seventeenth-Century England*, edited by Adam Smyth, 69–87. Cambridge: D. S. Brewer, 2004.

Mehl, Jean-Michel. *Les jeux au royaume de France du XIIIe au début du XVIe siècle.* Paris: Fayard, 1990.

Meldrum, Tim. "London Domestic Servants from Depositional Evidence, 1660–1750: Servant-Employer Sexuality in the Patriarchal Household." In *Chronicling Poverty: The Voices and Strategies of the English Poor, 1640–1840*, edited by Tim Hitchcock, Peter King, and Pamela Sharpe, 47–69. London: Macmillan, 1997.

Melis, Federigo. *I vini italiani nel medioevo*. Florence: Le Monnier, 1984.

Mendelsohn, Oscar A. *Drinking with Pepys*. London: Macmillan, 1963.

Mendelson, Sara, and Patricia Crawford. *Women in Early Modern England, 1550–1720*. Oxford: Clarendon Press, 1998.

Miczek, Klaus A., Elise M. Weerts, and Joseph F. DeBold. "Alcohol, Aggression, and Violence: Biobehavioral Determinants." In *Alcohol and Interpersonal Violence: Fostering Multidisciplinary Perspectives*, edited by Susan E. Martin, 83–119. Rockville, MD: National Institutes of Health, 1993.

Midelfort, H. C. Erik. *A History of Madness in Sixteenth-Century Germany*. Stanford: Stanford University Press, 1999.

Misraki, Jacqueline. "Criminalité et pauvreté en France à l'époque de la Guerre de Cent Ans." In *Etudes sur l'histoire de la pauvreté*, edited by Michel Mollat, 535–46. Paris: La Sorbonne, 1974.

Monckton, H. A. *A History of English Ale and Beer*. London: Bodley Head, 1966.

Montanari, Massimo. *L'alimentazione contadina nell'alto Medioevo*. Naples: Liguori, 1979.

Moulin, Léo. "Bière, houblon et cervoise." *Bulletin de l'Académie royale de langue et de littérature françaises* 59 (1980): 111–48.

———. *La vie quotidienne des religieux au Moyen Age, Xe–XVe siècle*. Paris: Hachette, 1978.

Muchembled, Robert. "Les jeunes, les jeux et la violence en Artois au XVIe siècle." In *Les jeux à la Renaissance*, edited by Philippe Ariès and Jean-Claude Margolin, 563–79. Paris: J. Vrin, 1982.

———. *Popular Culture and Elite Culture in France, 1400–1750*. Baton Rouge: Louisiana State University Press, 1985.

———. *Société et mentalités dans la France moderne, XVIe–XVIIIe siècle*. Paris: Armand Colin, 1990.

Muir, Edward. *Ritual in Early Modern Europe*. Cambridge: Cambridge University Press, 1997.

Murray, Alexander. *The Violent against Themselves*. Vol. 1 of *Suicide in the Middle Ages*. Oxford: Oxford University Press, 1998.

Myatt-Price, Evelyn M. "A Tally of Ale." *Journal of the Royal Statistical Society*, series A (general) 123 (1960): 62–67.

Nahoum-Grappe, Véronique. "Histoire du vin: Un choix socioculturel et technique dans la France d'ancien régime." In *L'imaginaire du vin*, edited by Max Milner and Martine Chatelain, 297–307. Marseille: Jeanne Laffitte, 1983.

Neveux, Hugues. "Déclin et reprise: La fluctuation biséculaire." In *L'âge classique des paysans, 1340–1789*, edited by Emmanuel Le Roy Ladurie, 11–173. Vol. 2 of *Histoire de la France rurale*. Paris: Seuil, 1975.

Newbigin, Nerida. "*Cene* and *Cenacoli* in the Ascension and Pentecost Companies of Fifteenth-Century Florence." In *Crossing the Boundaries: Christian Piety and the Arts in Italian Medieval and Renaissance Confraternities*, edited by Konrad Eisenbichler, 90–107. Kalamazoo, MI: Medieval Institute, 1991.

Nicolas, Jean. "Le tavernier, le juge et le curé." *L'histoire* 25 (July–August 1980): 20–28.

Niero, Antonio. *Tradizioni popolari veneziane e venete: I mesi dell'anno: Le feste religiose.* Venice: Studium Cattolico Veneziano, 1990.

Norberg, Kathryn. *Rich and Poor in Grenoble, 1600–1814.* Berkeley: University of California Press, 1985.

Nussdorfer, Laurie. *Civic Politics in the Rome of Urban VIII.* Princeton: Princeton University Press, 1992.

O'Callaghan, Michelle. "Tavern Societies, the Inns of Court, and the Culture of Conviviality in Early Seventeenth-Century London." In *A Pleasing Sinne: Drink and Conviviality in Seventeenth-Century England,* edited by Adam Smyth, 37–51. Cambridge: D. S. Brewer, 2004.

Oestreich, Gerhard. *Neostoicism and the Early Modern State.* Cambridge: Cambridge University Press, 1982.

O'Hara, Diana. *Courtship and Constraint: Rethinking the Making of Marriage in Tudor England.* Manchester: Manchester University Press, 2000.

O'Hara-May, Jane. *Elizabethan Dyetary of Health.* Lawrence, KS: Coronado Press, 1977.

Origo, Iris. *The Merchant of Prato, Francesco di Marco Datini.* Harmondsworth: Penguin, 1963.

Owst, G. R. *Literature and Pulpit in Medieval England: A Neglected Chapter in the History of English Letters and of the English People.* Oxford: Basil Blackwell, 1961.

Palliser, D. M. *Tudor York.* Oxford: Oxford University Press, 1979.

Paronetto, Lamberto. *Chianti: The History of Florence and Its Wines.* London: Wine and Spirit Publications, 1970.

Patrone, Anna Maria Nada. "Bere vino in area pedemontana nel Medioevo." In *Il vino nell'economia e nella società italiana medioevale e moderna,* 1:31–60. Florence: Accademia economico-agraria dei Georgofili, 1988.

———. *Il cibo del ricco ed il cibo del povero: Contributo alla storia qualitativa dell'alimentazione: L'area pedemontana negli ultimi secoli del Medio Evo.* Turin: Centro Studi Piemontesi, 1981.

———. "Il consumo del vino nella società pedemontana del tardo medioevo." In *Vigne e vini nel Piemonte medievale,* edited by Rinaldo Comba, 281–99. Cuneo: L'Arciere, 1990.

———. "I vini in Piemonte tra medioevo et età moderna." In *Vigne e vini nel Piemonte rinascimentale,* edited by Rinaldo Comba, 247–80. Cuneo: L'Arciere, 1990.

Pavan, Elisabeth. "Police des moeurs, société et politique à Venise à la fin du Moyen Age." *Revue historique* 264 (1980): 241–88.

Pellegrin, Nicole. *Les bachelleries: Organisations et fêtes de la jeunesse dans le Centre-Ouest, XVe–XVIIIe siècles.* Poitiers: Mémoires de la Société des Antiquaires de l'Ouest, 1982.

Penning-Rowsell, Edmund. *The Wines of Bordeaux.* Harmondsworth: Penguin, 1976.

Pernanen, Kai. *Alcohol in Human Violence.* New York: Guilford, 1991.

Phythian-Adams, Charles. *Desolation of a City: Coventry and the Urban Crisis of the Late Middle Ages.* Cambridge: Cambridge University Press, 1979.

Picco, Leila. "Gabelle, commerci e consumi: Il prelievo fiscale sul vino nel cinquecento." In *Vigne e vini nel Piemonte rinascimentale,* edited by Rinaldo Comba, 189–203. Cuneo: L'Arciere, 1990.

———. "Un viaggiatore in incognito: Il vino piemontese fra Cinquecento e Settecento." In

Il vino nell'economia e nella società italiana medioevale e moderna, 235–66. Florence: Accademia economico-agraria dei Georgofili, 1988.

Pini, Antonio Ivan. *Vite e vino nel medioevo*. Bologna: CLUEB, 1989.

Platt, Colin. *Medieval Southampton: The Port and Trading Community, A.D. 1000–1600*. London: Routledge and Kegan Paul, 1973.

Popham, Robert E. "The Social History of the Tavern." In *Research Advances in Alcohol and Drug Problems*, edited by Yedy Israel, Frederick B. Glaser, Harold Kalant, Robert E. Popham, Wolfgang Schmidt, and Reginald G. Smart, 4:225–302. New York: Plenum, 1978.

Porter, Roy. "Consumption: Disease of the Consumer Society?" In *Consumption and the World of Goods*, edited by John Brewer and Roy Porter, 58–81. London: Routledge, 1993.

Prestwich, Michael. *Armies and Warfare in the Middle Ages: The English Experience*. New Haven: Yale University Press, 1996.

———. "Victualling Estimates for English Garrisons in Scotland during the Early Fourteenth Century." *English Historical Review* 82 (1967): 536–40.

Pullan, Brian. *A History of Early Renaissance Italy from the Mid-Thirteenth to the Mid-Fifteenth Century*. London: Allen Lane, 1973.

Quaife, G. R. "The Consenting Spinster in a Peasant Society: Aspects of Premarital Sex in 'Puritan' Somerset, 1645–1660." *Journal of Social History* 11 (1977): 228–44.

———. *Wanton Wenches and Wayward Wives: Peasants and Illicit Sex in Early Seventeenth-Century England*. London: Croom Helm, 1979.

Raftis, J. Ambrose. *Tenure and Mobility: Studies in the Social History of the Mediaeval English Village*. Toronto: Pontifical Institute of Mediaeval Studies, 1964.

Rappaport, Steve. *Worlds Within Worlds: Structures of Life in Sixteenth-Century London*. Cambridge: Cambridge University Press, 1989.

Reay, Barry. "The Muggletonians: An Introductory Survey." In *The World of the Muggletonians*, edited by Christopher Hill, Barry Reay, and William Lamont, 23–63. London: Temple Smith, 1983.

Redon, Odile. "La réglementation des banquets par les lois somptuaires dans les villes d'Italie (XIIIe–XVe siècles)." In *Du manuscrit à la table: Essais sur la cuisine au Moyen Age et répertoire des manuscrits médiévaux contenant des recettes culinaires*, edited by Carole Lambert, 109–19. Montreal: Université de Montréal, 1992.

Rees, R. N. K., and Charles Fenby, "Meals and Meal-Times." In *Englishmen at Rest and Play: Some Phases of English Leisure, 1558–1714*, edited by Reginald Lennard, 203–34. Oxford: Clarendon Press, 1931.

Renouard, Yves. *Etudes d'histoire médiévale*. Paris: SEVPEN, 1968.

———. "Le vin vieux au Moyen Age." *Annales du Midi* 76 (1964): 447–55.

Revel, Jacques. "A Capital City's Privileges: Food Supplies in Early-Modern Rome." In *Food and Drink in History*, edited by Robert Forster and Orest Ranum, 37–49. Baltimore: Johns Hopkins University Press, 1979.

Riccetti, Luca. "Il naso di Simone: Il vino ad Orvieto nel Medioevo." In *Dalla vite al vino: Fonti e problemi della vitivinicoltura italiana medievale*, edited by Jean-Louis Gaulin and Allen J. Grieco, 117–55. Bologna: CLUEB, 1994.

Richardson, R. C. *Puritanism in North-West England: A Regional Study of the Diocese of*

Chester to 1642. Manchester: Manchester University Press, 1972.

Rivière, Daniel. "Le thème alimentaire dans le discours proverbial de la Renaissance française." In *Pratiques et discours alimentaires à la Renaissance*, edited by Jean-Claude Margolin and Robert Sauzet, 201–17. Paris: G.-P. Maisonneuve et Larose, 1982.

Roberts, S. K. "Alehouses, Brewing, and Government under the Early Stuarts." *Southern History: A Review of the History of Southern England* 2 (1980): 45–71.

Rocke, Michael. *Forbidden Friendships: Homosexuality and Male Culture in Renaissance Florence*. New York: Oxford University Press, 1996.

Rodgers, Edith Cooperrider. *Discussion of Holidays in the Later Middle Ages*. New York: Columbia University Press, 1940.

Romillat, Anne. "Les femmes, la parole et le vin." In *Actes de la Rencontre Internationale: Cultures, Manières de Boire et Alcoolisme*, edited by Guy Caro and Jean-François Lemoine, 243–47. Rennes: Bretagne, Alcool et Santé, 1984.

Rosenthal, Joel T. *Old Age in Late Medieval England*. Philadelphia, University of Pennsylvania Press, 1996.

Rosser, Gervase. "Going to the Fraternity Feast: Commensality and Social Relations in Late Medieval England." *Journal of British Studies* 33 (1994): 430–46.

———. *Medieval Westminster, 1200–1450*. Oxford: Clarendon Press, 1989.

Ruff, Julius R. *Crime, Justice and Public Order in Old Regime France: The Sénéchaussées of Libourne and Bazas, 1696–1789*. London: Croom Helm, 1984.

———. *Violence in Early Modern Europe*. Cambridge: Cambridge University Press, 2001.

Ruggiero, Guido. *Violence in Early Renaissance Venice*. New Brunswick: Rutgers University Press, 1980.

Sadoun, Roland, Giorgio Lolli, and Milton Silverman. *Drinking in French Culture*. New Brunswick: Rutgers Center of Alcohol Studies, 1965.

Salgādo, Gāmini. *The Elizabethan Underworld*. London: J. M. Dent and Sons, 1977.

Salzman, L. F. *Building in England Down to 1540: A Documentary History*. Oxford: Clarendon Press, 1952.

———. *English Industries of the Middle Ages*. Oxford: Clarendon Press, 1923.

Sambrook, Pamela. *Country House Brewing in England, 1500–1900*. London: Hambledon, 1996.

Sauzet, Robert. *Contre-réforme et réforme catholique en Bas-Languedoc: Le diocèse de Nîmes au XVIIe siècle*. Paris: La Sorbonne, 1979.

Schaefer, James M. "Drunkenness and Culture Stress: A Holocultural Test." In *Cross-Cultural Approaches to the Study of Alcohol: An Interdisciplinary Perspective*, edited by Michael W. Everett, Jack O. Waddell, and Dwight B. Heath, 287–321. The Hague: Mouton, 1976.

Schen, Claire S. *Charity and Lay Piety in Reformation London, 1500–1620*. Aldershot: Ashgate, 2002.

Schofield, John. *Medieval London Houses*. New Haven: Yale University Press, 1994.

Scully, Terence. *The Art of Cookery in the Middle Ages*. Woodbridge: Boydell, 1995.

Seaver, Paul. "Introduction, Symposium: Controlling (Mis)Behavior." *Journal of British Studies* 37 (1998): 231–45.

Shagan, Ethan H. "Rumours and Popular Politics in the Reign of Henry VIII." In *The Politics of the Excluded, c. 1500–1850*, edited by Tim Harris, 30–66. Basingstoke: Palgrave, 2001.

Sharp, Buchanan. *In Contempt of All Authority: Rural Artisans and Riot in the West of England, 1586–1660.* Berkeley: University of California Press, 1980.

Sharpe, James A. "Crime and Delinquency in an Essex Parish, 1600–1640." In *Crime in England, 1550–1800,* edited by J. S. Cockburn, 90–109. London: Methuen, 1977.

———. *Crime in Seventeenth-Century England: A County Study.* Cambridge: Cambridge University Press, 1983.

———. "Domestic Homicide in Early Modern England." *History Journal* 24 (1981): 29–48.

———. "'Such Disagreement betwyx Neighbours': Litigation and Human Relations in Early Modern England." In *Disputes and Settlements: Law and Human Relations in the West,* edited by John Bossy, 167–88. Cambridge: Cambridge University Press, 1983.

Shepard, Alexandra. "Manhood, Credit and Patriarchy in Early Modern England, c. 1580–1640." *Past and Present* 167 (May 2000): 75–106.

———. *Meanings of Manhood in Early Modern England.* Oxford: Oxford University Press, 2003.

Shoemaker, Robert B. "Male Honour and the Decline of Public Violence in Eighteenth-Century London." *Social History* 26 (2001): 190–208.

———. *Prosecution and Punishment: Petty Crime and the Law in London and Rural Middlesex, c. 1660–1725.* Cambridge: Cambridge University Press, 1991.

Simon, André L. *The History of the Wine Trade in England.* 3 vols. London: Holland, 1964.

Singh, R. U. "History of the Defence of Drunkenness in English Criminal Law." *Law Quarterly Review* 49 (1933): 528–46.

Slack, Paul. "Poverty and Politics in Salisbury, 1597–1666." In *Crisis and Order in English Towns, 1500–1700: Essays in Urban History,* edited by Peter Clark and Paul Slack, 164–203. London: Routledge and Kegan Paul, 1972.

Soman, Alfred. "Deviance and Criminal Justice in Western Europe, 1300–1800: An Essay in Structure." *Criminal Justice History* (1980): 3–28.

Soriga, R. "La vite e il vino nella letteratura e nelle figurazioni italiane del medioevo." In *Storia della vite e del vino in Italia,* edited by Arturo Marescalchi and G. Dalmasso, 127–89. Milan: E. Gualdoni, 1933.

Sournia, Jean-Charles. *A History of Alcoholism.* Oxford: Basil Blackwell, 1990.

Spooner, Frank. "Régimes alimentaires d'autrefois: Proportions et calculs en calories." In *Pour une histoire de l'alimentation,* edited by Jean-Jacques Hémardinquer, 35–42. Cahiers des annales 28. Paris: A. Colin, 1970.

Spufford, Margaret. "Puritanism and Social Control." In *Order and Disorder in Early Modern England,* edited by Anthony Fletcher and John Stevenson, 41–57. Cambridge: Cambridge University Press, 1985.

———. *Small Books and Pleasant Histories: Popular Fiction and Its Readership in Seventeenth-Century England.* Cambridge: Cambridge University Press, 1981.

Stouff, Louis. "L'approvisionnement des ménages et des maisons religiueuses (communautés religieuses, écoles, hôpitaux) aux XIVe et XVe siècles." In *Alimentazione e nutrizione: Secc. XIII–XVIII,* edited by Simonetta Cavaciocchi, 643–702. Florence: Le Monnier, 1997.

———. *Ravitaillement et alimentation en Provence aux XIVe et XVe siècles.* Paris: Mouton, 1970.

Summers, Montague. *The History of Witchcraft and Demonology.* Secaucus: Citadel, 1974.

Taveneaux, René. *Le catholicisme dans la France classique, 1610–1715.* 2 vols. Paris: Société d'Edition d'Enseignement Supérieur, 1980.

Taylor, William B. *Drinking, Homicide and Rebellion in Colonial Mexican Villages.* Stanford: Stanford University Press, 1979.

Thibault, Pierre. "Les parisiens et le vin à la fin du XVe siècle." *Mémoires de la Fédération des Sociétés Historiques et Archéologiques de Paris et Ile-de-France* 35 (1984): 231–49.

Thomas, Keith. *Religion and the Decline of Magic: Studies in Popular Beliefs in Sixteenth- and Seventeenth-Century England.* Harmondsworth: Penguin, 1973.

Thompson, Edward P. "Time, Work-Discipline, and Industrial Capitalism." *Past and Present* 38 (Dec. 1967): 56–97.

Thompson, Janet A. *Wives, Widows, Witches and Bitches: Women in Seventeenth-Century Devon.* New York: Peter Lang, 1993.

Threlfall-Holmes, Miranda. "Durham Cathedral Priory's Consumption of Imported Goods: Wine and Spices, 1464–1520." In *Revolution and Consumption in Late Medieval England*, edited by Michael Hicks, 141–53. Woodbridge, Suffolk: Boydell, 2001.

Titow, J. Z. *English Rural Society, 1200–1350.* London: George Allen and Unwin, 1969.

Tlusty, B. Ann. *Bacchus and Civic Order: The Culture of Drink in Early Modern Germany.* Charlottesville: University of Virginia Press, 2001.

Trexler, Richard C. *Public Life in Renaissance Florence.* New York: Academic Press, 1980.

Trout, Andrew. *City on the Seine: Paris in the Time of Richelieu and Louis XIV.* New York: St. Martin's, 1996.

Turgeon, Laurier, and Denis Dickner, "Contraints et choix alimentaires d'un groupe d'appartenance: Les marins-pêcheurs français à terre-neuve au XVIe siècle." In *Du manuscrit à la table: Essais sur la cuisine au Moyen Age et répertoire des manuscrits médiévaux contenant des recettes culinaires*, edited by Carole Lambert, 227–39. Montreal: Presses de l'Université de Montréal, 1992.

Ultee, Maarten. *The Abbey of St. Germain des Prés in the Seventeenth Century.* New Haven: Yale University Press, 1981.

Underdown, David. *Fire from Heaven: Life in an English Town in the Seventeenth Century.* New Haven: Yale University Press, 1992.

———. *Revel, Riot, and Rebellion: Popular Politics and Culture in England, 1603–1660.* Oxford: Clarendon Press, 1985.

Unger, Richard W. *Beer in the Middle Ages and the Renaissance.* Philadelphia: University of Pennsylvania Press, 2004.

Unwin, Tim. *Wine and the Vine: An Historical Geography of Viticulture and the Wine Trade.* London: Routledge, 1991.

Vaissière, Pierre de. *Gentilshommes campagnards de l'ancienne France.* Geneva: Slatkine-Megariotis, 1975.

Valenti, S. "La taverna comunale nella Giudicarie ulteriori: Piccolo contributo alla storia del pubblico diritto italiano." *Tridentum* (1904–1905): 442–58.

Vaultier, Roger. *Le folklore pendant la Guerre de Cent Ans d'après les lettres de rémission du Trésor des Chartes.* Paris: Guénégaud, 1965.

Venard, Marc. "La fraternité des banquets." In *Pratiques et discours alimentaires à la Renais-*

sance, edited by Jean-Claude Margolin and Robert Sauzet, 137–45. Paris: G.-P. Maisonneuve et Larose, 1982.

Walker, Garthine. *Crime, Gender and Social Order in Early Modern England*. Cambridge: Cambridge University Press, 2003.

———. "Expanding the Boundaries of Female Honour in Early Modern England." *Transactions of the Royal Historical Society*, 6th ser., 6 (1996): 235–45.

Wall, Alison. *Power and Protest in England, 1525–1640*. London: Arnold, 2000.

Wallace, David. "Chaucer and the Absent City." In *Chaucer's England: Literature in Historical Context*, edited by Barbara A. Hanawalt, 59–90. Minneapolis: University of Minnesota Press, 1992.

Walter, John, and Keith Wrightson. "Dearth and the Social Order in Early Modern England." In *Rebellion, Popular Protest and the Social Order in Early Modern England*, edited by Paul Slack, 108–28. Cambridge: Cambridge University Press, 1984.

Walzer, Michael. *The Revolution of the Saints: A Study in the Origins of Radical Politics*. New York: Atheneum, 1971.

Warner, Jessica. "Before There Was 'Alcoholism': Lessons from the Medieval Experience with Alcohol." *Contemporary Drug Problems* 29 (1992): 409–29.

———. "Good Help Is Hard to Find: A Few Comments about Alcohol and Work in Preindustrial England." *Addiction Research* 2 (1995): 259–69.

Watt, Tessa. *Cheap Print and Popular Piety, 1550–1640*. Cambridge: Cambridge University Press, 1991.

Watts, Sheldon J. *A Social History of Western Europe, 1450–1720: Tensions and Solidarities among Rural People*. London: Hutchinson, 1984.

Wear, Andrew. *Health and Healing in Early Modern England*. Aldershot: Variorum, 1998.

Weiss, Susan F. "Medieval and Renaissance Wedding Banquets and Other Feasts." In *Food and Eating in Medieval Europe*, edited by Martha Carlin and Joel T. Rosenthal, 159–74. London: Hambledon, 1998.

Weissman, Ronald F. E. *Ritual Brotherhood in Renaissance Florence*. New York: Academic Press, 1982.

White, Helene Raskin, Stephen Hansell, and John Brick. "Alcohol Use and Aggression among Youth." *Alcohol Health and Research World* 17 (1993): 144–50.

Wilson, Adrian. "The Ceremony of Childbirth and Its Interpretation." In *Women as Mothers in Pre-Industrial England: Essays in Memory of Dorothy McLaren*, edited by Valerie Fildes, 68–107. London: Routledge, 1990.

Wilson, C. Anne. *Food and Drink in Britain from the Stone Age to Recent Times*. London: Constable, 1973.

———. "Keeping Hospitality and Board Wages: Servants' Feeding Arrangements from the Middle Ages to the Nineteenth Century." In *Food for the Community: Special Diets for Special Groups*, edited by C. Anne Wilson, 43–68. Edinburgh: Edinburgh University Press, 1993.

Woodward, Donald. *Men at Work: Labourers and Building Craftsmen in the Towns of Northern England, 1450–1750*. Cambridge: Cambridge University Press, 1995.

Woolgar, Christopher. "Fast and Feast: Conspicuous Consumption and the Diet of the Nobility in the Fifteenth Century." In *Revolution and Consumption in Late Medieval England*, edited by Michael Hicks, 7–26. Woodbridge: Boydell, 2001.

———, D. Serjeantson, and T. Waldron. "Conclusion." In *Food in Medieval England: Diet and Nutrition*, edited by C. M. Woolgar, D. Serjeantson, and T. Waldron, 267–80. Oxford: Oxford University Press, 2006.

Wrightson, Keith. "Alehouses, Order and Reformation in Rural England, 1590–1660." In *Popular Culture and Class Conflict, 1590–1914: Explorations in the History of Labour and Leisure*, edited by Eileen and Stephen Yeo, 1–27. Brighton: Harvester, 1981.

———. *English Society, 1580–1680*. London: Hutchinson, 1982.

———. "Two Concepts of Order: Justices, Constables and Jurymen in Seventeenth-Century England." In *An Ungovernable People: The English and Their Law in the Seventeenth and Eighteenth Centuries*, edited by John Brewer and John Styles, 21–46. London: Hutchinson, 1980.

———, and David Levine. *Poverty and Piety in an English Village: Terling, 1525–1700*. New York: Academic Press, 1979.

Wyczanski, Andrzej. "Structure sociale de la consommation alimentaire en Italie au XVIe siècle." In *Mélanges en l'honneur de Fernand Braudel: Histoire économique du monde méditerranéen, 1450–1650*, 637–81. Toulouse: Privat, 1973.

About the Author

A. Lynn Martin is an award-winning historian, a fellow of the Royal Historical Society and of the Australian Academy of the Humanities, and a recipient of a Centenary Medal from the Australian government for his contribution to Australian society through history.

Born in Iowa, Professor Martin received his education at the University of Oregon and the University of Wisconsin before moving to Australia in 1973. In a previous incarnation as a historian, he specialized in the history of the Jesuits and his books included *Henry III and the Jesuit Politicians*, *The Jesuit Mind: The Mentality of an Elite in Early Modern France*, and *Plague? Jesuit Accounts of Epidemic Disease in the Sixteenth Century*, plus shorter pieces on Roman prostitutes, insanity in the sixteenth century, the Saint Bartholomew's Day Massacre, the family, and papal policies during the wars of religion.

More recently he abandoned the Jesuits for drink and now specializes in the history of drinking in traditional Europe. This phase of his career has resulted in a book on *Alcohol, Sex, and Gender in Late Medieval and Early Modern Europe* and articles on national reputations for drinking, the baptism of wine, unruly women, English alehouses, and the consumption of alcohol by the old and by the clergy.

In 1997 Professor Martin became founder and director of the University of Adelaide's Research Centre for the History of Food and Drink, a position he held until 2004. As director, he was responsible for the establishment of the University's Graduate Program in Gastronomy and was the program's first managing director. He also edited with Barbara Santich two books that resulted from the Research Centre's series of conferences and symposia, *Gastronomic Encounters* and *Culinary History*. Although retiring at the end of 2003, Professor Martin still keeps active as a visiting research fellow.

Index

enforcement of, 150–51
violations of, 3, 9, 29, 84, 135, 144, 209,
      218

D

Dante, 20–21
Davis, Robert C., 50
Deadly Danger of Drunkenness, 17, 25
*Débat des hérauts d'armes de France et
      d'Angleterre,* 53
Debate of the Carpenter's Tools, 35–36
Defoe, Daniel, 34, 35–36, 38, 64
Dekker, Thomas, 25, 29, 136, 153
Delamare, Nicolas, 208–9
Description of England, 39–40, 63
"despair drinking," 81, 155
devil's church, alehouses as the, 26–29,
      32–33
Devon, 62, 125, 147, 149, 207
Devonshire, 31, 37
D'Ewes, Simon, 106
diet and alcohol, 2, 3, 13, 53–54, 64–65, 106,
      159, 187, 217
Dijon, 53, 105, 127, 163, 172, 177
Dion, Roger, 23, 30, 51, 72–73, 74
disorder
      alcohol's ambivalent role in, 13, 133, 154,
            185, 216
      in alehouses and taverns, 26, 78–79,
            108–9, 112–19, *113, 120,* 121–27,
            130–31, *165*
      campaigns against, 11–12
      among clergy, 138–39
      court cases against, 134–42, 144–45
      curfews and, 144, 150–51
      defining and interpreting, 109–11
      drinking establishments as centers of,
            3–4, 158, 216
      and government slander and sedition,
            149–50
      and poverty, 34–36
      prostitution and, 8–9, 15, 31, 124, 127
      on the Sabbath, 145–48, 155
      and sacrilege, profanation, and
            blasphemy, 145–48, 155
      among servants and apprentices, 142,
            144–45, 155
      and sexual misconduct, 136–38, 152–54

and theft and vandalism, 151–52
and verbal abuse, 139–40, 155
among youth, 141–45, *143*
See also drunkenness; sexual disorder
      and misconduct; violence and
      disorder
Domesday Book, 189
Dorchester, 110, 146, 151, 153–54, 159–60,
      164, 182
Dorset, 109, 111, 222
Doughty, Robert, 160
Downame, John, 32
Dreadful Character of a Drunkard, 17
Drinke and Welcome, 62
drinking establishments
      and antisocial behavior, 219–20
      and curfew, 4, 29, 113, 114, 115, 132, 200,
            203
      and disorder, 3–4, 13, 78–79, 108–9,
            112–19, *113, 120,* 130–32, *165,* 216
      disorderly clientele of, 26, 86, 121–27,
            161–62
      in England, 87–91
      in France, 85–87, 116–17, 121, 123, 125,
            127, 194–95
      and gambling, 125–26, 202–3
      in Italy, 84–85, 116, 193–94, 195
      legislation governing, 4, 185, 187,
            193–200
      moralists' condemnations of, 13, 29, 31,
            32–33
      music in, 88–89
      and recreational drinking, 80, 84–91
      regulations on clientele and behavior at,
            198–203
      regulations on hours of operation of,
            203–5
      religious and political dissidents and,
            127–30, 131
      and sexual activity, 124–25
      students and, 87–88
      as the "third place," 86, 87, 90–91, 108, 118,
            121, 131–32, 142, 159, 216, 220
      violence and, 158, 161–63, 162n22, 172–79,
            183, 218, 219–20
      See also alehouses and taverns
drunkenness
      as a criminal offense in England,
            209–12, 216